A Writer's Handbook 3[

Writing with a Voice

Second Edition

Writing with a Voice
A Rhetoric and Handbook

Diana Hacker
Betty Renshaw

With a section on research writing
by Lloyd Shaw

SCOTT, FORESMAN AND COMPANY
Glenview, Illinois   Boston   London

Library of Congress Cataloging-in-Publication Data

Hacker, Diana, 1942–
  Writing with a voice.

  Includes index.
  1. English language — Rhetoric. 2. English language — Grammar — 1950–   — Handbooks, manuals, etc.
I. Renshaw, Betty. II. Title.
PE1408.H278 1988   808'.042   88–33710
ISBN 0–673–39670–3

1 2 3 4 5 6 7 8 9 10–KPF–94 93 92 91 90 89 88

Printed in the United States of America

To our students

Preface

Writing with a Voice, second edition, is a rhetoric, handbook, and student essay reader for college students. Today's college students, whether they attend a four-year university or a community college, are a diverse group. They include grandmothers and eighteen-year-olds, dorm residents and commuters, honors students and former drop-outs. Most, but not all, read on the college level. A few are budding writers, but the writing goals of most are more modest. We mean to reach all of these students with a book that is readable but not simplistic, supportive but not patronizing.

Furthermore, we have made *Writing with a Voice* adaptable to a variety of teaching styles. The parts of the book may be assigned in nearly any order; the rhetoric chapters and the sample student essays can be used either with or without further elaboration; the supporting exercises suggest many kinds of activities for both in-class and out-of-class use; the handbook invites classroom discussion, if desired, or it can be used exclusively for reference.

For those of you looking at *Writing with a Voice* for the first time, here are its principal features:

Use of Student Writing. We have illustrated the text throughout with student writing, frequently presented in draft form. Students learn what has worked for their peers at all stages of the writing process — from brainstorming to drafting to revising, polishing, and editing. Simply by reading successful essays written by their peers, students pick up strategies with which they too can succeed. *Writing with a Voice* contains more than thirty full student essays.

Hand-edited Student Drafts in Progress. The second edition includes twelve student drafts in progress, each illustrating a different revision strategy: adjusting the voice, improving the focus, strengthening the content, varying sentence structure, and so on. The twelve drafts appear in the rough — with the students' handwritten revisions — and they are fully annotated on facing pages.

Appeal to a Variety of Students. Because the student illustrations in the text were written by a diverse population, they appeal to a wide range of students, both traditional and nontraditional. Included are writings by eighteen-year-olds and returning adults, men and women, working people and full-time students, whites, and people of color.

A Friendly, Never Condescending Tone. Because we believe that student writers are not inherently different from other writers (including ourselves), our tone is straightforward and helpful, never patronizing. Adult students in particular appreciate our assumption that they, like us, are members of a community of writers.

Two Full Chapters on the Research Paper. The research paper guide, now divided into two chapters, introduces students to the research process and helps them with the aspects of research writing that they find most troublesome: choosing and narrowing a topic, designing a search strategy, formulating a thesis, avoiding plagiarism when taking notes and while drafting the paper, citing sources, and incorporating quotations smoothly into the text. A sample research paper annotated on facing pages reinforces the points raised in the chapters.

Documentation models are based on the third edition of the *MLA Handbook for Writers of Research Papers* (1988). As you are no doubt aware, the Modern Language Association now recommends a system of in-text citations and a list of works cited instead of the traditional footnotes and selected bibliography.

A Handbook Designed for Quick Reference. We have designed the handbook section for quick review and quick reference. Rules and subrules in a second color highlight important information, and examples are clearly set off from the text and from each other. The rules and subrules are coded with numbers and letters so that you can send students directly to the information they need: 5d for a comma after an introductory element, 17 for wordy sentences, 31a for vague pronoun reference, and so on. If you prefer to use symbols instead, a list of commonly used symbols appears on the back endpapers.

A Section on Dialect Interference. Students who speak a dialect will find special help in the handbook section of *Writing with a Voice*. Through the technique of contrastive analysis, we show students how to correct problems such as dropped -s endings, which may have been caused by dialect interference.

Numerous Writing Topics. The Appendix contains nearly two hundred topics organized by subject. Additional writing topics appear in the chapters on describing, narrating, reporting, and arguing a point.

Comprehensive Coverage.   Because it is a rhetoric, a handbook, a research paper guide, and a student essay reader, *Writing with a Voice* may be used without a supplementary text.

Those of you who are familiar with the first edition of *Writing with a Voice* will find numerous improvements in this second edition:

- a greater range of invention strategies
- fuller treatment of revision: global revision, sentence-polishing, editing, and proofreading
- advice on writing with a word processor
- more exercises requiring writing
- numerous exercises in peer review
- twelve hand-edited student drafts in progress
- two full chapters on the research paper
- a clearer page design, with the second color used throughout

In this second edition, we continue to hope that *Writing with a Voice* reflects an up-to-date and practical philosophy of the teaching of writing. Like many of you, we believe that writing is a process, that rhetorical choices are central to every phase of the process, and that when our students are *coached* throughout the process, many of them will indeed begin to write with a voice.

Acknowledgments

For their extensive reviews of this edition of *Writing with a Voice*, we would like to thank Chris Anson, University of Minnesota, Minneapolis; Jeffrey Gross, Memphis State University; Steve Hahn, William Paterson College; Robert Schwegler, University of Rhode Island; and Barbara Weaver, Ball State University.

We would also like to thank Lloyd Shaw for revising the research paper chapter; LeRoy Badger for drafting the section on mind-mapping; and Peter Adams, LeRoy Badger, Constance Coyle, Nancy Hume, Jean Hunter, Alice O'Melia, and William Peirce for contributing a number of excellent examples and exercises.

We are grateful to the many students whose writing appears in this edition: Elizabeth Anderson, Louise Barr, Lisa Bennett, Henry Bertagnolli, Emily Boyle, Joan Bradley, Kirk Brimmer, Michael Buongiorne, Judith Burgin, Marjorie Carson, Dolores Cockrell, Frank Cohee, Gloria Connor, Jacqueline Cosey, Barbara Crossley, Nick Culver, John Curley, Joan

Easterling, Helen Eisenberg, Michael Elmore, Deborah Fletcher, Lisa Fortunato, Charles Ganley, Alan Goldsticker, Clarence Hayden, Robert Jeanotte, Beverly Johnson, Mary Kenny, Renee Klar, Catherine Knudsen, Martha Krause, Cathy Lawson, Kathleen Lewis, Daniel MacFarland, H. C. McKenzie, Pat Napolitano, Ruth Parker, Nancy Powell, Nolan Presnell, Irene Rabun, Ethel Ramsey, Johnnie Randolf, Anne Reeves, Ruth Rezendes, Betty Ricketson, Martina Riley, Daryl Roe, Jenny Shelton, Jon Singleton, Margaret Smith, Martina Solliday, Joyce Spring, Margaret Stack, Jefferson Stewart, Karen Sutton, Cleopatra Tyson, Marie Visosky, Tom Weitzel, Linda White, Melvin White, Tom White, Andrew Woycitsky, Sharon Wultich, and William Zachem.

Finally, special thanks go to English Editor Joseph Opiela, for taking an active interest in all aspects of our book — from its philosophy to its design; and to Book Editor Virginia Shine and to P. M. Gordon Associates for guiding the book so expertly through production.

We continue to welcome suggestions from other instructors for improving this book.

Diana Hacker
Betty Renshaw

Contents

Part One

The Writing Process

1   *Getting Started*

*If I start very early in the morning, with a fresh pot of coffee,
sharp pencils, plenty of paper, a cat on my lap, and total silence, I
might come up with something.* — A STUDENT

Some people think they should be able to sit down at a desk, take
out a clean sheet of paper, and begin to write. They believe that their
sentences should flow from pen to paper almost magically, the product
of instant inspiration. But the experience of just about everyone we
know or have read about, including ourselves, says that this is rarely
the way good writing happens. What has to happen first, often long
before you sit down to write, is a less consciously directed, more random
kind of thinking. You begin by musing, exploring, discovering — by
letting your ideas unfold. You give yourself time for creative thinking.

Creative thinking can occur almost anywhere, often while you are
doing something else. Agatha Christie, creator of classic English mystery
stories that have delighted generations of readers, found that the best
time for planning a book was while doing the dishes. Another English
writer, Virginia Woolf, planned much of her work during long bubble
baths. And Toni Morrison, a contemporary American writer, tells us,
"I brood, think of ideas, in the automobile when I'm driving to work
or in the subway or when I'm mowing the lawn. By the time I get to
the paper something's there — I can produce."

Most writers do at least some of their creative thinking on paper.
They jot ideas on the backs of envelopes, on recipe cards or paper bags
or cocktail napkins or scraps of cardboard — whatever happens to be
handy at the time. Ann Tyler, a writer and mother of two, remarks:
"In the evenings, occasionally — between baths and other sorts of chaos
— a sudden idea will flash into my mind . . . I write it down on an
index card and take it to my study."

Initially, it's a good idea to keep such jottings informal, in order to
promote creativity and allow for those sudden insights and accidental
discoveries that are so typical of the creative process. In this chapter
we'd like to suggest a number of ways in which you might generate
ideas informally on scratch paper: listing, clustering, branching, mind-
mapping, and informal outlining.

Listing

Listing, also known as "brainstorming," is a good way to begin. Write your topic at the top of a piece of scratch paper and quickly list ideas in the order in which they occur to you. Don't let yourself worry at this point about the order or even the quality of your ideas. Save these concerns for later.

One of our students, Mary Kenny, jotted down the following list as the first step in writing an essay about her favorite art gallery, the Phillips Collection, located in Washington, D.C.

> 1612 21st Street, close to Mass. Ave.
> near Dupont Circle, in an interesting neighborhood
> hard to find a parking space; better to take subway
> elegant red brick townhouse, once home of Duncan and Marjorie
>   Phillips (art collectors)
> turned into a museum in 1918
> facade reminds me of a bygone era — teas and debutante balls
> free concert on Sundays
> mostly Impressionists, Postimpressionists, and modern masters
> Renoir's "Luncheon of the Boating Party" — warm and joyful —
>   you can almost smell the breeze off the Seine and hear the
>   hum of conversation
> you can wander through small rooms filled with paintings by Van
>   Gogh, Degas, Cezanne, Bonnard, and Klee
> the Rothko room, with huge color paintings — pulsating,
>   sensuous reds, yellows, blues, greens
> the new wing — no more bygone era — clean and uncluttered
>   lines appropriate for modern masters like Picasso, Pollack,
>   Dali, Braque
> a walled garden
> a gift shop

The purpose of this list was to generate ideas, not to bring order to those ideas. Later, working with this list, Mary Kenny turned to the technique of branching to produce a more orderly blueprint for her essay (see page 7). If you are interested in reading the final draft of the essay, you will find it on pages 314–315.

Clustering, Branching, and Mind-mapping

Like outlining, the techniques of clustering, branching, and mind-mapping bring order to ideas. But because they are less rigid than outlining, they tend to be more useful early in the writing process. They promote experimentation and creativity, allowing you to discover an order in your ideas; they do not tempt you to impose order prematurely.

To cluster ideas, put your key idea in the center of a page, draw a circle around it, and then surround it with related ideas, connected to it with lines. Then circle those ideas, surround them with related ideas, and continue the process until you have produced a wealth of details. For an essay describing the most remarkable woman he had ever met, student Tom Weitzel began with the cluster diagram on page 6. A draft of Weitzel's essay appears on pages 301–302.

To branch ideas, put your subject at the top of a page and then list several major supporting ideas underneath, leaving plenty of space between them. To the right of each major idea, draw lines branching to more specific ideas and, where possible, branch out to further details. On page 7 is a branching diagram for Mary Kenny's essay on the Phillips art gallery. As mentioned earlier, Kenny turned to the technique of branching after she had already generated a list of ideas.

Mind-mapping* is a colorful and creative method of generating, organizing, and remembering ideas. To mind-map, write your topic in the center of a blank page within a visual representation of your topic, such as a giant musical note, a sailboat, or scuba gear. If no central image comes to mind, use a box, heart, circle, or other shape. Then use various colors of ink to color-code related ideas. From the central figure draw radiating lines like the rays of the sun or branches and roots of a tree. Then, as you think of parts of the subject you wish to discuss, jot down pictures, key words, or phrases on or near these lines. Also add examples and subparts using branching lines and more images and words. If you do not already have a central focus for your essay, watch for a key phrase or image as you complete your exploration.

After spreading your topic out in an explosion of images and words, you can begin to bring order out of chaos by assigning Roman numerals to the main parts of the topic and capital letters to the subparts of each point. From this ordering you can later construct a logically organized outline.

The mind-map on page 8 was drawn by John Curley as he explored ideas for his essay "Journey Under Water" (pages 271–277). Curley drew his mind-map on a large sheet of paper with blue, green, yellow, and orange Magic Markers. Later he added the outline elements — Roman numerals and capital letters — in red.

---

* Mind-mapping was invented by Tony Buzan. See his books, *Use Both Sides of Your Brain* (1976) and *Use Your Perfect Memory* (1984), both published by E. P. Dutton, New York.

Branching

The Phillips Collection

where
- in a red brick town house —— at 1612 21st St.
  recalls a bygone era
- close to Dupont Circle

what
- The art collection of Duncan and Marjorie Phillips
- Impressionists, Post-impressionists, modern masters

The old wing
- Van Gogh
- Degas
- Cezanne
- Renoir's "Luncheon" —— warm, joyful
  party on the Seine

The new wing
- Picasso
- Pollack
- Dali
- Braque
- Rothko's color paintings —— blazing reds and yellows
  soothing blues and greens

mind-mapping

DEEP SEA DIVING

PILOT

© INTRO VICTIMS

Ⓑ H₂O SKIER

Ⓐ SCUBA DIVERS

Ⓓ DIVING INSTRUCTOR

JAWS I + II

Ⓒ NEW JERSEY – OIL TANKERS

Ⓑ AUSTRALIA (WEDDING)

Ⓐ THAILAND

Ⓓ CARIBBEAN (FAVORITE)

I. LOCATIONS

II. DAVIS BEACH (ST. CROIX)

V. RESURFACING

Ⓐ CORAL FANS

Ⓑ (LAND COMPASS)

IV. 60'

Ⓑ MURKY

Ⓒ SALAD OIL

CONCL.

III.

8' STING RAY

30'

Ⓒ PARROT FISH

Ⓓ BUTTERFLY FISH

Ⓐ CORAL

Ⓑ DAMSELS (YELLOW) (RED)

MO MOARY EELS MAUREEN

Ⓐ DEPTH GAUGES

Ⓔ 80°

Ⓓ GENTLE TRADE-WINDS

Ⓑ SWAYING PALMS

Ⓒ PEACOCKS

Ⓐ DESERTED BEACH

Informal Outlining

An informal outline is a simple blueprint for an essay. It lacks the conventions of formal outlining: Roman numerals, capital letters, and Arabic numerals; careful parallelism; and fully articulated sentences. Although formal outlines can be useful for lengthy writing projects, such as research papers, for most essays you will want to keep your outlines simple. The following informal outline was written by one of our students, Kathleen Lewis. The final draft of her essay appears on pages 294–295.

Life as a Stewardess

How I was hooked
-- TV ad (Broadway Joe)
-- first-class flight to Dallas, with champagne
-- good interview -- I came off poised, sophisticated, very much an adult
-- excitement of being accepted

The reality
-- six week course, with curfews and room searches, emphasis on beauty, pretended emphasis on safety
-- first trip: I was more a coffee and soda dispenser than a safety expert
-- lonely layovers, such as Christmas in Kansas City (of course I could always check my stack of businessmen's calling cards!)

Exercise 1   Written

Browse through the Appendix of this book in search of a topic on which you might be able to write an essay. Then brainstorm a list of ideas on your topic, making sure that your list is at least as long as the one on page 4.

Exercise 2   Written

Find a topic in the Appendix and use the technique of branching, clustering, or mapping to explore your ideas.

Exercise 3   Written

Take the list you generated in Exercise 1 and turn it into an informal outline. Feel free to delete items from your initial list and to add others.

Exercise 4   For Discussion

Read the following student essays, all mentioned in this chapter, and be prepared to discuss them in class: "The Phillips Collection," pages 314–315; "Goat Woman," pages 301–302; "Life as a Stewardess," pages 294–295; and "Journey Under Water," pages 271–277.

2 *Writing and Rewriting*

I used to worry considerably about my writing. Yes, I used to fret,
but that was out of fear. Now, though, I have enormous confidence
because I know that I can always rewrite it. — TONI MORRISON

If you're like most writers, you'll do almost anything to avoid writing
that first sentence. Suddenly your car needs washing, your refrigerator
has to be defrosted, your closet demands a thorough cleaning. Even
when you've all but chained yourself to your desk you find ways to
avoid that blank sheet of paper. Your typewriter ribbon must be changed,
the desk has to be cleaned, and your notes must be arranged in an
elaborate, color-coded outline. Writer Jacques Barzun advises us at this
point to "suspect all out-of-the-way or elaborate preparations. You don't
have to sharpen your pencils and sort out paper clips before you begin."

Professional writers have discovered ways of forcing themselves to
get started. Barzun, who assures us that "no writer has ever lived who
did not at some time or other get stuck," begins by letting his first
sentence "be as stupid as it wishes." Another author we know of types
or scribbles gibberish, just to warm up his cold brain and get his fingers
moving. Both these professionals assume that their first sentence will
be thrown away; knowing this, they're not afraid to write it.

Southern writer Flannery O'Connor set aside a regular time of day
for her work. As she told a group of students, "Every morning between
nine and twelve, I go to my room and sit before a piece of paper. Many
times I sit for three hours with no ideas coming to me. But I know
one thing: if an idea does come between nine and twelve, I am there
ready for it."

Finding a Time and Place to Write

If any magic is connected with writing, it may come from your
writing place. The more at home you are in the place where you write,
the more relaxed you will feel. And there is likely to be a particular
time of day or night when writing will come most easily for you.

11

Carson McCullers did her writing "in a quiet room in the early morning hours." Van Wyck Brooks, on the other hand, believed that "as against having beautiful workshops, studies, etc., one writes best in a cellar on a rainy day." One of our students reports: "I write in the quiet of night, when the children are sound asleep." Another says he writes "whenever there's free time, wherever there's free space . . . and lots of coffee."

Certain items — coffee, cigarettes, soda, milk, a favorite pen, a legal pad, music — seem to be essential to some people as they write. We suggest you surround yourself with whatever you need to get started. Carson McCullers said that she took a thermos of tea to her quiet room. Ernest Hemingway wrote his more poetic descriptive passages with a pencil; he said he needed to hear the lead move on the paper. But he typed out his sharp-edged action sentences while standing at a chest-high desk. Thomas Wolfe did much of his writing while leaning on the top of a refrigerator; he was so tall that he was most comfortable in that position.

Another writer we know does all her first-draft writing seated in the corner of a worn sofa, with containers of both hot coffee and iced water at hand. She writes on a beat-up clipboard, with a large supply of freshly sharpened yellow No. 2 pencils close by. She cannot write very well anywhere else. Nor can she write at night. On the other hand, one of our students says she can write anywhere she can get comfortable: "in the tub, in bed, on the floor, in a semidark room, almost anywhere."

Drafting

Let's get you into your writing place, at a good writing time, surrounded by whatever makes you feel at home. You have your lists, diagrams, and informal outlines close at hand. And before you is that blank sheet of paper. . . .

Now you're ready to write. At this point, treat your essay as a *rough draft* that will be improved later. Don't worry about neatness and spelling and precise word choice, or even about sentence structure and grammar. Go with the flow, roughing out the essay, leaving blanks when you get stuck, moving forward without stopping. You can fill in the blanks later, after the essay has begun to take shape. The trick, says writer Gene Olson, "is to keep the words flowing, rolling, sliding onto the paper. . . . Before your eyes, a few words turn into a sentence, a sentence into a paragraph, and a paragraph into a composition . . . in the rough."

It's a good idea to double-space a rough draft. That way you'll have room between the lines for changes you may want to make later. And you should leave margins, again so you'll have space in which to experiment with improvements.

If you are a reasonably fast typist, try composing your drafts on a typewriter or a word processor. Because typing is faster than writing longhand, you'll be better able to keep up with the flow of your ideas. A typed draft is also easier to read than handwritten copy, and therefore it will be easier to revise.

Getting Distance

A first, rough draft is seldom a satisfying piece of writing. Even professional writers cannot control their rough drafts perfectly, so they take their writing through several drafts, or revisions. You will need to do so too. ✗ *I'm sure*

But how do you decide what revisions your rough draft needs? Like most writers, once you have finished a draft, you probably feel too close to it to view it objectively. So you'll need to get "distance" from your writing. You'll need, somehow, to begin to see your essay as if you hadn't written it — as if you were your reader.

One way to get distance is to allow your draft to cool off, preferably overnight, or even for a few days. After this cooling-off period, try to read the essay as if you were your audience. The hard-to-read parts will confuse even you, and you'll begin to see what changes are needed.

Whenever possible, ask someone else — a friend, parent, instructor, writing center tutor, or fellow student — to serve as your reader. Choose someone whose judgment you trust, preferably someone who will level with you. Ask this person to tell you where your essay is most effective and where it is unclear, awkward, or hard to read.

Many composition instructors set aside class time for "peer review." In pairs or small groups, students exchange essays and respond to one another's drafts, often using a checklist such as the one printed inside the back cover of this book. Notice that the checklist includes separate questions for early drafts, later drafts, and final revisions. For early drafts, you should comment on overall effectiveness, not on fine points. Begin by considering the writer's purpose and audience, and then help the writer see how well his or her essay succeeds. Save your comments on word choice, sentence structure, grammar, punctuation, and mechanics for later. *Hope that Dr. Bovie knows this!*

Occasionally, you may decide that a rough draft lacks promise. If you are certain that you can't turn your rough draft into an essay worth reading, toss it out and begin again. One professional writer claims that the most important piece of furniture in her office is a ten-gallon wastebasket. Her mistakes go into the wastebasket, sometimes with a dramatic hook shot. What doesn't go into the wastebasket is good enough to be rewritten.

Rewriting: Making Global Revisions

"Rewriting," as we are using the term, means making global revisions — revisions that affect blocks of text longer than a sentence. They include improvements in focus, organization, content, paragraphing, and any other matters that involve deleting, adding, or moving chunks of text.

You will save yourself time if you handle global revisions before turning to sentence-level revisions, because in the process of revising globally, you may decide to delete sentences, paragraphs, or even larger blocks of text. There is little sense in polishing and editing sentences that may not even appear in your final draft.

Let's say that your essay is good enough to be rewritten. The first step in rewriting is easy and painless: Look over your rough draft in search of its strengths. Why is it worth rewriting? You will want to keep and perhaps embellish the strong parts.

Next decide whether you should delete anything. One of the hardest parts of rewriting is throwing out material that is repetitious, weak, or off the point. Train yourself to be merciless. As Sir Arthur Quiller-Couch puts it, be prepared to "murder your darlings." No matter how interesting a detail or an example or an idea may seem to you, if it does not clearly develop the main focus of your essay, then it must go.

Once you have scratched out any material that doesn't belong, check to see if the remaining sentences and paragraphs are ordered in the best possible way. If not, try moving chunks of text. When you are working on a word processor, this is a simple matter involving a few keystrokes. When working with typed or handwritten copy, cut apart the pieces, reassemble them, and tape them into place. Or circle and label the material to be moved (insert A, insert B, and so on) and repeat the label at the point where the material should be inserted. Whichever technique you have used, check to see whether the material fits smoothly into its new position in the essay. You may need to tinker with your sentences to make it fit.

At this point, read through your essay again in search of possible gaps — places where you may need to add new material — and begin drafting. If you get stuck, circle back to the earliest stage of the writing process, brainstorming on scratch paper, before attempting to draft the new material.

Let's see how the rewriting process worked for one student, Martha Krause, as she wrote an essay encouraging parents to send their children to Sunday school. Krause's first draft, too preachy to convince many parents, found its proper home in the wastebasket. When she tackled the essay again a few days later, Krause produced a draft (written in the form of a letter) that was more carefully aimed at her readers. This time Krause decided that her draft was good enough to be rewritten. As you read the draft, printed below, consider its strengths and weaknesses. If you were Krause, what would you decide to keep, to delete, to add? Focus on large decisions rather than on the finer points of sentence structure, word choice, punctuation, or grammar.

Dear Parent,

I missed your child in my Sunday School class this past Sunday. I can not help remembering something you said when I visited your home a few weeks ago. You said, "I don't want to force my children to go to Sunday School, it may turn them against it. I leave the decision of going to church up to them."

This morning when I got up there was six inches of snow on the ground and I wondered how many parents leave the decision to the child as to whether to wear a coat, shoes, boots, mittens, etc., or did they say something like: "You are not going outside until you are properly dressed for this kind of weather." If they did, their child may not ever want to wear clothing again and they may find themselves selling their home and moving to a nudist colony.

How about the skateboard or bicycle that belongs to our neighbor's child and our child would like to keep it. Do we allow them to steal it or a candy bar or two when they go the the 7-11 store? If so, we may have hindered them on their way to becoming a well-known bank robber.

The course of least resistance is popular and just what it says, "of least resistance."

The government does not ask whether our children want to learn or to go to school, nor does it say if it is raining outside today they can stay at home. Don't we make them go to bed early so that they can get up and go to school the next day? If we force our children to go to bed early, does that mean they may never want to sleep again? If we force them to go to school to learn to read and write when they grow up they may never want to read or write again?

How about other areas of our children's lives? Aren't we concerned that we buy and prepare the right kinds of food, and don't we try to give them a diet that includes the basic four food groups each day?

If we force our children to go to Sunday School they just might like all of the love and friendliness they find there. They might like Bible study and the good sermons they will hear about Jesus Christ, who died for them and someone whom they can learn to pattern their lives; also the stories of men and women who were very human but had faith in God. They just might get enthused about the activities that are planned for them.

To take our children to Sunday School and church can be the most effective, enjoyable, and peaceful part of our week.

If we "force" our children to go to Sunday School by taking them with us on our way to church that word "force" seems to disappear. When we share in that love and friendliness of the church atmosphere, the children will want to be a part of it, too. When they see that Bible study and learning, singing, giving our tithes, and listening to a good sermon are important to us, and that this is part of worshipping God they will want to worship him, too.

> Your child's Sunday School teacher,
> Martha Krause

Krause put this draft aside for a few days, knowing that she needed to get some distance from it. When she returned to it later, she began by congratulating herself on the parts she had handled well. She was especially proud of her introduction, which addresses an imaginary reader, "Dear Parent," and then quotes the most common reason parents give when they fail to send their children to Sunday school. This introduction, Krause felt, would make direct contact with her readers. As she scanned the body of the letter, Krause admired her comparisons, although she suspected that she was providing too many of them. When she looked again at her final paragraph, she liked its message but found it too flat for a conclusion. She hoped she would be able to come up with a livelier finish.

As she got to work deleting paragraphs and sentences that weren't carrying their weight, Krause was visited with new inspirations. A couple of fresh paragraphs flowed from her pen onto scratch paper. These she inserted into the paper by cutting her typed draft apart and taping the handwritten paragraphs in place.

As you read the new and improved draft printed below, notice that at this point Krause wasn't worrying about sentence structure, wording, punctuation, or grammar. She was focusing on global revisions, knowing that there would be time enough later for polishing, editing, and proofreading.

Dear *Mr. and Mrs. Hart,* ~~Parent~~,

I missed your *daughter, Susan,* ~~child~~ in my Sunday School class this past Sunday. I can not help remembering something you said when I visited your home a few weeks ago. You said,

"I don't want to force my children to go to Sunday School, it may turn them against it. I leave the decision of going to church up to them."

This morning when I got up there was six inches of snow on the ground and I wondered how many parents leave the decision to the child as to whether to wear a coat, shoes, boots, mittens, etc., or did they say something like: "You are not going outside until you are properly dressed for this kind of weather." ~~If they did, their children may not ever want to wear clothing again and they may find themselves selling their home and moving to a nudist colony.~~

How about the skateboard or bicycle that belongs to our neighbor's child and our child would like to keep it. Do we allow them to steal it or a candy bar or two when they go to the 7-11 store? ~~If so, we may have hindered them on their way to becoming a well-known bank robber.~~

~~The course of least resistance is popular and just what it says, "of least resistance."~~

The government does not ask whether our children want to learn or go to school, nor does it say if it is raining outside today they can stay at home. ~~Don't we make them go to bed early so that they can get up and go to school the next day? If we force our children to go to bed early, does that mean they may never want to sleep again?~~

(If we force them to go to school to learn to read and
write *does that mean that* when they grow up they may never *want to* read or write

again?

~~How about other areas of our children's lives?~~
~~Aren't we concerned that we buy and prepare the right~~
~~kinds of food, and don't we try to give them a diet that~~
~~includes the basic four food groups each day?~~

If we force our children to go to Sunday School they
just might like all of the love and friendliness they find
there. They might like Bible study and the good sermons
they will hear about Jesus Christ, ~~who died for them and~~
someone *after* whom they can learn to pattern their lives; also
the stories of men and women who were very human but had
faith in God. They just might get enthused about the
activities that are planned for them.

There is just one catch - it might cost us
something. We might have to get up just a
little earlier on Sunday mornings. Ouch!
The only morning that we have to sleep in.
We would get up early to take them to catch a
ride to go to King's Dominion, or to majorette
practice, bowling, and go to see them perform
at the ball game, wouldn't we?
Isn't it worth nurturing that part of
them that will live beyond this earthly
life?

To take our children to Sunday School and church can be the most effective, enjoyable, and peaceful part of our week.

If we "force" our children to go to Sunday School by taking them with us on our way to church, that word "force" seems to disappear. When we share in that love and friendliness of the church atmosphere, the children will want to be a part of it, too. When they see that Bible study and learning, singing, giving our tithes, and listening to a good sermon are important to us, and that this is part of worshipping God they will want to worship him, too.

We would not let our children go out into bad weather improperly dressed. Should we let them walk out into life spiritually undressed?

Susan's Sunday School Teacher,
Martha Krause

You can probably guess why Krause decided to delete certain sentences and paragraphs. She scratched out the last sentences in paragraphs two and three because their humor didn't quite work. These sentences were more distracting than entertaining. As for the fourth paragraph, which consisted of a single sentence, it interrupted the reader's pattern of thought. The letter flows better if the reader can move from one example to the next without interruption.

Krause made cuts in paragraphs five and six because she felt she was overloading the reader with comparisons. She cut the ones she thought were weakest. In paragraph seven, the line "Jesus Christ, who died for them and someone whom they can learn to pattern their lives," aside from being awkward, was too preachy. So part of it had to go.

The handwritten additions, we hope you'll agree, are definite improvements. And you may have noticed another small but significant improvement. "Dear Parent" has become "Dear Mr. and Mrs. Hart," and "your child" is now "Susan." This personalized touch makes Krause's appeal even more direct and more difficult for her readers to ignore.

Martha Krause later polished, edited, and proofread the draft of the letter that you have just read. You may be interested to know that the final version appeared in *The Wesleyan Witness*, the newsletter of Krause's church.

Some Final Notes

Obviously, there is much more to writing and rewriting than we have covered in this chapter. All the rest of this book is intended to help you as you write and rewrite. As you learn more about focusing and organizing and paragraphing, you'll be better able to put together a workable draft that may need only polishing, editing, and proofreading. In the meantime, we suggest that even before you've read the rest of the book, you keep an imaginary reader looking over your shoulder whenever you write. That reader will help you decide what to delete, what to rearrange, and what to add.

We have tried to discuss the writing-rewriting process so that you can follow it step by step. But we know you won't always follow the steps in just the way we've presented them. Because writing is an act unique to each individual, there are as many different ways to go about putting a piece of writing together as there are writers. We like what Ezra Pound has to say here: "It doesn't matter which leg of your table you make first, so long as the table has four legs and will stand up solidly when you have finished it." You will discover which leg *you* find it easiest to make first as you write — and write. We say "as you write — and write" because you will soon realize that nothing reinforces good writing like writing.

Exercise 1   Written

Choose a topic from the Appendix and brainstorm ideas on scratch paper, as suggested in Chapter 1. Then, when you feel ready, draft an essay fairly quickly, without worrying too much about grammar, punctuation, and spelling. The essay should be about five hundred words long, the equivalent of two typed, double-spaced pages. Once you have produced a draft that is good enough to be rewritten, bring it to class, even though it is not yet perfect. In class either your instructor or your fellow students will help you get distance from the draft and plan a strategy for revision.

Exercise 2 Classroom Activity

Interview someone you know who does quite a lot of writing, either on the job or in college. Find out from this person in as much detail as possible how he or she approaches writing tasks. In conducting your interview, you might use the following questions as guidelines:

1. What do you do, if anything, before you begin a first draft? For example, do you jot down ideas on scratch paper, talk about your ideas with anyone willing to listen, or mull over ideas late at night and then sleep on them?

2. How do you organize your ideas — in your head or on paper? Do you use outlines, and if so, how formal are they?

3. Where and when are you most comfortable writing?

4. Do you type rough drafts, write them in longhand, or put them on a word processor? Are you addicted to any sort of paper and pen? Do you single-space or double-space a draft; do you write on both sides of the paper?

5. Do you use a dictionary, a thesaurus, or a grammar handbook? If so, when do you usually consult these references — while writing the draft or later?

6. How do you "get distance" from a draft? Do you have someone read what you have written, get advice, and then rewrite? Or do you usually handle revision all on your own? Which of your friends, relatives, and colleagues can be trusted to offer helpful advice?

7. Do you make major revisions in a rough draft — revisions that go beyond the level of the sentence? For example, do you consider adding, deleting, or moving whole paragraphs? If so, how do you handle such changes — by making them on a word processor, by cutting and taping, by using circles and arrows, or by recopying the whole draft?

8. What sorts of sentence-level revisions do you make?

9. How do you handle proofreading?

10. How much time do you usually spend on a writing task? Do you spread your work over several days or wait until the last minute? What proportion of the time you spend is devoted to each of these stages of the writing process: prewriting, writing, and revision?

Bring notes on your interview to class and be prepared to share them with the group. If possible, also bring a page or two of rough copy from the person you interviewed, so other members of the class can get some sense of what your writer's in-process writing looks like. Be prepared to tell why — for what exact purpose — your writer writes.

Exercise 3   For Class Discussion

A friend has just written his first draft of a review of the Pines Steak House, and he has asked you to help him get distance from the paper. Begin by saying something positive. Why is the paper good enough to be rewritten? Then suggest possible improvements, focusing on large-scale changes, not on sentence structure, wording, punctuation, or grammar.

The Pines Steak House is a nationally known, underclassed chain of restaurants. Its main entrée, of course, is steak and potatoes.

I think that the Pines, as it is often called, is underclassed because people usually compare it with fast-food restaurants such as McDonalds and Hardees. If these people would just take a good look at the advantages of the Pines, however, they would surely stop comparing it with fast-food joints.

One good factor of the Pines is the prices that they charge for their dinners. The dinners are quite inexpensive when compared to other restaurants that specialize in steak. Consider the meat used by the Pines. It is fresh, tasty, and prepared to order. The meat used by some fast-food restaurants is probably not even 100 percent pure beef.

When you visit the Pines you will do well to select the baked potato instead of the french fried potatoes because a baked potato not only tastes better, but is also better for you. McDonalds prepare their french fries by using grease. If you select a baked potato, I suggest using butter, salt, and pepper to enhance its taste.

The Pines' soft drinks are cold and thirst-quenching; their hot rolls are fresh and soaked with butter.

For vegetarians the salad bar is ideal. The bar is stocked with fresh lettuce, juicy tomatoes, crisp onions, beans, pickles, peppers, and several types of dressing that go with salads. The purchase of a dinner entitles a diner to all the salad he or she can eat.

The seven or eight dinner choices range from chopped steak on a roll to a belt-tightening and satisfying T-bone special. A diner at the Pines also has plenty of choices for dessert: strawberry cheesecake, chocolate pudding, Jello, cake, and pie.

When you go to the Pines and there is a long line of people waiting to order dinner, do not be discouraged; just wait the few minutes it takes to get a great dinner. You definitely will not be disappointed.

Take your steak dinner to the beautiful dining area and take your time eating so you can savor every bite.

Exercise 4   For Thought and Discussion

If the idea of *re*writing — perhaps even several drafts — sounds like just too much trouble to you, maybe the following comments by both professional writers and successful student writers will help to convince you. Think about the comments and be ready to talk about them in class.

1. What is written without effort is in general read without pleasure.
   — SAMUEL JOHNSON, BRITISH WRITER AND CRITIC

2. The best reason for putting anything down on paper is that one may then change it.
   — BERNARD DE VOTO, AMERICAN WRITER

3. There is no such thing as good writing, only good rewriting.
   — LOUIS BRANDEIS, SUPREME COURT JUSTICE

4. I read my paper over and over. I think about it a lot. I use a great deal of paper. I rewrite and rewrite until it says what I want it to say.
   — A STUDENT

5. I have never thought of myself as a good writer. . . . But I'm one of the world's great rewriters.
   — JAMES MICHENER, AMERICAN WRITER

6. Easy writing makes hard reading.
   — ERNEST HEMINGWAY, AMERICAN NOVELIST

7. My goal in everything I write is simplicity. I'm a demon on the subject of revision. I revise, revise, revise, until every word is the one I want.
   — BEN LUCIEN BERMAN, AMERICAN AUTHOR

8. I can't write five words but that I change seven.
   — DOROTHY PARKER, AMERICAN WRITER

9. I keep rereading what I have written, making changes where needed. I do this about six or seven times until I feel it is right.
   — A STUDENT

10. Writing and rewriting are a constant search for what it is one is saying.
    — JOHN UPDIKE, AMERICAN NOVELIST

11. He would scratch and then put in a word and scratch and work and then paste on another piece of paper and the whole thing would be new. And then when the typed script would come he was still working on it.
    — RAPHAEL HAMILTON, ABOUT J.R.R. TOLKIEN

Exercise 5   For Discussion and Action

Professional writers tell us that rewriting is an essential part of the writing process. But in spite of all the talk about the importance of rewriting, most writers — especially beginning writers — are tempted not to rewrite. If you find yourself tempted to skip the rewriting stage, try to discover *why*. When urged to be honest in an anonymous poll, our students came up with this list of reasons. Are any of these *your* reasons?

1. I wait until the last minute, so there's no time to rewrite.

2. My first draft is the best I can do. I can't improve it.

3. I don't know whether my first draft is any good or not, so how can I improve it?

4. I don't know where to begin, and I wouldn't know when to stop.

5. Well, frankly, I'm lazy.

6. When I tinker with my sentences, they just turn out worse.

7. I don't really care about what I'm writing, so I just want to get it over with.

8. Rewriting is too messy. I like to work with clean-looking pages.

9. I'm such a bad writer I hate to read my own writing.

10. Rewriting is my instructor's responsibility.

11. Rewriting is painful. I can't stand the agony.

12. If I can't get it right the first time, I must be stupid.

What can you do to overcome the temptation not to rewrite?

Exercise 6 Just for Fun

I've always tried out my material on my dogs first. You know, with Angel, he sits there and listens and I get the feeling that he understands everything. But with Charley, I always felt that he was just waiting to get a word in edgewise. — JOHN STEINBECK, AMERICAN NOVELIST

3 Polishing, Editing, and Proofreading

Blot out, correct, insert, refine
Enlarge, diminish, interline;
Be mindful, when invention fails,
To scratch your head, and bite your nails. — JONATHAN SWIFT

Once you are satisfied with your global revisions, you are ready to think about some finer points — polishing, editing, and proofreading. We suggest you work on these sentence-level concerns only after dealing with the global revisions discussed in Chapter 2.

Polishing

Polishing consists of a variety of improvements in sentence structure and wording. Here, for example, is a rough-draft paragraph from our first chapter as it appeared after it was polished.

> *Most writers do at least some of their creative*
> ~~Getting something down on paper at once may prove in-~~
> *thinking on scratch paper.*
> ~~valuable to you when you finally sit down to write.~~
>   *I jot*
> ~~Professional writers know this, so~~ *t*hey ~~scribble~~ ideas on
>   *or cocktail napkins*
> the backs of envelopes, ~~on~~ recipe cards or paper bags, or
>   *handy*
> scraps of cardboard -- on whatever happens to be ∧~~around~~ at
>   *remarks*
> the time. Anne Tyler, a writer and mother of two, ∧~~says~~:
> "In the evenings occasionally -- between baths and other
> sorts of chaos -- a sudden idea will flash into my mind
> . . . I write it down and take it to my study."

An important part of polishing is deleting excess words. In the opening lines of our sample rough-draft paragraph, for example, we condensed twenty-four words into twelve, with very little loss of meaning. The opening sentence, relieved of the clutter of excess words, is easier to read. It is also more pleasing to the ear.

As you work to delete excess words, you'll probably notice words that need changing for one reason or another. Maybe you used the wore *attire* when the more ordinary word *clothing* would have sounded better; or perhaps you wrote *friend* when *benefactor* would have been more precise. You may have any number of reasons for deciding to change words, as you can see from the examples below.

Already the gale-force winds ~~came~~ *roared* through the walls.

(more vivid verb)

Until recently, ~~those individuals fortunate enough to further their knowledge with a college education~~ *college professors* were always in demand. (less pretentious -- and fewer words too)

The ~~loud~~ *raucous* cry of the seagulls greeted us as we neared the shore. (more precise adjective)

The doctors all had very ~~expensive~~ *lucrative* practices. (correct word to replace word improperly used)

My first time at bat I struck out, and every time after that / ~~This was probably due to the fact that~~ *because* I would swing at anything that came my way. (less wordy)

If you think these strangely named sandwiches will ^*empty* ~~cost~~
your wallet,
~~you an arm and a leg,~~ don't worry. (more vivid image to

replace cliché)

The ^*rat-a-tat-tat* ~~pecking~~ of the woodpecker woke me early the first

morning of our camping trip. (livelier word to replace

awkward repetition of "peck")

^*Tension*
~~Emotion~~ began to build as the union committee debated the

wage-and-inflation spiral. (more specific word for exact

emotion felt)

Just as you may have different reasons for changing words, you may
have a variety of reasons for deciding to restructure sentences. A re-
structured sentence might be clearer, more emphatic, or more rhythmic
than the original. It might connect more smoothly with the sentences
that come before, or point more clearly to the sentences that come after.
To give you a feel for the variety of reasons you might have for changing
sentences, we print the following polished sentences from students'
rough drafts.

We agreed ^*that the arrival and departure of the Concorde* ~~to the idea that it~~ must have been an impressive

sight. ~~to have seen the Concorde arrive and depart.~~ (more

forceful, more rhythmic —— and less wordy)

Slowly ~~the realization had taken place~~ *I realized* that this was some-

thing I could not control. (more direct)

The officers told us that someone ^*in our seating section had been* ~~was throwing particles~~

~~of ice from the vicinity of our seats,~~ pelting the inno-
with pieces of ice
cent fans below^ (more straightforward, less pretentious)

This is the first day of Carnival in Trinidad, West

Indies,/ ~~This~~ *a* celebration *that* occurs two days prior to Ash

Wednesday each year. (more emphatic, more fluid)

~~The thunderous roar of~~ *T*he waves ~~can be heard as they~~

crash into the stone breakers. *with a thunderous roar.* (more vigorous and

emphatic)

The spinner bait is a V-shaped object with two metal

spoons at one end,/ *and* ~~At the other end is~~ a hook, ~~with~~ *camouflaged by* a

skirt, ~~which is camouflaging it~~. *at the other.* (more balanced and

smoother)

For more detailed advice on polishing sentences, read Chapters 11 and 12 and consult sections 17–21 of "A Writer's Handbook" (Part Seven of this book).

Editing

Editing is correcting errors in grammar, punctuation, and mechanics. You will save yourself time if you edit by crossing out and inserting letters, words, and marks of punctuation instead of recopying the whole sentence. The following sentences have been edited for the very errors they are warning us against:

Don't use ~~no~~ double negatives.

A verb ~~have~~ *has* to agree with its subject.

Watch out for irregular verbs that have ~~came~~ *come* to you in the

wrong form.

Discriminate ^*carefully* ~~careful~~ between adjectives and adverbs.

Don't write a comma splice ^; you must connect the clauses correctly.

It's ~~Its~~ important to use *apostrophes* ~~apostrophe's~~ correctly.

When choosing pronouns, follow the example of ~~we~~ ^*us* teachers, ~~whom~~ ^*who* always speak correctly.

Proofread to see if you ^*left* any words out.

The handbook section of this book, Part Seven, will serve as a reference as you edit. It includes advice about common problems such as subject-verb agreement, comma splices, the proper use of *who* and *whom,* and errors in punctuation. We suggest that you scan the handbook's brief table of contents (inside the front cover of this book) to get a sense of what you can find there.

If you are familiar with the major rules of grammar, punctuation, and mechanics, you'll be able to handle most editing problems on your own. When in doubt about a particularly tricky matter, you can simply look it up in the handbook. However, if your background in grammar is weak and you tend to make a lot of mistakes, you will need to become familiar with the rules of English that are causing you problems. Either your instructor or your college's writing center can help you devise an individualized program of self-study.

Proofreading

After polishing and editing, you are ready to type or handwrite your final draft. Then only one task remains. It is a very important, if not a very exciting task — proofreading. Proofreading is a slow and careful reading in search of typographical errors, spelling mistakes, and omitted words or word endings.

Many students have difficulty proofreading. Several times a semester we hear comments like this one, from a frustrated student: "I've tried proofreading, but I just don't see my own errors. When they're pointed out, the mistakes are so obvious — so stupid. Why can't *I* catch them?"

One answer is that proofreading requires special skills. Your tendency when reading is to scan individual words quickly in search of the meaning of a whole passage. To proofread, you need to fight your ordinary reading habits. Since the purpose of proofreading is not to grasp meaning but to spot errors, you need to pay more attention to surfaces than to content. This special kind of reading is difficult, because your usual habits keep pulling your attention away from the errors you are trying to spot. Professional proofreaders become skilled only through practice, and with practice you too can improve.

The best way to proofread is to read your paper out loud, making yourself say aloud *exactly* what is on the page — not just what you intended to write there. If you read this way, slowly and deliberately, word by word, your ear will often tell you that you've added an unnecessary comma, dropped a letter from a word, or left out an entire word. When you read silently, these errors can slip right past you.

As we mentioned earlier, proofreading is not the most exciting part of the writing process, but it is nevertheless important, not so much because errors confuse readers — often they don't — but because they're distracting and annoying. They suggest too much haste and too little care.

We know that the writing process may not occur quite as systematically as we have suggested in these three chapters. We have deliberately divided the procedure into definable steps, so that we can talk about everything that might need attention as you rework your early drafts. But certainly you may spot a misspelled word at the same time that you are considering reorganization. So much the better. We would caution you, though, against consciously trying to deal with the big questions and all the little errors at once. That can get to be overwhelming and counterproductive.

Letting It Go

After so much serious talk about reworking your paper, we want to warn you against perfectionism. It is possible to worry a paper to death: Are my sentences varied enough? Shall I use this word or that one here? A comma or not there? A writer needs to know when to quit — when to release his or her writing to the world, to let it go.

Perhaps there is a fine line between not caring enough about your writing and caring too much. We don't know how to help you draw that line. But it is only fair to warn you that if you are a perfectionist in other areas of your life, you may tend to be the same way toward your writing. Our best advice here: Remember that there is no such thing as a perfect piece of writing; there will always be alternative ways to handle every part of it. Just try to make your writing clear, readable, and at least somewhat interesting — a piece of work you yourself can reasonably respect. Then let it go.

Exercise 1   For Class Discussion

Below are a number of rough-draft sentences that have been polished. Why do you suppose the writers made these changes?

1. I flopped down on my belly and slid about fifteen feet
    until my skis ~~hit~~ *grabbed* a tree.

2. Sister *Charity* got her kicks from passing out writing punish-
    ments: translate the Ten Commandments into Latin, type a
    ~~hundred~~ thousand-word essay on good manners, write the <u>New</u>
    <u>Testament</u> with a quill pen.

3. My husband, fearing his head might be snapped off, was
    ~~apprehensive~~ *afraid* to approach me.

4. For the first time in a long ~~time,~~ *while* I ~~put~~ *shouldered* my $300 Raleigh
    ~~on my shoulder~~ and brought it up from the basement.

5. We learned to listen to a lecture and take *well-organized* notes.~~in a~~
    ~~much better organized train of thought.~~

6. The odor of burnt grease permeated the room and a
    thick, gray cloud of smoke hung low.~~over the vicinity.~~

7.　Where else could you get an entire steak dinner for

three dollars?

about ~~two dollars and ninety four cents?~~

link with the doctors.

8.　The nurse is our ~~middleman~~.

restated

9.　The plainclothes officers ~~reinstated~~ their demand that

we leave with them.

As we　　　　　*up to*

10.　~~We had just~~ pulled ~~into~~ the entrance gate, ~~when~~ a man

put out his hand　*demanded*

~~approached my car~~ and ~~asked for~~ three dollars.

Exercise 2　*For Class Discussion*

Below are three paired paragraphs. One in each pair is a rough draft, and the other is the writer's polished revision. Which one do you think is the new and improved version, and how is it better? (*Note:* Each paragraph is taken from a whole paper. The first is from the middle of a paper, the second is an introduction, and the third is a conclusion.)

1a.　The receptionist at the counter tells the owner to have a seat until the doctor is ready. To the client the room is cheerful, with its plants, bright red floor, and picture window. The dog, hiding under a glass table, thinks of plans of escape. The counter is too high to jump over and the window is too risky. A cat across the room hisses and he loses control. The owner is embarrassed and cleans up the puddle on the floor.

1b.　The receptionist at the counter tells the owner to have a seat until the doctor is ready. "My, what a cheerful little room," thinks Mrs. Williams as she notices the plants, bright red floor, and picture window. Pootchie, hiding under a glass-topped table, is thinking of escape routes. But the counter is too high to jump over and the window is too risky. A cat across the room hisses and poor Pootchie loses control. Embarrassed, Mrs. Williams cleans up the puddle on the floor.

2a.　On our wedding day some nineteen years ago, I did not know just how much "to love and to cherish" would mean to that man in my life. He is such a lover — of football, baseball, basketball, tennis, golf, boxing, and horse racing.

2b. On that very important day some nineteen years ago, I did not realize just what "to love and to cherish" was going to entail. He is such a lover of football, baseball, basketball, tennis, golf, boxing, horse racing, and (if there are others) many more.

3a. As I was entering my apartment I heard the noise coming again, and I was furious. Upon reaching the door of the offender, I noticed something was on there. What was it? It looked like a doorbell. Why would she have a doorbell in an apartment? I decided to push the button, and in a few seconds the door opened. Standing there was this lady. In a boisterous voice I said this noise has to stop. I worked hard today and I want some peace and quiet. She put a finger up as if to say just a minute and closed the door. Boy, she is weird. The door opened and she handed me a piece of paper as if she wanted me to write down my problem. This puzzled me, but I wrote my complaint in plain English. She then responded with a note of her own: "Sorry for the noise. I did not know the children were disturbing you. I'll try to do my best to keep it down. I cannot hear or talk. Thank you, Mrs. Johnson."

3b. As I was entering my apartment, I heard the thumping again, and I was furious. When I reached the door of the offender I noticed a doorbell, which seemed odd since no one else in the building had one. I decided to push the button, and in a few seconds the door opened. Standing there was an attractive young woman. In a loud voice I proclaimed, "This noise has got to stop. I worked hard to-day and I want some peace and quiet." She put her finger up as if to say "just a minute," then closed the door. "Boy, is she weird," I thought. When the door opened, she handed me a piece of paper as if she wanted me to write down my problem. This puzzled me, but I wrote down my complaint in plain English. She then responded with a note of her own: "Sorry for the noise. I did not know the children were disturbing you. I'll do my best to control them. I cannot hear or talk. Thank you, Mrs. Johnson."

Exercise 3   Small Group Activity

Working with other students in small groups, read through the following essay in search of sentences that need polishing. Have one member of your group read the essay out loud, and as he or she reads, listen for wordiness, inappropriate choice of words, awkward sentences, unemphatic sentences, and other such problems. Then discuss the problems you heard and be prepared to explain to the rest of the class why your group thinks particular sentences need revision.

One of the places in our community where you can find a good evening's entertainment is the Hayloft Dinner Theater. Too few people seem to be aware of this local cultural attraction on Route 450. As its name suggests, the Hayloft offers you not only a great evening of enjoyment but also includes in the price of an $11.00 ticket your evening meal.

The Hayloft is open Tuesday, Wednesday, Thursday, Friday, Saturday, and Sunday nights. Dinner is served buffet style, with a waiter coming to your table to take drink orders and menu preferences; this begins at 5:30. There is a salad bar to which everybody is invited to go, featuring many chopped vegetables, cottage cheese, bacon bits, and lots of kinds of salad dressings. You can almost stack up a meal at the salad bar itself.

When my father, mother, brother, sisters and I ventured out to the Hayloft recently, we ordered several different main dishes. A list of these is chicken kiev, ham supreme with pineapple, crab imperial, stuffed veal, lasagna, and egg rolls with fried rice; the variety of food at the Hayloft is very varied. Each serving was really enormous and everything tasted good. I could have left the Hayloft truly full and happy after that fantastic meal.

But of course we stayed for whatever else was to come. That night the Hayloft Hayseeds had planned to perform "Fiddler on the Roof." The Hayseeds are especially well-known around these parts for the musicals they put on — and they certainly did a good job when they acted in "Fiddler." Everyone seemed to get into the spirit of the evening, and by the time we all stood up to give the cast a big hand of standing applause, it was hard to believe that it was nearly 11:00. Just then someone shouted, "Chef! Chef!" so that we were able to express our appreciation of the food as well as the play.

So gather your family or friends and head for the Hayloft. I assure you that you will find there a night of cheap fun.

Exercise 4 Written

Bring the rough draft of a paper you are working on to class. Then, working with one other student, read each other's rough drafts aloud and try to spot sentences in need of polishing, either for clarity or for smoothness. As your partner reads your paper aloud, mark any problem sentences. Then go off by yourself to polish those sentences. Ask your partner to read your new version to check on its clarity and smoothness.

Part Two

The Writer's Voice

4 *Finding a Voice*

The personality I am expressing in this written sentence is not the same as the one I orally express to my three-year-old who at this moment is bent on climbing onto my typewriter. For each of these two situations, I choose a different "voice," a different mask, in order to accomplish what I want accomplished. — WALKER GIBSON

"False starts in writing," says writing teacher Gerald Levin, "are often failures to discover the right voice." The right voice will be one you're comfortable with, one that suits your personality. But more than that, it will be a voice appropriate to your *purpose* in writing and to the particular *audience* you have in mind.

Purpose and Audience

Often you will know exactly what you hope to accomplish in a piece of writing. Consider on-the-job writing, for example. Usually your audience will be quite clear: perhaps your supervisor, a client, a board of directors, or your coworkers. And you will nearly always know why you are writing: maybe to inform your supervisor about a workshop he or she did not attend, to ask a client to pay an outstanding bill, to present next year's budget request to the board of directors, or to encourage coworkers to cooperate with you in implementing a training program.

In such writing situations, which have a given purpose and audience, common sense often tells you which writing voice to adopt. You might decide to sound businesslike in the memo to your supervisor, diplomatic but firm in the letter to the client, impersonal and objective in the budget request, and relaxed and friendly in the letter to coworkers.

Finding the right voice is not always easy, however, and this is especially true in college English, a writing situation that does not automatically supply you with a purpose and an audience. You may seem to have a specific audience — your instructor — and a clear purpose — to impress him or her with your writing ability. But if you write merely to impress your instructor, the result is almost certain to be voiceless "assignment prose," a kind of writing that in fact impresses few teachers of writing.

Consider, for example, the following student paragraphs, written at the very beginning of the semester:

> *Psycho*, directed by Alfred Hitchcock, is an excellent movie. This contemporary classic is seen occasionally on television and is released to movie theaters quite often. Probably the most well-known scene from *Psycho* is the one in which Janet Leigh is murdered. In this scene and throughout the entire film, Hitchcock combines suspense, symbolism, and an ingenious plot.
>
> It is advisable to see *Psycho* more than once. Many seemingly obscure details will become important after the second viewing. Hitchcock's twists and turns make *Psycho* a truly exciting movie.

The voice in these paragraphs does not speak to readers because the writer hasn't decided who they are. Did the student write for an audience interested in hearing about an exciting, suspense-filled movie? Is she trying to get these readers so excited about the film that they'll want to see it? Or is she writing for another group of readers, perhaps those interested in the film's artistic merits? Is she analyzing *Psycho* for them, the way one might analyze a poem by Emily Dickinson or a play by George Bernard Shaw?

Most likely the writer had neither group of readers clearly in mind. Since she wasn't sure who she was writing to, or for what purpose, our student couldn't decide what to say. She mentions that *Psycho* is an excellent movie; a classic; an artistic film with suspense, symbolism, and an ingenious plot; a film so complex it requires several viewings; and an exciting movie. But notice that none of these messages has been developed. Readers truly interested in hearing about the film's complexity, or those who would like a vivid description of the "well-known scene in which Janet Leigh is murdered," are disappointed. The brief essay mentions these points and others, then drops them all.

You may feel that we're being too hard on this student writer. After all, her vocabulary is impressive, her sentence structure is sophisticated, and she hasn't made a single grammatical mistake. True enough. But we nevertheless persuaded her to toss these paragraphs out and try again, perhaps on another topic. We weren't sorry, and neither was the student. A week later she wrote an essay not in "assignment prose," but in a voice that speaks to readers. Here is her final draft:

The Therapeutic Parachute

Troubles of the mind have continued to perplex doctors, nurses, and patients alike. Now, as a student nurse I've been told that a parachute is going to unlock the minds of some of these troubled patients. The whole idea is insane — or is it?

I was handed a folded army surplus parachute and told to accompany ten uptight psychiatric patients and a movement therapist to the gym. My first impression: the gym's a convenient place to rid the psychiatric ward of these patients, thus relieving the nurses. The movement therapist is a surrogate nurse hired to play games with the disturbed.

"Everyone take your shoes off. Hard soles have been known to mar the surface of the floor," shouted the therapist. Reluctantly everyone did as instructed. With the removal of our shoes, formality was banished.

Barefooted, we all hurried onto the floor to help unfold this khaki-colored bundle of cloth. This was a job in itself and it took all available hands to unfold it. With mission accomplished, we awaited our next step. What on earth could this wacky therapist have planned for us and this monstrous-looking mass of cloth?

Again we were hustled into activity. "Take hold of the parachute and shake it. Shake it hard. That's good . . . now less forcefully."

Just then I looked up into the faces of my patients. Faces that were once expressionless, angered, frightened, or sad were undergoing change right before my very eyes.

Myra, who had been without expression and in an almost catatonic state, had the look of belonging. Gary, my favorite, a fifteen-year-old boy who was filled with anger and hostility, seemed tranquil. This sudden release of energy without reprimand or repercussion had freed him plenty.

I believe the most rewarding transformation came over Lee. Lee, husband and father of two, was a deeply depressed man. He had tried to take his life just days before. As we were shaking the parachute, it created a breeze that felt to me like a wind from a mild autumn day. The gentle surge of air made me feel so warm and relaxed. As I looked into Lee's face I could see that I was not the only one experiencing this warmth and relaxation. It looked as if the weight of the world had been momentarily lifted from his shoulders.

Next we spread the parachute out flat on the floor. Each person was encouraged to lie on it while the rest of us took hold of the chute and tried to create different sensations for the rider. Most of us preferred the slow walk of the group, which created a rocking-chair effect. When I took my turn in the center of the chute, with eyes closed, the wavelike motions enveloped me in a serenity that I had not experienced in years.

As we left the gym that day, we did so united. We no longer felt alone, at least for the time being. If this hunk of army surplus can lighten the load of a troubled mind, if only momentarily, it is indeed of great value for the well-being of a psychiatric patient. — JENNY SHELTON

Here our writer has a clear sense of who her readers are. They are people who are skeptical, as the writer once was, about using a parachute for psychiatric therapy. Her purpose is to convince those readers that a "hunk of army surplus" can indeed "lighten the load of a troubled mind."

Probably the most important advice we can give you this semester is to write for readers you can envision, as this student did. If you're writing about the junk food in the vending machines at your child's school, don't tell your instructor about it. Aim your paper at other parents and write with a purpose — to get the parents to help you take action. Or if you're contrasting the merits of a Suzuki and a Harley-Davidson, write to readers who are interested in buying motorcycles; help them decide how to spend their money. When giving advice on the care of hanging ferns, imagine readers who don't know how to care for them but want to learn. Or if you think you have the secret to success in tennis, imagine readers eager to improve their game. Don't worry if your instructor is not a plant lover or a tennis player. Your instructor is interested in your ability to communicate purposefully, not in your ability to figure out what he or she is interested in.

Writer and Readers

As we mentioned in Chapter 1, the early stages of the writing process are creative, mysterious, hard to pin down. This is true partly because writing involves people, and because only one of them happens to be present: you, the writer. As you mull over ideas while weeding petunias or repairing your bicycle, as you jot down notes late at night, or as you sharpen pencils and pour yourself another cup of coffee, you're becoming acquainted with your future readers. They aren't there, of course, but you're thinking about them, sometimes even inventing a role for them. And at the same time, you're beginning to discover your own role as writer, or to invent it.

For example, one young woman, who wrote about a strange plant that she had recently discovered, began to see her readers as gardeners desperate for an easy-care houseplant that wouldn't die on them. Once she envisioned these readers, she understood her own role as writer. She would be the self-confident expert with the perfect answer to their problem: the air fern, a plant that couldn't die on them because it was already dead

Having settled on one role for herself as writer (the expert) and another for her readers (desperate gardeners willing to try anything), this student was able to find the right voice for her essay, as you can see from her first paragraph:

Do you love plants, yet they always seem to die on you? You can't decorate your indoors with greenery because the little devils shrivel up to an ugly brown? If you weren't born with a green thumb, I have the perfect plant for you. It's the poriferan, more commonly known as the air fern.

Even if you don't happen to be in search of the perfect houseplant, you are probably willing, as you read on, to play the role of the desperate gardener. Sensing from the opening paragraph that this is the role the writer has created for you, you are willing to cooperate with her, and to enjoy her tongue-in-cheek humor along the way.

The air fern is a gorgeous, delicate little plant that really isn't a plant at all. It's dead. Aside from its dainty appearance, being deceased is its greatest asset. It needs no tender loving care to sustain its life, because it has already passed on.

Under no circumstances will you have to prune, weed, repot, or fertilize your air fern. This is one plant you'll never have to sing to or talk to or play classical music for. Now you won't have to hide your plants in the other room when you're having a loud party. Play any type of music *you* want to hear — it doesn't care.

Are you worried about where to put your new houseplant? Well, your worries are over. Put it anywhere — in a corner, on a table, on a shelf, or even in a closet. Air ferns can survive anywhere.

No need to fuss about getting a neighbor to water your air fern while you are on vacation; in fact, no need to water the beauty at all. Which of course eliminates the problem of measuring water, counting days between watering, and misting. Never, never water the air fern.

Cost? An attractive vase of air fern will cost approximately two dollars. To make it thrive, you'll need no expensive food or plant lights. And you'll never need to replace it, because it can't die on you like the more costly, temperamental plants.

Follow the simple instruction "Leave your air fern alone" and you will be the green thumb of your neighborhood. When your friends compliment you on your healthy ferns, just smile, relax, and enjoy the fact that they are dead. — ANNE REEVES

The Writer's Stance

As you're deciding on roles for yourself and your readers, you'll need to choose a stance or a point of view from which to deliver your message. Will you address readers from the first-person point of view (*I* or *we*), putting yourself into the essay? Will you write from the second-person point of view (*you*), pitching your message directly to readers? Or will you choose the more distant third-person point of view (*he/she, one,* or *they*)?

You may have to experiment awhile before discovering a comfortable stance. In the following rough-draft introduction, for example, the writer is having trouble finding his footing:

> Psychology is a course which will arouse one's curiosity about such subjects as mental illness, suicide, dreams, forgetfulness, and your everyday routine. After learning about these and other subjects, you will begin to understand yourself and others a little better.

Notice that the writer begins in the distant third-person point of view ("*one's* curiosity"), then shifts to the second person (*your* everyday routine . . . *you* will begin"). This wavering commitment to a point of view plagued the writer's entire rough draft. Some of the later paragraphs addressed readers in the third person: "Dreams are another subject that proves interesting to many *students* of psychology." Other paragraphs spoke more directly, in the second person: "Do *you* have a fear of high places (acrophobia), open spaces (agoraphobia), or darkness (nyctophobia)?"

As the writer reread his rough draft, he realized that he would have to settle on one stance or the other. After thinking about his purpose — to convince fellow students to sign up for a psychology course — he decided on the direct approach. He rewrote the paragraph that began "Dreams are another subject that proves interesting to many *students* of psychology," this time from the second-person point of view: "Have *you* ever dreamed that you were falling from a cliff, running from wild animals, or choking on ashes?" He aligned the openings of all of the other paragraphs in the body of the essay with this one, and rewrote the introductory paragraph as follows:

> Psychology is a course that will get *you* interested in mental illness, suicide, dreams, forgetfulness, and even your everyday routine. After learning about these and other subjects, *you* will begin to understand yourself and others a little better.

But, you may be wondering, what ever happened to the prohibition against using the word *you*? Shouldn't the writer have stuck to the impersonal third-person point of view throughout?

We don't think so. Some instructors might argue, with reason, that students need practice writing in the third-person point of view, but few would claim that the use of *you* is never effective. Our student writer decided, quite intelligently, that given his purpose and audience, addressing his readers as "you" was more effective than writing about "psychology students" in general.

Consider another well-known prohibition: the rule against using the word *I*. It's true that sometimes this little pronoun can sound intrusive. Sometimes it puts too much emphasis on the writer, too little on the subject. But once again, the choice depends on what the writer is trying to accomplish. For certain purposes the "I" point of view is the best.

For example, Kathleen Lewis, the former flight attendant whose essay is mentioned in Chapter 1, first drafted her essay from the third-person point of view, carefully removing herself from her subject, the supposed glamour of her former profession. But nearly everything she wanted to put into the essay came from personal experience, so she had to rethink her approach. Here is the rough draft of her opening paragraph, written from the distant third-person point of view:

> On the surface the life of an airline stewardess seems ideal. Advertisements on television portray the stewardess as a beautiful girl with a fascinating and exciting job. Upon closer scrutiny, however, this occupation is not as glamorous as it may seem.

Not bad, really, but the revised version, drafted from the "I" point of view, is better:

> Broadway Joe enters the cabin, smiles at the camera and says, "When you've got it, flaunt it." Such an inducement was hard for a nineteen-year-old to ignore, so I sent in my application for the position of airline stewardess.

Once she had shifted her stance, Lewis improved her voice just as dramatically later in the essay. Consider, for example, this paragraph from her original draft, written from third-person point of view:

> A social life can be difficult to arrange when one is on short layovers or working different shifts. The stewardess may fly to exotic places; however, very often the plane must make the return trip immediately. So, if she is on a "run" to Paris, she may never see it! Nor is she likely to get to know many Parisians.

Again, this is not bad writing. But it's uninspired, because in avoiding the use of the word *I*, Lewis has put an unnatural restriction on herself. Once she decided to tell us what her own social life was like, instead of writing about stewardesses' social lives in general, she wrote a much more powerful paragraph:

> The most lonely times were the "layovers," a normal part of the working trip. They involved spending the night in a motel room, eating

cold sandwiches for dinner, and washing out a dirty uniform for the next day's flight. Sometimes I wasn't lucky enough to make it to a motel. I can remember spending my first Christmas eve away from my family sleeping on a bench in the Kansas City airport. Of course when I was really lonely, I could always refer to the stack of calling cards that were passed out by deplaning salesmen — "if you're ever in Chicago, give me a call and I'll show you around."

Writers often attempt the third-person point of view when the "I" or "you" stance would be more appropriate. But there are situations, of course, in which the third person is the appropriate choice. Business writing, technical writing, and much college writing are often best composed from the impersonal third-person point of view.

The third-person stance puts both writer and reader behind the scenes, where they frequently belong. In the following introductory paragraph, for example, the writer decided to put his subject up front, without injecting himself or his readers into the discussion:

> Although the sixties saw blacks struggling to attain civil rights, they are still a long way from the equality they need. However, for a group that has been oppressed in this country for two-hundred-odd years, the black population has been socially significant. Blacks have influenced the white middle class by their modes of dress, language, music, and dance.

Here the third-person stance was an appropriate choice. If the writer had mentioned his own identity as a black or a white, or if he had assumed certain racial attitudes on the part of his readers, he would have distracted us from his message: that the black culture has had a significant impact on the life-styles of white Americans.

Like the students we have quoted in this chapter, you'll be able to find the right voice for an essay once you've experimented awhile. But don't expect to sound like the same person every time you write. You might be an experienced mountain climber in one essay, an outraged victim of discrimination in another, the devoted parent of a retarded child in still another. Writers are something like actors. As Walker Gibson puts it, "Somehow the writer has to evoke, out of mere ink marks on the paper, a character whose language the reader will trust, enjoy, profit from."

Exercise 1   For Thought and Discussion

Writers often speak of the importance of the human voice behind a piece of writing. Here is what some have said. Think about their observations in relation both to writing you have read and to your own writing.

1. Style usually means some form of fancy writing — when people say, oh yes, so and so is such a "wonderful stylist." But if one means by style the voice, the irreducible and always recognizable and alive thing, then of course style is everything.
   — MARY MCCARTHY, AMERICAN AUTHOR

2. The audience fails to understand the writer because the writer has failed to understand the audience.
   — ANONYMOUS

3. The ideal reader of my novels is a lapsed Catholic and failed musician, short-sighted, colorblind, auditorily biased, who has read the books that I have read. He should also be about my age.
   — ANTHONY BURGESS, BRITISH WRITER

4. Who touches this book touches a human being.
   — WALT WHITMAN, FIRST PAGE OF *LEAVES OF GRASS*

5. I've enjoyed writing in a course where I've been encouraged to experiment with my own voice.
   — A STUDENT

6. Writing, when properly managed (as you may be sure I think mine is), is but a different name for conversation.
   — LAURENCE STERNE, ENGLISH NOVELIST

Exercise 2   For Class Discussion

Discuss the writer's stance in each of these introductory paragraphs. Does the choice of first-, second-, or third-person point of view seem appropriate, considering the writer's apparent purpose and audience? If not, what would you suggest instead?

1. As I sit at a table with my friends, I invite you to join me at an African party. Although it is half past twelve o'clock, the party is just beginning. Drain the glass that has been set before you, clean your plate, and be prepared to dance 'til your legs fall off. Welcome to Moses' and Sylvia's wedding reception.

2. Most people learning to shoot want to learn as a sport. No one wants to get hurt, but accidents can happen through negligence and oversight. Novice shooters need to learn the correct and safe methods of operating a firearm. Some of the basics are discussed in this paper.

3. When I was a teenager, I used to feel sorry for pregnant women. I thought that they felt fat and ugly and sloppy and embarrassed. I even

felt embarrassed when I saw them. No one ever corrected this impression, so I was in for a few surprises when I finally became pregnant.

4. Grab your most comfortable jeans and your tennis shoes. Pack a bag lunch and bring a deck of cards. You'll be waiting a long time. Where are we going? Why, we are going to see the King Tutankhamen exhibition at the National Gallery of Art.

5. When my mother became ill three years ago with a heart condition, she was put on a low-salt, low-calorie diet. Today we are convinced that a good nutritional diet may prevent and even cure some illnesses. It worked for our family, and it can work for yours.

6. Sports heroes come and go. Some dominate their particular sport for a few years, then fade away, later to become answers to trivia questions. A handful obtain a level of greatness and are inducted into a hall of fame. Still fewer surpass all others before them, yet strive to improve their game. In the world of golf, one man stands above all others. His name is Jack Nicklaus.

Exercise 3   For Discussion

Read the student essays listed below and consider the purpose and audience of each. What relationship with his or her audience does the writer assume? What is the writer's purpose in addressing this audience?

Also consider the writer's stance or point of view: first, second, or third person. Is the point of view appropriate, given the purpose and audience?

Irish vs. American Education, pp. 229–235.
So He's Driving You Crazy? pp. 295–297.
A Viennese Waltz It Was Not, pp. 308–310.
Children's Hospital, pp. 318–320.

Exercise 4   For Thought

Unless you choose writing topics that will work for *you,* you'll have a hard time finding your voice. Wayne C. Booth, an English professor, tells a story that makes this point very well:

> Last fall I had an advanced graduate student, bright, energetic, well-informed, whose papers were almost unreadable. He managed to be pretentious, dull, and disorganized in his paper on *Emma,* and pretentious, dull, and disorganized on *Madame Bovary.* On *The Golden Bowl* he was

all these and obscure as well. Then one day, toward the end of the term, he cornered me after class and said, "You know, I think you were all wrong about Robbe-Grillet's *Jealousy* today." We didn't have time to discuss it, so I suggested that he write me a note about it. Five hours later I found in my faculty box a four-page polemic, unpretentious, stimulating, organized, convincing. Here was a man who had taught freshman composition for several years and who was incapable of committing any of the more obvious errors that we think of as characteristic of bad writing. Yet he could not write a decent sentence, paragraph, or paper until . . . he had found a definition of his audience, his argument, and his own proper tone of voice.

When this graduate student finally discovered something he wanted to say — to someone who wanted to hear it — he found his voice.

Exercise 5   For Discussion in Small Groups

Working in small groups, discuss the following draft of an essay by one of our students, Sharon Wultich. Pretend that Wultich is a classmate who has come to your group for advice about the point of view of her essay. Where is her point of view inconsistent? Would you advise her to revise the essay in the third person or the second person? If your group has time, revise one or two of Wultich's paragraphs for her. After your discussion, turn to Wultich's own revisions (pages 219–221) and compare them with your suggestions.

Population Explosion

    Anyone wishing to start an aquarium of live-bearing fish needs to be aware of how prolific fish such as black mollies, guppies, sunsets, and swordtails can be. They may return from the pet shop with a pair of these fish only to wake up the next morning and find thirty new arrivals squirming through the filter's air bubbles. Soon these newcomers grow and contribute to the mass production of live-bearing fish that knows no forty-hour work week. They will fill your bathtub and your kitchen sink; and the sewers of this country must know plenty of their cousins.
    The prospective buyer may think that he'll just buy one, or all of the same sex. That logical solution is struck down when his single, but once impregnated female mollie has three broods of fifty fish, each without a father in sight; she left him back at the pet shop. Once

a live-bearer is pregnant, she may seem to be so continuously. If the buyer does find a group of nonpregnant
females, he shouldn't be surprised if within a week a few
have changed their sex. Why not have all male fish?
Because they will chase each other in dizzying circles,
getting so confused that they will eventually commit the
ultimate in aquatic suicide -- and jump out of the tank.
    Fans of the velvet swordtail should not despair,
however, because I have found the solution to the
underwater population explosion. The tank can be supplied
with two or three large angel fish, who will delight in a
feast of newborn swordtails. Those who decide to raise a
few live-bearing offspring in the same tank can plop a few
plants on the surface for their protection. Anyone who
decides to become a really serious breeder should set up
separate maternity tanks for the expectant mothers. There
will be plenty of future occupants waiting in line.
Plenty.

                                        Sharon Wultich

5   *Choosing Appropriate Language*

"How am I to know," the despairing writer asks, "which the right word is?" The reply must be . . . "The wanted word is the one most nearly true. True to what? Your vision and your purpose."

— ELIZABETH BOWEN

As a speaker, you command several varieties of English. When applying for a job or addressing the congregation at church, you speak formally; but when you relax with friends on Saturday night, you relax your language as well. When explaining your latest modification of a VW engine to your little brother, who knows nothing about the inner workings of automobiles, you use easy-to-understand, nontechnical English. But explain the same thing to your best friend, who has just modified his Corvette, and your language is suddenly filled with cams and crankshafts and cc's.

Among strangers you keep your language distant, but with your in-group — people of your age, your social class, or your ethnic or geographic background — you use language common to that group. If you're from Appalachia, you might talk one way to people from your part of the country and a slightly different way to outsiders. If you're an Afro-American or a Puerto Rican–American or Mexican-American, you may have the ability to shift, depending on the situation, between an ethnic language and a more neutral language common to all.

Perhaps you come from a highly educated family around whom your grammar is perfect. If so, you probably adjust your speech when hanging out with friends from a different background. Or maybe you're a middle-aged veteran who has returned to college. On campus you make friends with a crowd of younger vets, and before long you find yourself picking up all their latest slang. When you get together socially with people your own age, you may throw in just enough of the new slang to be interesting, but not so much that you'll look like you're showing off.

In speaking, then, you have an amazing ability to choose, on the spot, from a number of language varieties. It's as if you were computerized to judge every complex social situation in which you speak. Your computer gives you the answer immediately: It tells you how formal, how technical, how slangy, how ethnic, how intimate, how youthful, how class-conscious, how personal, how regional you should be. Sometimes you may make mistakes; for example, you may speak too informally for the situation, or you may choose language too technical for your listeners. But on the whole your instincts — and those of almost all native speakers of our language — are remarkably accurate.

Writing, like speaking, requires you to choose from among a number of language varieties. Often the same instinct that guides you as you speak will help you as you write — but not always.

When you write, you are more likely to adopt a formal tone when an informal one would be more suitable, to use slang or jargon where they're not appropriate, or to mix styles in odd ways. The question to ask yourself is, "What language is *appropriate* to the situation in which I am writing?"

Formal or Informal?

You will choose a relatively formal voice when applying for a job, explaining your aesthetic beliefs in a philosophy paper, or arguing in a letter to the editor that a traffic light should be installed at a dangerous intersection. In such writing situations an informal voice would be inappropriate.

But there are also situations in which a formal voice would be inappropriate. In a letter to a friend or in a memo to a coworker, a formal voice might sound too distant or too unfriendly. Similarly, if you were describing your first blind date, the absurdities of a soap opera, or the recent pranks of your six-year-old, a formal voice might sound pretentious.

Occasionally we encounter students who have been taught that the more formal a piece of writing, the better. No matter what the subject, they do their best to sound like encyclopedias. We think you'll agree that the writer of the following paragraph needs to relax her language a bit, especially in light of the personal nature of her material. The assignment — to be included in a journal — was to describe a personal response to one of several short stories.

> I had a very high level of response to that fine work of fiction by Mrs. Kate Chopin, "The Storm." This phenomenon happened because the masterpiece evoked significant memories of my early years in New Orleans, where I lived between the ages of nine and twelve. My brain still records the uniqueness of a rainstorm in that grand old city, where rain fell on one side of the street while the sun shone on the other. At

times the rain precipitated so violently that it appeared to be descending sideways. Then suddenly that miracle of nature would occur: a rainbow.

The journal entry continued with a reference to "magnificent" chinaberry trees on whose berries the birds "became inebriated." Further on, our writer referred to a sentence of Cajun dialect she had memorized as "the patois of the inhabitants of antique New Orleans."

A peer review session helped the writer see that her message had been obscured by a too formal style. Here is her revision:

> The short story "The Storm" by Kate Chopin brought back pleasant memories of my childhood in New Orleans, where I lived when I was nine to twelve. I remember rain falling on one side of the street and the sun shining on the other side; I always thought there was magic involved, especially when the rainbow came out. We would run in and out of the rain, one minute wet and the next dry. Sometimes the rain fell so hard it seemed to be coming down sideways.
>
> Chopin's reference to a chinaberry tree also took me back to my childhood, reminding me of two large chinaberry trees in our front yard. My dad had told me birds would get drunk from eating chinaberries, so I spent hours waiting to see whether they would fall off the limbs, drunk. Our Creole friends in New Orleans made chinaberry wine, so maybe what he said was true.
>
> Chopin's use of dialect also appealed to me; in it I could hear the singsong of Cajun speech. My brothers and I thought we could speak Cajun because someone taught us the sentence: "Youseemycowdowntheroad-youpush'imhome'eh?" If you repeated that very rapidly, you were speaking Cajun.

The new version sounds more like pleasant memories of childhood.

"In-group" or Standard?

Years ago students were taught to avoid all "in-group" language in their writing. "Never use slang," preached English teachers, "and never write in an ethnic or a regional dialect. Always use standard English." But today most English instructors agree that in-group language is sometimes appropriate, even though in most writing situations it is not.

When are slang and dialect likely to be appropriate? They are clearly acceptable when you are quoting the words of people who actually speak in slang or dialect. If you are quoting Sojourner Truth's famous "And Ain't I a Woman?" speech, you wouldn't "correct" Truth's dialect as some misguided English teachers once did. You would let ex-slave Sojourner Truth speak with the ringing authority of her own voice:

That man over there. He says women need to be helped into carriages and lifted over ditches and to have the best everywhere. Nobody ever helps me into carriages, over mud puddles, or gets me any best place. *Ain't I a woman?* Look at me! Look at my arm. I have ploughed. And I have planted. And I have gathered into barns. And no man could head me. *And ain't I a woman?*

I could work as much, and eat as much as any man — when I could get it — and bear the lash as well. *And ain't I a woman?* I have borne thirteen children and seen them sold into slavery, and when I cried out with a mother's grief, none but Jesus heard me. *And ain't I a woman?*

It is appropriate, then, to quote the special language of others. No one is likely to disagree with this. But when is it appropriate for you to put your own slang or dialect into your writing? Here we are on more dangerous ground; any guidelines are likely to be controversial.

In general, dialect and slang are more appropriate in creative, "expressive" writing than in practical or intellectual writing. Slang and dialect can also be appropriate when you're appealing to an in-group audience. The common language is a way of expressing your solidarity with the group. A union leader, for example, might write campaign literature in the language of the steelworkers who will be voting in the election. Or a Chicano community leader will write to his or her constituents in the language they all share. Here, for example, are the words of José Ángel Gutiérrez, addressed to fellow Chicanos.

You've got a handful of gringos controlling the lives of *muchos Mexicanos.* And it's been that way for a long time. . . . In 1960 there were twenty-six Texas counties in which Chicanos were a majority, yet not one of those counties was in the control of Chicanos. If you want to take that you can. You can be perfectly content just like your father and your grandfather were, *con el sombrero en la mano.*

As you are no doubt aware, however, most writing situations require standard English. Slang and dialect attract a reader's attention to the writer's *way* of speaking, and most of the time this is distracting. If you want readers to focus on *what* you're saying, you won't make them too conscious of *how* you are saying it. We think you'll agree that the writer of the following letter to the editor needs to translate his message into standard English:

The way some creeps let their kids act in public really bugs me. I've seen parents allow their little dumplings to play hide and seek in a busy Howard Johnson's or to play catch on a city bus. In the A&P last week a mother grabbed an extra cart for her five-year-old to push through the aisles, and into my shins it went. It's bad enough when the parents are too busy to notice, but it really gripes me when they cheer the kids on, thinking their behavior is cute. People like me, who don't have children, have a right not to be stressed out by other people's spoiled brats.

Because of the slang, it is hard for us to take this writer seriously.

In most writing situations, then, slang or dialect is out of place. Avoiding it is often a matter of courtesy. It's bad manners to assert one's uniqueness too strongly in a business letter or a college essay, especially when readers may not share the in-group language. Standard English is more appropriate because it is a language accessible to all.

Technical or Plain English?

Sometimes you'll need to choose between technical English, understandable only to specialists, and plain English that everyone can understand. Usually your audience will determine your choice.

A lawyer, for example, will use legal language when writing a brief for other lawyers but will shift to nontechnical English when summarizing that same brief for a client. Someone we know who supervises computer technologists finds that she must write technically accurate directives for her staff and simplified memos in plain English for her own supervisors. If she writes the directives in ordinary English, her staff will make mistakes. If she writes technical memos for her supervisors, who are not specialists, they won't understand her — and they'll be annoyed with her for wasting their time.

Writers often use technical language when plain English would be more appropriate. Doctors, lawyers, scholars, and government or military officials are sometimes so impressed with themselves for having mastered a sophisticated vocabulary that they use it whenever they get a chance — even when it's clearly inappropriate. For example, a scholar once asked a farmer if he was "excavating a subterranean channel." The farmer replied, "No, sir, I am only digging a ditch."

Supreme Court Justice Oliver Wendell Holmes, himself a highly educated man, once complained about such misuse of technical language. Said Holmes, "I know there are professors in this country who 'ligate' arteries. Other surgeons only tie them, and it stops bleeding just as well." Like Holmes, we think it's best to avoid specialized language when ordinary English will do as well. Don't write "This semiautomatic, small-caliber, shoulder-fired weapon, because of mechanical derangement, ceased to function." Just tell your readers that the rifle jammed.

Let's conclude with a useful guideline. In general, choose plain English. Use technical English only when (1) you are knowledgeable enough to use it correctly; (2) your readers are knowledgeable enough to understand it; and (3) your purpose in writing truly requires it.

Nonsexist Language

Sexist language is inappropriate in our society because it demeans women and girls simply by not recognizing them. Such language emphasizes maleness as the human norm, with the inevitable consequence that femaleness becomes less than human. Think of how often you encounter such expressions as *mankind, the brotherhood of man, man and his universe, All men are created equal, The Norsemen settled along the coast of . . .* , and *Anthropology is the study of man.* None of these common expressions recognizes that at least one-half of the human beings in the world are female.

You might argue, of course, "Oh, everybody knows those uses of *man* mean *all* people." But even if that were absolutely true, there is a wide gap between possible inclusion and clear, equal recognition. Because women remain invisible in such "man-words," there is at least a fifty-fifty chance that they will not be equally recognized in the consciousness of the writer — or the reader. You can be sure that your reader will know you mean everybody when you substitute for these man–words such words as *human, humanity, person, people,* and *individuals.* Some of these substitutions may feel awkward to you at first, but every expression in our language was new and awkward at some time.

Just as *mankind* does not clearly include everybody, neither do the pronouns *he, him,* and *his* when used in a generic sense, as in a sentence like this: "A lawyer typically spends a great deal of *his* time researching and writing." Restricting yourself to masculine nouns and pronouns can indeed lead to some strange sentences, such as this one, uttered by a New York state legislator: "Everyone should be able to decide for himself whether or not to have an abortion." Or this one, which appears in a children's book: "Man, like the other mammals, breast-feeds his young."

Instead of using masculine pronouns in a generic sense, you nearly always have two options. You can use the singular forms *he and she* and *his and her:* "A lawyer typically spends a great deal of his or her time researching and writing." Or you can switch to the plural: "Lawyers typically spend a great deal of their time researching and writing." In addition, you can frequently recast the sentence. For example, in our sample sentence, we can simply delete the pronoun: "A lawyer typically spends a great deal of time researching and writing." For further advice about these revision strategies, see section 30 in "A Writer's Handbook," Part Seven of this book.

Another way to remove sexism from your language is to avoid sex-linked occupational and organizational terms. As more careers attract both men and women, our former occupational terms are gradually becoming false designations. You will be more accurate if you say *worker* instead of *workman, flight attendant* instead of *stewardess, firefighter* instead of *fireman,* and so on. And if you listen, you will notice that in many organizations *chairperson* is replacing *chairman.*

When we first wrote this chapter, in 1978, sexist language was becoming inappropriate in our society. Now, in 1989, we can report that it *is* inappropriate. You have probably noticed this yourself. Newspapers refer to *police officers,* not to *policemen,* and few writers today would risk the term *police lady.* Government offices routinely edit sexist language from their publications. *He* has become *he or she, congressman* has become *member of Congress,* and words such as *mankind* are taboo. Writers and speakers everywhere are learning to recast their sentences in the plural so that the issue of sexist pronouns doesn't even arise.

Why, you may ask, are people going to all this trouble? The answer is simple, really. More and more readers, both men and women, are finding sexist language offensive. And most writers, no matter what their personal feelings on the issue might be, don't want to offend their readers. Nonsexist English is a matter of courtesy — of respect for and sensitivity to the feelings of others.

Exercise 1 Written

The student writer of an essay about ways to relieve the monotony of dull jobs had some trouble maintaining a consistent voice. Read the following paragraph from his essay to decide whether a formal or an informal voice is more appropriate. Then revise the paragraph so that it is all in the voice you choose.

At my job, whenever the tedious routine begins to get to me, I rely on Butch to come up with something to break the monotony. One such instance immediately comes to mind. While I was busy working one day, I noticed Butch waving for me to "come over here." Noting the level of his enthusiasm, I promptly moved toward him. As I drew near, he revealed to me a frog, which he had just found. "So what?" I commented. With a gleam in his eye, Butch said, "Let's put it in the new guy's lunch pail!" A smile immediately materialized on my face. Butch recognized my approval, and we made our way toward the truck. As the lunch hour approached, we compared expectations as we anxiously anticipated what we imagined would occur. Eagerly the new guy opened his lunch pail — and out popped the frog, landing right under his nose. By that time, Butch and I were laughing so hard we were about to explode.

Exercise 2 *Written*

The following paragraph seems too formal and intimidating. Try rewriting it in a more informal and friendly voice, one that makes the students feel welcome. Before you begin to revise, think about how you might change the writer's stance or point of view to avoid sexist English.

When the student arrives for registration, he must have in his possession appropriate identification, his high school transcript or report cards, and a number two pencil. He must proceed directly to room 201 of the Administration Building, following the appropriate signs, and pick up registration materials. At this point he will be given instructions as to the procedure to be followed for the remainder of the registration process.

Exercise 3 *For Class Discussion*

What kind of language would you choose for each of the following writing situations? Would you write formally or informally? Would you use technical language in any instances? Where would you consciously avoid technical language and take care to write in plain English? Would in-group slang or jargon be appropriate in any case? As you think about how you would handle each of these writing situations, you might begin to make notes on some of the topics that interest you, to use in developing essays later.

1. Write an enthusiastic review of a campus theatrical production for your college newspaper.
2. Write an article for publication in the monthly bulletin of a large agency with many employees, in which you argue for child-care facilities at the work site.
3. If you know about a diet prescribed for a particular physical condition, describe the diet and explain its benefits to persons who have been recently diagnosed as having the condition.
4. Write an article for your church newsletter encouraging all members

of the congregation to donate items for the spring fair that funds summer activities for children of the church.

5. Convince other students to sign up for a course that you have found especially interesting.

6. If you are dissatisfied with one of your professors and talking with him or her has not helped, write a letter of complaint to the head of the department in which the professor teaches (no names, please).

7. Write a description of what you do at work to be included in a directory of local occupations being compiled by career counselors at your college.

8. Warn readers about a job or position that is not all it was advertised to be.

9. If you work for an agency that can help people in some way, write a brief article for your local newspaper explaining how clients can obtain aid.

10. If you have ever been the victim of police brutality, describe the incident. Your audience is a citizen's review board.

11. If you are very good at a particular sport, summarize your qualifications to impress a coach or a scholarship committee.

12. Write a positive description of your ethnic background — Italian, Polish, Irish, Afro-American, Jewish, or whatever.

13. Write a review of a local child-care center. Your review may be positive, negative, or mixed.

14. If you have attended school in another country, contrast some aspect of that country's educational system with an aspect of ours.

15. If you have served in a war, write about a personal experience with violence.

Exercise 4   *For Reading and Listening*

For at least a week, look and listen for examples of sexism in language in your day-to-day life — at work, at school, in advertisements, at home, in stores, on radio and television, at social events, wherever you go. Try to be alert to all the sexist language problems pointed out in this section: man-words, pronouns, occupational and organizational terms, and so on. Bring your five choicest items to class; then experiment with ways to remove the sexism.

Exercise 5 Just for Fun

One of our students wrote the following poem about language:

Nostalgia
(or, Getting with It)

I remember
    when a chick was the offspring of a hen,
    when a dude was a ranch vacationer,
    when a greaser was a garage mechanic,
    when a square was a geometric figure,
    when a freak was a side-show performer,
    when a sucker was a lollypop,
    when a shrink was a dry-clean-only dress,
    when a pig was a farm animal,
    when cool was the opposite of warm,
    when making out was being successful (at anything),
    when flipping out was missing the mat in tumbling,
    when to dig had to do with ditches,
    when a hangup was Monday's wash on the line,
    when my bag was the grocery sack,
    when a bug was an insect,
    when pintos, mustangs, and cougars had legs,
    when uptight was how a corset was laced,
    when grass was something you mowed,
    when tea was something you drank,
    when pot described grandpa's belly,
    when a weed was a nuisance (to anyone),
    when high was the sky,
    when a joint was a hangout,
    when hash was mashed corned beef,
    when upper referred to the department store level,
    when a trip involved packing a suitcase,
    when rock had to do with geology,
    when acid had to do with chemistry,
    when a bust was part of the anatomy,
    when bread was something to butter,
    when a head-shop was a beauty parlor,
    when long-haired described classical music,
    when a turn-on involved a light switch,
    when a ripoff meant getting out the sewing basket,
    when a pad was something you wore, periodically. — RENEE KLAR

Exercise 6   For Discussion in Small Groups

Working in small groups, discuss the following draft of an essay by
one of our students, Joan Bradley. Pretend that Bradley is one of your
classmates and that she has come to your group for help in establishing
an appropriate voice. Where in her essay would you advise her to adjust
her language and perhaps even her content in order to reach her audience
more effectively? After your discussion, turn to Bradley's own revisions
(pages 209–217) and compare them with your suggestions.

Euthanasia for Animals

Euthanasia, the process of helping an animal die by
administering certain drugs, is legal and accepted in the
veterinary profession. It is also the hardest part of my
job as a technician in an animal hospital. Sometimes I
feel that it is justifiable to put an animal to sleep
because the creature is suffering and needs to be put out
of misery, but at other times I feel it is a waste of an
animal's life.

An animal brought to the hospital to be put to sleep
is called an "E and D" patient. "E and D" means "euthanasia and disposal." This is the most difficult task I must
perform. It is done by injecting the drug T–61 into the
animal. It is usually put directly into the vein. I am
not a professionally trained technician, but I was taught
how to inject drugs into the vein of an animal. It isn't
easy, so sometimes I would get out of administering the
drug by claiming I couldn't do it. Putting an animal to
sleep is a very hard thing for me to do, and it took a
long time for me to get used to it. The process is done
by tying the foreleg off above the elbow with a tourniquet. The fur is wetted down with a moist cotton ball and
the needle is inserted. The tourniquet is then loosened
and the drug is injected. I was surprised to find that
animals don't close their eyes and look peacefully asleep
when they die. Cats and small dogs have very small veins
which are hard to find, so T–61 is injected directly into
the chest cavity. This is easier for the technician but
harder for the animal because it takes longer for the drug
to take effect and to go through the body. I often wonder
what the animal feels, and sometimes I have nightmares of
a burning sensation going throughout my body, with animals
all around me asking, "Why?"

Animals are put to sleep for many different reasons.
As I mentioned, some are justifiable, and some are not. A
good example of justifiable euthanasia is Trixie. She was
a thirteen-year-old fox terrier who began to feel her age,
which would have been the equivalent of ninety-one in a
human. Her owners wanted to do all that was possible to
keep her alive, but each day she became weaker. Soon she
gave up eating and drinking and waited painfully for her
time to come. There was nothing anyone could do for
Trixie. Veterinarians can cure sickness but cannot
restore youth. Instead of watching Trixie suffer, the
owner brought her to the hospital for euthanasia.

Another example was the litter of three puppies that
some idiot had abandoned in a burlap sack along a road-
side. After the sack had been struck by a car, a passerby
found the puppies and brought them to the hospital. One
puppy was in shock, one had a broken pelvis, and the other
had serious internal injuries. They were going through
too much pain and suffering, so each puppy was euthanized.
I believe these two examples are justifiable because these
animals were better off being put to sleep than being
allowed to suffer.

Some humans are pig-headed and cruel. Those people
who have their pets put to sleep for selfish reasons are
examples of unjust euthanasia. Ms. Olsen brought two
beautiful cats to the hospital to be euthanized -- an
adult blue point Siamese that someone had given her and a
young healthy black cat. When asked why, she replied,
"I've just bought a new beige carpet for my living room
and these cats are constantly shedding hair on it." And
then there was the woman who wanted her beagle put to
sleep because she was moving and couldn't find a suitable
home for it. By coincidence a man came in at the same
time who just happened to be looking for a beagle. He was
looking for one to train into a hunting dog to add to the
few he already had. When I tried to arrange for him to
take the dog, the woman refused, saying that she didn't
want her dog to be trained to hunt. Because of her feelings about hunting, this silly woman was actually willing
to deprive her dog of a good long, happy life! These
examples of euthanasia are the hardest for me to perform
because the animal seems to know that it hasn't had a full
life and fights the euthanasia.

Whenever I must euthanize an animal, I tell myself
that it is part of my job and that I must do it, no matter
what the reason. I certainly can't save them all or give

them homes. But I can't help wondering who or what can
give the right to me to do this. I can see where it is
needed in some cases, but why not then in people? If
euthanasia was allowed with people, perfectly healthy
people wouldn't be put to sleep, so why are perfectly
healthy animals allowed to be? My point is that euthanasia
on animals should have restrictions. I do it as part of
my job, then try to forget it, but the look in an animal's
unclosed eye and the nightmares will be impossible to
forget.

Joan Bradley

Part Three

Drafting and Revising Essays

6   *Focusing on a Point*

Have something to say, and say it as clearly as you can.
— MATTHEW ARNOLD

Try this reading test. Read the paragraph *once* only.

Suppose an elevator starts at the first floor with six passengers, and stops at the next floor where four people get out and two get on; it continues upward to the next floor where three get on and no one gets off, but at the following floor two get off; at the next floor two get on and three get off.

Now answer the question: How many times did the elevator stop?

Chances are you did not "pass" this reading test, even if you are a very good reader, because the test was rigged against you from the start. Most readers think they're supposed to be watching for the number of people on the elevator, so they focus their attention on the people getting on and off the elevator, not on the elevator stops.

If you failed this test, it was the writer's fault, not yours. Suppose for a moment that you were giving the test. If you really wanted the readers to watch for the number of times the elevator stopped, you would tell them what to look for. You would let them know why they were reading.

As you write essays this semester, how can you show readers what to look for? The answer, for most writing tasks, is surprisingly simple: State your main point clearly and concisely, preferably in one sentence, and put that sentence early in your essay, either at the beginning or at the end of an introductory paragraph. This one-sentence declaration of your main point is called a *thesis statement.*

The thesis statement is arguably the most important sentence in your essay, for all other sentences must relate to it.

Writing a Thesis

A successful thesis statement has three characteristics: It is a generalization, not a fact; it is limited, not too broad; and it is sharply focused, not too vague.

First, a thesis statement must be a *generalization;* it cannot be merely a fact. A simple statement of fact, such as "Edgar Allan Poe was born in 1809," doesn't communicate a main point, so it just won't do as a thesis. It takes a generalization to state a main point. "Edgar Allan Poe's life was filled with bitter disappointments" — a general statement requiring specific development later in the essay — would make a good thesis. So would "According to his biographers, Poe had difficulty relating to women sexually." That's a generalization about Poe's life, not just a fact about it. You could develop it into an essay filled with facts about Poe's relationships with women.

Although a thesis should be a generalization, it should not be *too* general. It should be a *limited* generalization, one that can be adequately developed within your word limit. When your generalization is too broad, you are promising readers too much, unless you happen to be writing a book. Common sense will tell you when a thesis statement is too broad. For example, if you love Italian food, you might be tempted to work with a thesis like "San Francisco has more first-rate Italian restaurants than any other major American city." But common sense would lead you to a more limited generalization instead: "At the top of my list for good food, friendly service, and a charming atmosphere is a little Italian restaurant called Luigi's."

The third characteristic of a successful thesis is that it is *sharply focused.* It is not too vague. A thesis like "Edgar Allan Poe is an interesting writer," for example, is too vague. You could write about Poe's life, about his theory of poetry, about his horror stories, about almost anything connected with Poe, and still be more or less sticking to your thesis that Poe is an "interesting writer." So the thesis is poorly focused.

Usually the vagueness of a thesis can be traced to a word that could mean too many different things — a word such as *interesting* or *enjoyable* or *lousy*. Where precisely is an essay going when it promises to show us that Poe's life is "interesting" or that swimming is "enjoyable" or that *Citizen Kane* is a "lousy" movie? Your guess is as good as ours.

Sharpening a too-vague thesis is part of the process of discovering what you really want to say. Each of these students, for example, began with a blurred focus and ended with a sharp one:

Too Vague	*Sharpened Focus*
The Parkdale Community College cafeteria serves bad food.	At the Parkdale Community College cafeteria you will search in vain for a nutritious meal.

Conquering a weight problem can be rewarding.	After trying every diet that's been popularized in the past five years, I finally found one that worked: old-fashioned calorie counting.
The Moto-guzzi is a better bike than the BMW.	The Moto-guzzi is a better all-round touring bike than the BMW.

A precise thesis, though it may be harder to write than a vague one, gives you more control over the rest of your essay. So it is worth the extra effort.

To sum up, a thesis statement is a one-sentence declaration of the main point of your essay. A good thesis statement has three characteristics: it is a generalization, not a specific fact; it is limited, not too broad; and it is sharply focused, not too vague.

We have devoted much of this chapter to just one sentence in your introduction because it is so important. Now let's consider your introductory paragraph as a whole.

Writing an Introductory Paragraph

Remember that readers come to your essay cold, not knowing what to expect. They have no idea what your point is. So your job, in your very first paragraph, is to announce it.

Your thesis statement — the one sentence that most clearly announces your main point — should nearly always appear either at the beginning or at the end of your introductory paragraph. Where you decide to place it depends on the effect you want to achieve. For a slow-paced effect, put the thesis at the end; for a blunter, more straightforward effect, put it at the beginning.

For a slow-paced effect, you begin a few steps back from your thesis, orienting readers and giving them a feel for the subject area into which you are taking them. Then you zoom in on your thesis, the last sentence of the paragraph. If you think of a zoom-lens movie camera, you'll have some notion of how this kind of paragraph works. With a zoom lens you can film a broad panorama as background for your actual subject, then zoom quickly to the subject itself. Here is an example of what we might call a zoom paragraph:

Little League sports were developed many years ago as amateur sports for young people. Little League's purpose was physical development, sportsmanship, and the advancement of peace and good will through athletic competition. However, if our local organization is a good example, Little League sports have strayed far from these goals. *The Palmer Park Little League is clearly run for the benefit of the adult coaches and parents.*

The writer begins broadly, speaking of Little League sports in general, and then zooms in on the message of his paper: that one specific Little League organization (the one the writer is familiar with) is run for the benefit of adults, not children.

The zoom paragraph allows you to chat awhile with readers before getting to your main point. The effect is polite and friendly, as if you were inviting readers into your essay. Notice, for example, how smoothly this student writer eases us into her essay on the violence in Grimms' fairy tales:

The Brothers Grimm have always seemed a friend to parents at bedtime. They have helped get the kids into bed without too much trouble, and they've sent them quickly off to dreamland. But little do parents realize, when they leave the room and turn out the lights, that their children dream of wicked witches in gingerbread houses, trolls under bridges, and poisonous apples. *In their own way, the Brothers Grimm have been teaching children that life is no fairy tale.*

As you have seen, the zoom paragraph builds toward the thesis. For much of the writing that you will do this semester, the zoom paragraph will serve very well. Sometimes, though, you may decide to get to your point faster — with what we'll call a pointed paragraph. A pointed paragraph begins with the thesis:

Karate teaches a philosophy of respect, self-discipline, and nonviolence. I learned this a few years ago when I was looking for an answer to a problem my son was having.

Pointed paragraphs are often appropriate in practical writing situations, when readers expect you to get right to the point. This kind of introductory paragraph can be short, sometimes as short as the thesis statement alone. Although it may lack the graceful flow of the zoom paragraph, the pointed paragraph has the advantage of being straightforward.

Whether you begin with a zoom or a pointed paragraph, your readers should understand immediately, without consciously thinking about it, that your introduction is an introduction. And they should understand, again without effort, what to expect as they read on. The primary function of your introduction is to let readers know your point. It's as simple as that.

Rewriting Your Introduction

Don't be surprised if you go through several false starts before coming up with an introductory paragraph that's workable. It would be helpful if you always knew before putting pen to paper (or fingers to word processor) just what your main idea would be. Then, as you wrote your opening paragraph, you could confidently introduce readers to your paper — before you had even written it. But you won't always have that kind of control over your material right from the start.

Often you'll need to write an introductory paragraph not to reveal your focus, but to discover it. And discovery is not a neat and tidy process; it almost always involves false starts. Here, for example, is one student writer's first attempt:

> The women's movement, which originated in the 1960s, is a well-intentioned movement. And I agree with its basic goals. *At the same time I do have some disagreements with its goals.*

Not bad for a first try, but the focus is pretty foggy. The student's next effort was better:

> I agree with the economic goals of the women's liberation movement, such as equal pay for equal work and the right to credit. *However, the women's movement goes too far in challenging two traditional roles for women: the role of wife, and the role of mother.*

It's a good idea to experiment awhile, as this student has done, before settling on an introductory paragraph. Keep writing introductions until you've got the focus you want, and then turn to the business of writing the paper. Don't worry too much at this point about how your opening sentences sound. Why not? Because you may need to rewrite them later, after you've written the rest of the essay.

Essays have a way of changing as they are being written, and this is not necessarily a bad thing, as long as you are aware of the changes — and as long as you are prepared to rewrite your introduction later. Sometimes an essay becomes more clearly focused as you write it. Other times the focus changes as you discover, through writing, what you really want to say.

For example, once he began drafting the body of his essay, the student who wrote the introductory paragraph criticizing the women's movement discovered that he couldn't write a convincing argument in support of his main point. He had said that he was in favor of the economic goals of the women's movement but that he did not support its challenges to the roles of wife and mother. Once into the essay, he realized that the roles of wife and mother were more tied to economics than he had thought, because in a society where divorce is common, these traditional unpaid roles leave women economically vulnerable. As soon as our writer saw this problem, he scanned his rough draft in search of a main point that he would be able to develop convincingly.

As it turned out, the strongest section of this student's rough draft was a description of his wife's job as mother of their six children. At the time the essay was written, the women's movement seemed to be saying that women such as his wife weren't leading meaningful lives. It didn't give full-time mothers the recognition this student felt they deserved. So he revised the essay, focusing on his new point: that motherhood, though unpaid, can be a full-time job that deserves our respect. Here is the student's revised introductory paragraph. Notice how much his introduction has changed since his first effort.

> The women's movement should be applauded for helping women make economic gains. But the movement should be careful, in its push for economic goals, not to lessen our respect for women's traditional unpaid roles — particularly the role of mother. *If you think motherhood is not as challenging, meaningful, and rewarding as other full-time jobs, let me show you a day in the life of my wife, Lurleen, mother of six.*

You may be surprised to hear that a student writer spent so much effort rewriting his introduction. But successful student writers, like professionals, often spend more time on the introduction than on any other section of the essay. One professional writer claims he puts 85 percent of his effort into his opening paragraph. That's pretty extreme, but not as extreme as you may be tempted to think.

Conclusions: Echoing the Point

The final paragraph of an essay should drive home the essay's main point. Ordinarily either the first or the last sentence of the conclusion should echo the thesis that was stated in the introduction.

If you decide to echo your thesis in the first sentence of your conclusion, use the remaining sentences of the paragraph to drive home the point. That's what this student has done, for example, to end an essay arguing for the rights of nonsmokers:

> Though I recognize the right of others to smoke privately, public smoking infringes on the rights of nonsmokers. It is more plausible for the smoker to curtail smoking than for the nonsmoker to stop breathing.

The first sentence echoes the main point of the essay, that public smoking infringes on the rights of nonsmokers. The final sentence drives home that point with a witty remark: "It is more plausible for the smoker to curtail smoking than for the nonsmoker to stop breathing."

Sometimes you may decide to end your concluding paragraph with an echo of your thesis. In that case, the earlier sentences of the paragraph will build toward the restatement of your main point. Here, for example, is how one student writer constructed a final statement of her main point:

> The mother-at-home situation may produce secure, well-adjusted children. But not necessarily. It may result in a happy home. But not necessarily. The question of whether mothers of small children should work has no single answer. Since family situations are different, the answer to the question must be tailored to meet the needs of every family member — wife, husband, and children.

Whether you choose to echo your main point at the beginning or at the end of your final paragraph, remember that this is your last chance to drive home that point. So don't settle for a dull restatement of your thesis. Try to put some life into your concluding words, so readers will leave your paper with a strong impression.

This is not always easy to do, as you probably know. Strong conclusions sometimes seem to be a matter of instinct. Occasionally, as you near the end of a rough draft, just the right finish will come to you in a flash of inspiration. More often, though, you'll probably find yourself dully restating your thesis instead of forcefully driving it home. If that happens, try to get away from your essay awhile, even for a few minutes. Then reread the essay, getting into its spirit, and try again. Hemingway claimed that he rewrote one ending thirty-nine times before he was satisfied. When an interviewer asked what the problem was, Hemingway paused for a moment, then gave his answer: "Getting the words right." You too may have to try more than once before getting those final words right.

Exercise 1   For Class Discussion

In each of the pairs below, which sentence might work well as a thesis? What is the problem with the other one? Is it too factual? Too broad? Too vague?

1a. Fresh foods are more economical than frozen foods or commercially prepared mixes.

1b. Fresh foods are preferable to frozen foods or commercially prepared mixes.

2a. A good set of golf clubs costs at least $150.

2b. If you've never played golf before but are thinking of trying it, consider first whether you have the funds to support this expensive hobby.

3a. A number of toys on the market provide safe and effective outlets for your child's aggressive feelings.

3b. There are many ways to provide children with outlets for their aggressive feelings.

4a. The Physical Education Department at City College is more interested in promoting winning teams than in teaching lifetime sports to average students.

4b. City College's physical education teachers are too biased.

5a. Mountain climbing is a very dangerous sport, regardless of the climber's ability.

5b. Mountain climbing is a thrilling sport.

6a. History 157, taught by Professor Baldwin, is offered at 10:00 on Tuesdays and Thursdays.

6b. Whoever said that history is nothing but polishing tombstones must have missed History 157, because in Professor Baldwin's class, history is very much alive.

7a. I nearly crashed to my death in a "55" helicopter.

7b. Although it looks innocent enough, the "55" is an extremely dangerous helicopter.

Exercise 2 For Class Discussion

Below are several paired introductory paragraphs. One in each pair is a rough draft, and the other is the writer's revision. Which paragraphs do you think are the new and improved versions, and in what ways are they better?

1a. I belong to a baby-sitting club. One of the greatest assets of belonging to the club is that you're almost guaranteed to find a sitter whenever you need one. The club's bylaws give detailed information as to what is expected of its members.

1b. I belong to a baby-sitting club. Because I am a member of this club, it has never taken me more than fifteen minutes to find a sitter. And my sitters have always been mature, reliable, and free. Let me tell you how you can start such a club in your own neighborhood.

2a. I do not think prayer should be allowed in schools. During most of my school years, the Lord's Prayer was part of our opening exercises. I never thought about it one way or another. I never heard anyone complain about it. When prayer in the schools became an issue in the courts, I was surprised. I never thought of the Lord's Prayer as being a threat to individual rights or as a breakdown in the division between church and state.

2b. During most of my school years, the Lord's Prayer was a part of our opening exercises. I never gave it a second thought, and I never heard anyone complain about it. So when prayer in the schools became an issue in the courts, I was surprised to hear that anyone viewed it as a threat to individual rights or as a violation of the division between church and state. But now that I've thought about it, I would not like to see the practice of prayer in the schools reinstituted.

3a. After reading many self-improvement books, I finally got up enough gumption to fulfill an ever-returning dream of enrolling in college. Since the psychological theories I had been reading about were all so positive, I signed up for a psychology class. I was convinced that a psychology professor, having majored in such a humanistic subject, would be sensitive to students' feelings. However, by the end of the evening of my first class with Dr. Crumb, I was not so sure.

3b. After being out of school for fifteen years, I finally got up enough gumption to enroll in college. This in itself was a feat. In the past years, I had felt intimidated by most authority figures and most college graduates. Last year I experienced a family crisis and sought counseling to get through a difficult time. I read many self-improvement books and decided psychology would be a very interesting subject.

4a. Beauty is in the eye of the beholder, but glamour is for anyone who can afford it. Head-to-toe miracles are performed on both sexes, young and old alike. Nature no longer binds people to their bodies; if they desire to add to or subtract from their frames to create a new image, the change agent may be as close as the nearest drugstore or as advanced as the tip of a plastic surgeon's scalpel.

4b. Nature no longer binds people to their bodies. If they desire to create a new image, the change may be as close as the nearest drugstore or as advanced as the tip of a plastic surgeon's scalpel. Beauty is in the eye of the beholder, but glamour is for anyone who can afford it.

Exercise 3   For Class Discussion

How well does each of the following introductory paragraphs serve to orient you, then focus your attention on the writer's main point?

1. When you bought your home or leased your apartment, you signed a contract. Did you read it before you signed it? Did you understand it? If you've taken Business Law 105, the answer to these questions will be "yes." Business Law 105 is the most informative and useful course I have taken at City Community College.

2. Child abuse is physical or emotional harm to children by parents or guardians. Physical abuse includes intentionally inflicted bruises, fractures, burns or other wounds, attempts to drown, and so forth. Emotional abuse is battering with words that reject or ignore a child.

3. Traditional Japanese architecture and furnishing are so different from those of the West that it is virtually impossible to reproduce the style of a formal Japanese dinner party outside Japan. Nevertheless, I would like to venture a simple account of the basic essentials which a Western hostess can adapt.

4. Without a doubt our daughter Nicole suffered academically from not entering Forestville Elementary at the beginning of her kindergarten year. Instead she was computerized, zoned, and bused to Brookline. Though by all outward appearances our community's two elementary schools are comparable, Forestville is academically superior to Brookline.

5. After spending about a month in the hospital I believe that it is safe for me to say that the hospital is not a very nice place to be. When I was injured I weighed about one hundred and sixty pounds and was in very good condition. But by the time I was released I was down to about one hundred and thirty pounds, I had a bad case of jittery nerves, and I had broken out in pimples again. Most of the weight was lost because the first week I was on a liquid diet. Then when I was able to eat, I found the food was so bad that I didn't want to eat. Then there were the damn holes in the roof. There were millions of them and after staring at them for a short time I would look away and everything would have holes in it.

6. Most kids can hardly wait for Saturday morning so they can turn on their television sets. They look forward to the superheroes such as Superman, Wonderwoman, Spiderman, and Shazzan. Television is the highlight of their morning.

7. During my childhood I had to pass the city jail to get to town. The barred windows of the jail were easily visible from the street. Of the many times I passed that jail I recall seeing only black faces behind those bars. It was years later when I realized why that was so. The

primary reason for the disproportionate number of blacks in our jails and prisons is their low economic status.

Exercise 4 *Written*

Look through the topics in the Appendix. Choose three on which you think you could write essays in support of a point, then try to come up with a good thesis statement for each of your three topics.

Working in small groups, ask your classmates to evaluate each of your thesis statements, using these questions as guidelines: (1) Is it a generalization, not a specific fact? (2) Is it limited, not too broad? and (3) Is it precisely focused, not too vague?

If the thesis statements of some of your group's members are weak, help each other out. Make sure each member of the group ends up with at least one successful thesis statement that could lead to an essay the other group members would be interested in reading.

Exercise 5 *Written*

Turn to the topics in the Appendix and scan them until you find two topics on which you think you might be able to write essays. Write an introductory paragraph for an essay on each topic, but don't write the essays. Bring your introductory paragraphs to class to test them out on sample readers.

Working in small groups with other students, test each introduction on your sample readers. Does each introduction orient them, make them feel at home? Does it let them know the main idea in a clear thesis statement? Does it get them interested in reading further?

As you work in class, be on the lookout for your classmates' successful efforts. You can learn much about writing by seeing what works for others.

Exercise 6 *For Discussion in Small Groups*

Working in small groups, discuss the following draft of an essay by one of our students, Dan MacFarland. Pretend that MacFarland is a classmate who has come to your group for advice about the focus of his essay. Where in his essay might he clarify his main point? After

your discussion, turn to MacFarland's own revisions (pages 223–227)
and compare them with your suggestions.

```
                    Hollywood Trucking

      A beautiful new tractor and trailer rig comes barrel-
ing up the highway, heat waves shimmering on the road.  A
small red convertible is in the way.  The horn blares, the
girl smiles, and the movie begins.
      Perhaps Hollywood's greatest misconception surround-
ing the trucker concerns the CB radio, that magic box that
tells the drivers where the bears are hiding.  Using the
CB, Burt Reynolds and Jerry Reed avoided Sheriff Jackie
Gleason throughout Smokey and the Bandit.  The Rubber Duck
was able to hold together one thousand trucks which toured
the country in song and movie, recklessly breaking toll
gates and speed limits galore.
      Real-life truckers use CB's to find parts, equipment,
food, lodging, and whatever else they may need.  Channel
9, an emergency channel reserved for emergency transmis-
sions only, is monitored by a national organization called
REACT.  Many times a trucker has been the first to respond
to an emergency call.  But is this service shown in the
movies?
      Did you ever notice the type of tractor and trailer
rigs the stars drive?  Their brand new trucks are equipped
with every chrome ornament available -- chrome gas tanks,
chrome exhaust stacks, even chrome wheel lugs.  The paint
is clean, bright, and unscratched.  As for the trailers,
there's not a hint of road dirt on the mudflaps.  All in
all, the rigs are spotless, with no dust on the wind-
shield, no bugs on the grill, not even exhaust deposits on
the trailer.  And who owns these rigs?  Why, the driver,
of course.
      Most rigs, however, are company owned or leased.  The
few privately owned rigs actually belong to the banks.
The trucks are often dirty, with dull paint and bent bump-
ers, and little or no chrome.  In the movies, if a tractor
breaks down, a tow truck is called and a genuine mechanic
works on it.  In real life, nine times out of ten the
driver is also the mechanic.
      Many people believe, thanks to Hollywood, that a
truck driver is a young, free-wheeling, single guy who is
good-looking enough to pick up a beauty queen within
minutes of hitting the asphalt.  But most drivers are
```

actually middle-aged and attached to a family. If the
driver is lucky enough to own a rig, he (or she) also owns
a house, a station wagon, and a dog.

Trucking is a vital form of commercial transportation. But it's dull. To make it sell, producers had to
create an appealing image, dispelling the loneliness of
the long haul. So the screen trucker was born. Although
the image may be attractive, it's wrong.

Daniel MacFarland

7   *Supporting Your Point*

*It is easy to write a check if you have enough money in the bank,
and writing comes more easily if you have something to say.*

— SHOLEM ASCH

You can think of your introduction, particularly its thesis statement, as a contract between you and your readers. You are contracting with readers for a bit of their time. In return, you promise to show to the reader's satisfaction that what you claim is true. Readers who don't care whether the thesis is true probably won't read past the introduction unless they have to. But readers who do care will expect persuasive evidence in return for their investment of time.

Think for a moment about the writing that will be required of you after this course is over, in other college courses and on the job. Most of you are familiar enough with school writing to know that professors are impressed with fact-filled presentations. You know very well that an essay exam filled with unsupported generalizations gets a lower grade than one packed with relevant details in support of a point. And work-related writing requires as much substance as school writing, sometimes even more. Most supervisors are busy people who do not appreciate having their time wasted, so they request substantive writing — writing filled with relevant and necessary information.

In other college courses and in on-the-job writing, you probably won't have much trouble coming up with appropriate content. Usually the material is almost given to you, or you know where to find it. For example, let's say you are writing a paper for Ancient History 103. Your instructor has asked you to compare two culture heroes, Gilgamesh and Job, to show the difference between Babylonian and Hebrew values. Because your content comes from the reading you have done in the course, you won't have much difficulty filling out your paper; as a matter of fact, you may have trouble trimming down such a wealth of material. The same is true of on-the-job writing. If your writing task, for example, is to summarize for your supervisor the important decisions made in a meeting that he or she was unable to attend, your problem will be deciding what to include. You'll have more information than you'll need.

But college composition may present you with a unique writing situation. Because it is a course in *how* to write, it doesn't necessarily provide you with content to write about. Whereas the details for supporting your points are almost given to you in other college classes and in on-the-job writing, in composition classes you may have to come up with them on your own. And let's face it, this is not always easy.

Choosing a Thesis You Can Support

Be careful to choose a thesis you will be able to support. Unless you are writing a research paper (in which case you will get your supporting material from written sources), we advise you to write about what you already know. To help you discover how much you already know, we have printed approximately two hundred writing topics in the Appendix in the back of this book. These topics cover a wide range of subjects: sports, religion, race, men and women, violence, and so on. At least some of them will touch on your areas of expertise.

You may be a police officer, a government worker, a basketball player, an amateur actress, a mountain climber, a vegetarian, a nurse's aide, a sports-car enthusiast. Such people have special knowledge worth communicating to readers. If you think you know nothing worth communicating, we believe that you, like the students we have taught, will find that you have a great deal to say once you look through our topics.

To illustrate how you can use your own knowledge to support a thesis, here is a list describing other students' successes.

1. Trained as a helicopter pilot at Ft. Walter, Bob Zeigler experienced firsthand the dangers of helicopter school. He was especially aware of the dangers of the "55," a helicopter in which he nearly died. He had more than enough knowledge to write a convincing essay on the dangers of the "55."

2. Brenda Jenkins, a mother concerned about the quality of her neighborhood high schools, had done some investigating. She had talked to school officials, to teachers and counselors, to other parents, and to students. Finding that the schools were just barely adequate to prepare a student for college, she wanted to share her discovery — and her alarm — with other residents of her community.

3. Mary Kenny, a lover of art galleries, took her readers on an appetite-whetting tour of her favorite gallery, the Phillips, in Washington, D.C. She visited the gallery again right before writing the paper, so the details would be fresh in her mind.

4. An avid ice-hockey fan, Lloyd Cash was disturbed by the violence of the game — not because he was squeamish, but because the violence was making the skills of the players almost beside the point. He wrote a paper arguing that if the violence were reduced, the players would be better able to display the true skills of the game.

5. Steve Brown had gone to most of the Italian restaurants in town in search of the perfect pizza. Having finally discovered it at Geppetto's, he shared his discovery with fellow pizza lovers in a glowing review of the restaurant.

6. Tom Kramer had been hearing a number of arguments against allowing girls into Little League baseball, and he was struck by the absurdity of the arguments. So he wrote a paper that simply displayed these arguments in all of their absurdity, leaving his readers to conclude that girls should be allowed to participate in Little League.

7. Lurleen Alston, a young woman whose father had recently died of cancer, was bothered because everyone, herself included, had pretended to her father that he wasn't dying. She had read a book, *On Death and Dying*, which made her wish even more that she had spoken honestly with her father. So she wrote a paper, based primarily on her own experience, to share her insights with readers.

8. Ken Beale, who had spent several years in Japan, was fascinated by Japanese sports, especially Sumo wrestling. Because most Westerners know very little about this unusual sport, he put his readers on the scene with ringside seats in an action-packed essay.

Getting Close to Your Subject

But, some of you may be thinking, I haven't gone to helicopter school or to Japan or even to local art galleries; I have not discovered the perfect pizza, have rarely attended ice hockey games, and couldn't care less about my neighborhood schools. *I* don't have anything to write about.

We doubt that this is true, but if you think it is, here's some practical advice. If you are having trouble developing your papers because you lack material with which to fill them out, you can always choose a topic that requires you to look for material. Select topics that ask you to seek out material in the world you live in. Some of our topics in the Appendix encourage you to do just that. Here are a few examples.

1. Interview someone who does work that is interesting. Describe the job to readers who are considering that line of work.

2. Choose an instructor from whom you are taking a course this semester. Describe in detail one actual class period in such a way as to communicate either your admiration of or your distaste for his or her teaching style. *No real names,* please.

3. Visit your child's school for at least half a day. Report on what you observe to interested parents in your community.

4. Review a play (or a film, an opera, a ballet, or a concert). Either encourage readers to attend the performance or discourage them from attending. Take notes during the performance or immediately after it.

5. What picture of American Indians, black Americans, Italian-Americans, southern whites, Chinese, or another minority group is presented in movies and television dramas? Limit this topic radically, perhaps by discussing the image of one of these groups as presented in one film or one TV series.

6. Take your reader on a tour of an art museum you have visited. Write the essay to encourage a visit by your reader.

7. Write a review of a cafeteria, fast-food chain, or local restaurant.

8. Interview a police officer — or better yet, accompany the officer on his or her beat (many communities have ride-along programs). What did you learn about the officer, the job, or both? Give the essay a focus.

9. Write a letter to your local TV news program suggesting any improvements you would like to see in its sports coverage. Or write a letter praising the sports coverage. Before attempting to write the letter, watch the program for at least a week and take detailed notes.

10. If you are happy in your neighborhood, describe its virtues to readers looking for a place to live.

To do a good job with any of these topics, you would need to get close to your subject. Then the necessary details, the material for your writing, would be right there in front of you. Literally getting close to your subject is a good method for writing, even if you already know something about your subject. As Stuart Chase put it, "It is much easier to sit at a desk and read plans for a billion gallons of water a day, and look at maps and photographs; but you will write a better article if you heave yourself out of a comfortable chair and go down in tunnel 3 and get soaked."

Your instructor may have his or her own way of helping you get close to a subject. Some instructors, for example, use a collection of essays to provide material for writing. Others ask students to write about literature or great books. When you write about a particular essay, story, or book, your material is right at hand. If you read carefully, you'll be close enough to your subject to write a paper filled with details.

Brainstorming on Scratch Paper

Let's say you have selected a thesis you think you can support, and you have written a first-draft introductory paragraph that either begins or ends with a thesis statement. Your next step is to decide just how you will support your point. What you're really deciding, of course, is how to write the rest of the paper.

Unless you have a very clear idea of how to support your point, it's a good idea to stop and brainstorm on scratch paper. Put your thesis statement at the top of the sheet, then jot down as many details, facts, or examples as you can think of to back it up or support it.

One student brainstormed this list before writing a paper showing the difficulties of enduring a five-day Navy "survival" school.

> *Thesis:* If you think it's easy to survive off the land, let me set you straight. Here's how I managed to get through a five-day Navy "survival" school.
>
> found 50 crabs — for 105 hungry men
> captured a dozen limpets (tasted like art gum erasers)
> followed a recipe for grass soup — tasted like weeds!
> chased a tiny ground squirrel, not really enough to serve one person — and didn't catch it anyway
> discovered the yucca plant, very tasty — but had the effect of a bushel of dried prunes
> raunchy-looking grubs and lizards — not so bad when you're desperate

With this list as a guide, the student wrote a fact-filled paper showing readers just how hard it is to survive off the land.

If you think it's easy to survive off the land, let me set you straight. Here's how I managed to get through a five-day Navy "survival" school.

The first evening the instructors dumped 105 of us onto a deserted beach. All we had were eight parachutes to use for tents, some string, and instructions on how to make nets and crab traps. In about three hours we had managed to trap about fifty crabs. Do you know how far fifty crabs go among 105 hungry men? Later that evening, after wandering along the beach, I found about a dozen limpets, which I had been told were edible raw. I was so hungry at that point I would try anything once. But eating raw limpets, I found out, is like trying to eat art gum erasers. After chewing on about half of them, I decided I wasn't really as hungry as I'd thought.

The next morning the instructors took us up to Warner Springs, where we were to survive four days in the mountains. The days were spent looking for food and the evenings were spent preparing it and feeling sorry for ourselves. On days two and three we ate a lot of soup made from the grass that we were able to gather. We had been told it was healthy and good. It tasted like weeds. The fourth day, while scavenging for food, a group of us stumbled upon a ground squirrel. Five grown men chased that squirrel for three hours, though even if we had caught it it wouldn't have been enough to feed one. Well, we didn't catch it, so we headed back to camp with a few handfuls of weeds for the community pot.

On the fifth day we discovered the yucca plant, which grows abundantly in the mountains. The stalks of the plant are similar to sugar cane. They were sweet and much better than the weeds we had been eating, so we gorged ourselves. An hour later we learned that yucca has the same effect as a bushel of dried prunes. Well, after losing my bout with Montezuma's revenge, I was ready to eat just about anything. One of the group brought back a load of grubs and some small lizards. Realizing how hungry I was, I decided they wouldn't kill me. Actually, as raunchy as grubs and lizards look, they weren't really all that bad. Roasted lizard tastes a little like beef jerky.

That night I dreamed of the steak dinner that I felt sure would be waiting for us back at base. As we helicoptered out of Warner Springs the next day, all talk was of food: sirloins and filet mignon, pork chops and ribs, baked potatoes with sour cream, dumplings with gravy, and beer, beer, beer. After landing, we raced to the mess hall for the Navy's reward to its 105 heroic survivors. But the hall was closed, and a notice was pinned to the door: "All personnel report to the command post for evasion course. You have three hours to get from one side of the course to the other, a distance of about two miles, without getting captured. If you are not captured, you will be rewarded with a piece of fruit and a sandwich." — ANDREW WOYCITSKY

The main purpose of brainstorming is to get enough details down on paper, as this student did, so you won't have to stop to think them up as you're writing. But brainstorming sometimes has a side benefit. Occasionally it will show you before you even attempt to write a paper that you don't have enough evidence to support your thesis. For example, one student began with the thesis, "Single people are often discriminated against in job interviews." Once he began brainstorming on scratch paper, it became clear that he had too little evidence to support his point. As it turned out, his only evidence was that he suspected he had once been discriminated against in a job interview because he was single. Since this one example was not enough to prove his point, and since this student saw no way to get the evidence he needed in the time available, he decided to give up on the topic. He found another thesis instead, one he could support more convincingly.

For further advice about brainstorming on scratch paper, see Chapter 1.

Revising the Content

As an essay is being written, it can begin to have a life of its own. You probably know from experience what we mean. Maybe you once wrote a thesis in favor of capital punishment, but found that your essay slanted in the opposite direction. Or perhaps you intended to show that the Ten Commandments are important rules for twentieth-century Americans to live by, yet were unable to justify more than six of them. Or maybe you just went off on a tangent as you were writing. For one reason or another, then, your rough draft won't always turn out the way you have planned. So once you've finished a rough draft, it's a good idea to read it over with a critical eye. Ask yourself: Does the body of this essay adequately support its thesis statement?

A good technique is to read the rough draft as if you were someone who *disagreed* with your thesis. If you find it impossible to pretend that you disagree, find a test reader, preferably one who *does* disagree with your thesis. Or ask your instructor or someone else who is likely to be objective to read the essay.

Though a test reader will help you see whether you've presented enough evidence in support of your thesis, your own common sense will take you a long way. Just ask yourself whether your essay contains enough facts to convince even skeptical readers. If your answer is *yes,* fine. If it's *no,* you have some more work to do. You'll need to strengthen your supporting material so that readers who do not already agree with your thesis will be forced to take it seriously, even if they do not end up completely in agreement with you.

Exercise 1   For Class Discussion

Consider what evidence a writer could use to support each of these thesis statements.

1. Fresh foods are more economical than commercially prepared frozen foods or prepared mixes.

2. Though by all outward appearances our community's two elementary schools are comparable, Forestville is academically superior to Brookline.

3. Poe, according to his biographers, had difficulty relating to women sexually.

4. Whoever said that history is nothing but polishing tombstones must have missed History 157, because in Professor Baldwin's class history is very much alive.

5. Though it looks innocent enough, the "55" is an extremely dangerous helicopter.

6. If you've never played golf before but are thinking of trying it, I'd advise against it — unless you have the funds to support this expensive hobby.

7. At the top of my list for good food, good service, and a charming atmosphere is a little Italian restaurant called Luigi's.

8. A number of toys on the market provide a safe and effective outlet for your child's aggressive feelings.

9. The Palmer Park Little League is clearly run for the benefit of the adult coaches and parents.

Exercise 2   For Class Discussion

Comment freely on the following quotations.

1. There is no need for the writer to eat a whole sheep to be able to tell what mutton tastes like. It is enough if he eats a cutlet. But he should do that.
   — W. Somerset Maugham, British Writer

2. If I had sat down to read everything that had been written — I'm a slow reader — I would never have written anything.
   — E. B. White, American Essayist

3. Do not be grand. Try to get the ordinary into your writing — breakfast tables rather than the solar system; Middletown today, not Mankind through the ages.
   — Darcy O'Brien

4. To tell about a drunken muzhik's beating his wife is incomparably harder than to compose a whole tract about the "woman question."
— Ivan Turgenev, Russian Novelist

5. An abstract style is always bad. Your sentences should be full of stones, metals, chairs, tables, animals, men, and women.
— Alain, French Philosopher

6. I'm a bit like a sponge. When I'm not writing I absorb life like water. When I write I squeeze the sponge a little — and out it comes, not water but ink.
— Georges Simenon, French Mystery Writer

7. A writer who does not speak out of a full experience uses torpid words, wooden or lifeless words, such words as "humanitary," which have a paralysis in their tails.
— Henry David Thoreau, American Writer

8. Writers get ideas . . . from real life. It's OK to lock yourself in the broom closet to write, if you have spent 95 percent of your time involved in life.
— A Student

9. I always start writing with a clean sheet of paper and a dirty mind.
— Patrick Dennis, Creator of Auntie Mame

Exercise 3   For Discussion in Small Groups

Working in small groups, discuss the following draft of an essay by one of our students, Margaret Stack. Pretend that Stack is a classmate who has come to your group for advice about the content of her essay. Where in the essay would you like to hear more details? Are any sentences or other chunks of text unnecessary or off the point? After your discussion, turn to Stack's own revisions (pages 229–235) and compare them with your suggestions.

```
                Irish vs. American Education

     During my junior year of high school, my family moved
from a suburban American community to a small village in
rural Ireland.  The change was pleasant once we got over
the initial cultural shock, and we learned a great deal
from the visit.  My biggest discoveries came from being
enrolled in the local convent, a school that was very dif-
ferent from my old high school.  The difference lay not in
the subjects that were taught, but rather in the way they
```

were taught and the surroundings and atmosphere they were
taught in.

In contrast to my ordinary brick high school, the
convent was a Gothic mansion with tall, narrow windows and
doors, vaulted ceilings, and endless, winding corridors.
To run or yell in a hallway was unthinkable.

Unlike its American counterpart, the convent was
badly heated and had almost none of the educational facilities or equipment believed necessary in America. There
was no cafeteria or food service. There were no science
labs (although one day my biology teacher did bring in a
dead frog and dissect it for us). The home economics department was equipped with only the bare necessities.
There was no library, really, just a box of paperback
books that the English teacher let us borrow from. In
contrast, just think of the many facilities in almost any
high school in America.

Strangely enough, instead of being academically inferior to my American high school, the Irish convent was
superior. In my class at home, Love Story was considered
pretty heavy reading, so imagine my surprise at finding
Irish students who could recite passages from War and
Peace. In high school, I didn't even begin algebra until
the ninth grade, while at the convent seventh graders (or
their Irish equivalent) were doing calculus and trigonometry.

Not that the Irish were completely superior in educational standards. Many of the students at the convent had
never even heard of chemistry, much less sex education.
The average Irish student seemed to have a firm knowledge
of the classics but was out of touch with the world of
today.

The main reason for this contrast may be the way the
classes were taught. In America the teacher is usually
approachable, and his or her teaching style is informal.
Disruption and disorder are normal. The students feel
relaxed, and very often daily life is discussed, ranging
anywhere from politics to personal problems, even at the
risk of wasting time. Why are American teachers so willing to let students get them off the point? The nuns at
the convent would be shocked.

At the convent there was no disruption, no disorder,
no wasted time. Classes ran smoothly and on a tight
schedule. Unfortunately, this made for dull, regimented
classes where tension ran very high. We never asked ques-

tions for fear of being singled out and drilled for lack
of knowledge.

After experiencing these two systems of teaching, I
am not sure which is better. Perhaps a combination of the
two would be ideal -- a system in which there is order and
discipline but without suppression and fear.

Margaret Stack

8 *Organizing*

Writing is not the dainty arranging of superficialities, it is the solid construction of thoughts. — DONALD MURRAY

An essay will probably start to take shape in your head; its form will become clearer as you sketch a plan on scratch paper or perhaps write an outline; then, after you have written the rough draft, you may find yourself rearranging it.

It's safest to plan a paper before you begin your rough draft. If you just plunge in, hoping to get your bearings as you write, you may write a well-organized paper, but the odds are against it. So plan the shape of your paper, at least sketchily, *before* you begin to write.

Organize before you write. This sounds like simple enough advice to follow, but you probably know from experience how tempting it is *not* to do so. Maybe you've tried organizing in your head, but found that one thought led to another which led to another and so on, leaving you with a string of loosely related ideas. Or perhaps you've turned to formal outlining in hopes of pinning down your ideas but found it more trouble than it seems to be worth. When students are required to submit formal outlines with their college essays, many of them write the outline after they've written the essay. Some of these students are probably just lazy, but we think many of them believe that formal outlining won't help them write a better essay.

Sketching a Plan

Organizing in your head and formal outlining are two ways of shaping an essay before you write, but they are not the only ways. Somewhere between the extremes of "just thinking" and Roman-numeraled outlining is a middle ground: planning on scratch paper. As you become a practiced writer, you'll discover that informal planning has advantages over both the extremes.

Sketching a plan on scratch paper helps you pin down your ideas. It gets them out where you can see them, so you can have some control over them. But unlike formal outlining, which can nail down your ideas too soon, informal sketching allows the shape of an idea to evolve. You'll feel free to move the parts around, to add new categories, or to delete whole sections — all before you've even begun the first draft.

Chapter 1 illustrates common methods for bringing order to ideas: clustering, branching, mind-mapping, and informal outlining. Of these, informal outlining is perhaps the simplest. For example, a student whose purpose was to persuade readers to try a local Italian restaurant sketched this brief plan:

> *Luigi's is a first-rate Italian restaurant*
> *charming atmosphere*
> *wide menu selection*
> *excellent food and wine*
> *efficient, friendly service*
> *moderate prices*

Mind-mapping, a technique that looks disorderly, can in fact lead to well-organized essays. On page 93 is the mind-map used by Tom Weitzel in preparing for his tightly organized essay "Who Goes to the Races?" (pages 259–263).

Formal Outlining

Sometimes, especially when you're writing long papers, you'll find that outlining gives you greater control over your rough draft than informal jottings. You might doodle a bit on scratch paper first, since that keeps you flexible as your ideas are taking shape. But once your ideas have begun to take shape, you may want to write a sentence outline.

A sentence outline with the thesis statement placed at the top pictures the logical relationships among your ideas. The thesis statement is the point you are going to support in your essay. The rest of the sentences in the outline are layered to picture their relationship to the thesis.

Thesis statement: _____.
    I. _____.
        A. _____.

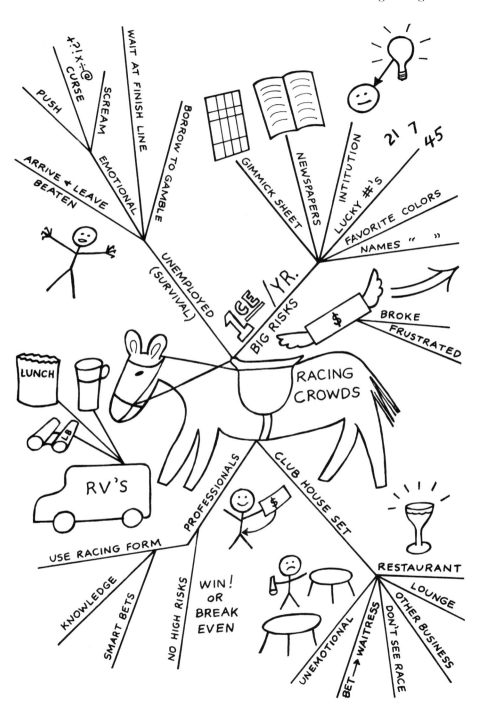

B. _____.
C. _____.
II. _____.
A. _____.
B. _____.
III. _____.
A. _____.
B. _____.
C. _____.
D. _____.

First-layer supports (the Roman numerals) are direct proofs of the thesis statement. They are indented and listed under the thesis statement to show that they support it. You think of them as propping up your thesis, which would collapse without them. Second-layer supports (the capital letters) prove the first-layer supports. Again, each one is indented and listed under the statement it supports, to picture that support relationship. You could of course have third- and fourth-layer supports, but unless you are writing very long papers, your outline should not be so detailed. Your outline is merely an overall picture of your paper. You fill in the details as you write the rough draft.

If you feel the need to write a two-layer outline, we suggest that you work on it a layer at a time. First block out the overall structure of the essay with a simple, one-layer outline. Then go back and work on the second layer. This way you won't get too bogged down in the details of the outline while you're still struggling with your essay's overall design.

We have learned through our own experience and the experiences of our students that complex outlines can paralyze writers. They force the writer to decide too much too soon. Simpler outlines will keep you flexible for the creative process of writing a rough draft. Because they picture the overall design of your essay, simple outlines leave room for new insights that may occur to you as you write.

Reorganizing

Even though it's a good idea to organize before you write, we're aware that writers — both students and professionals — don't always choose this method. A writer sometimes begins with just a hint of a plan and then writes awhile, hoping that the paper will take shape as it is being written. This is a perfectly acceptable, if risky, way to begin. Your rough draft may turn out so tangled that your only hope is to toss it out and try again. But if the draft at least begins to take shape as you're writing it, you will be able to reorganize it later. Even when you begin with a clear blueprint, sometimes your rough draft won't turn out quite the way you planned. Then, too, reorganizing is your answer.

To see where your draft needs reorganizing, try to look at it from the point of view of a reader. Reading expert Mortimer J. Adler tells us that good readers X-ray their reading material. They make every effort to see the skeleton that lies beneath the words on the page. The skeleton shows them how the parts of the essay are connected to each other and how they contribute to the main point of the whole essay. "The reader tries to *uncover* the skeleton," says Adler, and "the author starts with the skeleton and tries *to cover it up* . . . to put flesh on the bare bones."

Readers will look for the bones of your essay in certain key sentences, and in general you should make sure you've put these sentences in places where readers will be looking for them. The thesis statement is of course the key sentence for the whole essay; readers tend to look for it in the first or last sentence of the opening paragraph. Within the body of the essay, readers look for other key sentences that help them see how the parts of the essay are related to each other and to the whole; these are usually found at the beginnings of paragraphs. As you probably know, these key sentences are known as *topic sentences*. Although a topic sentence usually prepares readers for a single paragraph, it can also prepare them for chunks of text longer than a paragraph.

As a general rule, your thesis statement and topic sentences should interlock. Just by reading them, readers should be able to see the shape of the paper. Consider these key sentences, for example, taken from Tom Weitzel's "Who Goes to the Races?"

THESIS	After numerous encounters with the racing crowd, I have discovered that there are four distinct groups who appear at the track: the once-a-year bunch, the professionals, the clubhouse set, and the unemployed.
TOPIC SENTENCES	The most typical and largest group at the track are those who show up once a year.
	A more subtle and quiet group are the professionals.
	Isolated from the others are the clubhouse set.
	The most interesting members of the racetrack population are the unemployed.

As you can see, the skeleton of Weitzel's essay resembles an outline. Just by reading these key sentences, readers can see how the parts add up to the whole.

When you are trying to improve the organization of a rough draft, begin with the skeleton of your essay. Can a reader, just by scanning it, tell how the essay is organized? If not, strengthen that skeleton.

As you work to strengthen the skeleton, you may find yourself making other changes — deleting material, moving sentences or paragraphs about, even adding new material. With the help of scissors and tape you can take apart and reassemble your essay, experimenting with new arrangements. Don't worry if your pages look messy — this is your rough draft, after all. Of course, if you are lucky enough to be working on a word processor, you can do away with the scissors and tape. With a few keystrokes you can delete, add, and even move material; then you can print out a clean copy.

If you're having a hard time deciding whether a rough draft needs reorganizing or if you can't think of a way to reorganize it, ask someone for help. A friend, parent, classmate, writing center tutor, or instructor — anyone with a fresh perspective — may help you assess the possibilities. Sometimes just talking about the organization of your rough draft or sketching an outline will lead you to a new insight. Keep yourself flexible, experimenting with the possibilities, and sooner or later you will discover an organization that will work.

In this chapter we have given you three practical strategies for organizing an essay: sketching a plan on scratch paper, formal outlining, and re-organizing. If you're not in the habit of using these techniques — and many students aren't — give them all a try this semester. See for yourself the difference they can make.

Exercise 1   For Class Discussion

To outline or not to outline is often a question for novice writers. And whether to require an outline is a question for composition instructors. Some discussion in class of both the advantages and disadvantages of outlines could well be worthwhile. Here are some professional writers' observations that might help get such a discussion going.

1. [Outlining] too often becomes an artificial framework that a student has to justify. If writing is a learning process, then you will discover better ways of doing things as you go along.
   — CYRIL H. KNOBLAUCH

2. How can you tell what your house will look like or keep up with the building of it if you don't start with a blueprint?
   — ANONYMOUS

3. If you are used to starting every writing job with an outline, don't. Wait until you have felt the click. Before that, any outline will tie you down.
   — RUDOLF FLESCH

4. [The] writer may create a formal "Harvard" outline in which each point is in a complete sentence. It is more likely, however, that he [or she] doesn't follow the rules of Roman numerals and Arabic numbers, of capital letters and small letters, but draws what he has to say in a circle or a square, develops it in chart form, or scribbles it very informally, putting ideas down in random patterns and then drawing lines between ideas.
   — DONALD M. MURRAY

5. If you are the kind of person who loves card files, try dropping all your cards on the floor some time. It will do you no end of good.
   — RUDOLF FLESCH

6. Complicated outlines tempt you to think too much about the fine points of organization, at a time when you should be blocking out the overall structure.
   — ANONYMOUS

Exercise 2   Written

We know one woman who can take almost any subject and break it into three logical parts. How did she pick up this skill? Well, she's the daughter of a Southern Baptist preacher whose sermons were always divided, quite logically, into three parts. As a child our friend was forced to sit through her father's sermons twice every Sunday, so she learned how to organize almost without effort.

You too can increase your organizing skills by paying attention to the structures of sermons, classroom lectures, television documentaries, and sometimes even politicians' speeches. Sometime this week while you are listening to a sermon or a classroom lecture or a chalk-talk at the office, jot down notes that outline the structure of what you have heard.

Exercise 3   Written

Write a scratch-paper sketch or a sentence outline for a paper you are thinking about writing. Bring your sketch or outline to class and be prepared to discuss it with other students or with your instructor.

Exercise 4   For Discussion in Small Groups

Working in small groups, discuss the following draft of an essay by one of our students, Judith Burgin. Pretend that Burgin is a classmate who has come to your group for advice about the organization of her essay. How might she strengthen the skeleton of her essay? Should she move any sentences or larger chunks of text? Should she delete any material? After your discussion, turn to Burgin's own revisions (pages 237–241) and compare them with your suggestions.

Time Out

Howard Cosell is not the only offender. Most television sports announcers set my teeth on edge. I enjoy televised professional sports, especially football, but I cannot understand the low quality of sports broadcasting provided by the networks. I could forgive the numerous technical errors and the consistently mispronounced names if the persistent running commentary were tolerable.

Each rookie who displays any talent is proclaimed a future Hall of Fame nominee. Each participating team becomes the "toughest, meanest, and most fascinating to watch." Any pass completion is "fantastic," and every call by an official is "controversial." A second stringer having a good day is said to be the "most undervalued player in the league."

The local fans each week are dubbed "the most loyal in the world" and "the best to be found in any stadium." The head coach always seems to be "the most respected man around" and has always "done a great job with the boys." According to our announcers, there are no adequate athletes performing well, only superb superstars gaining glory. During the pre-game chit-chat, the weather is described as "picture perfect" or "unbearably miserable." Even the elements are not allowed to remain ho-hum in television land.

Quarterbacks are "men of great courage" and specialty teams are "suicide squads." Every person on the field is "a real man" with "a lot of heart." If a team is losing by twenty-eight points in the fourth quarter, we are instructed not to "count this team out" because those "tough competitors" have been known to "turn it around."

What ever happened to originality in broadcasting?

These guys are earning hundreds of thousands of dollars a year for sounding redundant.

When they deplete their supply of handy statistics, sportscasters turn to pathos. The viewer is informed that a certain hulking linebacker was a sissy in second grade. Another bought "dear old mom" her dream house with his first playoff bonus. We hear vivid descriptions of previous injuries and suffer through some poor guy's excruciatingly painful experience with a pulled groin muscle. One player, who was not expected to walk after his car accident, has a daughter with cerebral palsy for whom he "plays his heart out" weekly. Another is enduring a period of great stress. He wants to be near his family in California, but is forced by his contract to earn millions in Buffalo. If players are aware of these gushy interludes, they must find them embarrassing. "Dear old mom" could be watching and might not want her neighbors to realize that she doesn't make her own mortgage payments.

Why not allow the reality of a well-played game to project its own excitement, and let the tension of the competition provide the color? It doesn't seem like an unreasonable request. I wonder if Howard and friends could stop chattering long enough to consider it.

Judith Burgin

9   *Building Paragraphs*

The paragraph [is] a mini-essay; it is also a maxi-sentence.
— DONALD HALL

If paragraphing hadn't been invented, just how easily could we do without it? What would it be like, for example, to read a 300-page book that was not divided into paragraphs? Most of us would not even try to read such a book; if we did, we would find ourselves reading at a slow pace, with less comprehension than usual.

Paragraphs help readers in several ways. First, they ease the reader's eye by breaking up black print with restful touches of white. As writer Donald Hall puts it, "Paragraphs rest the eye as well as the brain. . . . Those little indentations are hand- and footholds in the cliff face of the essay." In addition to providing a rest, paragraphs outline the shape of an essay. Just by looking at the way the paragraphs are blocked out, readers begin to understand how the whole has been divided into parts and how the parts add up to the whole. Paragraphs also signal relationships among sentences, for the fact that several sentences are clustered together means that they belong together in some way. The topic sentence of the paragraph tells readers why they belong together, how they all add up.

This chapter will discuss only "body paragraphs," those used to develop the main idea of an essay. It will not consider paragraphs with special functions: introductory, concluding, and transitional paragraphs. These are discussed in other chapters.

Focusing with a Topic Sentence

The topic sentence of a paragraph is a mini-thesis statement. It announces the main point of the paragraph, preparing readers for the sentences to come. Notice, for example, how well this student writer has focused our attention with a topic sentence:

> *Because Tiet was an orphan in a country at war, my parents spent a lot of time cutting red tape and bargaining in the customary Vietnamese fashion — with monetary bribes.* The nuns of the orphanage, in a subtle way of course,

let my parents know that if money wasn't sent for a new well and milking machine then the Lord never meant for Tiet to be adopted. Money had to be sent to village heads and Saigon officials as a gesture of respect. Even the President of Vietnam, who must sign all citations of adoption, was sent a token of esteem — namely, one thousand dollars.

This student's topic sentence has all of the characteristics of a good thesis statement: it is a generalization that needs to be supported by more detailed information; it is limited (not too broad); and it is precisely focused (not too vague).

You should generally put your topic sentence at the beginning of a paragraph rather than in the middle or at the end. The topic sentence is designed to focus the reader's attention on the main point of the paragraph; it should therefore come first. Also, readers tend to look for topic sentences at the beginnings of paragraphs, so when you begin with a topic sentence you are fulfilling your readers' expectations, going along with their natural reading habits.

Occasionally you will have a good reason for violating your readers' expectations. You may decide, for example, to delay your topic sentence until the end of the paragraph because you want to surprise readers or even sneak up on them. We recall one student paragraph that ended with a topic sentence calling for increased taxes. The student felt, quite rightly, that if he had stated his point first, many readers would have been reluctant to read on. So he gave his arguments first, thinking he could get readers to go along with them, and saved his unpopular topic sentence for the end.

The writer of the following paragraph also had a good reason for delaying her topic sentence. Recognizing that her examples were more vivid than her topic sentence, she decided to dazzle her readers first, with a vivid opener, then let them know the point later, at the end of the paragraph. She judged that her readers would know from the context what the examples were supposed to illustrate, so by putting the topic sentence last she didn't risk confusing them.

> Our impressionable tykes read about homicidal old ladies offering poisoned apples long before they discover SWAT. They cope with Alice's encounter with madness and Red Riding Hood's mugging without tension or discomfort. No red-blooded American child would wince during Peter Pan's battle with the pirates or Dorothy's gruesome attack by winged monkeys. *These worldly little people are not likely to faint because of television crimes: more likely they will be disappointed by the quality of the violence.*

Rarely will you have a good reason for putting your topic sentence in the middle of a paragraph, but often you will have reason to delay it a bit. Sometimes, as you move from one paragraph to another in your essay, you'll find that you need a transitional or "bridge" sentence before your topic sentence. The purpose of a transitional sentence is to show readers the connection between what went before and what is about to come. Here is a student paragraph that opens with a transitional sentence followed by the topic sentence:

> Aside from sexual incompatibility, there was another problem. *Although David was a good and decent man, he lacked initiative.* All decision-making, regardless of importance, was relegated to me. "You decide" was his answer. Home and car repairs went untended until I either insisted he make repairs or saw to them myself. If the roof leaked, it continued leaking until I had it mended. If the furnace went out, I negotiated for repair and arranged for purchase of a new one. All of our financial affairs were left for me to handle.

As a general rule, then, put your topic sentence at the opening of the paragraph unless you have a good reason for putting it elsewhere. Sometimes you may even want to echo your topic sentence at the end of a paragraph in a "clincher" sentence. The topic sentence orients, prepares, and points ahead; the clincher sentence concludes, emphasizes, and points back. Clincher sentences work well for stressing a point, as the following student paragraph demonstrates.

> *It is true that I have had a few warning signals that I'm not as young as I used to be.* I do notice a slight shortness of breath after climbing several flights of stairs. Looking in the mirror, I see facial lines that weren't there before. The grocery boy at the store used to call be "Babe." Now his respectful reply is "Yes, Ma'am." As I sit here with aching feet and dead tiredness after a day at work, it hits me. *All of a sudden I'm over thirty.*

Filling out Paragraphs

Paragraphs, like whole essays, should be developed fully enough to satisfy a reader. Once you have focused on a topic sentence, ask yourself how much evidence and what kind of evidence your readers need to hear.

We think you'll agree that the writer of the following paragraph has some more work to do — if she is to convince us that her topic sentence is true:

> My aunt has a green thumb. She's very good at growing things. Whatever she plants seems to thrive. Yes, my Aunt Rose has a talent for making things grow.

Instead of developing the main idea, "My aunt has a green thumb," the writer has merely repeated it three times, with slight variations. No details are offered in its support.

Adequate support is not simply a matter of providing details, however. Though the following revision offers specific details, it too fails to prove the point:

> My aunt has a green thumb. She really enjoys gardening. Her house is full of books and magazines on the subject. She even has monogrammed garden tools. And I've never seen anyone who could work in the hot sun as long as she can. Yes, Aunt Rose grows things better than anyone in the neighborhood.

Here the details do not directly support the main idea. Rose's enthusiasm and devotion do not prove that she can make things grow.

To convince us that Aunt Rose does indeed have a green thumb, the writer needs to give us examples of Rose's successes, as in the revision below:

> My aunt has a green thumb. Anything she plants springs up strong and healthy. Her tomatoes are bright red and so heavy they almost break their stems. One year she planted onion seeds and forgot about them, only to discover a bumper crop of onions a few weeks later. In fact, her vegetables grow so plentifully she has to give half of them away to friends. As for flowers, her dahlias and roses always win first prize at the county fair. Yes, growing things respond beautifully to Rose's touch.

Here the specific examples — tomatoes, onions, flowers — have been selected to prove the writer's point. Even skeptical readers will be convinced.

Structuring Paragraphs

A paragraph should be structured around the kind of evidence most appropriate for proving its main point. There are many possible ways to prove a topic sentence, and in this section we discuss some of the most common: examples, illustrations, details, reasons, and comparisons and contrasts.

Examples

A few well-chosen examples will often satisfy readers as to the truth of a topic sentence. Three vivid examples are enough to convince us in the paragraph below:

> *Throughout history, women have resorted to many extremes in order to attain the standard of beauty popular at the time.* In China women's feet were bound

to keep them small, because men admired tiny feet. A tribe in Africa measured the affluence of the husband by the wife's weight, so women put on so much weight they could not move. In our own country we don't have to look too far back to a time when women were prone to fainting spells because they had cinched their twenty-five inch waists down to a fashionable eighteen.

"Yes," we think as we finish this paragraph, "women have been driven to some pretty bizarre extremes to reach their culture's standards of beauty."

The quality of a writer's examples is at least as important as their number. The mother who wrote this next paragraph could have given us many more examples of her daughter's "peculiar reactions to ordinary experiences," but she wisely chose to limit herself to a few of the most memorable.

> *When Julie was about two, I realized that she had peculiar reactions to ordinary experiences, but I did not know why.* She would see a toy across the room, crawl over to it, and then ignore it. She was afraid to sit on the edge of a chair. When I held up a favorite doll and cuddled it to me, she would laugh and seem to want it. When I offered it to her, the closer it got, the more afraid she became of it. You may have already figured out her problem. And I admit, it does seem simple with all those clues to think about at once. Yes, vision, Julie had a severe vision problem.

Though often just a few examples will do to fill out a paragraph, occasionally your purpose will require more. One student, while working in a day-care center, had discovered a number of toys that allowed children to blow off steam without hurting each other. Since the purpose of her paragraph was to acquaint parents with those toys, she decided to mention as many as she could remember.

> *A number of toys on the market provide safe and effective outlets for your child's aggressive feelings.* For example, you can buy a small punching bag for a small bully. In the case of fighting brothers and sisters, soccer boppers are quite effective. Soccer boppers are a primitive form of boxing gloves that protect the children from actually hurting each other, but allow them to keep on fighting until they feel better. When you have a child who likes to throw things, the "Nerf" airplanes and animals are your answer. With these toys not too much can get broken, because they are made of foam rubber. In the case of the child who enjoys biting, a rubber hand might be appropriate. You can always find these around Halloween. When you have a child with an uncontrollable amount of aggression, one solution is a padded room. However, these are not yet on the market for home use.

Had this paragraph been much longer, the writer would have split it at a natural pause between examples. A topic sentence sometimes introduces the material in more than one paragraph.

Illustrations

When an example is extended and told in the form of a story, it is called an illustration. Because readers enjoy stories perhaps more than any other form of writing, illustrations, when appropriate, can be a powerful way of proving a point.

> *Hospital workers know that at any moment they can be faced with a crisis.* For example, while I was running an EEG (electroencephalogram) one day, the pens started clacking and throwing ink around the room. I knew then that I was in trouble. My patient was having a seizure. Pressing the alarm button, I ran to the patient to immobilize her. Poor little thing, she was only four years old. Within seconds, three other members of my clinic rushed into the room. The physician started giving instructions and technicians rushed about, while the patient lay there helpless. As I drew the medication, the physician prepared her arm for the injection. When he gave the medication, a soft hush fell over the room. Slowly the pens stopped swaying and clacking. The patient's movements calmed. I knew then that everything would be all right for this child, this time — but that there would be other patients in my life just like her.

Notice that the writer carefully limited his topic sentence so that a single illustration would be enough to prove it: "Hospital workers know that *at any moment they can be faced with a crisis.*" If the writer had wanted to show us that such crises are commonplace, a single illustration wouldn't have been enough. To prove this broader point, he would have needed several illustrations; or, since several illustrations might have become too long, he could have resorted to short examples instead.

Details

To prove some topic sentences, you'll decide to sketch in relevant details. These might be statistics, facts, items, parts, facets, or other particulars. The best details are specific, as in the following student paragraph:

> *In our one-room schoolhouse in Green's Harbour, final exams were taken seriously.* These exams were written the third week of June after school closed for the summer. They were mailed from the Department of Education to the chairman of the school board, who had to be present during the

entire three-day exam period. We could not bring anything into the exam room except for pens, pencils, erasers, rulers, and a mathematical set. One of our parents had to be present to pick up anything we might drop because we could not bend over to pick it up. Our seats were spaced three feet apart in all directions, and there was a time limit for each exam. At the end of each day's work, the completed exams were placed in envelopes, sealed, stamped, and then delivered to the post office — by three people. The results of the tests were mailed to the chairman of the school board in August, at which time we learned of our success or failure.

We are left with few doubts as to the truth of this writer's point: At his school in Green's Harbour, Newfoundland, final exams were taken very seriously indeed.

To decide how many details to include in a paragraph, simply consider your purpose and audience. One student writer, for instance, hoped to convince readers that the form letters sent out from her desk were the best she could manage under the circumstances. Several statistics, she felt, would make this clear.

Those who complain about receiving form letters from our office should consider themselves lucky to receive any acknowledgement of their application at all. On the average we receive about 500 applications a month from every out-of-work attorney on this side of the hemisphere. During peak periods, our office (which consists of three people, only one of whom can type) answers nearly 2,000 applications in two to three weeks. I do not advise anyone to call or visit during this time, as tempers run extremely short. Too many of these 2,000 nameless faces feel that their submission makes us the best of buddies, so they phone, usually early on Mondays, to chat. The conversations often conclude with appeals to our "friendship": "Can't you pull some strings and find me a job?"

Reasons

Reasons are a fourth way of filling out paragraphs. They are appropriate when a topic sentence begs for an answer to the question "Why?" If a paragraph recommends that we install a wood stove or vote Republican or send our kinds to camp, we want to know why. The writer's job, then, is to tell us why — to give some reasons.

In a paper on the pros and cons of the open-space classroom, one writer included a paragraph explaining why such a classroom can be disastrous for students like her son, David.

Though the open-space classroom works for many children, it is not practical for my son, David, for several reasons. First, David is hyperactive. When he was placed in an open-space classroom, he became confused and frustrated. There were so many distractions because of the large number of children in one area that he was tempted to watch the movement going on around him instead of concentrating on his own work. Second, David has a tendency to transpose letters and numbers, a tendency that can be overcome only by individual attention from the instructor. In the open classroom he was moved from teacher to teacher, with each one responsible for a different subject at a different level. No single teacher worked with David long enough to diagnose his problem, let alone help him with it. Finally, David is not a highly motivated learner. In the open classroom he was graded "at his own level," not by criteria for a certain grade. He was in Area 1, not in second grade. He could receive a "B" in reading and still be a grade level behind, because he was doing satisfactory work "at his own level."

Notice that our writer has supplied readers with clear transition words — *first, second,* and *finally* — to help them see where one reason ends and the next begins. Without such help many readers would have lost the thread that ties the paragraph together.

Comparisons and Contrasts

To compare is to call attention to similarities; to contrast is to point out differences. If you're arguing that the $20,000 sports car your friend is thinking of buying is nothing more than a slickly packaged version of a much cheaper model, you'll use comparisons. You may mention a few differences, including the prices, but you will focus on similarities. If on the other hand your purpose is to help your friend decide between a 280 ZX and an RX-7, you'll focus almost entirely on differences.

Whether you need to compare or to contrast, you can use one of two basic ways to fill out your paragraph. You can discuss your two items point by point, or you can deal with them one at a time. Here is a paragraph of contrast developed by the point-by-point method:

> *Strangely enough, instead of being academically inferior to my American high school, the Irish convent was superior.* In my class at home *Love Story* was considered pretty heavy reading, so imagine my surprise at finding Irish students who could recite passages from *War and Peace.* In high school we complained about having to study *Romeo and Juliet* in one semester, whereas in Ireland we simultaneously studied *Macbeth* and Dickens's *Hard Times,* in addition to writing a composition a day in English class. In high school I didn't even begin algebra until the ninth grade, while at the convent seventh graders (or their Irish equivalent) were doing calculus and trigonometry.

Here the point-by-point method sharpens the contrast: *Love Story* vs. *War and Peace*; *Romeo and Juliet* vs. *Macbeth, Hard Times*, and a composition a day; elementary arithmetic vs. calculus and trigonometry. The writer could have dealt with the academic requirements of the American high school and then of the convent, but she decided that the point-by-point method highlighted her contrast more dramatically.

Sometimes your material won't lend itself to the zigzag structure of the point-by-point method. Then you'll deal with your two items one at a time. For instance, in a paper contrasting small-town and urban life, one student writer decided to put us on the scene, first in a small town.

> Let's go on a routine grocery trip in small-town America. First you get a cart and begin to make your selections. As you shop, people nod, agree that prices are outrageous, and they may even tell you, for instance, why they are buying green grapes today. As you pass the meat counter, you are told "hello," usually by name. The meat man knows just what type of meat you like and usually buy. Often he has put a special cut in the back because he thought you would like it, and he tells you to wait while he gets it to show it to you. You are not particularly flattered, because this is what you are used to.
>
> After you have finished shopping, you push your cart up to the line at the cash register. While you wait in line, everyone smiles and talks to each other. You may be told what nice apples you picked out. The weather, inflation, and even the latest hemlines are often discussed. When it is your turn, a bag boy takes your groceries out of the cart and places them on the counter. While the cashier adds up your total and chats with you, the bag boy is bagging your groceries. By the time you pay, your groceries are in a cart ready to go out as you do. Now you really get personalized service. The bag boy walks out with you, pushing your groceries to your car. He opens the trunk and loads them for you. As he leaves, he says with a smile, "Thank you, Mrs. Ricketson. Have a nice day."

Now that we have experienced small-town America, our writer takes us to the city.

> Let's shop now at the same grocery chain, but this time in the suburbs of a large city. From the start you are on your own. No one will talk to you or even look at you. The meat man has no idea who you are or what you might like, even if you shop there twice a week. When you finish shopping and get in line, no one will speak to you. If you are brave and say to the couple next to you, "Hi. Nice day, isn't it?" they will look at you as though you just threatened them. Maybe they will give you a quick reply, but there will be no conversation. When it is

your turn, *you* take your groceries out of the cart and place them on the counter. The cashier adds them up, silently. If you write a check and hand it to the cashier, even if you have been through her line many times, she will look you straight in the face and say, "Do you have a card on file?" When this happened to me last week, I couldn't resist the temptation. I looked right back at her and said, "No, I have never been here before." I thought she would laugh, but she didn't. She looked kind of strange and said, "Oh."

Usually you help bag your groceries and put them into a cart. Then you push them outside, go get your car, drive up to the curb, and wait in line to reach your groceries. If you are lucky, a bag boy will be on duty to put them into your car. And when he is finished, you will finally get a borrowed bit of small-town gentility, because he will say, mechanically and without smiling, "Have a nice day." — BETTY RICKETSON

These paragraphs echo the ones that came before. In the city suburb, as in the small town, we enter the store, pass the meat counter, stand in line, get checked out, walk to the parking lot, and leave with a word from the bag boy. Because so much is the same, the contrast is all the more vivid.

In this chapter we have surveyed some of the most common ways of filling out paragraphs: examples, illustrations, details, reasons, and comparisons and contrasts. Don't expect every paragraph you write to fit one of these models and feel free to use a combination of methods. Just consider your topic sentence, your purpose, and your audience, and then give readers the kind of evidence you think they need to hear.

How Long Should a Paragraph Be?

How long should your paragraphs be? Our general advice is to be flexible, because there is no one consideration that outweighs all others. Using a few rules of thumb, you will need to make decisions for yourself.

Often you can tell whether a paragraph is too long or too short just by noticing how it looks on the page. Remember that one major function of a paragraph is to rest the reader's eye, so if you have a 500-word paragraph (two pages typed, double-spaced), you can be pretty sure it's too long. You'll need to break up the 500 words into three or four, maybe even five paragraphs. By the same token, if you have divided 500 words into ten paragraphs, you can be fairly certain that readers are pausing too frequently. It's like taking them on a ten-mile hike and insisting that they rest every mile; you break their momentum and wear them out from too much starting and stopping.

Thus, you need to notice how long your paragraphs look on the page. And that, of course, depends on what kind of page we're talking about. As you write essays in college, your paragraph length will be determined to some extent by your decision to type or to write longhand. Typed paragraphs generally can be a bit longer than handwritten ones.

Earlier in this chapter we made the point that paragraphs help readers understand the shape of what they are reading. This is a very important consideration in determining the lengths of your paragraphs. If at all possible, let your paragraphs reflect the shape of your ideas. If, for example, you are writing a 500-word essay in which you give the reader three examples to illustrate your main point, you'll probably decide on five paragraphs: a paragraph of introduction, three body paragraphs (one for each example), and a short concluding paragraph. If one of your examples is much longer than the other two — so long that it will tire your reader's eye — you'll probably want to split it at some convenient point. The more closely your paragraphs reflect the shape of your ideas, the clearer your essay is likely to be.

One final word about paragraph length: How consistent should you be in the lengths of your paragraphs? Should you try to make them all about the same length, or should you vary them, playing off long ones against short ones? These questions are hard to answer. Paragraph lengths, like sentence lengths, give an essay a kind of rhythm that readers can feel but that is hard to talk about it. A very short paragraph can be just the right kind of pause following a long and complex one. Or a series of paragraphs of about the same length can give the reader a very satisfying feeling of balance and proportion. But let us say no more about this; you'll have to follow your own ear.

Exercise 1   Written

Select a topic from the Appendix that could be developed in a paragraph of 150 to 250 words. Before you write the paragraph, jot down a list of ideas on scratch paper. If your list shows little promise, throw it out and start another one, maybe on another topic. Once you have a workable list on scratch paper, write the paragraph. (Don't worry if the paragraph doesn't exactly fit the list — the list is there to give you control, not to straitjacket you.) Hand in your paragraph and your scratch-paper list.

Exercise 2 For Class Discussion

Identify the topic sentence of each of the following student paragraphs. If the writer chose not to place the topic sentence at the very beginning of the paragraph, do you see a good reason for its being elsewhere?

1. Now for those prepared mixes. I know that the Duncan Hines Cake Mix looks very tempting, but have you ever considered what you actually get for your ninety-nine cents? Let's take a look. For ninety-nine cents you get items that are usually already in your kitchen cabinets — flour, sugar, shortening and leavening. In addition, you get certain undesirable preservatives. After getting the mix home, you find that you must add your own eggs and in some cases butter for a better-tasting cake. Since the ingredients for a cake are usually in your cabinets, why not make your own mix and save your ninety-nine cents?

2. Soap opera characters are far from being realistic. They are all upper-class people, living in the finest of homes and wearing the latest fashions. You never see any poor people on these shows or anyone who has an ordinary job. No, these characters are all doctors or lawyers. The cities in which these soap operas take place must have to ship people in to do the less prestigious work.

3. Another example of research aimed at preventing sexual child abuse is under way at California State Hospital. Operating under the theory that most child molesters have led highly inadequate social and sexual lives, psychologists teach offenders how to talk and relate to adults. The California State Hospital program is so sophisticated that it even has volunteer counselors from local gay organizations coming in to teach homosexual offenders how to pick up adult partners.

4. Today the two oldest are out of college with well-paying jobs. The oldest one went into dentistry and then into the Navy. He is stationed in South Carolina, and has his own office to work in. The second child passed through college with high honors and now is a certified public accountant, working for the second largest firm in the United States, making $18,000 yearly and awaiting a $5,000 raise. The youngest is still in college, planning to go into business.

5. The atmosphere of the Berwyn Cafe was easygoing. Some of the customers who had finished their meals were washing their own dishes, talking and sharing vegetarian recipes with the cooks. As they left, people paid for their meals by dropping their money into a large wooden bowl, retrieving the change themselves.

6. The dream of every cyclist is to own a Cinelli. A Cinelli is the highest-quality, most expensive bicycle made. Each part on a Cinelli is machined

individually by hand. The wheels are laced and trued to the millimeter, by hand — a process which can take forty hours for just two wheels. The special lightweight tubing on the frame is thickened at the joints and thinned in the middle, a design known as double butting. A Cinelli could be all yours for just $1,300. At least that's how much I saw it advertised for on one of the rare occasions a Cinelli was ever advertised.

Exercise 3   For Class Discussion

Following are a number of student paragraphs developed according to the methods discussed in this chapter: examples, illustrations, details, reasons, and comparisons and contrasts. Identify the method that has been used in each paragraph.

1. *On the inside your worst fate was to be discovered as an informer or a "snitch."* One evening during our recreation period, when the cells were open, making it possible to go to the ground floor to play cards, watch TV, or just talk, I saw how snitches were dealt with on Cell Block One. This area, like all the cells, is separated from the guards by grill and screen. While I was playing cards with Hank, a small scuffle disturbed our game. Looking up, we saw two men, labeled as snitches, ritually getting their throats cut. The guards on the other side of the grill would not enter to offer any assistance until everyone had returned to his cell to lock in. In the meantime, the two men bled to death.

2. *The ambulance is well equipped.* There are neck braces in case of whiplash, eye pads for particles in the eye, sanitary napkins for extensive bleeding, air masks to help breathing, burn sheets for burn victims, restraining straps in case of seizures, a suction unit for getting blood out of the throat, and a complete first-aid kit. The kit includes all possible shapes and sizes of gauze bandages for cuts and scrapes and lacerations. The ambulance is also equipped with a radio that enables the medics to talk directly with the hospital to which they are en route, and a computer for monitoring vital signs.

3. *The Irish convent had almost none of the educational facilities or equipment believed necessary in America.* There was no cafeteria or food service. There were no science labs (although my biology teacher *did* bring a dead frog once and dissect it for us). The home economics department consisted of one stove and seven sinks. There was no library, really, just a box of paperback books that the English teacher let us borrow from. There was one record player for the entire school and a tape recorder that dated from World War II.

4. *Not that the Irish were completely superior in educational standards.* Many of the students at the convent had never heard of chemistry, much

less sex education. They knew by heart the exploits of Cuchulain (a legendary Irish warrior), but knew nothing of Freud or Marx or of any religion but their own. The average Irish student seemed to have a firm knowledge of the classics but was out of touch with the world of today.

5. *For the over-thirty gang who are overweight, out of shape, but healthy, I recommend rope-jumping as a most convenient form of exercise.* First of all, the equipment is simple and can usually be found in the home. All you need is a rope. A piece of clothesline will do, but if you want to feel a little more professional about it, go to a sports store and buy a leather rope weighted with ball bearings. A second convenience is that no special setting is needed. You can jump anywhere at any time to suit your schedule. You can jump outside — on the patio, the driveway, or the lawn — or inside — in the basement, attic, or even the living room. If you are traveling, you can jump rope in your hotel room. If you forgot your rope, just hook several belts together. Finally, since rope-jumping is a private exercise, you won't need to buy expensive sports attire. You may wear anything that's comfortable and won't get in your way.

6. *Hospitals are concerned with keeping the heart beating, not with the dignity of life.* The eighty-three-year-old father of a friend of mine, who had a slow-growing cancer of the prostate and whose veins were collapsing due to old age, was treated by the hospital staff as a collection of symptoms, not as a person. The nurses insisted on checking his blood pressure often, even though he found this very painful. In addition, they took blood tests every day, in spite of the fact that they had difficulty finding his veins. Before he died, he also had to endure the torture of being X-rayed to check the progress of the cancer. Mercifully, he died after being in the hospital only a few weeks. Unfortunately, an eighty-nine-year-old aunt of mine suffered for seven months in the hospital before she died. She went in and out of comas, had pneumonia a couple of times, and was pulled back to life to suffer more. She was a shrunken, senile old lady begging for death when she died.

7. *Since children learn a good deal by imitation and often have trouble distinguishing between fantasy and reality, parents should be cautious about what they expose their children to on television.* My older son's addiction to "Kung Fu" reruns, for instance, cost me a trip to the hospital last summer. During a particularly heated argument, he Kung Fu-ed his little brother on the head. As for "Batman," we've had a few jammed knees and wrists from jumping off picnic tables and porches with a towel pinned on as a cape. And once a bottle of perfume was emptied as "bat spray." Within the past year NBC featured an early evening film, "Born Innocent," which showed the sexual attack of a young girl with a broom handle by female inmates of a juvenile detention home. A

mother has sued the station, charging that the show inspired a similar attack on her nine-year-old daughter.

8. *Buying and maintaining their equipment requires quite an expenditure for the musicians.* Hundreds of dollars are spent just for an instrument. Each instrument (except drums) then needs an amplifier and a head, to produce the precise volume and sound needed for nightclubs. Amplifiers and heads also run hundreds of dollars apiece. Other necessary equipment — microphones for the vocalists, a PA board (the broadcast transmitter), and speaker cabinets — can total over a thousand dollars.

   Since this heavy equipment is transported from club to club and receives excessive use, blown tubes and fuses and wornout cords must be replaced frequently. A piano needs to be kept in tune. For this, the pianist either pays thirty to forty dollars per tuning or buys a $400 strobotuner and learns how to tune.

9. *Now that I'm over thirty, I'm not as naive as I was in my twenties.* I know how to resist a car salesman, how to handle an obscene phone call, what precautions to take when I'm out alone. I know how to handle a bank account, plan a week's menu, run a household, and raise a child. I know how to dress for an interview, how to find my way around a strange city, and how to vote. All of this I have learned through experience, by trial and error.

Exercise 4   *For Discussion in Small Groups*

Working in small groups, discuss the following draft of an essay by one of our students, Ethel Ramsey. Pretend that Ramsey is a classmate who has come to your group for advice about the paragraphing of her essay. Where might she combine or separate paragraphs? Should she delete any paragraphs? After your discussion, turn to Ramsey's own revisions (pages 243–249) and compare them with your suggestions.

Learning to Decide

To some extent, we are all affected by our environment. And among the most powerful influences upon us are the personalities of the significant people in our lives. These influential people can either nurture and promote our growth and development as individuals, or they can inhibit it.

Having been raised in the home of my father and mother and now living in my own home with my husband, I am acutely aware of the value of supportive personalities.

In our home, my father was the indisputable authority. Male supremacy was assumed by my father and accepted by my mother. He considered it to be his prerogative to govern every facet of life for anyone who resided in his domain. My mother was not even permitted to select a new piece of furniture or carpet. If he liked a particular chair but she thought the fabric or color was inappropriate for our large family, he bought it and she tried to keep it clean. With my mother having virtually no voice in most subjects, it followed that we, as children, had even less. This was inhibiting to all of us, but it was worse for my sister and me than for my brothers. Naturally my father did not share our interests, so he proclaimed them frivolous and unnecessary. On the other hand, since my brothers shared many of his interests, they had the opportunity to participate in activities they enjoyed. Dad insisted that we spend our leisure time together. He liked boating and fishing, so we all went boating and fishing. And my being subject to motion sickness was completely irrelevant. Therefore I spent countless Saturdays and Sundays with clenched teeth and a queasy stomach. Although there were four children in our family, we never went to the zoo or to an amusement park. Only once did we ever go to a movie. But we never missed the annual boat and auto shows. We were expected to enjoy Dad's interests and given little opportunity to enjoy normal childhood activities.

What little individuality Dad did not crush, Mom discouraged. An "A" in algebra—trig was trivial, because she managed a house and family with a knowledge of only basic mathematics. But a disinterest in home economics was unforgivable. She totally rejected the idea that I might be anything other than a wife and mother. Any mention of a career was met with murmurs concerning the immoralities of unmarried women and her opinion that a mother's place was with her children. Between the two of them, my parents tried to mold us into duplicates of themselves, complete with their hobbies, professions, and opinions.

After marrying, I found it confusing to be expected to have my own point of view. My new husband insisted upon knowing my preference before purchasing any household items. At first, this was extremely difficult for me, because I discovered that I usually did not have a preference. Whenever that occurred, Bill would assume that I needed more time to decide, so he would suggest that we wait until I had made my decision. After a week of stum-

bling around in our dark apartment, I selected some lamps.
Eventually, forming my own opinions and making decisions
became easier. Vacations, activities, and purchases were
mutually planned. I truly realized how much progress I
had made when we started to build our house.

We had decided, for economic reasons, to use a precut
or package—style house. After obtaining floor plans and
brochures from several companies, we found ourselves over—
whelmed by the task of selecting the right house. Finally
I sorted through the plans and eliminated those that did
not meet our minimum requirements or that were too large.
Next I considered which ones either included the extras we
wanted or could be altered to include them. I was left
with three plans, one of which I felt was the best house
for us. When I showed Bill the plans and explained my
method of selection and ideas for alterations, he immedi—
ately agreed that my first choice was the best house for
us. It was built, complete with the alterations I had
suggested. Five years before I could barely choose a
lamp, but now I felt confident enough to select a house.

As a child, I was expected to accept the opinions and
obey the decisions of others without questions. Now I am
encouraged to think, to reach, and to achieve whatever is
within my capabilities.

For the first time in my life, I am expected to be
me, with my own interests, hobbies, opinions, and dreams.

Ethel Ramsey

10 *Making Connections*

Word carpentry is like any other kind of carpentry: you must join your sentences [and paragraphs] smoothly. — ANATOLE FRANCE

We come now to what may at first strike you as a minor detail: the coherence of your writing, or how the parts connect with one another. Sentences and paragraphs should meet one another smoothly, without gaps, outcroppings, or rough edges. They should flow so naturally, one to the next, that readers are barely aware of the movement.

Whenever sentences are disjointed, seeming almost to bump into one another, readers must waste energy trying to make them connect. Some readers will refuse to go to this kind of trouble; others, even after struggling, won't quite see the connections the writer had in mind.

Logical Connections

If sentences are not arranged in logical order, or if unrelated sentences appear, coherence suffers. For example, consider this paragraph, which describes the way in which sculptor Louise Nevelson arranges shapes in wood:

> The sculpture of Louise Nevelson relies on her placing unlikely pieces of wood together to create interesting surfaces that emphasize light and shadow. Nevelson's appearance is striking, almost bizarre; she wears unusual clothes combinations and many chains and beads. Her studio is in New York City. Nevelson collects bedposts, two-by-fours, mantels, spools, dowels, and other shaped wood and then begins to experiment with these shapes in various arrangements. One summer her work was being shown in three different galleries at the same time. Sometimes Nevelson paints the finished sculpture — gold, silver, flat black, perhaps white; sometimes she leaves the piece in its natural state. Once arranged, the protruding pieces of wood stand out as if highlighted and create shadows on the recessed areas. She nearly always ends up with an exciting collection of wood that distinguishes her as a sculptor.

The flow of the paragraph is broken by irrelevant details: Nevelson's appearance, the location of her studio, the fact that her work was shown

117

in three galleries at the same time. Although interesting, these details interrupt the description of the process by which Nevelson creates her sculptures.

Even after irrelevant sentences have been deleted, the paragraph still needs work, for the steps in the process have not been arranged in logical order: Nevelson is painting the finished sculpture one minute, assembling it the next. Once the logical order has been straightened out, the paragraph reads more smoothly:

> The sculpture of Louise Nevelson relies on her placing unlikely pieces of wood together to create interesting surfaces that emphasize light and shadow. Nevelson collects bedposts, two-by-fours, mantels, spools, dowels, and other shaped wood and then begins to experiment with these shapes in various arrangements. Once arranged, the protruding pieces of wood stand out as if highlighted and create shadows on the recessed areas. Sometimes Nevelson paints the finished sculpture — gold, silver, flat black, perhaps white; sometimes she leaves the piece in its natural state. She nearly always ends up with an exciting collection of wood that distinguishes her as a sculptor.

Logical connections can also break down if the writer omits certain facts crucial to the reader's understanding. The facts omitted are often so obvious to the writer that he or she simply forgets not everyone is aware of them. For example, one student wrote the following note to his instructor:

> I'm sorry I was late to class this morning. I got a ride with my friend Joe in plenty of time, but halfway to school we were caught in a heavy thunderstorm. As a result, I had to return home and change clothes before coming to class.

The instructor was puzzled until she learned that the student had ridden to class on the back of Joe's motorcycle. This fact was so obvious to the student that he had forgotten to include it in his note.

Consistency in Perspective

Coherent writing maintains a consistent perspective. If a writer switches tenses without warning or suddenly begins using *you*'s in place of *they*'s, readers will be left wondering why. Consider your own reaction to the following paragraph, which contains a number of such jarring shifts.

> Isaac Asimov's short story "The Ugly Little Boy" shows how much a human being needs to be loved and needed. The nurse becomes very attached to the little boy as she cared for his physical needs and taught

him to speak. She loves him so much that she risks her own life. People will do that if someone or something means enough to them. She knows that she may die if she stays with him, but her need to be loved and needed is too great. By the end of the story, you understand why she is willing to take the risk.

Notice that the writer has shifted from the present tense (*becomes*) to the past tense (*cared* and *taught*) and then back to the present (*loves*). Such shifts are a common problem in essays discussing a literary work, since either the present or the past tense may seem appropriate for fictional events. The literary convention, however, is to use the present tense when writing about literature, so in her revision, our writer changed the two past-tense verbs to the present.

Notice also that the writer has shifted in her last sentence to the second-person point of view ("you"), a shift that is awkward since the rest of the paragraph is written from the third-person point of view. Our writer fixed this problem by changing *you* to *readers*: "By the end of the story, readers understand. . . ."

There is one other shift in the paragraph that is worth mentioning. Did the fourth sentence of the paragraph suddenly take you away from the nurse and the little boy? Such a general-observation sentence, which reads as if it has been dropped into a paragraph, is called an aside. The paragraph reads more smoothly without it.

All shifts in perspective startle and confuse a reader. It's fairly common for shifts to slip into a rough draft; just be on the lookout to correct them as you polish a paper. For more about shifts, see "The Writer's Stance" in Chapter 4 and section 25 in the handbook.

The Echo Effect: Repetition and Parallelism

One device that helps your writing to cohere is the repetition of key words or phrases or ideas, which produces a sort of echo effect. Such repetition keeps reminding readers of the main point within a paragraph and focuses their attention on major ideas throughout an essay. In the essay printed below, the writer echoes whole sentences. "The husbands comfort their wives" is echoed in the beginning of paragraph 2 and at the end of paragraph 3. In addition, the question "Who is to comfort the husbands?" creates an echo effect to open paragraph 4.

The first thing I saw when I opened my newspaper this morning was a photograph of two sets of parents at the graveside of their young daughters, brutally murdered recently. The caption beneath the photograph, in which the mothers were clearly grieving, ended with the sentence "The husbands comfort their wives." Those last five words leave an important question unanswered: Who is to comfort the husbands?

"The husbands comfort their wives." I believe that the women in the picture are indeed receiving comfort from their men. But I believe they are getting more comfort in the open release of their emotions. Such open release allows twofold benefits. First, the women's display of emotion elicits a sympathetic reaction from others, who rush to comfort the grieving. Second, and I believe most important, their open grieving allows for a release of tensions that would otherwise build up inside. Such public display of emotion is therapeutic, and it is acceptable behavior for women.

I look more closely at one of the husbands. He sits there with his "stiff upper lip," surrounding his wife with his comfort-giving arms. I look closely at his eyes and the circles under them. In even such a poor-quality photograph I can see the grief in his eyes longing for release. But that release cannot come, not in public, for he is "strong"; he is a "man." He is expected to give comfort to the "weaker" female. And so this husband comforts his wife.

But who is to comfort the husband? He is expected to "take it like a man." And he will. He will hold his grief and allow the tensions to build, until an acceptable time and place for release. Meanwhile, he acts "like a man" — in a display that is not very healthy, but that is acceptable behavior for men.

Another way to achieve the echo effect is to use synonyms, a device that also helps to avoid the monotony of simple repetition. The following paragraph uses synonyms for the word *marijuana* in this way.

The effects of *marijuana* are hotly debated. And whether the *drug* will be decriminalized largely depends on the outcome of the controversy now under way. Whether the pleasurable results from smoking *grass* should be considered worth the possible risks of its use is a real question in a free society. What are the long-term effects of the substance affectionately known among its advocates as *Mary Jane* — and how much should its detractors be listened to? Let us try to take an objective look at *marijuana*.

You can also create an echo effect by using parallel structure, in which parallel elements of a sentence or a paragraph are expressed in the same way. In the following paragraph, for example, five successive sentences begin with a verb that invites an art museum visitor to enjoy a painting in various ways.

Suddenly, in the midst of your musings, you find yourself in a room ablaze with light, color, and life. There on the wall is Renoir's "Luncheon of the Boating Party." Take a seat and treat yourself to a longer look. Settle back and feel the joy and warmth of the painting. Smell the early summer breeze off the Seine. Hear the rustle of the leaves and the hum of the conversation. Stay as long as you like, but remember, there is more.

Here are the sentences listed so that you can more readily recognize the parallel structure:

Take a seat and treat yourself to a longer look.
Settle back and feel the joy and warmth of the painting.
Smell the early summer breeze off the Seine.
Hear the rustle of the leaves and the hum of the conversation.
Stay as long as you like, but remember, there is more.

In our next example, parallel structure has been combined with repetition to produce an echo effect.

You come up on the desert of the White Sands from the cultured East or the deep South or the industrial North and suddenly you breathe. The sand beneath you is white and the sky above you is blue and there is no need even to define the colors, for the white is the whitest you have ever seen and the blue is the bluest. There is nothing else. You take off your shoes and slide your feet quietly onto the whiteness and walk. You address the blue sky and walk. You breathe.

Parallel structure can also be used to carry along an entire piece of writing. In a paper by Jo Goodwin Parker entitled "What Is Poverty?" eight of the fifteen paragraphs begin "Poverty is. . . ." Here are the topic sentences of Parker's opening paragraph, and several of her other paragraphs:

You ask me what is poverty?
Poverty is being tired.
Poverty is dirt.
Poverty is staying up all night on cold nights to watch the fire, knowing one spark on the newspaper covering the walls means your sleeping child dies in flames.
Poverty is looking into a black future.
Poverty is an acid that drips on pride until all pride is worn away.

Transitional Bridges

The final coherence device we want to tell you about is one of the simplest, and also one of the easiest to learn how to use. It is providing bridges to carry your reader from one part of your essay to the next. You can use these bridge words or phrases, sometimes called transitions, to move your reader from sentence to sentence or from one paragraph into the next.

Below is a chart of some bridge words and phrases. You can train yourself to use these bridges by asking yourself certain questions as you write: Does the next thing I am going to say simply make an *addition* to something I've just said? Or does the content of my next sentence set up a *comparison* or a *contrast* with what is in my last sentence? Am I involved in a *cause-and-effect* discussion? Am I about to illustrate my point by using an *example?* You can ask yourself the same questions as you begin a new paragraph, of course.

Transition to indicate:	*Bridge words and phrases:*		
1. Addition	furthermore	or	third
	also	nor	next
	in addition	moreover	last
	further	again	finally
	besides	first	
	and	second	

Example: For the fruit-testing project we tasted sour green apples; furthermore, some of us consented to try very green bananas.

2. Time	while	immediately	never
	after	later	always
	when	soon	whenever
	mean-	in the	sometimes
	while	meantime	now
	during	afterwards	once
	next	following	simultaneously
	then	at length	

Example: For the fruit-testing project we tasted sour green apples. Soon several of us developed stomach cramps.

3. Place	here	beyond	adjacent to
	there	wherever	neighboring on
	nearby	opposite to	

Example: For the fruit-testing project we tasted sour green apples; nearby another group of volunteers was trying very green bananas.

4. Exemplification
or Illustration

for example
as an illustration
to demonstrate
specifically

for instance
to illustrate
e.g. (means
"for example")

Example: For the fruit-testing project, volunteers were expected to taste a variety of samples; our group, for instance, tried very green bananas.

5. Comparison

in the same way
by the same token
similarly

in like manner
likewise
in similar fashion

Example: For the fruit-testing project we tasted sour green apples; in similar fashion, some of us tried very green bananas.

6. Contrast

on the contrary
in contrast
nevertheless
but
at the same time
although that may
   be true
nonetheless
on the other hand

yet
and yet
notwithstanding
otherwise
however
after all
though
instead
rather

Example: For the fruit-testing project we tasted sour green apples; however, most of us refused to try very green bananas.

7. Clarification

that is to say
in other words
to put it another
   way
to explain

to clarify
to rephrase
i.e. (means
   "in other words")

Example: For the fruit-testing project we tasted sour green apples. In other words, we experimented with the possible effects of green fruit on our health.

8. Cause

owing to
because

since
for that reason

Example: Since we were afraid they·would make us sick, several of us refused to try very green bananas during the fruit-testing project.

9. Effect   therefore   thus
                  consequently   hence
                  as a result   accordingly

Example: For the fruit-testing project we ate sour green apples; consequently, we were all in bed the next day with stomachaches.

10. Purpose   in order to   to that end
                  for this purpose   so that

Example: For the fruit-testing project we tasted sour green apples. In order to earn full pay for volunteering, some of us tried very green bananas.

11. Qualification   almost   perhaps
                  nearly   maybe
                  probably   although

Example: For the fruit-testing project we ate sour green apples. Perhaps I shall never feel more uncomfortable than I felt following that experiment.

12. Intensification   indeed   undoubtedly   doubtlessly
                  to repeat   in fact   certainly
                  by all   without   surely
                      means   doubt   of course
                  even more
                      so

Example: For the fruit-testing project we ate sour green apples; without doubt, that was one of my most unpleasant sensory experiences.

13. Summary   to summarize   in short   in brief
                  in sum   to sum up   in summary

Example: We ate green apples for the fruit-testing project. Then we were handed very green bananas to try. Next came pears almost as hard as rocks. In brief, we were provided a steady diet of green fruit throughout the afternoon.

14. Conclusion   in conclusion   to conclude   finally

Example: To conclude my report on tasting green fruits, I would simply advise my readers to find another way to contribute to the health studies of the nation.

Here is the rough draft of a student paragraph before the writer attended to his transitions. Notice how his pile-up of unconnected short sentences makes the paragraph jerk along when you read it aloud.

> Kid porno is highly immoral. I don't care for adult pornography because it is violent. That does not seem as wrong to me as child pornography. Adult pornography uses adults. They know they are being used and they consent. Children don't understand how kid porno exploits them. It uses them to sell products. It can encourage promiscuous sexual activity. They are too young to realize what they're doing. Kid porno can promote such sexual behavior among other children. Kid porno is highly immoral. It is more immoral than adult pornography.

Rewriting, this student built in transitional bridges to weave those jerky sentences together. His new version reads more smoothly, as you can see. The added bridges are in italics.

> Kid porno is highly immoral. I dislike adult pornography because it is violent, *but* it does not seem as wrong to me as child pornography. Adult pornography uses adults. They know they are being used and they consent. Children, *on the other hand,* don't understand how kid porno exploits them; *for example,* it uses them to sell products. *Furthermore,* it can encourage them toward promiscuous sexual activity *while* they are too young to realize what they're doing. Kid porno can *also* promote such sexual behavior among other children. *Therefore,* kid porno is highly immoral — *even more so* than adult pornography.

You will want to take care not to overuse transitional words and phrases. If you do, your writing may begin to sound mechanical, almost as if it had been written by a computer instead of a human being. Can you hear such a mechanical effect as you read the following paragraph aloud?

> Watching football on television is my favorite way to relax. First, I put on my grungies in order not to be worried about wrinkling my business clothes. Second, I turn off the telephone; therefore, my game won't be interrupted. Third, I chase everybody else from the room so I can be alone with my game. Fourth, I have a bowl of popcorn and a jug of root beer close by; consequently, I don't have to get up for refreshments. Finally, I become totally involved in the action on the screen, with the result that I totally escape from my real life. In conclusion, this is how I relax in my favorite way — with football on television.

Did you hear any bridges you as reader did not need? Or any necessary ones that stuck out as mechanical? Would some other bridge sound better in those places? Remember, you don't need to overconnect your writing; just build in the bridges without which your reader can't get along.

Transitions are not always merely single words or phrases. Sometimes whole sentences or even paragraphs work as bridges to smooth the way for your reader. Here is a student paper that uses a transitional paragraph:

> This paper is a salute to black women all over our nation who have suffered almost unendurable hardships trying to keep their families together in the face of relentless day-to-day oppression. American history and American literature are slowly beginning to show us some of these strong black women, their struggles, their heartaches — and, always, their pride.
>
> I can think of no better example of these proud, tenacious women than Phoenix, in Eudora Welty's short story "A Worn Path."
>
> Old Phoenix was a product of the cruel institution of slavery. She had been freed by the Emancipation Proclamation, and had had no formal education. However, she was able to survive in a country hostile to freed slaves. . . .

The second paragraph, one sentence long, is transitional. Transitional paragraphs can be composed of one, two, or perhaps even three sentences, but they are unlikely to be very long.

Exercise 1 Written

Read the following paragraphs aloud for problems in coherence. Each one needs to be improved by establishing consistency, creating parallel structure, or adding bridges. Improve the paragraphs, restructuring sentences if necessary.

1. One summer I worked as a camp counselor. Each counselor was in charge of a cabin of ten boys. The nine-year-olds were in my cabin, Tahoe. All my campers were white except one. He was a black youngster named Jonathan. The rest of the campers ignored Jonathan in the beginning. Sometimes they outright excluded him from their activities. The camp master had told the counselors that each cabin should function as a unit. I worked hard to create a unit of those nine-year-olds. I succeeded. My most treasured object from that summer is a photograph of Jonathan hoisted on the shoulders of three new friends with six more nine-year-olds crowded around — all of them Jonathan's cabinmates from Tahoe.

2. The Chuckling Oyster at Land's End serves delicious seafood. It is known that their specialties are crab imperial, oyster stew, fried clams, salmon steak, and stuffed flounder. The last time we were at the Chuckling Oyster, I ordered salmon steak and my wife ordered crab imperial. Most salmon steak comes from the Pacific Northwest, but it tastes fresh at the Chuckling Oyster on the East Coast. First, our

waiter brought us a large salad with house dressing and salty rye bread. We were served the next course — corn on the cob with plenty of butter — by another waiter. After that, a waitress delivers lime sherbet "to cleanse the palate for the specialty." By then you are almost too full to eat your main course. When we finally finished, I left the Chuckling Oyster convinced that it must be one of the best seafood restaurants in the United States.

3. Have you ever known a hermit? A hermit named Mr. Joe was a special part of my childhood. Mr. Joe knew about everything, or so it seemed to us children: how to catch minnows by hand, cracking walnuts so the meat came out whole, the sun as a record of time. Mr. Joe lived way back in the woods in a log cabin he had built himself. The hammock in his yard had been hand-tied by him. He dug his trout-breeding pond himself. All the flowers around his cabin had been dug up in the woods and transplanted by him. But the best thing about Mr. Joe was that, even being a hermit, he loved us kids and always carried treats for us — sweet, juicy oranges; shiny, crunchy apples; lollipops that were sometimes stale but were candy nonetheless; and, always, fresh, forbidden Juicy Fruit chewing gum.

Exercise 2 *Written*

Though repetition of key words makes a piece of writing flow, too much repetition of the same word can be jarring. Improve the following paragraph by substituting synonyms for the word *just* or its echoes. You need not change the word in every instance, but vary the language enough to keep the passage flowing.

The question of justice for all in our courts is of great concern to me. It seems only just that all should be treated equally when being tried under our system of justice. But surely that does not happen. Too often, affluent, well-educated, white-collar individuals in our society are treated more justly than the poor, who are often less-educated minority persons. Since that is true, can our court system really be called just?

Exercise 3 *Written*

Though use of transitions generally improves coherence, their self-conscious use becomes awkward. In the following paragraph, printed in this chapter, transitions seem too mechanical. Try smoothing them, restructuring sentences and changing words where necessary.

Watching football on television is my favorite way to relax. First, I put on my grungies in order not to be worried about wrinkling my business clothes. Second, I turn off the telephone; therefore, my game won't be interrupted. Third, I chase everybody else from the room so I can be alone with my game. Fourth, I have a bowl of popcorn and a jug of root beer close by; consequently, I don't have to get up for refreshments. Finally, I become totally involved in the action on the screen, with the result that I totally escape from my real life. In conclusion, this is how I relax in my favorite way — with football on television.

Exercise 4 Peer Review

Bring your most recent rough draft to class with you. Working in pairs, check your writing for coherence by having your partner read your paper out loud to you. Listen for rough, bumpy-sounding spots in your writing. Then, with your partner's help, try to discover the source of each problem. Is there a failure in logical connections, a lack of consistency in perspective, an absence of transitions, a need for the echo effect? By the end of your work session you should be ready to revise your paper for coherence.

Exercise 5 For Discussions in Small Groups

Working in small groups, discuss the following draft of an essay by one of our students, Kirk Brimmer. Pretend that Brimmer is a classmate who has come to your group for help with coherence. Where in the essay would you advise him to reorder ideas, to clarify connections, to eliminate confusing shifts, or to supply appropriate transitions? If your group has time, revise one or two of Brimmer's paragraphs for coherence. After your discussion, turn to Brimmer's own revisions (pages 251–257) and compare them with your suggestions.

Working the Water

Chesapeake Bay watermen have always been known as hard-working individualists, and Robin Collier lives up to this reputation. Robin has lived on Deale Island all his life. He learned his trade from his father, who learned from his father. Working the water is hard and dangerous work, but Robin swore that there is no better way of life. At the age of eight Robin began working the water with his father. He began working as a carpenter when he

turned eighteen, but after two years he was back. "I
didn't like having a boss. When you work the water, you
are your own man."

Robin's main source of income comes from the summer
crab season, but he also works in the off season. Occasionally he tongs for oysters (pronounced "arsters" on the
shore) at the mouth of the Moniac Bay and Menoken Creek,
but mainly he works as a custom cabinet maker. He also
carves decoys and has been known to act as a guide for a
hunting party every now and then.

A typical day for Robin during the crabbing season
starts at 2:00 A.M. He begins by powering up the Chrysler
engine of his twenty-seven-foot Baycraft, and then he
heads for Fox Island to buy ale-wives and menhaden, used
for bait. By 3:00 he is checking his six hundred crab
pots. He pulls up the pots, sunk in eight to twenty-five
feet of water, rebaited each of them and sorted the crabs
into three different groups. They are males, females, and
crabs about to molt. Robin sells the crabs that are about
to molt for five dollars a bushel to a friend. Why does
he sell them so cheaply? "There's too much work involved
with soft-shelled crabs," said Robin. You have to check
the boxes every two hours, and I am out on the water up to
ten hours a day.

The crabbing season begins April 1st, on the last day
of the oyster season. Maryland watermen can't enter the
market until June because the crabs haven't yet moved into
their pots, but the Virginians on the other side of the
bay start dredging for crabs from the opening day on.
Robin said a few choice words about the Virginia watermen;
he explained that when you dredge for crabs you take all
the crabs off the bottom, large and small. "Some Virginians keep 'em all, even the ones under four inches." The
practice of dredging keeps many of the young crabs from
even reaching Maryland waters and is just one of many reasons why there is so much hostility felt toward the Virginia watermen.

I asked Robin what he disliked about working the
water besides the Virginians, and he replied, "These days
if people can't find jobs they work the water, and right
now the market is flooded. The price for bait is up, and
the price of a bushel is down." He also said, "With so
many people on the water you have some jokers fishing your
pots and sometimes stealing them." And then there are the
jellyfish. When the water warms up, the jellyfish move up
the bay, and they make crabbing miserable. When the
jellyfish are bad, Robin's arms are covered with red welts

up to his shoulders, and sometimes the poison got into his eyes and he could hardly see.

It's hard to make a living from crabbing. In Robin's words, "Anything can go wrong." Robin is kept from his pots if his boat breaks down, and some storms can keep him from going out. "You can crab in the rain but not in the wind. And when the wind whips up the waves, I also lose pots. The current will roll the pots and pull the floats right down under."

Although working the water is a hard life, Robin plans to stay with it. "I like being my own boss. I know that if I don't work hard, I'm not hurting anyone but myself." He ended with, "You see things on the bay that you can't see anywhere else. I probably see more sunrises in a month than most people see in a lifetime."

Kirk Brimmer

11   *Constructing Sentences*

A sentence should read as if its author, had he held a plough instead of a pen, could have drawn a furrow deep and straight to the end.
— HENRY DAVID THOREAU

If you're like most writers, your success with sentences varies. Sometimes your sentences flow onto the page smoothly, with grace and clarity. Other times they sound as if they were cranked out by a rusty machine. Listen to these sentences, for example, written by a student on a bad day. Listen out loud:

> *Prostitution* for centuries has been a word that was seldom mentioned in society, and when it was mentioned, it was in a negative manner. However, now for many reasons I feel that we as citizens of the United States of America need to take another look and to re-evaluate the positives of prostitution. The legalization of prostitution would drastically cut down the number of rape cases reported each year which is one of the worst violations that could occur to a woman's body; not to mention the psychological effect. Not only are women affected by this kind of experience, but children as well.

Pretty bad, we hope you agree. But if you're tempted to dismiss this student as a poor writer, listen to some sentences she wrote the week before:

> On a day that was of no particular significance to the country or the state of North Carolina — it was not a holiday — on May 31, 1969, I was born, the fifth of seven children. I am reasonably certain that there was nothing exciting about my birth except for the fact that Mother no longer had to "look ugly with her belly sticking out." Mother often said that she never wanted more than four children. Throughout my childhood, she let me know it.

Yes, that really is the same writer. Here she is clearly in command of her sentences. But a week later, when she wrote the essay on prostitution, she seemed to have lost her touch. How is it that a writer's command over sentences can vary so dramatically?

When we talked with the writer of these paragraphs, she told us that

she had not felt at home with the topic of prostitution. She had had only a vague sense of where the paper was headed, so as she wrote, every sentence was burdened with decisions: "What am I going to say next, how does it connect with my thesis, where are my facts going to come from," and so on. Each new sentence was a problem — a number of problems, really. She had to do so much stopping and starting as she wrote, it's no wonder her sentences jerk along.

This student's smooth sentences appeared in an essay she obviously wanted to write, one showing the effects on a child of a mother's rejection. She knew exactly what she wanted to say to readers, and she knew where her material was going to come from — her own experience — so every sentence wasn't laden with decisions. Her writing could flow.

The more comfortable you feel about your writing, the more your sentences are likely to flow. One way to make yourself comfortable is to sit with stacks of scratch paper, close to a wastebasket. Beginning writers often forget that wastebasket. Apparently feeling that they have only one chance to write a sentence, they stiffen up. If they would move closer to a wastebasket, they might relax a bit. Good sentences are more likely to flow from a writer willing to take chances, secure in the knowledge that bad sentences can always be thrown out or rewritten.

As you write a rough draft, you can't afford to worry too much about sentence structure. You should of course try to write in English sentences, but don't fuss over them. You can do that later, as you revise the paper. When you read over your rough draft — especially if you read it aloud — your ear will often tell you which sentences need revising. You'll hear that you need to weave together the too-short sentences, trim down the wordy ones, and straighten out the crooked ones.

Your ear will take you far in making sentence decisions, particularly with practice. But in this chapter we would like to supplement your good ear with an understanding of basic sentence structure. If you understand the basic architecture of sentences, you'll be able to make more intelligent choices as you revise them.

Sentence Cores and Modifiers

Let's begin by looking at sentences in the simplest possible way. A sentence is primarily composed of a *core,* where its message is centered, and *modifiers* that give readers additional information about the core. Simplified sentence diagrams will help you visualize the relationship between the core and its modifiers. The core appears on the top line;

the modifiers, which expand the core with further information, appear on the lines below. Study these simplified diagrams of two sentences to get a feel for this very basic relationship between the sentence core and its modifiers.

Uncle Will's favorite instrument was a six-string dulcimer made out of cherry.

instrument	was	dulcimer
Uncle Will's favorite		a six-string
		made out of cherry.

During most of his working life, my father held two jobs, since one usually did not pay enough.

father	held	jobs
my		two
	During most of his working life	
	since one usually did not pay enough.	

Modifiers add to the meaning of the sentence core. You can think of them as answering questions about it. For the first sentence diagramed, you might ask, "Which instrument?" The modifier is the answer: "Uncle Will's favorite." And you might ask, "What kind of dulcimer?" Your answer is "a six-string" one "made out of cherry." For the second diagramed sentence, the modifier *my* tells you whose father; *two* tells you how many jobs. The other modifiers answer two questions: "When did he hold two jobs?" — "During most of his working life" and "Why did he hold two jobs?" — "Since one usually did not pay enough."

You probably already have a feel for this basic structure of sentences. You may not know how to label all the parts of a particular sentence, but you have a radar that detects sentence cores as you read. As you

are reading these words right now, your RADAR DETECTS our SEN-
TENCE CORE, because you know that the sentence's message is carried
in its core. Skilled readers pay more attention to the cores of sentences
than to modifiers.

If you can improve your sentence radar, you'll be better able to revise
weak sentences. In a rough draft, you may unintentionally bury important
information in modifiers, thus drawing your readers' attention to the
wrong part of the sentence. The following sentence will help you see
what we mean:

> At 10:00 on the night of December 14, a Chinese HOME on Chien Ying
> WAS ENTERED by eleven Japanese soldiers, who raped four Chinese
> women.

The sentence core is HOME WAS ENTERED, so those are the words
the readers' attention is drawn to. But let's hope the writer of the
sentence didn't think this was the sentence's most significant content.
The sentence should be revised to emphasize its most important
information:

> At 10:00 on the night of December 14, after breaking into a home on
> Chien Ying, eleven Japanese SOLDIERS RAPED four Chinese WOMEN.

This revision puts SOLDIERS RAPED WOMEN into the sentence
core, so that the sentence emphasizes its most important content.

As you revise the sentences in your rough draft, watch for weak
sentence cores. One student, for example, discovered, as she read over
her rough draft describing a recent visit to a prison, that she could
strengthen a number of sentences. For example, at one point she had
written:

> The VISITING PERIOD WAS NEARLY OVER when the guard tapped
> me on the shoulder.

The sentence core tells us that the visiting period was nearly over, but
this was not the information the writer wanted to emphasize.

To stress the point she wanted readers to notice, she revised the
sentence like this:

> Shortly before the visiting period was over, a GUARD TAPPED ME
> on the shoulder.

At another point in this paper, the writer wanted to emphasize how
impersonal her visit with the prisoner had been. Her first-draft sentence
read like this:

> I SAT in a chair, viewing the prisoner through the glass as we talked on
> the visitor's telephone.

When the writer reread this sentence, she noticed that it pulled her readers' attention to the fact that she was sitting in a chair. The information about viewing the prisoner through the glass and talking to him over the phone — the facts she really wanted to emphasize — were buried in modifiers. To improve the sentence, the writer revised it to:

> Sitting in a chair opposite the prisoner, I VIEWED HIM through a glass wall and SPOKE TO HIM over the prison telephone.

Here the important information appears in the sentence core, and the lesser information about sitting in the chair has been turned into a modifier.

When you check over your rough drafts, make sure your sentences are working with you, not against you. If you want to stress your close call with death, don't write "THE ROTOR HIT, gouging a hole about an eighth of an inch deep in my helmet." Write "When the rotor hit, IT GOUGED a HOLE about an eighth of an inch deep in my helmet." Or if you want to emphasize your shock upon meeting a monstrous snake at eye level, don't write "I YANKED OPEN the DOOR, whereupon I saw a 48-inch blackish-grey snake resting at eye level on the ledge of our storm door." Write instead: "When I yanked the door open, at eye level on the ledge of our storm door LAY a 48-inch blackish-grey SNAKE."

Compound Sentences

Whether you're conscious of it or not, the structure of a sentence — content aside — sends its own messages. Take compound sentences, for example. A compound sentence is made up of two independent clauses (word groups that could have stood alone as sentences) hooked together with a comma and a coordinating conjunction or with a semicolon. The following diagram includes all of the coordinating conjunctions in English and the semicolon.

$$
\underline{\text{[Independent clause]}}
\begin{array}{l}
\text{, and} \\
\text{, but} \\
\text{, or} \\
\text{, nor} \\
\text{, for} \\
\text{, so} \\
\text{, yet} \\
\text{;}
\end{array}
\underline{\text{[Independent clause]}} \, .
$$

The structure of a compound sentence sends certain messages to readers, no matter how you fill in the blanks. First, it tells readers that the sentence contains two relatively important ideas, each one deserving its own independent clause. Second, it tells readers that these two ideas are approximately equal in importance, since they are balanced as a pair. And third, it alerts readers to the relationship between the two ideas, depending on the connector. For example, *and* suggests that the two ideas are being added together, *but* indicates that they are being contrasted, and *or* tells us that they are alternatives. A semicolon suggests balance between two similar or sharply contrasting statements.

Thus, the structure of a compound sentence sends certain messages. Don't let the structure of a sentence send one message while the content relays another. Listen to the clashing messages in this senence, for example:

> Once Betty was driving to our house, and her daughter accidentally fell out of the car window.

The compound structure tells us that we are dealing with two ideas of about equal importance. The content, however, suggests the opposite: The daughter's falling out of the car window is surely more important than the fact that Betty was driving to someone's house. Moreover, the connector *and* suggests that the relation between the two parts of the sentence is one of addition. But is this really accurate? Isn't the relationship more clearly expressed as follows:

> Once when Betty was driving to our house, her daughter accidentally fell out of the car window.

With this simple revision, we have a sentence designed to carry its message. "Once when Betty was driving to our house" is a modifier appropriate for carrying the information of lesser importance. And the time-word *when,* placed as it is, serves much better than *and* to convey the relation between the two ideas in the sentence.

Unfortunately, it is easy to overuse compound sentences in your rough drafts. As you compose sentences, ideas sometimes come haltingly. To keep them going, you may string them together with *and* or *but.* Some of these compound sentences will turn out to be perfectly in tune with their content, but others will need to be revised.

The original versions of the following student sentences were ineffective compounds. In each case, the student has revised the sentence by turning one of the independent clauses into a subordinate clause functioning as a modifier.

I told her that *since* this might be my last meal ~~and~~ I wanted to enjoy it.

When
∧I entered high school, ~~and~~ I had a male teacher for the

first time.

which
Nutritious foods∧can be easily prepared, and they give the
          ∧

body the basic carbohydrates, fats, minerals, and

         can be easily prepared.
proteins/,∧

The words *since* and *when* are subordinating conjunctions, words that turn an independent clause into a subordinate clause modifying a verb. Other frequently used subordinating conjunctions include *although, as, as if, because, before, if, unless, until, where, while.* The word *which* is a relative pronoun, a word that can turn an independent clause into a subordinate clause modifying a noun. Other relative pronouns include *who, whom, whose,* and *that.*

Not all compound sentences are ineffective. When properly used, so that the structure is working with the content, compound sentences can be strong. Consider these student examples:

Uncle Will's dulcimers disappeared as soon as he put them up for sale, but he always kept one for himself.

Sometimes we would end up at a big red brick teacher's college across town, and sometimes we would just follow the railroad tracks.

A man was respected for his money, power, or intelligence; a woman had to rely on her books.

In each of these compound sentences, the content fits naturally within the structure. Two important ideas, about equal in significance, are balanced together. And they are joined with a connector that reveals the relationship between them — *and, but,* and a semicolon.

Simple Sentences

The structure of a simple sentence — one statement that stands alone — also sends messages to readers. It tells them that the content is fairly important, deserving a statement all to itself. The simple sentence also suggests to readers that its content does not closely depend on that of sentences close by. So a simple sentence should contain fairly important material that doesn't beg to be pulled into any neighboring sentences.

It's common to overuse simple sentences in a rough draft. Look at these sentences, for example, taken from a student's paragraph describing the chests in a museum exhibit:

> The last chest is the most impressive. It is carved from ivory. There is a painting in the lid showing King Tut and his queen. This painting is bordered with engraved flowers and animals.

Your ear tells you that some of those simple sentences ought to be woven together. But which ones? The answer is easy. Just decide which sentences carry important ideas and let them stand. Then find the sentences that contain less important supporting information, and hook that content into the sentences you're allowing to stand. If you followed this advice, you might pull the first two sentences together like this:

> The last chest, carved from ivory, is the most impressive.

And the next two together like this:

> On its lid, within a border of engraved flowers and animals, is a painting of King Tut and his queen.

In each revision we have woven supporting information into the sentence that it seemed to support naturally.

Simple sentences, like compound ones, can be effective when the content works well with the structure. In the following paragraph, for example, strong simple sentences (italicized) draw the reader's attention to important content.

> *The ultimate test, in my child mind, for finding out the difference between black and white occurred one day in a bus station in Alabama.* While waiting with my parents at the station, I studied the two water fountains against the far wall. *Side by side they stood. A big sign above one read "whites only." The sign above the other fountain read "colored only."* I decided that once and for all I would satisfy my curiosity about the water fountains which always carried the signs above them. Was the water colored in the "colored only" one, or did it taste different? Since no one was watching me, I slipped over and quickly took a sip of the water in the "colored only" fountain. When I found it was every bit the same as the water in the "whites only" fountain, I ran back to my parents and shouted, "Dad, I just drank some water from the 'colored' fountain and it tasted just the same as the other." *My father's answer was a quick, hard slap. That day I learned not to question the difference between black and white.*

Each simple sentence carries information important enough to deserve a whole statement all to itself. The cores of these sentences emphasize significant content:

> The ultimate TEST, in my child mind, for finding out the difference between black and white OCCURRED one day in a bus station in Alabama.

Side by side THEY STOOD.

A big SIGN above one READ "WHITES ONLY."

The SIGN above the other fountain READ "COLORED ONLY."

My father's ANSWER WAS a quick, hard SLAP.

That day I LEARNED NOT TO QUESTION the difference between black and white.

Simple sentences, especially short ones, draw attention to themselves, particularly when they follow longer, more complex sentences. Probably the most emphatic simple sentence in the paragraph we've been discussing is "My father's answer was a quick, hard slap." This relatively short sentence follows several longer sentences, so it has a blunt impact on readers. The sentence core — ANSWER WAS SLAP — overpowers everything else you've been reading.

Parallel Structure

When you want to stress the similarity of two or more ideas, you can put them into parallel grammatical structures, as this writer has done:

> On March 14, 1988, Karen Riley was admitted to Suburban General Hospital with three broken ribs and a punctured lung. On July 8, 1988, Denise Porter was admitted with a broken arm and severe facial lacerations. These women were not victims of terrible automobile accidents, nor were they attacked as they walked down a dark city street. Both were products of an age-old phenomenon called wife-beating.

Here are two sentences printed so you can see how very closely the second one has been modeled on the first:

On March 14, 1988,	On July 8, 1988,
Karen Riley was admitted to SGH	Denise Porter was admitted
with three broken ribs and	with a broken arm and
a punctured lung.	severe facial lacerations.

Wanting to stress the similarity of the two cases, the writer structured the sentences almost identically. He deliberately used parallel structure to reinforce parallel content. As you revise a rough draft, you may spot opportunities for stronger or more effective parallelism. For example, one of our students found this sentence in her rough draft:

> *Roots* is the story of a black boy stolen from his native land, chained and treated as though an animal, to be brought by ship here to America to be a slave.

The sentence reports that the black boy was stolen, chained, treated like an animal, and brought to America. Since these items were similar — all brutal events that happened to the boy — the writer saw that she could strengthen the sentence with parallel structure, like this:

> *Roots* is the story of a black boy stolen from his native land, chained like an animal, stowed on a ship like cargo, transported to America, and enslaved.

A much stronger sentence. The parallel structure underscores the inhumanity of the treatment of the young black boy. Let's print the sentence so you can see the parallel structure more clearly. Read the sentence aloud so you can hear its strength.

> *Roots* is the story of a black boy stolen from his native land,
> chained like an animal,
> stowed on a ship like cargo,
> transported to America,
> and enslaved.

Sentence Variety

When you read through a rough draft, especially if you read it aloud, your ear will pick up any sentence monotony. Sentences will begin to sound monotonous when they are nearly the same length or when they repeat the same structures over and over.

When you combine short, choppy sentences and restructure weak compound sentences (as suggested earlier in this chapter), the problem of sentence monotony may take care of itself. But if your sentences still seem too similar, consider varying your sentence openings. Instead of beginning every sentence with the subject, begin some sentences with an introductory phrase or clause or with a transitional expression. In the following paragraph, taken from the rough draft of a student essay on jogging, the writer has combined sentences and also varied her sentence openings.

```
Jogging is different from most other popular physical fit-
         Unlike weight-lifting,
ness programs. Weight-lifting, isometric exercises, and
         which
calisthenics emphasize muscle-building, Jogging improves
                                    although other
the heart, lungs, and circulatory system. Other body mus-
                              t
cles are exercised as well, The most important benefit
```

comes from improving the way the heart and lungs work.

Bulging biceps and pleasing pectorals may boost the ego.
But when
~~When~~ you're past thirty, as I am, your life and health may
∧
depend upon the fitness of the heart and lungs.

Exercise 1 *Written*

Try your hand at revising the following rough draft so that the sentences all emphasize the writer's main point, as summed up in the topic sentence. Put important ideas in sentence cores and lesser content in modifiers.

A typical hot lunch at City College has little nutritional value. For example, one day's menu might be zippy pot roast, mashed potatoes, creamy green beans, an ice cream sandwich, and milk. The zippy pot roast contains more fat than lean meat. The mashed potatoes are instant flakes mixed with water, causing them to turn out dry and thick. They contain a low amount of protein and vitamins. The creamy green beans are usually cold, watered down, and faded in color, which causes them to lose vitamins. The frozen ice cream sandwiches consist of artificial flavoring, instant milk, and nitrochloric acids. The last item on the menu is milk, which has the most nutrition. The milk is whole milk consisting of iron, certain vitamins, and calcium. So the hot lunch at City College does not provide much of nutritional value, except for milk.

Exercise 2 *Written*

Assume that the sentences below are from the rough draft of a paper describing your mandolin-playing career. As you look back over the rough draft, you notice that you have written quite a few compound sentences. Which ones do you decide to keep because their content fits well into a compound sentence? Which ones need revising? Try rewriting at least five of the compound sentences that you think are ineffective.

1. Owen had an antique mandolin from Italy, and it had a round back and beautiful wood inlaid on the front.

2. Owen's mandolin intrigued me, so I borrowed it in hopes of figuring out how to play it.

3. Later that weekend Owen left for England, and he took his old mandolin with him.

4. My mandolin career might have ended there, but I found a used instrument listed in the classified ads for ten dollars.

5. The mandolin had been in someone's shed for almost thirty years without a case, but the price was right.

6. The mandolin player for "The Seldom Scene" had made his own instrument, and we spent most of an afternoon in the shade of his camper pickin' bluegrass music.

7. My new mandolin was a Gibson "A" model from 1911, and it sounded, and played, like solid gold.

8. By the time I had played with "Kinfolk" for a month, I felt like a professional; after two months, I was a professional.

9. Playing at the Berwyn Coffeehouse was rewarding, and the people there loved us.

10. As my music got better my grades in school got worse, so I decided to leave my regular gig to study full time.

Exercise 3 Written

The following paragraphs by a student contain some ineffective compound sentences. Revise the sentences that need improvement.

> I've known Sugar Ray for four years now, and he was always determined to succeed as a fighter. Each morning at about six o'clock you could find Ray jogging and training very hard. After his workout each morning he would go home, clean up and leave for school. Then, after school, each evening Ray could be found down at the community recreation center training.
>
> Sugar Ray's training paid off, and he became one of the best young fighters in the country, and he was chosen to represent the United States in the Olympics. Ray attended the 1976 Olympics and he brought the gold medal back home with him. A few months after the Olympics were over, Ray received an offer to turn professional. Ray accepted the offer and turned pro.

Below are some passages from student papers containing too many short, choppy sentences. Rework each passage by pulling subordinate information into the sentence it seems to support naturally.

1. My father works for the Washington Trucking Company. Right now he is district manager for several different terminals. I believe he has twelve different terminals, all of which are located in the mid-eastern

region of the country. Traveling is very important in his work. He travels about three times a month.

2. I had an appointment with one of my physicians. It was on a hot, humid September day. My appointment was at four o'clock in the afternoon.

3. The jewelry found in King Tut's tomb is perhaps the most exquisite of all the relics. There are gold necklaces, beaded bracelets, gold rings, and earrings. Many of the above are decorated with colored glass. This glass was usually shaped as a scarab, the symbol of the sun god. The most magnificent of all of the jewelry is the necklace that had been placed on King Tut's mummy. It is in the form of a vulture goddess with spread wings. Different shades of red and blue glass are used to decorate the necklace. This ornament was supposed to provide magical protection.

4. Have you ever wanted to find the perfect Mexican restaurant? I found the perfect restaurant for me. It is located on Riverdale Road in Riverdale, Maryland. The place is called the Alamo.

Exercise 4 For Class Discussion

Eldridge Cleaver wrote *Soul on Ice* while serving time in California's Folsom State Prison. In this spiritual autobiography Cleaver expresses himself powerfully, often using parallel sentences. Here are four such sentences, with discussion questions for each. We have printed the sentences so that you can see the parallel structure. As you discuss the sentences, be sure to read them aloud:

> I'm perfectly aware
>   that I'm in prison
>   that I'm a Negro,
>   that I've been a rapist,
> and that I have a Higher Uneducation.

This sentence, which appears early in the book, has a powerful effect on readers. Can you account for its power? What do you suppose Cleaver means by "Higher Uneducation," and why does he put this item last? Why is Cleaver putting all these facts about himself in one parallel-structured sentence?

Our next sentence from *Soul on Ice* describes the nighttime longings of a man behind bars:

> Because we were locked up in our cells before darkness fell, I used to lie awake at night racked by painful craving
>   to take a leisurely stroll under the stars, or

> to go to the beach,
> to drive a car on a freeway,
> to grow a beard,
> or to make love to a woman.

What impact does this sentence have on you as a reader? How does the sentence's parallel structure contribute to this impact? Why does Cleaver order his "cravings" as he does?

The following sentence was not written by Eldridge Cleaver. Cleaver quotes it, from Malcolm X, to explain his own one-time hostility toward white people:

> How can I love the man who raped my mother,
> killed my father,
> enslaved my ancestors,
> dropped atomic bombs on Japan,
> killed off the Indians
> and keeps me cooped up in the slums?

What does Malcolm X mean by "the man"? How do you interpret "raped my mother" and "killed my father"? Why has Malcolm X included the Japanese and the Indians as recipients of "the man's" atrocities? Why has he ordered the atrocities in just this way, and why does he end with "keeps me cooped up in the slums"? To which words in the sentence does the parallel structure draw your attention, and how does this contribute to the sentence's power?

For the next sentence, you need some background information. While Cleaver was in Folsom, he was impressed by the Christ-like quality of a philosophy professor who taught at the prison. Cleaver wrote this one-sentence paragraph about this man, whom he called "the Christ" as a mark of respect:

> The Christ could weep
> over a line of poetry,
> over a single image in a poem,
> over the beauty of a poem's music,
> over the fact that man can talk,
> read,
> write,
> walk,
> reproduce,
> die,
> eat,
> eliminate, —
> over the fact that a chicken can lay an egg.

good sentence structure

use for emphasis

This sentence should be read aloud more than once, as you discuss it; its power will grow on you. What kind of man is Cleaver describing? Why does Cleaver order the sentence as he does? Why end with "over the fact that a chicken can lay an egg"? Why begin with three lines about poetry? Why put that long list of human activities just where it is in the sentence? Why does Cleaver use *eliminate* instead of a synonym?

Exercise 5 *For Thought*

In an article entitled "Why I Write," Joan Didion compares sentence structures with camera angles:

> To shift the structure of a sentence alters the meaning of that sentence, as definitely and inflexibly as the position of a camera alters the meaning of the object photographed. Many people know about camera angles now, but not so many know about sentences. The arrangement of the words matters, and the arrangement you want can be found in the picture in your mind. The picture dictates the arrangement. The picture dictates whether this will be a sentence with or without clauses, a sentence that ends hard or a dying-fall sentence, long or short, active or passive. The picture tells you how to arrange the words.

Exercise 6 *For Discussion in Small Groups*

Working in small groups, discuss the following draft of an essay by one of our students, Tom Weitzel. Pretend that Weitzel is a classmate who has come to your group for help with sentence variety. Where in the essay would you advise him to combine or restructure sentences, to vary his sentence openings, or to vary his language? If your group has time, revise one or two of Weitzel's paragraphs for sentence variety. After your discussion, take a look at Weitzel's own revisions (pages 259–263) and compare them with your suggestions.

```
                  Who Goes to the Races?

     A favorite pastime of mine is observing people, and
my favorite place to observe is at the horse races.  After
about fifteen encounters with the racing crowd, I have
discovered that there are four distinct groups who appear
at the track.  There are the once-a-year group, the
professionals, the clubhouse group, and the unemployed.
```

The most typical and largest group at the track are those who show up once a year. They know little about horses or betting. They rely strictly on racetrack gimmick sheets and newspaper predictions for selecting possible winners. If that doesn't work, they use intuition. They also use lucky numbers, favorite colors, or appealing names. They bet larger amounts as the day goes along, betting on every race. They even bet on exactas and daily doubles (long-shot bets). The vast majority go home broke and frustrated.

The professionals are a more subtle and quiet group. They follow the horses from track to track and live in campers and motor homes. Many are married couples and some are retired. All are easily spotted with their lunch sacks, thermos jugs, and binoculars. Most are familiar with one another, so they section themselves off in a particular area of the stadium. All rely on the racing form and on personal knowledge of each horse, jockey, and track in making the proper bet. They bet only on the smart races, and rarely on the favorites. They always avoid exactas and daily doubles. More often than not they either break even or go home winners.

In addition, there exists the clubhouse group. They can be found either at the cocktail lounge in the restaurant, usually involved in business transactions. They rarely see a race in person and do their betting via the waiter. It's difficult to tell whether they go home sad, happy, or in between. They keep their emotions to themselves.

The most interesting are the unemployed and welfare group. They won't be found in the clubhouse, but right down at the rail next to the finish line. The real emotion of the track — the screaming, the cursing, and the pushing — is discovered here. The unemployed are not sportsmen. It's not a game for them, but a battle for survival. They usually lose, and then they must borrow enough money to carry them until the next check comes in, and then, of course, they head right back to the track. This particular group arrives at the track beaten and leaves beaten.

Financially speaking, I have probably lost more money than I have won at the track, but these four interesting groups of people make it all worthwhile.

Tom Weitzel

12 *Choosing Words*

The difference between the right word and almost the right word is the difference between lightning and the lightning bug.
— MARK TWAIN

One of the secrets to building strong sentences is careful, conscious choice of words. Choosing words carefully will make your writing clearer and more vivid.

We have placed "Choosing Words" near the end of this section of the book because we feel that writing will be easier for you if you do not worry too much about single words until late in the writing process. Stopping to think about every word when you first begin an essay will slow down your writing, and when that happens, you risk sacrificing your flow. So we advise you to attend first to focusing and shaping your material into paragraphs made up of strong sentences, and only then to concentrate on words.

Pruning Wordy Sentences

When you are ready to think about words, we suggest that you first look for wordy sentences — sentences that can be pruned without loss of meaning. Sentences filled wih "deadwood" drag along, blurring your meaning and boring your reader. Consider the following sentences, for example. Trimmed of their deadwood, they are easier to read. And they move at a more sprightly pace.

The roses ~~that grow~~ in my largest rosebed are flame orange

and pale yellow.~~in color.~~

~~There were~~ *T*wo women ~~who~~ ran for senator in ~~the state of~~

Virginia last year.

To our great disappointment, the circus did not get to

town on time, ~~This was~~ because one of the elephants decided to go AWOL during the long march from the train station.

~~It was known for a fact by~~ /their families ^knew^ that John and David had left San Francisco to surf in Hawaii without enough money ~~to live on in Hawaii~~.

George Orwell, one of the most effective writers in the English language, has suggested a sort of ground rule about wordiness: "If it is possible to cut a word out, always cut it out." Listen to the difference between the following loose, wordy student paragraph and its revision:

~~This summer~~ While I was vacationing in Switzerland, *this summer, the kindness and friendliness of the* ~~the one thing that impressed me most was how kind and~~ *Swiss impressed me more than anything else.* ~~friendly the people were. The people who worked in~~ /the *staff* hotel ^where we stayed were extremely nice.~~ ~~They~~ went out of their way to make our stay ~~an even more enjoyable one~~ *pleasant.*

The maids and bellboys greeted us with /a smile, the women behind the desk always asked how we were, and ~~the people~~ ~~in the hotel~~ *the* restaurant *personnel* ~~always went out of their way to~~ ~~give~~ *gave* us excellent service. Although ~~there was~~ a language barrier *existed,* everyone we ~~would~~ talk to was very patient while we tried to communicate ~~and get our point across~~ with the ~~few words of~~ German and French *words* we knew. *Indeed,* /The friendly ~~people of Switzerland~~ *Swiss* added to ~~a wonderful trip to their~~ *the pleasure of our visit* ~~beautiful country~~ *to Switzerland.*

You have probably noticed that the revisions make the paragraph considerably shorter than the original. But nothing important has been lost. When you write, don't let yourself be tempted into leaving in the deadwood just for the sake of quantity. On the other hand, we would caution you against worrying so much about wordiness that you sacrifice essential content. Leaving out needed material is not the same thing as deleting wordiness. One has to do with content — what you have to say; the other, with form — how you go about saying it.

The idea, then, is to make your writing as concise, and hence as direct and clear, as possible, while including what needs to be included. Every word you choose should be working to make your writing strong and interesting and alive. As the poet Wallace Stevens said, "Life is the elimination of what is dead."

Saying It Simply

Worse than wordiness alone is verbal fog, language that makes the simplest of ideas complicated and important-sounding. Sometimes used deliberately to obscure meaning, verbal fog often emerges from the government, the military, the educational establishment, and other large institutions.

For example, here is a quotation from a release by the Bureau of Land Management (BLM) of the United States Department of the Interior:

> Because the heavy mistletoe infestation in the Kringle Creek area has rendered the residual timber useless for timber production, the ultimate goal is to establish a healthy new stand of Douglas Fir.

The BLM release apparently means to say:

> Because mistletoe has taken over the timber in the Kringle Creek area, we need to plant a new stand of Douglas Fir.

OSHA, the Occupational Safety and Health Administration, wrote this thirty-nine-word definition of *exit:*

> That portion of a means of egress which is separated from all other spaces of the building or structure by construction or equipment as required in this subpart to provide a protected way of travel to the exit discharge.

But government is not the only source of verbal fog. Representatives of our other institutions use it, too. The following sentence appeared in a letter to the editor from a doctor: "If home births are an indictment of impersonal and dehumanized health care in our hospitals' obstetrical units, then attempts should be directed toward increasing the human factor in our health-delivery systems."

Verbal fog often plagues college textbooks. Beware of it; it could find its way into your own writing almost by osmosis. This student writer, for example, may have been unduly influenced by a textbook for a speech course:

Effective listening requires the senses of hearing and seeing, working in harmony, to correctly interpret incoming communications. Now, more than ever before, body language — that nonverbal part of a communication — contributes significantly to the intent of a transmission and how it is received.

The student who wrote the following paragraph had spent years in the military and had gone from there into a career in business:

> As a supervisor I am charged with the responsibility of insuring maximum production through utilization of all resources, both manpower and machines. However, the increasing level of the younger employee and the state of the art in business has created a problem for supervisors in trying to find new techniques to use in motivating subordinates. This group of individuals expects rapid growth and promotion and wants to take an active role in the decision-making process.

Getting rid of such swollen sentences was the most difficult part of freshman composition for this writer. However, he learned to simplify his writing enough so that the above paragraph was transformed like this:

> As a supervisor I am responsible for seeing that all our resources — both personnel and machines — are as productive as possible. One of my challenges is how to motivate those persons working under me. Younger employees, especially, expect to advance rapidly, and they also want to be involved in decision-making.

Writers addicted to verbal fog often resort to euphemisms. A euphemism (pronounced *you-fuh-miz-em*) occurs when less direct and less vivid phrasing is substituted for words that might be considered offensive. Journalist Meg Greenfield refers to them as "verbal chloroform." Some euphemisms, substituted for more straightforward English, are deliberately misleading, as you will recognize as you read the list below. Here the euphemisms have been translated into plain English.

Euphemism	*Plain English*
selected out	fired
over-aggressive self-initiative	anger
attitude adjustment hour	cocktail hour
therapeutic misadventure	medical malpractice
energetic disassembly	nuclear power plant explosion
plutonium has taken up residence	plutonium contamination after nuclear explosion

radiation enhancement weapon	Pentagon's designation for the neutron bomb, which destroys only people

Though an occasional euphemism may be used for the sake of politeness ("released" for "fired" or "passed away" for "died"), on the whole euphemisms should be avoided, for they diminish the strength and honesty of language.

All forms of verbal fog ignore the reader's need for simplicity and clarity. We like a piece of advice attributed to a "wise old woman": "Keep away from fancy words because you can never tell what they mean." Or as John O'Hayre, who tried to eliminate verbal fog from the Bureau of Land Management, suggests, "To kill this big word bug, stop [writing] like a mechanical nobleman who has been stuffed to overflowing with impressive, exotic words, and start [writing] like the genuine, natural human being you are."

Saying It Vividly

If some words are too fancy, too big and heavy, there are others you will want to avoid because they are weak. Some began their existence as slang, and most are used commonly in speech. But all have become "tired," for they have been used to the point of exhaustion. Here is a list of such words.

amazing	fantastic	incredible	really
awful	fascinating	interesting	stupendous
bad	funny	lovely	terrible
beautiful	glorious	magnificent	terrific
big	good	marvelous	thing
colossal	gorgeous	neat	tremendous
enjoyable	great	nice	very
exciting	horrible	outstanding	wonderful
fabulous	huge	pretty	

You will probably be able to think of some more tired words.

Using these words occasionally is of course all right; attempting to avoid such everyday words completely could make your writing sound awkward and unnatural. However, if you discover that your writing is dotted with weak words, you will need to revise. Consider the following paragraphs, for example, from an early draft of a paper describing Seattle. The weak words are italicized.

Seattle is a *beautiful* city, full of *wonderful* sights and *interesting things* to do. It is surrounded by *big* bodies of water that the sun dances off of in *marvelous* fashion. More water greets visitors to Seattle as they discover the city's several *fabulous* fountains. Furthermore, the city has many hills, providing *really glorious* views. One of these views is of Mount Rainier, with its *gorgeous* snow-covered peak. In addition, Seattle has some *magnificent* buildings — its public library and the IBM building, to name two. There are *interesting things* to do in Seattle, too, at its playhouse, its opera hall, and its science center. And I must not forget to mention a visit to the *incredible* Space Needle, that features an *amazing* revolving restaurant at its top.

The weather varies greatly in Seattle, it is true, and some people say that all those rainy days in a row must be *awful*. But, believe me, one *nice* day of *glorious* sunshine on those fountains and mountain peaks and buildings makes one forget weeks of rain. Surely Seattle must be one of the *neatest* cities in the United States.

When the writer of these paragraphs read them over, she realized they would not make readers experience Seattle vividly. Using a dictionary of synonyms, she was able to find more precise and lively words to substitute for many of the weak ones. And drawing upon her memory of Seattle, she managed to replace some of the duller words with new descriptive details. Here is the beginning of a new version of her paper:

Seattle is a splendid city that offers breathtaking scenery, striking buildings and varied activities. The sun dancing off the water that surrounds Seattle makes the whole city seem to sparkle. More water greets visitors to Seattle as they discover the city's several fountains. Some of these fountains, like the one by the City Library, are constructed of sculptured metal. However, the most unusual fountain in Seattle is one in which the rise and fall of the water is synchronized with both music and varicolored lights. In Seattle, mountain-views exist side by side with water-views. One such view is of the glistening snow-covered peak of Mount Rainier.

Now readers will come closer to experiencing Seattle with our writer.

We do have some suggestions about how to use your synonyms book. Once you have located the synonym list for your weak word, be sure to read all the way through the list before choosing your substitute word; the one you most need may not be among the first two or three listed. Try, too, to find a word that will read smoothly in your sentence. If you are not sure about the exact meaning of a particular synonym, turn to your regular dictionary and look it up to be sure that you finally use the most appropriate word.

You will also want to be alert to clichés that may slip into your writing. A cliché (pronounced *klee-shay;* a term borrowed from French) is a worn-out phrase, an expression that you have heard so often that it is empty of meaning. You will probably recognize some clichés in the following paragraph:

> The mechanic rescued us, cold and miserable, from beside the road and towed our car in. He saw that we were safe and sound, and then, as the hours wore on, he looked after us above and beyond the call of duty. We found it hard to believe, in this day and age, that someone would be so kind to total strangers who had appeared in his life out of nowhere. It was indeed a moving experience.

Did you pick up the clichés? They are included, along with others, in this list:

above and beyond the call of duty	in this day and age
all walks of life	ladder of success
appeared in his life	last but not least
at this point in time	moving experience
believe it or not	on a silver platter
beyond a shadow of a doubt	out of nowhere
brought back to reality	pride and joy
cold and miserable	rude awakening
easier said than done	safe and sound
facts of life	sink or swim
first and foremost	straight and narrow
hours wore on	total stranger
	tried and true

Don't let clichés weaken your own writing. Either delete such phrases entirely, or rephrase flat, cliché-ridden sentences to make them more vivid and lively.

Selecting Just the Right Word

As you are no doubt aware, words with the same meaning (or *denotation*) can carry widely different feelings (or *connotations*). Many words are emotionally loaded, either positively or negatively. For instance, different expressions connected with growing old, though they all denote old age, affect us differently. Consider the image and the accompanying feelings the following phrases create. To which do you react positively? To which negatively? Are any of the expressions relatively neutral?

the elderly	the aged
senior citizenship	the golden years
the declining years	old age
old man (or old woman)	old folks
growing older and wiser	older person

Here are some other sets of words with essentially the same meaning but with varying connotations. As you read a set, observe how each word affects you, what it "says" to you:

run	alternate life-style	stubborn
bolt	homosexuality	persistent
dash	sexual deviancy	resolute
flee	sexual preference	persevering
rush	the gay life	hardheaded
scamper	perversion	tenacious
dart		determined

Use this emotional loading of words when you write. For example, if you want readers to visit a space museum you have just discovered, appeal to them by describing its display area as *vast* or *expansive,* instead of using *cavernous,* which sounds more threatening. Or if you are recommending an instructor whose only flaw is a soft voice, say that his or her delivery is *low-keyed* rather than *inaudible.* On the other hand, if you are writing a letter to your local newspaper about a popular child's toy that worries you, referring to the toy as *hazardous* will be more effective than merely saying it is *unsafe.* Use a dictionary of synonyms or thesaurus to locate the best word for the connotation you want.

There is one more matter of word choice you will want to attend to: accuracy. When writing is flawed by careless word choice, its entire effect may be lost.

Sometimes inaccurate word choice produces hilarious sentences. Just for fun, here are a few such sentences collected from the business world:

A study is underfoot.

Bulldozers have left the earth baron.

We hope that all employees can remain relapsed and calm.

He has worked in several places. Most recently, he put in a stench at HUD.

They treated him as if he had Blue Bonnet plague.

The Barbie and Ken dolls are so realistic that the Ken doll even has a full set of Gentiles.

Let's wait and see whether there is any follow-out from the incident.

Do you think she was speaking thumb-in-cheek?

Collecting Words

Increasing your supply of words, by whatever means, is absolutely basic to becoming a good writer. A writer needs to be on the lookout for new words all the time: while listening to TV or the radio, during conversation, while reading, during lectures and class discussions, even eavesdropping while traveling — wherever he or she encounters words, written or spoken.

You can train yourself to be aware of words in exactly the same way you train yourself to concentrate on anything else, whether it's basketball, singing, cooking, or karate. The payoff is that you will be a better writer — because a more precise one — for the rest of your life. It doesn't have to cost you any extra money, and you can start right away. Turn to the editorial page of your newspaper, or leaf through *Time* or *Newsweek*, in search of words you don't ordinarily use. Use some of them, as you talk and as you write, as often as possible during the next two weeks. They will soon belong to you.

Exercise 1   *For Thought and Discussion*

E. B. White said it succinctly: "Omit needless words." After mulling over the following quotations, discuss why this is an important principle of good writing.

1. In composing, as a general rule, run a pen through every other word you have written; you have no idea what vigor it will give your style.
   — Sidney Smith

2. I apologize for this long letter; I didn't have time to shorten it.
   — Pliny

3. Clutter is the disease of American writing. We are a society strangling in unnecessary words, circular constructions, pompous frills, and meaningless jargon.
   — William Zinsser

4. I once said his prose is dipped in chicken fat.
   — Oscar Levant, Referring to David Susskind

5. To write simply is as difficult as to be good.
   — Somerset Maugham

6. He can compress the most words into the smallest ideas of any man I ever met.
— Abraham Lincoln, Speaking of a Fellow Lawyer

7. If you give me an article that runs to eight pages and I tell you to cut it to four, you'll howl and say it can't be done. Then you will go home and do it, and it will be infinitely better. After that comes the hard part: cutting it to three.
— William Zinsser

Exercise 2   Written

Remove the deadwood from the following sentences, taking care not to change the meaning of the originals. Bring your revised sentences to class for discussion.

1. In this age of fierce competition for a limited number of well-paying jobs, I have found that in order to be successful at a career I need to put all of my available time and resources toward my education.

2. The atheist, who did not believe in God, avoided church regularly each Sunday.

3. In "Raisin in the Sun," a black family decides to buy a house which is in an all-white neighborhood where no blacks have been allowed to buy in the past.

4. During our tour of New England in the hot summer month of August, cool glasses of iced coffee were served every afternoon.

5. The student answered the question that Mr. Battle asked with a negative answer of no.

6. The principal finally located the injured child's parent by means of the telephone after 3:00 P.M. in the afternoon.

7. There are problems that confront an educated black person who applies for a job that may not affect a white person of exactly the same level of education.

8. The food that is included in an actual Chinese meal is quite a bit different from what you find on the menu in many Chinese restaurants.

9. Sociologists claim that in the case of hardened criminals rehabilitation is rarely achieved.

10. The image of the American Indian through the eyes of the TV media is, to put it mildly, an insult to American Indians.

Exercise 3 Written

Make a list of all the words you can think of that mean the same thing as any five of the words below. Work first without your dictionary of synonyms or thesaurus, then go to that source to complete your list.

1. advise	**7.** fat	**13.** serene
2. agree	**8.** fix	**14.** straightforward
3. ask	**9.** get	**15.** thin
4. conscious	**10.** inactive	**16.** walk
5. disagree	**11.** sensitive	
6. evaluate	**12.** sentimental	

Bring your sets of words to class for a discussion of connotation.

Exercise 4 Written

Connotation can be used to slant a piece of writing. Write on one of the following topics in two ways. In one paper, attempt to prejudice your reading audience *for* the idea; in the other paper, attempt to prejudice your audience *against* the idea. Deliberately choose words with either positive or negative connotations to strengthen your position.

1. A mother of a two-year-old wants to go to work. The income she would make is not required for the family to live. In one paper, support her going to work; in the other, argue against her taking a job.

2. Introductory psychology is being considered as a required course for all first-semester freshmen in a community college. Argue in one paper in support of the requirement; in another, attempt to defeat the requirement.

3. A university establishes a coed dormitory in which unmarried couples can live together. Write papers (perhaps letters) from two sets of parents with students enrolled; one set supports the idea, the other rejects it.

Exercise 5 Classroom Activity

Try to translate the following euphemisms. Listen for others to bring to class to challenge your classmates. Advertising, political statements, work memoranda, and hospital language are some likely sources for euphemisms.

1. adult entertainment
2. correctional facility
3. down-sized car
4. encore telecast
5. Egyptological pornoglyphic sarcophagi
6. engage the enemy on all sides
7. expired, passed away, left us
8. for motion discomfort
9. grief therapist
10. inner city
11. nervous wetness
12. powder room
13. preowned automobile
14. protective reaction strike
15. twilight years

Exercise 6 Written

Revise the following passage primarily for word choice. Turn to a dictionary or thesaurus where necessary.

A way of life is dying out in that part of the state of Maryland known as the Eastern Shore. For several hundred years watermen have worked the waters of the Chesapeake Bay bringing in fish, oysters, clams, and especially crabs. They lived a lifestyle that was incredible. At the crack of dawn they were out on the bay. They returned in the afternoon to sell their ketch and clean their boats. By eight o'clock they were in bed asleep. It was a hard but rewarding life.

What is now happening to this entire way of life is awful. Today, most active watermen are in the upper age brackets. Pollution has reduced the size of their catches. Conservationists have restricted the methods they may use. And the allure of the big cities is draining off many of the younger watermen. In lean years American farmers receive subtleties from the federal government; watermen receive none. If something isn't done soon about the predicate of watermen, then a way of life will disappear and will no longer exist.

Exercise 7 Just for Fun

My husband had lost his temper at the church ballgame on Saturday, resulting in an embarrassing scene, so I decided to pay an impromptu visit at the pastor's house and apologize for his temper.

The pastor and I chatted briefly; then, intending to emphasize my husband's good qualities, I blurted out, "I sure wish Allen could learn to control his temper. He is good in so many ways. He's thoughtful. Kindhearted. Very generous. But *most* of all, he is so passionate!"

Unaware of the inevitable phone call, I returned home feeling satisfied that my mission had been accomplished. Opening the front door I called out, "Hon, I'm home."

There he stood in the kitchen with arms folded and a Cheshire grin to greet me. With a chuckle he said, "Hi, hon. By the way, the word is *compassionate!*"

Exercise 8   For Discussion in Small Groups

Working in small groups, discuss the following draft of an essay by one of our students, H. C. (Cal) McKenzie. Pretend that McKenzie is a classmate who has come to your group for help with wordiness. Where in his essay would you advise him to eliminate redundancies, to streamline sentence structures, and to cut needless background information or philosophizing? If your group has time, revise one or two of McKenzie's paragraphs for wordiness. After your discussion, turn to McKenzie's own revisions (pages 265–269) and compare them with your suggestions.

```
             Conflict, Black and White

        I once served as an aide to one of the United
States's most powerful senators.  He was and still is not
only a powerful senator; he was also once a high-ranking
man in the military.  The senator made me more aware than
I had ever been before that some of our Caucasian leaders
are still the victims of an early-nineteenth-century men-
tality; they're still stereotyping black people.
        I don't think I will ever forget the time that I had
the unhappy experience of being alone with the senator.  I
had been assigned the task of driving the senator from his
senate office to Washington National Airport.  As soon as
he got into the car, I could feel his extreme apprehension
and total uncertainty as to what he should say to me or
how he should say it.  He shook my hand and said, "Good
afternoon, young man."  Then he sat silently, without
speaking, for a few seconds.  Finally, he began by asking
me my age, my educational background, and my place of
birth.  I wondered if he was going to ask me if I liked
girls; he didn't, and I breathed a sigh of relief.
```

For approximately two miles, total silence filled the
air. And then the senator began telling me about a
friendship he and his wife had with a "colored girl."
According to the senator, this young "colored girl" was a
classmate of his daughter, and his daughter attended a
prestigious university. According to the senator, whenever he and his wife visited their daughter at this prestigious university, they would always request the presence
of the "colored girl." She would play the piano and sing
while he and his family had a merry time. I sat there
behind the steering wheel, listening, but my mind was in a
state of utter boredom. When we finally reached our des-
tination, I breathed another sigh of relief.

My drive back to my office was not a pleasant one. I
wondered to myself: What is the senator telling me? Is he
saying that all black people have musical talent? Is he
saying that his only exposure to black people has been on
a master-servant level? I finally concluded that the senator is still living in the early nineteenth century when
black slaves would sing and dance while their masters
drank whiskey and clapped their hands. A dangerous state
of mind for a modern-day, senator, I thought to myself.

I wondered how the senator would react if the world
conflict between black and white came to a state of armed
warfare. Would he order total destruction of the enemy?
I shudder at the thought.

H. C. McKenzie

Part Four

Common Purposes for Writing

13 Describing

> *It is a good deal easier for most people to state an abstract idea than to describe and thus re-create some object they actually see.*
>
> — FLANNERY O'CONNOR

Let's say your uncle has given you for graduation a thirty-day bus pass to travel around the United States, and you want to thank him by sending him your impressions of the Grand Canyon, a part of the country you know he especially likes. Or say the department for which you work is to be renovated, and all employees are being asked to describe in writing their ideal new working quarters.

Perhaps your history professor has assigned a project in local history, for which you are to write about some building at least one hundred years old. Or the editor of the weekly family section of your local newspaper has called to ask if you would like to send in a feature article about your family's recent reunion. Or a friend who has applied to serve on a local commission on human rights has asked you to write a personal recommendation for her.

In each of these situations, you will be doing descriptive writing. How will you go about it?

Observing and Selecting Details

When preparing to write a description, you need first to be sure you are thoroughly familiar with what you are describing. You need to have *observed* carefully enough to be able to convey an exact picture. In her statement at the beginning of this chapter, writer Flannery O'Connor recognizes that this kind of "re-creating" by describing is not easy. But careful observation — "actually seeing," as O'Connor puts it — is the key.

You will need a *focus* around which to collect details. For instance, if you wanted to share with your uncle the awesomeness of the Grand Canyon as a spectacle of nature, you would focus on details of size and perhaps the overwhelming variety of texture and color the canyon presents. However, if you were most interested in emphasizing the canyon as a geological phenomenon, you would highlight details of its rock formations, the variation in color created by different minerals in the rock, and the way in which water continues to carve away the rock bed. Your focus tells you which details to delete as well as which to include.

Let's watch a student as she observes and selects details and then shapes them into a descriptive report. At the beginning of one fall semester, students in a science course were assigned to take a botany walk where flowers grew wild and to identify as many flowers as possible. The students were to report the identifications, with brief descriptions of each flower, in a paper. One student walked around several blocks in an overgrown area near her apartment complex. She repeated the walk to look more closely at the flowers she had identified and to see whether she could spot any others. As soon as she got home, she made a list of what she had seen while the walk was still fresh in her mind:

> thistles/heads turning white
> goldenrod/gives me hayfever
> large yellow-black spider, spinning remarkable web
> trumpet vine/flaming
> sumac — leaves turning/maroon berry cones
> two white flowers I didn't know
> white honeysuckle all over everywhere

When she was ready to write up her botany walk, our student checked her assignment one more time. She realized immediately that her list included some details she could not use. She was to report on flowers she could identify and briefly describe each. So she wrote at the top of her list:

FOCUS: TO IDENTIFY AND BRIEFLY DESCRIBE FLOWERS SEEN ON A BOTANY WALK

This focus told her right away not to use that large spider in the remarkable web, even though it was one of the most interesting things she had seen. Nor should she talk about goldenrod causing hayfever. And she would not mention that she had seen two white flowers she didn't know; she was only to write about flowers she could identify, so a mention of unidentified ones would hardly impress the professor. The student marked through all the unrelated details on her list.

As you can see, our writer deleted the details that were outside her focus *before* she began to write. That way she did not waste time writing a paper that wandered around, and her report ended up unified and in focus:

On a botany walk in my neighborhood I saw several flowers I could name. First, standing high above the undergrowth were spiny purple thistles, going to seed in white puffs. Nearby I spotted goldenrod, which deserves both halves of its name; it's gold like rich butter and it grows in a proud, upright rod. The trumpet vine I saw next boasted flaming red-orange blossoms shaped like the trumpet mouth they are called after. Sumac bushes further down the block were reaching their height in color, with bright green leaves turning ruby-red and maroon-colored cones of berries. White honeysuckle, with tiny blossoms but bold vines, tried to take over everything else I saw. I finished my botany walk glad that I grew up with a grandfather who taught me the names of some flowers.

Appealing to the Reader's Five Senses

Because well-done description plays on a reader's five senses, you will want to take particular care to get as much sensory detail as possible into your descriptive writing. When readers encounter strong descriptive writing, they find themselves experiencing what is being described; they identify with the situation through sight, smell, sound, touch, taste, or some combination of these.

For example, this student writer manages to appeal to four of our five senses (all but touch):

> I shall always remember those Sunday morning breakfasts I used to have as a child. At seven in the morning the smell of fresh-perked coffee would snake its way down the long hall which led to my room and fill it with an indescribable aroma, awaking me to tell me breakfast was ready and waiting. And what a breakfast it was! I first see a tall frosty glass of just-made orange juice filled with orange pulp. Steaming hot coffee is being poured into a small mug with sugar and country cream already in the bottom. Pancakes cooked to a golden brown are stacked almost a foot high, with butter oozing down the sides. Warm maple syrup covers the cakes with a soft glaze and slowly drips down to form a small pool in my plate. In a side dish are oven-baked apples sprinkled with cinnamon, nutmeg, vanilla, and raisins and served hot with the cooking juices still bubbling. Thick-sliced country bacon rounds off the meal. Whose mouth would not water, just thinking about this kind of breakfast served on a cold wintry morning — an "old fashioned breakfast"?

A useful rule of thumb to follow in descriptive writing is "Show your readers; don't just tell them." The breakfast paragraph does just that, through its specific sensory details. The writer has piled detail on detail: from the smell of the coffee "snaking its way down the long hall" to a "tall frosty glass" of juice to baked apples with their "cooking juices bubbling."

We should warn you, however, against overdoing the pile-up of detail that we have just advised. Overdone description is so lush that it overwhelms; there is simply too much to digest. The following sentence about the cliffs around a lake in Oregon is an example: "The shores are lined with searing, blood-red clay cliffs that produce a staggering display of fluorescence and kaleidoscopic colors at sunset." A reader could feel overpowered by that sentence.

In overdone description, details tend to be used for their own sake, not because they contribute to a particular effect. The writer of the following paragraph, for example, is trying too hard to reach for details — so hard that the description seems unreal:

> On a summer morning Eagle Rock Camp is the most captivating and blissful place in the world. The camp, located high in the mountains of upper New York State, is tucked away in the midst of mighty oak trees that seem to be reaching out elegantly in a creative dance movement. The exquisitely sweet summer breeze floats softly through the air, bending the slim blades of grass and kissing the golden buttercups.

Overdone description can often be improved, usually by deleting the excess details. Another kind of description is much harder to fix: the kind that floats off into abstractions existing more in the writer's mind than in reality. One of our students, for example, intending to describe a walk on the beach, turned inward instead:

> When I take a walk on the beach I am a king surveying his kingdom. Gulls soar ahead to herald my approach and the waves bow at my feet. The sea belongs to me as far as I can see. And yet I am lonely, as lonely as a man lost on an empty desert. The seagulls have become hawks circling above their prey. The waves are mirages that retreat as I move toward them. And the expanse of the sea merely intensifies my loneliness. I realize my intense aloneness, my place as an almost nonexistent speck in the universe. I am a king no more.

Too much of this takes place internally, inside the writer's head; he leaves the physicality of the beach, and with it the kind of details a reader could identify with: the gleam of sun on water, the feel of sand and pebbles underfoot, the plaintive sound of a bell buoy.

Creating Word Pictures

In descriptive writing, you can often use word pictures to good effect. Word pictures give your reader a concrete image on the page with which to identify. You can use three major devices to produce such pictures: the simile, the metaphor, and personification.

A *simile* creates a word picture by comparing what is being described with something else, using *like* or *as* to express the comparison. In his novel about migrant workers, *The Plum Plum Pickers*, Raymond Barrio uses a simile to describe apricot harvesting: "The plump orange balls plopped pitter patter like heavy drops of golden rain into his swaying, sweaty canvas buckets." Annie Dillard, in *Pilgrim at Tinker Creek*, finds two similes to describe the translucent entrails of a rotifer (a water creature): "Something orange and powerful is surging up and down like a piston, and something small and round is spinning in place like a flywheel."

In a *metaphor,* the thing described in a sense becomes the object with which it is being compared. In a passage from Frank Waters's novel *The Man Who Killed the Deer*, a sacred lake becomes an eye as an American Indian describes it: "We wanted the mountains, our mother, between whose breasts lies the little blue eye of faith. The deep turquoise lake of life." In a student paragraph about Washington in midspring, a cloud formation becomes "little sheep flocks" of cloud and the Washington Monument is "a sharp, clean sword." Here is one more especially effective metaphor: "A burning silver sword slit through the heavy cloud's fat stomach and it bellowed in rage . . . and then cried like a child." Do you recognize the image?

Personification makes descriptive writing more vivid by giving life to inanimate objects. Sappho, a poet of ancient Greece, made dawn perform a human act in these lines: "Standing by my bed in gold sandals/Dawn that very moment woke me." A student writer gives life to the sun as she describes an afternoon on the beach: "The sun takes an afternoon break while the clouds bluff a storm. Now the sun returns to work, laughing at his naive victims below." Playful images like this one are often especially appealing to a reader.

You can increase your skill at creating word pictures if you consciously try to do so. First you concentrate on what it is you want to describe — an object you see while driving, an aroma you pick up during a walk, the sensation you experience when sand runs through your fingers. Then you set your mind to work trying to think of different ways you could compare the object or the aroma or the sensation with something else. Your skill will increase with practice, and you will develop a store of images to draw on when you need them.

We should caution you against getting too caught up in a word picture. This one, for example, may be overdone: "Morning comes over the bay like a young woman gowned in palest blue chiffon trimmed with billowing white lace, as cloud puffs drift across the sky." A reader gets lost trying to follow this image all the way through.

It is also possible to create an *absurd image,* a word picture that doesn't quite make sense. Here are some illogical or nonsensical images: "You can hear the ruffling of lifeless leaves as the trees embrace you"; "She accepted her husband's death with open arms"; "The insurance agent stepped over our heads and signed a renewal contract without our permission."

Mixed images don't make sense either — images like "At this point in my life I sit in a stew that smacks of irony" (a stew cannot "smack"); "The talk I had with my grandmother helped to dissolve the generation gap between us" (a gap is bridged, not "dissolved"); "Gales of the late November wind glide around you" (gales would not "glide").

Finally, let us warn you again to beware of tired images or clichés in your writing. "White as a sheet," "cool as a cucumber," "pretty as a picture," "hungry as a bear," "hot as hell," "tired as a dog," and "cold as a clam" are only a few of the many clichéd images you will want to avoid. One way to test for clichés in your writing is to consider whether you can automatically supply the second half of a comparison when you hear the first half.

To get a feel for the difference between clichés and original expression, consider two versions of the same paragraph:

> Pollution had made its mark on the town, and the first thing that caught your eye was the dirty brick of the houses and buildings. It was a town of machines and tall chimneys out of which blew a steady stream of black smoke. The canal and river had also paid the price of pollution. The waters of both were smelly and dirty. As for the buildings, most of the windows rattled like tin cans while the piston of the steam engine worked like a Trojan pumping up and down like a seesaw all day long.

> It was a town of red brick, or of brick that would have been red if the smoke and ashes had allowed it; but as matters stood it was a town of unnatural red and black like the painted face of a savage. It was a town of machinery and tall chimneys out of which interminable serpents of smoke trailed themselves for ever and ever, and never got uncoiled. It had a black canal in it, and a river that ran purple with ill-smelling dye, and vast piles of buildings full of windows where there was a rattling and a trembling all day long, and where the piston of the steam engine worked monotonously up and down like the head of an elephant in a state of melancholy madness.

The first version is filled with clichés. The second, from Charles Dickens's *Hard Times,* vividly conveys what the writer has felt, seen, heard, and smelled; and its word pictures are original enough to surprise.

Animating Descriptions

Robert Lewis Stevenson once remarked that he'd never heard anyone speak of scenery for more than five minutes at a time, which made him suspect he heard too much of it in literature. Purely static descriptions, in other words, are hard to sustain. They should be used only in small doses.

Static descriptions may appear as part of a larger piece of writing, perhaps to embellish an example proving a point or to set the scene for a narrative. But extended descriptions should be animated in some way. If your subject is an elderly, self-sufficient woman, for example, describe her in action, as this student has done:

> A typical day for Gladys starts at four in the morning. She walks to the barn to milk about 125 goats. After milking she releases the goats to the countryside, chasing them to a particular area that she wants them to feed on. She then cleans the barn, shovels manure, and spreads clean hay around the milking stalls.

Or if your subject is Muhammad Ali, get him talking:

> The world champion could, as he put it, "float like a butterfly and sting like a bee."

Or if you want to describe the world you've experienced underwater, on a scuba expedition, take readers with you:

> After snorkeling around a few rocks, we begin the dive. . . . Descending, we see the clear water turning dark, the effect of the warm water settling on the darker, colder water like that of oil floating on vinegar.

The idea, then, is to get the description moving, to give it life and human interest. If the paper begins to resemble a narrative, that is not necessarily bad. The boundaries of the various forms of writing are fluid. A description can tell a story, and a story can include descriptions.

Exercise 1 For Class Discussion

Below are several pieces of descriptive writing by students. Be ready to discuss in class why each is effective and what devices have been used to make it so.

1. My childhood home, a large white Cape Cod cottage with a red roof and dormered windows, stands at the end of a long, straight driveway. My room is behind one of those dormer windows. As a child I spent

long hours on the window seat, reading and daydreaming. From that window I could see apple trees, sweet-scented in spring, heavy with red fruit in summer, gay with yellow leaves in fall, and etched in snow during the winter. Returning home now all I see is concrete and asphalt. I miss my apple trees.

2. You can smell the pier before you can see it. Walking up the narrow oystershell road bordered with high marsh grass and cattails, you pick up the odor of old wood, fish, and creosote tar. The crunch of the oyster shells underfoot gives way to a hollow sound at your first step onto the plankings which form ragged vertical lines between the pilings. Here and there a new board of bright tan breaks the seemingly endless rows of older boards, brown and rough from years of wear. The old timber creaks and sways as the rushing tide pushes against the pilings driven deep into the bottom of the bay.

3. In the early sixties, Framingham, Massachusetts, was a small town with bicycle paths worn into the grass wherever the sidewalk didn't go. Sometimes in my dreams I ride back over those trails, feeling the bumps, the jars, and the tree roots just as they were under the wheels of my new English racer. I can even recall some of the places where if I didn't duck I'd get a mouthful of clothesline.

4. Small groups of people huddle under umbrellas to protect themselves from the burning sun, waiting for some sound, some movement. Then it happens. The street dancers, so beloved in Trinidad, round the corner ahead. Suddenly you feel a surge of energy, like an explosion throughout your body, as each nerve comes alive. Everyone rises and starts to dance, throwing up their arms and shouting for the favors being tossed by the official dancers. You forget the heat and the wait as you are caught up in the excitement — and you know it is worth everything to be here.

5. We're on our way down the Hudson on the Manhattan Excursion Line. When the motor revs up, the band revs up, and the excitement begins. As the boat slowly pulls away from the dock, it is already vibrating with rock music. The buildings and people behind us look smaller and soon disappear as though they were never there. Our boat rides so smoothly through the water that the city seems to be moving instead of us. The skyline is like a Rembrandt, as the setting sun casts an orange glow along the shore.

Exercise 2 For Class Discussion

The following descriptions are less effective than those in the preceding exercise. Based on what you have learned in this chapter, try to determine how each description got off the track.

1. Picture the sunrise over the bay. You are standing on the beach. Bulky waves bounce between the ancient towering rocks with a deafening crash, while the undersized ripples wash the miniature boulders of earth from beneath your feet. Suddenly the dark, peaceful, moonlit sky is filled with a kaleidoscope of light and color. Now you can see a colossal, fiery, luminous sphere rising from the hidden depths of the ocean. As you look up into the endless space, morning brings you a multitude of seagulls who seem to be gazing back down at you in the early morning light.

2. The most interesting city I know is Jacksonville, Florida. I made my first trip there when I was fourteen years old. We have relatives there and went there for our summer vacation. I was amazed to see how crowded the beaches were, because I was so used to seeing Bayside's beaches. Also, in Jacksonville there is no boardwalk with all the side stores and pizza parlors. Another interesting thing is that the cars drive right up to the beach to the edge of the water, which is rather unique compared to other beach resorts. Jacksonville is really a great city full of many wonderful sights and people, and I hope to go there again in the future.

3. The wind rushes again almost like the surf. The air feels like a rainstorm — but the sun won't let me down. I wish I were a leaf, tossing about, free and flying. Up, up, up from the ground into the blue and white sky, and then I'd float back, touching on a jeweled lake. I guess I shouldn't ask myself what it's all about so often. I feel the wind coming up stronger now. It's almost dark — I'll have to work tomorrow.

4. Like a multicolored centipede inching its way, the jammed traffic crawls through the choked, rain-drenched streets. Furiously dancing rain ricochets off everything in sight. The dark and menacing sky, seen through blurred windshields, rests on the tops of buildings like a filthy layer of gauze. Swirling wisps of gray, shaved off the billowing clouds by the buildings' granite edges, spill over into the deep concrete canyon. In the floor of the canyon, amber taillights ignite brilliantly all along the curving spine of the centipede. A line of hazy headlights hangs in the air like shimmering disks suspended from an invisible wire, reflected in water-spotted mirrors. Blaring horns add a shuddering wail of protest to the already clamorous language of the city. Undaunted, the wet, sluggish mechanical creature continues its methodical journey home.

Exercise 3 Written

Make up word pictures for three or four of the following sensory situations, using similes, metaphors, and personification. Observe carefully first. Be as creative as possible; don't let yourself resort to clichés. Bring your word pictures to class to share with your classmates.

chewing taffy
stroking a long-haired dog or cat
listening to *little* waves as they reach the shore
watching a fire burn down
feeling polished marble, bronze, or aluminum
smelling ripe peaches, watermelon, or bananas
feeling fine rain hit your face
smelling charcoaled hamburgers
tasting curry, spinach, bittersweet chocolate, or cinnamon
hearing rock music
seeing tulips, lilacs, or dogwood
walking barefoot on packed wet sand
walking barefoot on dry sand
motorcycling on a bumpy road
seeing a horizon of trees of five different shades of green, or
    seeing the same horizon in autumn

Exercise 4   Class Activity in Small Groups

Before coming to class, take notes for a descriptive paper while directly observing the person, place, or thing that you plan to describe. Bring your notes to class, and in small groups present your description orally, asking your listeners where they would like clarifications and/or further details. Below are some possible topics.

the people or performers at a concert
one room in your house, dorm, or apartment
a house for sale in your area (visit during an "Open House")
an animal or bird
a garden
some family treasure (such as an unusual piece of furniture)
a favorite painting in an art gallery
a walk through the woods
a walk down a city street
a classic car
the interior of a church
a unique building
the details of a dream that you recollect upon awaking

Exercise 5   Written

Write a descriptive essay on one of the topics suggested in exercise 4. Be sure to observe carefully before you begin to write.

Exercise 6   For Discussion in Small Groups

Working in small groups, discuss the following draft of an essay by one of our students, John Curley. Pretend that Curley is a classmate who has come to your group for help with his description. Where would you advise him to delete overdone (or overly abstract) descriptions, to simplify and clarify his descriptions, or to choose concrete rather than abstract language? If your group has time, revise one or two of Curley's paragraphs for him. After your discussion, turn to Curley's own revisions (pages 271–277) and compare them with your suggestions.

```
                 Journey Under Water

        Each time I've tried to describe the beauty I have
   discovered under the rolling waves of the sea, my friends
   have countered with their movie-going experience from Jaws
   and its toothy sequel, Jaws 2, which portray divers as
   fools treading water where angels fear to go.  In Jaws 2,
   you may recall, the bride of Jaws snacked on two scuba
   divers, a fast-moving water skier, a helicopter pilot, and
   the resident diving instructor before the local sailboat
   regatta became the main course.
        In my travels over the past ten years, I have experi-
   enced a far more peaceful world under water: from coral
   gardens along the Pacific shores of Thailand, to an under-
   water wedding in Australia, to oil tankers sunk by Nazis
   along the New Jersey coast, to the pastel hues of the
   Caribbean Sea.
        A description of the ultimate might be appropriate
   enticement to urge you to join me undersea.  My favorite
   spot is Davis Beach, St. Croix, in the Virgin Islands.
   Picture, if you will, a deserted sandy beach graced with
   palm trees.  Of course, although there is no McDonald's,
   we may come upon a little squirrel monkey or a strolling
   peacock taking an interest in our visit.  Usually the wel-
   comed tradewinds sway the palms in the 80 degree tropic
   heat.  Here even the waves pause, taking an indolent
```

pleasure in inviting the sunbeams to play upon them as
they break over the reef.

Let's wade out through a century-old crevasse in the
reef which it is believed was made by early Danish
explorers.

After snorkeling around a few rocks, we begin the
dive. As we descend to the first level, about thirty feet
down, colorful parrot fish, butterfly fish, and damsels
greet us in a field of red and yellow coral. This coral
is yellow, courtesy of Mother Nature, but the effect of
the nibbling parrot fish is to turn it as red as rubies.
Enormous sponges ensconced at this depth become our royal
thrones.

The coral reef guides our downward path, which is
carefully monitored with frequent and meticulous readings
on the depth gauge that I carry. The living reef of coral
drops to 1,800 feet. Our limit is 100 feet. Descending,
we see the clear water turning dark in color as it becomes
colder. This appearance is analogous to oil floating on
vinegar in a salad dressing.

Now, down to sixty feet. We look about for Mo and
Maureen, a photogenic couple who have startled divers new
to the North Star Cliffs. These moray eels have never, as
far as anyone knows, behaved like the famous -- or should
I say infamous -- man-eaters of movie notoriety but prefer
instead the snacks the divers have saved from their lunch.

On our way back, we ascend slowly, relaxing and hov-
ering over purple fields of filigree coral fans reminis-
cent of old Spanish lace. Not only beautiful, they are
functional navigational guides. The waves, rolling into
shore, create an underwater current which flutters the
fans in an off-shore and on-shore undulating motion. Thus
guided by the reef, we head for the land, loitering along
the way in crystalline waters warmed by the sun.

Perhaps on our next dive we will chance upon a sting-
ray, as I did recently off the coast of St. Thomas. With
a little encouragement, he spread out his magnificent
wings, and with more grace than a ballet dancer, lifted
himself to unfurl an eight-foot wing span. He then with-
drew, feeling perhaps his obligation to perform completed.
Awed by his performance, I forgot to snap a picture. But
there will be other journeys under water for me, and, if
I've whetted your interest, I hope for you too. It is all
there, just waiting for you, whenever you are ready.

John Curley

14 *Narrating*

*I was trying to write . . . and I found the greatest difficulty . . .
was to put down what really happened in action; what the actual
things were which produced the emotion that you experienced.*
— Ernest Hemingway

Your daughter is away at college, and you want to send her a full
report of her younger brother's first high-school band parade. Or you
are helping to expose police corruption in your town, and you plan to
relate what happened during a raid on a music store that was fronting
for a drug supply source. Or you have been invited to speak to a civic
group that may be interested in sponsoring a scholarship for your college,
and you have decided to begin with a funny anecdote.

You are interested in becoming a sports announcer, and the local
station where you are training has asked you to prepare a five-minute
account of the Little League playoffs. Or you are planning to argue
before your city council for a stoplight at a street corner in your neighborhood, and as part of your evidence you want to highlight a fatal
accident that occurred there last month.

Each of these situations calls for narrative writing. You do narrative
writing whenever you tell about something that happened within a
defined time span. Narrative writing, then, relates an event, usually in
simple chronological order. In other words, it tells a story.

Some Ground Rules

A few ground rules can be applied to most narrative writing: (1) Put
readers on the scene immediately. (2) Select details for a specific effect.
(3) Keep the story moving. These ground rules can be diagramed like
this:

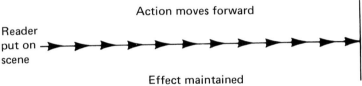

Action moves forward

Reader
put on →
scene

Effect maintained

This brief narrative follows these ground rules very well:

> It happened at the dinner table at the Greenbrier Hotel, a fancy resort where I, a young bride from the country, felt even less sophisticated and more awkward than usual. My new husband and I were on our honeymoon, and the social manager of the hotel had invited us and three other honeymooning couples to a celebration dinner in the main dining room. For my dinner I ordered beef burgundy with noodles.
>
> After a while, the very French waiter returned from the kitchen and said to me, in rather breathless Parisian English, "The beef, it is strucken off."
>
> "Oh," I responded, "that's okay. I'll have ham in pineapple sauce, then."
>
> "Oh, no, Madame, the beef is all right, but it is strucken off!"
>
> "Ham is fine," I said again.
>
> "No, no, no, Madame! Beef, beef — but is *strucken off!*"
>
> This dialogue continued for longer than I care to remember — until finally another, more sophisticated new bride "translated" for me, in a tactfully quiet voice, "I believe he is saying the beef dish is beef Stroganov, rather than beef burgundy with noodles."
>
> "Oh-h-h." My eyes must have been as wide open as my mouth.
>
> So I had beef Stroganov for that celebration dinner, instead of either beef burgundy with noodles *or* ham in pineapple sauce, but you can be sure that I have never eaten it since without remembering with a chuckle the Greenbrier beef Struckenoff.

Here is the working list the writer of this essay made up as she prepared to write:

```
Desired specific effect: My relative lack of
                         sophistication in a
                         setting that assumed a
                         certain amount of
                         sophistication

     where event happened ⎫
     when event happened  ⎬ background
     the circumstances/   ⎭
          situation

              why we chose the Greenbrier
              what I wore
              describe other couples --- no, keep
                   focus on me and my funny
                   story
              what I ordered originally
```

~~what others ordered~~
conversation between waiter and
   me -- ham as alternate dinner
~~my new husband's discomfort~~
another bride, from St. Louis,
   "rescues" me
my reaction when I realized what
   was going on
~~how beef dish tasted~~

characterize waiter -- briefly --
   to add humor

Readers learn right away that this narrative is going to occur at the dinner table at an exclusive hotel during the honeymoon of an unsophisticated young woman. We are on the scene immediately, ready to get on with the story. If the writer had told us why she and her husband had chosen the Greenbrier or what she was wearing at dinner, we might have felt impatient, bogged down in needless, boring background information.

Now note what else our writer decided to delete before she began to write. As her specific effect, she wants to emphasize her relative lack of sophistication in a setting that assumed a certain amount of sophistication. So she gets rid of such details as what the others ordered, her new husband's discomfort as the situation got more and more out of hand, and where her "rescuer" was from. The spotlight needs to stay on the action between herself and the waiter. Details about her dinner partners are irrelevant. They would blur her intended effect.

The deletion of irrelevant details is one reason this piece of writing keeps moving. Another is the use of dialogue, a device that helps convey the you-are-there effect to a reader. The essay moves rapidly enough that you want to keep on reading to see what happens next.

Finding a Lively Opener

It's a good idea to involve your reader in your narrative right away with a lively opener. In her narrative about the honeymoon incident, our writer catches readers at once with her opening words: "It happened at the dinner table. . . ." To what does "It" refer? she wants readers to ask.

Generally, it is wise to avoid beginning a narrative with something like "I am going to tell you a story about . . ." unless what follows "about" is so intriguing that a reader could hardly resist it. The original opening sentence of the honeymoon dinner narrative read: "One of my favorite funny stories on myself has to do with my lack of sophistication in a very sophisticated setting." Pretty flat, isn't it?

Here are some lively openers taken from student narratives:

> While I was running an EEG (electroencephalogram) one day, the pens started clacking and throwing ink around the room.

> Celery sticks served as slugger bats; olives substituted for baseballs to be smashed across the kitchen.

> Pipsqueak, a freshwater selvini, would eventually grow to be a terror in the tank, but only if he could manage to live long enough to become one.

> "Breaker one nine . . . breaker one nine!" It's two o'clock in the morning and I am heading toward the beach.

We would guess that you would want to hear each of these narratives once you had read their opening sentences.

Arranging Events in Time

You will probably choose to write narratives in chronological order most of the time. But occasionally you may decide to begin in the middle or near the end, then flash back to an earlier part of your story. The student writer of the following football narrative opens his story at its climax, as an overtime field goal is being placed at the end of a tied game. Then he pauses to take his readers back through some of the semiclimaxes of the game, to build up to whether the field goal wins the game.

> The game is tied. The date is December 14, 1975. The place is Baltimore's Memorial Stadium. Everyone in the stands is on their feet for the overtime play. Down below, Toni Linhart, behind a wall of Colts, is set to kick the field goal.
>
> For a moment before Linhart's snap, I see the game so far in my mind's eye. At one point, my team, the Baltimore Colts, is behind 7–0. Then, late in the fourth quarter, the Colts seem to hear the pleas of the shouting crowd and start to move. Like a machine, Bert Jones marches the Colts over a determined Miami defense. Then, from the six-yard line, Lydell Mitchell bursts into the end zone. Touchdown! Linhart adds the extra point and the game is tied. The gun sounds, ending regulation time.
>
> In sudden-death overtime, the young Colt defense freezes Miami's offense and the Colts take over on their own four-yard line. Once again the Colts seem to grow stronger from the crowd's screams. Jones throws

to Chester, then to Mitchell, and completes a third pass to Carr. As the Colts get nearer to the goal line, the noise becomes almost deafening.

And now a strange silence falls over the stadium. I realize that Linhart is ready to try to win the game. The ball is snapped and an unbelievable roar pours out of the crowd. The stadium seems to rock and then explodes with screams of joy and excitement. The referee's raised hands only confirm what 60,000 frenzied fans already know. The field goal is good. The Colts have won.

Pacing Sentences

Your narrative writing will be more dramatic if the form in which you write it reflects the content about which you are writing. You can achieve this happy combination by being aware of the pace of different kinds of phrasing.

For example, note how this student's choice of expression reinforces the event she is narrating — the escape of a horse from her uncle's corral:

> The horse races away in exultation. He runs as if the world is his, his head trying to touch the sky, his body strong with spirit and muscles, his mane and tail flying as if to tell the wind which way to go. His skin glistens in the sun, his feet hit the ground in perfect rhythm, never missing a beat, never slowing down, but going faster and faster until the forest stops him.

The following sentence, with which Edgar Allan Poe opens his short story "The Fall of the House of Usher," demonstrates the pacing effect you can achieve with a long sentence piling detail on detail:

> During the whole of a dull, dark, and soundless day in the autumn of the year, when the clouds hung oppressively low in the heavens, I had been passing alone, on horseback, through a singularly dreary tract of country; and at length found myself, as the shades of the evening drew on, within view of that melancholy house.

This long, heavy, slow-moving sentence is exactly right to establish the despairing mood into which Poe wants to plunge his readers.

The following paragraph, on the other hand, immediately establishes for the reader the detached attitude of the central character who will narrate Albert Camus's novel *The Stranger:*

> Mother died today, or maybe yesterday; I can't be sure. The telegram from the Home says: YOUR MOTHER PASSED AWAY. FUNERAL TOMORROW. DEEP SYMPATHY.

We are not surprised, as we read on, by the uninvolved quality of a character who begins his story with such short, stark sentences.

One of our student writers uses short sentences in another way to pace a narrative. Here is her account of the final inning of a softball game for which she was catcher:

> Here comes the first pitch. It's outside. Ball one. The ball goes back to the pitcher. I return to my position behind the plate. My mind is racing. Relax. Keep your glove out there. Don't take your eyes off the ball. Here's the second pitch. It looks good. It's coming right over the plate. Smack! She hit it. I can't see it. I'm up off my knees in a split second. My glove is open. It seems like an eternity and then suddenly it's all over. The ball falls right on target into my glove. The game is over and we have won.

The student writer of the following paragraph invites readers to ride with him in a fantasy about the Grand Prix. He maintains the movement of that heady race through the steady, almost rhythmical pace of parallel structure, as he begins three successive sentences: "To feel . . ."; "To go flat out . . ."; "To know. . . ."

> To feel the wind in your face and hear the tires scream as you slide through the S-curves at Monza. To go flat out through the streets of Monaco, hearing the roar of that mighty engine and accelerating till you think you are going to be pushed through the seat. To know you are one of only twenty-four men in all the world who drive the giant V-12 Formula-1 cars in the Grand Prix National Circuit.

You can use sentences of different kinds and different lengths to vary the pace of a narrative, reflecting what is happening at a particular moment. The following paragraphs from a student narrative about a cross-country marathon use pacing in this way. Listen to how the sound of the writing echoes exactly what is happening as the race progresses:

> The runners are already at the line-up, pawing the ground like horses at a derby. The starter readies his pistol. He fires. Adrenalin surges through the runner's body, exciting every muscle into spontaneous movement. Dirt and gravel fly in faces as the human steeds head toward home.
>
> The first mile removes some of the competitive element of the race, as some runners overheat and retire to barking coaches and sympathetic parents. Others fall victim to injury and lack of stamina. But some persevere. They run — like they have never run before.
>
> The next turn marks halfway. The runners quicken their pace as the thundering hooves round the bend. The mind recognizes the hill ahead and instinctively shifts to a traction mode. Arms pump and spikes dig in while the words "work that hill" echo through the mind.

As we mentioned at the end of the last chapter, you will sometimes need to combine narrative and descriptive writing. For example, if you were writing about a trip you took with a learning-impaired relative, you might want to describe your companion; doing so would help you show how his or her handicap made the trip unique.

By the same token, narration often appears in other kinds of writing. One student who wanted to explain why her gospel choir broke up began her paper with a startling story about the infighting between two of the choir members. Another student writer was concerned about why crime among youth is on the increase. Her paper included an account of a teenage break-in at her apartment and the indifference of the police officers who answered her emergency call.

Exercise 1   Classroom Activity

Jot down some notes for a narrative you would be interested in writing. Then, working from your notes, tell your narrative to a classmate, to test it out. Watch to see if your story holds your listener's attention throughout. If it does not, talk with your partner about how you can improve it.

Exercise 2   Written

Write a narrative on one of the following topics. Pace your narrative by deliberately constructing sentences to reflect what is happening from moment to moment.

1. a bicycle, motorcycle, or auto race, perhaps over a bumpy course that includes several obstacles
2. the final minutes of a baseball, basketball, or football game — with the score nearly tied
3. a trip in a canoe or rowboat down a river with changing currents and small rapids
4. a frightening encounter with an animal, an authority figure, a criminal, or the like
5. giving birth or watching someone give birth
6. skiing down a challenging slope
7. a hurricane or other natural disaster you have lived through

8. an experience hiking, rock climbing, sailing, horseback riding, or the like
9. an experience working in an emergency room
10. a humorous story revealing some truth about human nature

Exercise 3 For Discussion in Small Groups

Working in small groups, discuss the following draft of an essay by one of our students, Mel White. Pretend that White is a classmate who has come to your group for help, feeling that he needs to quicken the pace of his narrative. Where would you advise White to cut needless explanations and descriptions or to improve his sentence pacing? If your group has time, revise one or two of White's paragraphs for him. After your discussion, turn to White's own revisions (pages 279–285) and compare them with your suggestions.

Fish Story

Pipsqueak, a freshwater selvini, would eventually grow to be a terror in the tank, but only if he could manage to live long enough to become one. Pipsqueak's problems began when I placed Dirty Harry, a larger selvini, in the tank, to ease his loneliness. I had hoped for peaceful coexistence, but Dirty Harry proved to be like a contemporary human being. He attacked Pipsqueak relentlessly, never allowing the child to rest. Dirty Harry pursued his "companion" as if Pipsqueak were a punching bag. This imbalance of power was so great and the ensuing battles were so alarming that something had to be done.

Since I had forced Pipsqueak to be subject to these inhuman acts of barbarism, I had to insure law and order, allowing this "little guy" the right to live peacefully until he was large and strong enough to defend himself and make it on his own. To establish law and order, I had several alternatives: I could separate the villain from the victim, I could destroy the evil one, or I could hire a policeman. After considering the homeland, I had to eliminate the first alternative. The homeland consists of twenty gallons of clean fresh water, rising from a base of immaculate white pebbles. The eastern end of the homeland consists of the grasslands, from which colorful elephant grass rises and flows with the tide. The far west end is rocky and desolate. Obviously, there was no way to separate the eastern and the western territories. The destruction of Dirty Harry would be nothing short of murder, a punishment far greater than the crime. Alas, I had no alternative but to seek the aid of a policeman.

After reviewing several potential employees, I found my man. His name, Big John. His breed, Jack Dempsey. His manner, tough. Big John wouldn't accept the job unless I allowed him to bring along his deputy, a mild-mannered Jack Dempsey who goes by the name of Murph. The stage was set; the day of reckoning had come. As the curtain rose for the main attraction, Dirty Harry was busy trying to mutilate poor Pipsqueak. At first Harry didn't realize that he was no longer top dog. Harry didn't quite understand that he was no longer king of the castle.

Big John made his rounds majestically, with Murph at his side. Pipsqueak hovered in fear among the weeds, hoping that the attacks upon his life would soon cease. Suddenly an eerie silence fell over the homeland. Dirty Harry stopped dead in his tracks. "Who the hell are you?" he bellowed. Ignoring him, Big John continued his patrol. He moved from the eastern boundary and strolled through the high grasslands toward a clump of orange vegetation hiding the skeleton of an unfortunate seaman. He examined the seaman's remains and moved into the west end, patrolled by an air-blowing dragon. Seeing the air bubbles coming from the dragon, he carefully approached. Realizing that the dragon was no threat, the peacekeeper, Big John, moved on, inserting his nose among the boulders where Dirty Harry loved to bask.

Dirty Harry could hold back no longer. His back arched and his fins stuck straight out. His whole body began to shake in the ritual manner that precedes attack. Big John did nothing. The shaking intensified. Fear and hate were in the air.

When the shaking stopped, the attack began. First Dirty Harry attacked face to face. The next attack came toward Big John's midsection. The counterblow sent Dirty Harry to a tunnel beneath the dragon to lick his wounds. When Dirty Harry emerged, executing a sneak attack from the rear, Big John whipped around and with a frontal assault drove Dirty Harry back to the tunnel. This time he suffered defeat without dignity. "They call me Big John and I was hired to keep the peace. There's enough room for everyone to live in harmony, Dirty Harry, so when you come outside again you'd better act right." Big John didn't have to say more.

Peace and harmony have finally come to the homeland. Pipsqueak has grown a little larger, and Dirty Harry has learned to respect the rights of others. Big John and Murph have adapted to their new positions well. Outside the homeland, however, there is another territory, a land filled with hatred, political unrest, and turmoil. I wonder if Big John has any friends.

Melvin White

15 *Reporting*

Never underestimate your readers' intelligence or overestimate their information. — AN OLD NEWSPAPER SAYING

A friend of yours wants instructions for making wreaths of nuts, cones, and other natural materials to sell at a Christmas bazaar. Or you need to write to your insurance company to claim compensation for several expensive items missing from your car. Or you have just discovered a new bluegrass musician, and you want to tell your friend on a submarine — a bluegrass fan — about the unique banjo-picking style of your find.

Your art history instructor believes in comprehensive exam questions; you expect one something like this on your final: Tell me everything you know about Chagall, or Rembrandt, or Georgia O'Keeffe. Or the owner of the summer camp where you serve as a counselor has asked for a report on all the special activities you designed for your campers this summer, to help her determine who to hire next year. Or your sister, who has a partially deaf ten-year-old, knows that a family on your block also has a youngster with hearing problems, and she has written to ask you about a hearing device that child wears.

To meet the needs of these situations, you will be reporting information. Informative writing explains, and often it instructs. It is intended to be useful and practical.

Complete, Accurate, and Clear

Because your readers do not already know the information you are reporting, you'll need to take special care to be complete, accurate, and clear. To help you understand the importance of these three guidelines, we would like to show you a sample informative essay on a subject you probably know very little about.

Our writer's purpose in this essay is to inform readers about hypoglycemia, a rather common metabolic condition that can radically affect the everyday lives of its unsuspecting victims. She wants to explain what hypoglycemia is, what symptoms might indicate it, why diagnosis is important, how to find out whether one has it, and what diet to follow if the tests are positive. The essay's focus is determined for her by what she wants to explain and how much information she chooses to convey.

> Facing the fact that you have hypoglycemia is somewhat like an alcoholic's facing the fact that he or she is an alcoholic. From that day forward, if you want to feel good and to function well, you know that you must generally avoid sugary foods — just as the alcoholic must avoid alcohol. And just as with alcoholism, hypoglycemia is much more prevalent than many people realize.
>
> "Hypoglycemia" (*high-po-gly-seé-mee-uh*) means, to put it simply, that you suffer from low blood sugar. What actually happens is that pure sugar in your bloodstream makes your pancreas overproduce insulin, which in turn burns sugar very rapidly. This explains why the "pick-up" candy bar so popular with the unaware, tired hypoglycemic provides the desired sudden spurt of energy — but at the price of a new low as soon as insulin gets to the sugar in the candy bar.
>
> The hypoglycemic person — depending on the rate at which he or she burns sugar — may have functioned fairly well for years prior to suspecting hypoglycemia. But even with a reasonable level of functioning, having yourself tested if you have certain symptoms — irritability, depression, fatigue, lassitude, blurring of vision, difficulty in concentrating — is very important. For hypoglycemia sometimes precedes diabetes, a much more serious condition.
>
> It may not be easy to talk your doctor into the blood sugar test used to discover hypoglycemia; for some reason, many doctors refuse to acknowledge hypoglycemia. If your regular doctor won't cooperate with you, go to another physician, probably an internist. If your sugar test does indicate hypoglycemia, then you will need to attend carefully to what you put into your body — if you want to be a healthy hypoglycemic.

The essay continues with a discussion of foods and beverages the hypoglycemic should include in his or her diet and those to be avoided. These are listed under appropriate headings:

Include: *Avoid:*   *May be used sometimes:*

Next she mentions the effect of both alcoholic beverages and drugs. Finally, the writer explains that the hypoglycemic will probably need to eat more frequently and in smaller portions than formerly, to slow down the insulin overreaction.

Let's look at this essay in terms of our three standards for informative writing: completeness, accuracy, and clarity.

The essay seems complete enough. It defines hypoglycemia, mentions some of the common symptoms, points out its relation to the more serious diabetes, talks about the sugar test used for diagnosis and tells how to get one, and details both an approved food and beverage diet and recommended eating habits for the hypoglycemic. It even notes that hypoglycemics are likely to be more susceptible to drugs than other people are.

How accurate is the information? Though the writer doesn't overwhelm us with medical terminology, she does give us enough technical information about blood sugar, insulin, the pancreas, and so on, to inspire our confidence in her discussion of hypoglycemia.

The essay is clear enough so that most readers could follow it and use the information if they needed to. Several specific factors contribute to its clarity. First, the writer has used everyday language rather than a lot of technical words that many readers might not understand. Second, she has been careful to define *hypoglycemia* early in the paper. She does not assume that her readers are familiar with the word. She has even taken the trouble to show the reader how to pronounce this big, rather strange-looking word — a minor tactic that can be more important than you might think. Letting readers in on how to say possibly intimidating words can make them feel more in command of what they are reading.

By referring to the "pick-up" candy bar so popular with hypoglycemics, our writer gives her readers a common hypoglycemic situation that they can identify with. This real-life situation helps to clarify early in the paper how hypoglycemia affects human metabolism. Finally, the information about what a person with hypoglycemia should and should not eat and drink is presented in list form for easy readability and quick reference.

You might want to try out your informative writing on a test reader before you write your final draft. In fact, you might want to use *two* test readers — one to check your rough draft for accuracy, another to test it for completeness and clarity. Choose an expert on your subject to test read for accuracy. For instance, our writer might have enlisted someone in either medicine or nutrition — perhaps a nurse, a medical student, a lab technician, or a dietitian — to test read for accuracy. But to check for completeness and clarity, she would need to ask an average, uninformed reader to help her out. Only an uninformed reader — her real audience, remember — could help her see where to fill in the information gaps and where to clarify. It is probably more important to test your paper on an uninformed reader than on an expert. Why? Because it is easy to assume that your readers know more than they do.

Opening Devices: Analogies and Rhetorical Questions

The writer of our sample informative essay opens with a device that often works well in informative writing: an analogy. In an analogy, an unfamiliar subject (in this case, hypoglycemia) is made clearer by being compared with a more familiar one (alcoholism). In addition to clarifying unfamiliar content, an analogy helps to make readers feel at home with new material. Many readers of this essay may never have heard of hypoglycemia before; however, the chances are good that they know at least something about alcoholism.

Using an analogy can be tricky, though, especially if you try to push it too far. Notice how our writer qualifies her comparison of hypoglycemia and alcoholism:

> Facing the fact that you have hypoglycemia is somewhat like an alcoholic's facing the fact that he or she is an alcoholic. From that day forward, if you want to feel good and to function well, you know that you must generally avoid sugary foods — just as the alcoholic must avoid alcohol.

She says that facing hypoglycemia is *somewhat* like facing alcoholism, and that hypoglycemics must *generally* avoid sugary foods in the same way that alcoholics must avoid alcohol. Both *somewhat* and *generally* are qualifying words; that is, they keep the sentences they appear in honest.

Our writer does not try to extend her analogy too far. No analogy will validly compare every point about an unfamiliar subject with a familiar one. For that to be true, the two things would have to be identical. Actually, this particular analogy could be applied at certain other points in this essay. However, it has served its purpose once it has made the reader feel at home with the unfamiliar subject it has been used to introduce. If you try to extend an analogy too far, it can take over your material, so that you risk losing the focus on your main points as you — and in turn your reader — get caught up in the fascination of the analogy.

There is another opening device you can use in informative writing to whet the curiosity of your readers and make them want to read on: the rhetorical question. This device poses a question that will be answered by what follows. A reader begins to wonder about the answer as soon as the question is asked — and right away you have an involved reader, one who is in the right frame of mind to absorb your information.

The student writer of an informative paper about some problems in owning an aquarium of live-bearing fish began her paper with two rhetorical questions:

You wish to start an aquarium of live-bearing fish? Are you aware of how prolific certain live-bearing fish can be?

Here are some other rhetorical questions calculated to engage readers:

1. Does extraterrestrial life exist?
2. How can you locate a doctor who believes in "treating the whole person"?
3. How — if at all — should pornography be controlled?
4. What is cloning, and how near is science to being able to clone humans?

Explaining a Process

When you explain to someone in writing how to do something — how to repair a guitar, execute the backstroke, groom a dog, carve a totem pole — you are doing a special kind of informative writing known as process writing. For process writing we would add three more standards to our original three of completeness, accuracy, and clarity: Be direct, concise, and orderly. By *direct,* we mean you should be straightforward and to the point; by *concise,* not waste words; and by *orderly,* put the steps of the process in proper sequence. After all, we usually explain a process so that someone else can do exactly the same thing in exactly the same way.

In the following paper, a student gives directions for constructing a piñata. Notice the clear list of all needed materials early in the paper. Using this list, anyone making a piñata would find it easy to assemble all the supplies ahead of time.

> To set the theme for a "south of the border" fiesta, you might make a colorful piñata, a figure filled with edibles and/or party favors, borrowed from Mexico. You will need to start your piñata several days ahead of time, since it contains paste that must dry.
>
> To make a piñata, you will need:
>
> a large balloon (shape depends on figure you want to create)
> paste
> newspaper (cut into many strips 1½" × 20")
> paint (any kind that will stick to newspaper)
> decorative materials, such as crepe paper, ribbons, sequins
> assorted treats: candy, nuts, miniature party favors, etc.
> a sheet of colored paper to match paint
> transparent tape

Inflate the balloon. Then dip the newspaper strips in the paste and apply them one at a time to the balloon, leaving a small space clear to put in the party treats later. Continue this procedure until you have four or five layers of newspaper strips on the balloon. Set the balloon aside to dry for a day or two.

When the paste has dried completely, paint your creation any color you want. If you like, you can add such materials as crepe paper, ribbons, sequins, and so on, to make the balloon resemble some figure — perhaps a donkey, or a drum, or a football. To finish off the piñata, fill it with assorted treats and patch up the hole with colored paper and tape. Your piñata is now ready to be hung from the ceiling for your fiesta — and to be smashed to bits for all the goodies to fall out, as the high point of your party.

Remember that a process paper must enable its readers to perform the activity it explains. There are ways you can test your process paper to insure this. One way is to go through the process yourself, step by step, following your own directions. With this method you must not let yourself take for granted any essential step that you have not actually included in your paper. Don't just fill in the gaps and move ahead; your reader won't be able to do that. Because filling in the gaps can occur so readily when you read your own writing, you may want to ask someone else to test your directions. Then if what you have written needs clarification, you can attend to that before you write your final draft.

If you are assigned a process paper for a college class, you will want to put some thought into choosing your process. Certain processes are almost impossible to explain in words; how to tie a shoe is an example. Furthermore, some process topics almost inevitably produce dull papers. Shoe-tying no doubt would, and tire-changing often does. One of our students decided to write his process paper about building a doghouse and came to class the following week muttering, "I never thought a doghouse could be so boring!" So it will pay you to try to think about what your process is likely to involve before you settle on your topic.

Formatting: Using Lists, Headings, and Other Visual Devices

Special formats are required for many types of informative writing: project proposals, employee evaluations, lab reports, case studies, and so on. Such formats make the information easily accessible. For example, readers familiar with the format of lab reports know that they will find an abstract (a brief summary of the report) at the beginning and a description of the results of the experiment near the end, before the conclusion and the list of references. Headings for the various sections of the report help readers locate information. A reader interested only in the summary can turn to it quickly, without needing to scan the whole document.

Even if a special format is not required, often you can strengthen a piece of informative writing by using lists, headings, and other visual devices such as charts, graphs, diagrams, and illustrations. Consider, for example, this first draft of a notice to be pinned on the bulletin board in the clubhouse of a retirement community.

> Due to the many requests from our residents seeking more information about the HMO medical plan which we have heard so much about lately, whereby you receive free medical care plus eyeglasses, certain dental work and free prescriptions, your board of directors has contacted the HMO medical center located at 1200 W. Maple Street, Oshkosh, and made arrangements with them to have one of their representatives come to the clubhouse at 7:00 p.m. on Wednesday, August 10, to give us full details of the plan. There will be a question-and-answer period at which time you should feel free to ask any questions pertaining to the above.

Only a committed reader would work through this version, which opens with a sentence eighty-three words long. If there were competing interests in the clubhouse, such as a pool table or a card game or a political discussion group, this announcement would almost certainly be over-looked.

When revised with the use of visual devices, this announcement is easier to read and more likely to be noticed.

> **HMO medical plan to be explained**
> Where: at the clubhouse
> When: Wednesday, August 10, at 7:00 p.m.
>   We have had many requests from our residents for information on the HMO medical plan. This plan provides
>
> 1. free medical care
> 2. eyeglasses
> 3. certain dental work
> 4. free prescriptions

One of the HMO plan's representatives will give us full details about the plan in a half-hour presentation. A question-and-answer period will follow, at which time refreshments will be served.

This revised announcement begins with a headline summarizing the most important information. Then it highlights the time and place of the meeting. Finally, it presents the details of the HMO plan in list form. Notice also that the revision, although shorter than the original, includes additional information of interest to readers: the lecture will be limited to a half hour, and refreshments will be served afterwards.

Exercise 1 For Class Discussion

Below are two informative papers on the same subject. Compare them according to the standards for informative writing discussed in this chapter.

1. Anyone can learn to play pinball. All you need is a good eye, a controlled arm, perseverance in practicing, a pocketful of loose change — and a lot of luck.

   You should approach the magic machine with respect; after all, it does contain all the answers to the riddles posed by its buttons, bumpers, and bells. After you have bowed before it with proper courtesy, pull back the arm — and say a prayer for luck. If you're lucky, your ball will stay in play and away from the flippers for a long time.

   You are bound to score points when you play pinball. But to be really good at it, you will have to "pop" the machine. To learn how to pop, stand and watch what several experienced players do in order to increase their scores; it never hurts to learn from the competition! If you pop regularly enough, you will soon feel that the money you have fed into the maw of this mechanical monster was well spent.

2. Although it looks rather easy, playing pinball well is an art few can master. Not many players can be termed "Pinball Wizards" * — although many lay claim to the title. On the way to becoming a wizard, first you need to understand how to play the game.

   After placing your quarter in the machine, gently pull back on the spring-loaded knob which sends the little steel ball into the playing area. The object is simple enough: to keep the ball in the playing area while scoring as many points as you can by hitting buttons, bumpers, bells, even moving targets. To help keep the ball in play, there are two button-controlled flippers, which flip the ball back into the playing area if it should near one of three or four exit holes. You do not want to let the ball get past a flipper and out of play.

   Scoring points in pinball isn't hard. You will always score at least 1,000 points per ball played, and there are five balls to a game. But

---

* Pinball Wizard: the greatest player of all; the movie *Tommy* was about him.

to become a great player, a master, you will have to consistently "pop" the pinball machine. Popping the machine means scoring beyond the point total needed to get a free game. This range is usually between 64,000 and 151,000 total points, depending on the machine. While even a good player may score 12,000 to 15,000 points per ball, to pop the more popular machines you would need at least 20,000 to 25,000 points per ball. Only one player out of 1,000 can accomplish this with regularity. And only that one can proclaim himself or herself a Pinball Wizard.

Exercise 2 Written

Write an informative essay (not one explaining a process) about something that at least some people in your class do not already know about. Bring your rough draft for uninformed persons to read. Is the draft complete and clear enough to satisfy your test readers? Is it accurate enough to satisfy you?

Exercise 3 Class Activity

First select a process that you can demonstrate or explain to the class in five minutes. You may wish to use objects, charts, pictures, or other props to illustrate your topic; if your demonstration requires another person, ask a classmate to participate. Some possible topics are listed below:

tuning a guitar	putting on scuba gear
riding a unicycle	flipping an attacker
quilting	sculpting or carving
decorating a cake	giving a ticket to a motorist
selling a used car	repairing a bicycle
arranging flowers	taking blood pressure

When choosing a topic, please remember the safety and well-being of your classmates and instructor. Demonstrations requiring the use of alcohol (mixing a favorite drink), firearms (cleaning a shotgun), or any other explosive, harmful, or illegal substances are completely out of place.

After selecting a topic, write a rough draft of a 350- to 500-word essay in which you explain step by step how to perform the process.

As part of your prewriting, practice the activity at home or at the dorm, noting each important step so that you will not leave out an essential part of the process.

In class, working from your rough draft, give a five-minute demonstration of the process. Strive for a well-organized, informative, enthusiastic, and possibly humorous presentation.

During and after your demonstration, make note of the audience response — questions, chuckles, looks of bewilderment, or knowing smiles and nods. What part of the process needs clarification or elaboration? Which explanations worked especially well? Based on this "field-testing" of your paper before a live audience, revise the draft. Hand in your final draft.

Exercise 4   For Discussion in Small Groups

Working in small groups, discuss the following draft of an essay by one of our students, Pat Napolitano. Pretend that Napolitano is a classmate who has come to your group for advice about the format of her essay. Where in her essay might she use a format other than traditional paragraphing? After your discussion, turn to Napolitano's own revision (pages 287–293) and compare it with your suggestion.

"Popsicle"

It makes me laugh when you say that we "spoil" Chris because she's handicapped — that we give her whatever she wants. Let me tell you what the procedure is in teaching a three-year-old deaf child one word.

One of the tools you'll need is a small table and chairs set so that the child can get up and down easily. Children generally are unable to sit still for long periods of time and get frustrated if they have difficulty climbing up and down when they need a break. Deaf children have a particular problem here since they do not expend the energy the rest of us do in talking.

Another necessary tool is a set of 3 X 5 cards containing pictures of the words that Chris has already mastered, such as pictures of her mom, dad, sister, a cat, and a dog. The other tools you will need are a lot of patience and a ready smile. Since deaf children cannot hear the tone of your voice, they "listen" to your expression and depend on your pleased response for reinforcement.

Okay, you're ready to start the warm-up exercises. Sit in one of the little chairs across from Chris. Show her each picture whose word she has already mastered; praise her when she says the word.

Now you're ready for the new word -- "popsicle." First, show her the picture of the popsicle and say "pop-sicle" slowly and distinctly. Next, hold the palm of her hand in front of your mouth and say "pah, pah" (so she can feel the puffs of air from the "p" sounds). Repeat this until she's mastered "pop."

Again hold her hand in front of your mouth while you make an exaggerated "s" sound. She must see how your teeth are positioned and feel that the "ssss" produces air from your mouth. For the "c" sound, place one of her hands in front of your mouth so she can feel the air. Place her other hand on your throat so she can feel the sound you make. Show her how to place her tongue on the roof of her mouth to get the hard "c" effect. Repeat all of this until she's mastered "kah."

Now practice the "s-c" sounds together, "sica," using the same methods as used for doing the sounds individually. Finally, show Chris how you roll your tongue to get the "l" sound. Hold your hand against your throat so that she feels the sound.

Now you're ready to put it all together. Show her the picture of the popsicle, place her hand on your throat, and say "pop-si-cul," exaggerating every syllable.

You may not get through all ten steps in one day. If she gets tired, push her further than she wants to go, but not to the point where she's frustrated. Or to the point where you're frustrated either. For if you aren't happy and smiling, you'll lose her for sure.

When at last she mastered the word "popsicle," give her a popsicle. After you've both gone through "popsicle" every day for two or three weeks, every time Chris says "popsicle" you will both want to celebrate the victory. What better way to let her know she's got the idea than by giving her a popsicle?

Imagine this process with every word Chris learns, and maybe you'll understand why we tend to give her everything she asks for. Everything she asks for is to be celebrated.

Pat Napolitano

16 Arguing a Point

We never fully grasp the import of any true statement until we have a clear notion of what the opposite untrue statement would be.

— WILLIAM JAMES

For a class in historic preservation, you have been asked to draft a letter to the city council protesting the proposed demolition of an Art Deco theater in your neighborhood. Or you are planning to write a letter to the editor of your local newspaper complaining about the newspaper's biased coverage of the candidate you are supporting for governor. Or you have learned that the required "great books" seminar on campus fails to include any works by women or minorities, and you wish to register your protest in the campus newspaper.

Each of these situations calls for argumentative writing. You are doing argumentative writing whenever you are attempting to prove a point or to justify a point of view on some controversial issue.

In argumentative writing, you should assume that your readers do not already agree with you. If you have asserted that the Chicago Cubs are headed for a pennant victory, aim your essay at Yankee fans who think the Cubs don't stand a chance. Or if you have claimed that alimony should not be awarded except in rare, isolated cases, pitch your argument to readers who believe just the opposite. Imagining a tough, skeptical audience — readers from Missouri who say "Show me" — will force you to write a more powerful argument. With a skeptical group of readers in mind, you will include a great deal of evidence in support of your point. And your paper will be the better for it, even for readers who aren't quite so hard to convince.

Setting Ground Rules

Arguments, like games, proceed better if certain ground rules are set up, so the participants know what counts as fair play. As a writer you have a certain advantage: Since you're the only participant present, you get to make the rules.

If you're planning to argue in favor of the Supreme Court decision outlawing prayer in public schools, for example, you can decide on the precise issues to address and on the type of evidence that will count in the argument. Usually you will make your ground rules clear in your opening paragraph, and especially in your thesis, as this student has done:

> Although the Supreme Court has ruled against prayer in public schools on First Amendment grounds, many people still feel that prayers should be allowed. These people, most of whom hold strong religious beliefs, are well-intentioned. What they fail to realize is that the Supreme Court decision, although it was made on legal grounds, makes good sense on religious grounds as well. Prayer is too important to be trusted to our public schools.

Notice that as the student has drawn it, the issue has little to do with the legal decision of the Supreme Court. Arguments over the wisdom of the Court's decision are put firmly outside the scope of this paper. Notice also that arguments concerning the value of prayer are swept outside the scope of the paper. The writer assumes that both he and his audience consider prayer important. Once these issues have been eliminated, we are left with the student's chosen issue, as stated in his thesis: *Prayer is too important to be trusted to our public schools.* The paper will argue this point alone, and the only evidence that the writer will allow into the discussion will be that which bears on this point.

Selecting Evidence

Once you've set the ground rules, you're ready to decide what kinds of proof are admissible in your argument. The student who wrote about school prayer decided that the following kinds of evidence would help him prove his point even to skeptical readers:

1. Evidence showing that public school teachers are often unqualified to lead students in prayer, and that ministers, priests, rabbis, and concerned parents are more qualified.
2. Evidence showing that school is a poor environment for prayer (the writer remembered from his childhood, for example, that students had thrown spitwads and fights had broken out during school prayers) and that churches, homes, and quiet, solitary places such as forests or lakesides are much more appropriate environments.
3. Evidence showing that school prayers are often so homogenized to avoid offending anyone that they are really not prayers at all.

In deciding on this evidence, the writer thought seriously about the *opposite* of his thesis: Prayer is too important to *leave out of our public schools.* The people who believe this, he surmised, must feel that (1) public school teachers are qualified to lead students in prayer; (2) school is an appropriate environment for prayer; and (3) school prayers are meaningful enough to deserve the label "prayer." The writer's job, then, was to show these readers that they were mistaken on all three counts. If he could do this, the writer felt, his readers might change their minds on the subject.

Changing people's minds on controversial subjects is not easy. As philosopher George Santayana put it, "People are usually more firmly convinced that their opinions are precious than that they are true." And as one novelist confided, in a moment of truthfulness, "I'll not listen to reason. . . . Reason always means what someone else has got to say." Thus, to get readers to give up their precious opinions is quite an accomplishment. If you don't at least try to look at your issue through the eyes of skeptical readers, you're not very likely to convince them.

Considering the Other Side

Let readers know you've looked at both sides of your issue, but in considering the other side, be careful not to allow opposing arguments to persuade readers. Instead of just presenting these arguments, do your best to disprove them. One student writer, for example, as he argued in favor of girls' participation in Little League baseball, confronted the opposing arguments directly:

> Along comes the traditionalist who announces that such athletic com-
> petition will cause unnatural muscular development in girls. This belief
> is unfounded. Girls have been playing softball in physical education classes
> for a long time, and they have always looked pretty good to me. Little
> League baseball provides girls with an excellent opportunity to develop
> strong, healthy, attractive bodies.
>
> One of the loudest arguments against boys and girls playing ball is
> risk of injury. But girls are no more susceptible to injury than boys.
> Moreover, baseball is essentially a noncontact sport. You must remember
> that we are talking about baseball, not football or field hockey.
>
> Recently I heard the most absurd argument of them all. A father stated
> during a news interview that he didn't want his daughter playing organized
> sports with boys for fear of having his little girl groped. Either the man
> is sick or he has never played any sport. In the heat of competition, the
> last thing on anybody's mind is a free feel. How would that look at
> second base?

These paragraphs leave most readers feeling that the traditionalists' arguments are misdirected, even absurd. Though we have been exposed to them, we are not convinced by them.

Another student, writing the first draft of an argumentative paper, was not quite so skillful. As you read her opening paragraphs, notice how dangerously close she has come in the second paragraph to asserting the opposite of her thesis.

> Abortion has always been a controversial issue in our society. The Catholic Church takes a firm stand against abortion because it sees it as murder. As a Catholic, I have to disagree with the Church. I feel that abortion should continue to be legalized — for the sake of the unborn child.
>
> Opponents of abortion have shown that by the time most abortions are performed, the fetus has the exact physical appearance of an infant. Therefore, destroying the fetus is the same as murdering a child. This is a good point to make. It would convince most people against abortion if it was the only thing considered. However, a more important aspect to consider is the kind of life the child would live if it were born rather than aborted.

The writer seems to be agreeing with those who believe abortion is murder, since she calls this view "a good point to make." But if she agrees with this point, how then can she argue in favor of abortion?

In fact, the writer did not believe that abortion is murder. She had simply presented this argument in an effort to be fair. Once she realized that her paragraph swayed readers in the wrong direction, she had to make a decision. Either she had to argue that abortion is not murder, or she had to sweep that issue outside the scope of her argument. As it turned out, she chose the latter approach, since the point she really wanted to make was that unwanted children are often neglected and abused. (The writer worked in an emergency room and saw all too many examples of child abuse.) The murder issue, she felt, was so complicated that it would take most of her paper to deal with it, thus pulling the reader's attention away from the point she actually wanted to press. In putting this issue outside the scope of her argument, the writer was of course giving up on the attempt to change the minds of those who truly believe that abortion is murder. Instead, she was directing her paper at readers she felt might be brought to her point of view.

Avoiding Fallacies

In any college community, writers are assumed to be in search of the truth. It is bad form, therefore, to load arguments emotionally, to fabricate links between ideas, or to ignore evidence. In other words, unfair or misguided argumentative tactics, sometimes called "fallacies," should be avoided. Some common fallacies are detailed below.

Hasty Generalization.   A hasty generalization, as the name suggests, is a claim made too hastily, on the basis of too little evidence. For example, you should not argue that marriage is essential for raising emotionally healthy children if your only evidence is that all of the single parents you know have disturbed children. Your own acquaintances are far too small a sample on which to justify such a sweeping claim.

To avoid hasty generalizations, be especially alert to unqualified statements. Such statements often contain words such as *always, never, all,* and *everyone.* Sentences with these words in them are quite likely to be untrue because there are exceptions to almost every possible situation.

Faulty Cause–and–Effect Reasoning.   The fact that two events occur in sequence does not necessarily indicate that the second results from the first. Let's say that I work in a hospital emergency room, where I see many children with concussions, broken limbs, and deep burns. Since it is well known that some of these "accidents" are actually cases of child abuse, I decide to write an essay arguing for more careful investigation of suspected child abuse.

I know that in one week my emergency room treats an average of ten accidents involving children from the inner city, where unemployment is high and much borderline poverty exists, and only two from the more affluent suburbs to the northwest. However, I cannot automatically assume that unemployment and poverty create more child abuse. I cannot use those two factors alone to argue that the most intensive investigation should be conducted in the inner city. I must take into account other possible factors. Perhaps most of the abused children in the suburbs are taken to other hospitals; perhaps the level of child abuse inflicted on suburban children does not as often reach emergency proportions; perhaps most of the cases reported as accidents in the inner city really *were* accidents, the inner city being a more dangerous place to live. I must consider all possible contributing factors before I try to analyze the cause of a particular effect — in this instance, child abuse.

Arguing in a Circle.   This fallacy occurs when a writer merely restates in the second half of a sentence what he or she has already said in the first half. The statement reads as if the second half is proof of the first half, when actually the statement simply circles back on itself.

For example, let's assume you have found a nursery school you want to recommend to other mothers and fathers who need care for their children while they attend classes. You write: "The days at Derry Dale

Nursery School are pleasant for the children because they have a good time from the moment they arrive until they are picked up." But then you notice that the second half of your sentence does not really expand upon the first half; it merely repeats it. To avoid arguing in a circle, you'll need some specific details to support your point that "the days at Derry Dale Nursery School are pleasant for the children." Such details might include, for example, the high level of individual attention the school provides, the variety of stimulating board games and puzzles, the challenging but safe outdoor play equipment, and the well-balanced lunches that include a special treat every day.

Name-calling. Writers who engage in name-calling are arguing against a person instead of arguing the point: "Don't listen to Amy Stein when she supports Planned Parenthood. She doesn't have any children, and besides, she's been divorced twice." This argument implies that Amy Stein's childlessness and two divorces automatically disqualify her as a supporter of Planned Parenthood. She may in fact be a thoughtful advocate of careful family planning.

Emotionally Loaded Language. Writers and speakers frequently avoid the argument at hand by resorting to emotionally loaded words and labels: "The federal government should not fund attempts to rehabilitate street drunks. Those bums are repulsive, filthy characters who should be put away for good instead of being allowed out on the street." Labeling all public alcoholics "street drunks" and "bums" and describing them as "repulsive, filthy characters" is more likely to alienate thoughtful readers than to win them over.

Audiences are sometimes swayed by fallacies, we must admit. But among writers and readers interested in the truth, fallacies have no place. Truth, after all, is hard enough to come by. As Emerson has defined it, truth is "such a fly-away, such a sly-boots, so untranslatable and unbarrelable a commodity, that it is as bad to catch as light." Fallacies should be avoided, then, because they push this precious commodity beyond our reach.

Exercise 1 *For Class Discussion*

Assume that you are going to write an argument in support of at least three of the following statements. Make a list of the points you would use to support each statement you select.

1. Because our society is coming to depend more and more on computers, no one can be considered educated today without basic computer literacy.

2. A week of camping in close quarters with at least two other people is a good way to test one's adaptability.

3. Even in a country that stands for freedom of expression, as does the United States, violent scenes should not be allowed on television during the family viewing hours.

4. Because a sensible diet is basic to good health — both physical and mental — one should plan his or her life so as to be able to eat well every day.

5. There are times when a person should be allowed to die — times, indeed, when one should be helped to die.

6. A fine arts course — in art, music, or theater, for example — is an important part of anyone's higher education and should be required in all curricula.

7. Working parents cannot adequately attend to the needs of their children; unless basic survival depends on both parents' holding jobs, one or the other should remain at home to be available to the children.

8. A job lifeguarding for a community pool is not as pleasant a way to spend a summer as some people may think.

9. Human beings need the kind of belief system and sense of community they can find in organized religion; therefore people need to belong to an established church or synagogue.

10. Although our college's program of developmental activities for handicapped children serves a limited population, the county should be fully funding the program. The parents of these children should not have to assume the added burden of paying for this special training.

Exercise 2   Written

Select a local, state, or national issue that needs to be addressed, such as one of those on the list below. Choose an issue that you feel strongly about and then narrow your focus to an argument that can be handled in 500 to 700 words. For example, instead of writing in general about group homes for troubled adolescents, argue for or against establishing such a home in your neighborhood. Or instead of writing about sex education in general, argue for or against the sex education course currently required in your local high school. Aim your essay at readers who do not already agree with your position on the issue.

drug abuse
gun control
air or water pollution
smoking on airplanes
racism
sexism
ageism
automobile safety

penalties for drunk driving
the drinking age
the cost of automobile insurance
    for young males
the homeless
sex education
the proposed demolition of a
    historic building

Exercise 3 *For Class Discussion*

Each item below contains one of the following fallacies: (a) hasty generalization, (b) faulty cause-and-effect reasoning, (c) arguing in a circle, (d) name-calling, or (e) emotionally loaded language. Mark each item with a letter from this list to identify the fallacy, and come to class prepared to discuss the flaws in the arguments.

1. The law requiring motorcyclists to wear helmets should be reinstated, despite the arguments of cyclists for freedom of choice. Last year fifty riders died following accidents.

2. That ore is ancient because it is carbon-dated 1200 B.C.

3. The reason ferns are not easy to grow is that they are difficult to care for.

4. Welfare mothers should be sterilized as soon as they have borne two children. I don't want my tax money used to support careless breeding by such loose women.

5. Unless the preparation of secondary-school teachers improves radically, nationwide test scores on the verbal skills of high-school students will continue to decline.

6. If you are an American citizen sixty-five or over, retirement holds little promise of pleasure for you unless you can afford to live in a retirement colony in Florida.

7. Those baby killers just don't appreciate the sweet joys of motherhood.

8. The chemicals buried by the government at Brown's Corner, Texas, have caused a wave of cancer in that town: Among fifteen families on one street, six women have had breast cancer, and two other people are suffering from bladder and throat cancer.

9. Everybody should exercise fairly vigorously each day.

10. Luther Wayne should not be allowed to coach the Little League because he drinks more than he should at political fund-raisers.

Part Five

Student Essays

17 Revision Strategies: Twelve Student Essays in Progress

This chapter highlights twelve different revision strategies by displaying actual student drafts as marked up by the students themselves. Here is a list of the revision strategies, along with the names of the students and the titles of their essays.

Adjusting the Voice: "Euthanasia for Animals," by Joan Bradley
Changing the Point of View: "Population Explosion," by Sharon Wultich
Improving the Focus: "Hollywood Trucking," by Daniel MacFarland
Strengthening the Content: "Irish vs. American Education," by Margaret Stack
Clarifying the Organization: "Time Out," by Judith Burgin
Reparagraphing: "Learning to Decide," by Ethel Ramsey
Improving Coherence: "Working the Water," by Kirk Brimmer
Introducing Variety: "Who Goes to the Races?" by Tom Weitzel
Pruning Excess Words: "A Dangerous State of Mind," by H. C. McKenzie
Refining the Style: "Journey Under Water," by John Curley
Quickening the Pace: "Fish Story," by Melvin White
Changing the Format: "'Popsicle,'" by Pat Napolitano

Although most of these students took their essays through several drafts, we are printing only one marked-up version of each essay. Because we want to focus on one revision strategy at a time, we have idealized the students' revisions to some extent. For example, Joan Bradley, the author of "Euthanasia for Animals," polished, edited, and proofread her essay *after* making the revisions you will see in her essay. However, to keep your focus on the revision strategy being illustrated — adjusting the voice of the essay — we have presented a somewhat cleaned-up version of her draft.

For the most part, the revisions, although idealized, are very close to the revisions the students actually made. In a few cases, however, we have added a flaw or two to a student's original draft, simply for our own teaching purposes. We are grateful to our students for giving us permission to use their drafts in progress in this way.

Adjusting the Voice

"Euthanasia for Animals," by Joan Bradley

1. Bradley's voice sounds more confident without the hedging phrases "I feel that" and "I feel." The revision is also more straightforward and emphatic than the original.

2. The description of the process of euthanasia has greater impact when it is not interrupted by sentences describing Bradley's personal feelings. In her revision, Bradley adopts a colder, more objective voice appropriate for this rather chilling technical description.

1

Euthanasia for Animals

Euthanasia, the process of helping an animal die by administering certain drugs, is legal and accepted in the veterinary profession. *But it is still* ~~It is also~~ the hardest part of my job as a technician in an animal hospital. Sometimes ~~I feel that~~ it is justifiable to put an animal to sleep because the creature is suffering and needs to be put out of misery, but at other times *euthanasia* ~~I feel it~~ is a waste of an animal's life.

An animal brought to the hospital to be put to sleep is called an "E and D" patient. "E and D" means "euthanasia and disposal." ~~This is the most difficult task I must perform.~~ *Euthanasia* It ~~It~~ is done by injecting the drug T-61 into the animal, ~~It is~~ usually ~~put~~ directly into the vein. ~~I am not a professionally trained technician, but I was taught how to inject drugs into the vein of an animal. It isn't easy, so sometimes I would get out of administering the drug by claiming I couldn't do it. Putting an animal to sleep is a very hard thing for me to do, and it took a long time for me to get used to it. The process is done~~ *The animal's is tied* ~~by tying the~~ foreleg off above the elbow with a tourni-

1

2

3. Bradley moved this sentence because she felt it worked well as a transition between the objective, impersonal tone of the technical description and the more emotional tone of the paragraph's conclusion.

4. The editorial comment about veterinarians interrupts the sad tale of Trixie. Although she liked the sentence, Bradley decided that the paragraph was stronger without it.

2

quet. The fur is wetted down with a moist cotton ball and
the needle is inserted. ~~The~~ *as the* tourniquet is ~~then~~ loosened,
~~and~~ the drug is injected. I was surprised to find that
animals don't close their eyes and look peacefully asleep
when they die. Cats and small dogs have very small veins
which are hard to find, so T-61 is injected directly into
the chest cavity. This is easier for the technician but
harder for the animal because it takes longer for the drug
to take effect. ~~and to go through the body~~. I often wonder
what the animal feels; ~~and~~ sometimes I have nightmares of
a burning sensation going throughout my body, with animals
all around me asking, "Why?"

Animals are put to sleep for many different reasons.
~~As I mentioned~~ some ~~are~~ justifiable, ~~and~~ some ~~are~~ not. A
good example of justifiable euthanasia is *the case of* Trixie. ~~She was~~
a thirteen-year-old fox terrier who began to feel her age,
which would have been the equivalent of ninety-one in a
human. Her owners wanted to do all that was possible to
keep her alive, but each day she became weaker. Soon she
gave up eating and drinking and waited painfully for her
time to come. There was nothing anyone could do for
Trixie. ~~Veterinarians can cure sickness but cannot~~

3

4

5. Referring to the person who had abandoned the puppies as "some idiot" is too intemperate and too casual for a subject deserving a more dignified approach. By substituting the phrase "a cruel person," Bradley projects a more reasonable image of herself to the reader.

6. The "I believe" phrase is not necessary, and it makes Bradley sound a bit apologetic, as if her conclusion were based only on opinion, not on a reasoned judgment. In the revision, Bradley sounds more confident.

7. The revision tones down the emotional language of the original. Bradley decided that the specific examples in the paragraph would be taken more seriously if they were not preceded by a judgmental outburst.

8. The original transition, while it might be appropriate in spoken English, is too casual for written English. The revision helps readers move smoothly from one example to the next.

3

~~restore youth.~~ Instead of watching ^*his beloved pet* ~~Trixie~~ suffer, the

owner brought her to the hospital for euthanasia.

Another example was the litter of three puppies that   5

a cruel person
^~~some idiot~~ had abandoned in a burlap sack along a road-

side. After the sack had been struck by a car, a passerby

found the puppies and brought them to the hospital. One

puppy was in shock, one had a broken pelvis, and the other

had serious internal injuries. They were going through

too much pain and suffering, so each puppy was euthanized.

~~I believe these two examples are justifiable because~~ ^T ~~T~~hese   6

animals were better off being put to sleep than being

allowed to suffer.
      Many times, though, I am asked to perform
~~Some humans are pig-headed and cruel. Those people~~   7
unnecessary euthanasia. For example,
~~who have their pets put to sleep for selfish reasons are~~

~~examples of unjust euthanasia.~~ Ms. Olsen brought two

beautiful cats to the hospital to be euthanized -- an

adult blue point Siamese that someone had given her and a

young healthy black cat. When asked why, she replied,

"I've just bought a new beige carpet for my living room

and these cats are constantly shedding hair on it." ~~And~~   8
               Another   *Ms. Ford,*
~~then there was the~~^ woman, ~~who~~ wanted her beagle put to

sleep because she was moving and couldn't find a suitable

home for it. By coincidence a man came in at the same

9. Here again, Bradley decided that her original tone was too judgmental. She also decided to remove an unnecessary comment on her own feelings.

10. The original conclusion rambles from one idea to another, in an almost stream-of-consciousness fashion.

4

time who just happened to be looking for a beagle. ~~He was~~
~~looking for one~~ to train ~~into~~ *as* a hunting dog. ~~to add to the~~
~~few he already had~~. When I tried to arrange for him to
take the dog, the woman refused, saying that she didn't
want her dog to be trained to hunt. Because of her feelings about hunting, this ~~silly~~ woman ~~was actually willing~~
deprived *long and happy life.*
~~to deprive~~ her dog of a ~~good long, happy life. These~~   9
~~examples of euthanasia are the hardest for me to perform~~
~~because the animal seems to know that it hasn't had a full~~
~~life and fights the euthanasia.~~

Whenever I must euthanize an animal, I tell myself
that it is part of my job and that I must do it, no matter
what the reason. I certainly can't save them all or give
them homes. ~~But I can't help wondering who or what can~~
~~give the right to me to do this. I can see where it is~~
~~needed in some cases, but why not then in people? If~~   10
~~euthanasia was allowed with people, perfectly healthy~~
~~people wouldn't be put to sleep, so why are perfectly~~
~~healthy animals allowed to be? My point is that euthanasia~~
~~on animals should have restrictions. I do it as part of~~
~~my job, then try to forget it, but the look in an animal's~~

11. The revised conclusion, which preserves the first two sentences of the original and half of its final sentence, makes a personal rather than a political statement. Since the essay as a whole does not support a political approach to her topic, Bradley decided that an honest assessment of her own feelings would be a more appropriate conclusion.

Note: For more about the voice of an essay, see Chapter 4, "Finding a Voice," and Chapter 5, "Choosing Appropriate Language."

5

unclosed eye and the nightmares will be impossible to
forget. I harden myself just like the
veterinarians and the other technicians do,
pretending not to think about it and making
jokes. I try to forget. But the look in an
animal's unclosed eyes and the unpleasant
dreams are hard to forget.

11

                                        Joan Bradley

Changing the Point of View

"Population Explosion," by Sharon Wultich

1. Wultich attempted to write her original draft from the third-person singular point of view (*"Anyone* wishing to start an aquarium"), but she had difficulty maintaining this perspective. In the opening paragraph, for example, her rough draft shifts to the third-person plural (*"They* may return") and then to the second-person point of view (*"your* bathtub and *your* kitchen sink").

   Wultich decided that the "you" point of view would lead to a livelier essay than the more distant third-person perspective. By pretending that her readers were interested in stocking their aquariums with live-bearing fish, Wultich could write conversationally, asking an occasional question, for example. Given the humorous nature of her subject, an informal, conversational approach seemed appropriate.

2. In the original draft of her second paragraph, Wultich maintains a consistent point of view, but she achieves that consistency by using sexist English, which offends many readers: "The prospective buyer . . . his . . . the buyer . . . he." Although Wultich might have eliminated the sexist English by using the phrases "his or her" and "he or she," the sentences would have become word heavy. Once she decided to rewrite the essay from the "you" point of view, the problem of sexist English disappeared.

1

Population Explosion

You wish

~~Anyone wishing~~ to start an aquarium of live-bearing

Let me tell you

fish? ~~needs to be aware of~~ how prolific fish such as black

You

mollies, guppies, sunsets, and swordtails can be. ~~They~~

may return from the pet shop with a pair of these fish

only to wake up the next morning and find thirty new

arrivals squirming through the filter's air bubbles. Soon

these newcomers grow and contribute to the mass production

of live-bearing fish that knows no forty-hour work week.

They will fill your bathtub and your kitchen sink; and the

sewers of this country must know plenty of their cousins.

You say that you'll

~~The prospective buyer may think that he'll~~ just buy

one, or all of the same sex;? That logical solution is

your

struck down when ~~his~~ single, but once impregnated female

mollie has three broods of fifty fish, each without a

father in sight; she left him back at the pet shop. Once

a live-bearer is pregnant, she may seem to be so continu-

you do

ously. If ~~the buyer does~~ find a group of nonpregnant

don't

females, ~~he shouldn't~~ be surprised if within a week a few

have changed their sex. Why not have all male fish?

Because they will chase each other in dizzying circles,

1

2

3. Although the word "you" does not appear in the opening sentences of this revision, it is understood: "Don't despair" means "You shouldn't despair," and "Supply" means "You can supply." The subject "you" is understood in imperative sentences, those offering advice or issuing commands.

4. Notice that throughout this essay, "you" refers to "you, the reader." It does not mean "you, anyone in general." The "you" point of view is appropriate when used to address readers directly, but many English teachers and usage experts discourage indefinite uses of "you." The accepted indefinite pronoun in English is "one," even though this word, commonly used in Great Britain, often sounds stilted in American English.

Note: For more about the point of view of an essay, see Chapter 4, "Finding a Voice."

2

getting so confused that they will eventually commit the

ultimate in aquatic suicide -- and jump out of the tank.
But don't despair, red velvet swordtail 3
~~Fans of the velvet swordtail should not despair,~~
fans,
~~however,~~ because I have found the solution to the
Supply your
underwater population explosion. ∧ ~~The tank can be supplied~~

with two or three large angel fish, who will delight in a
If you do
feast of newborn swordtails. ∧ ~~Those who~~ decide to raise a

few live-bearing offspring in the same tank ∧ ~~can~~ plop a few

plants on the surface for their protection. ~~Anyone who~~
On if you decide
~~decides~~ ∧ to become a really serious breeder, ∧ ~~should~~ set up

separate maternity tanks for the expectant mothers. There

will be plenty of future occupants waiting in line. 4

Plenty.

Sharon Wultich

Improving the Focus

"Hollywood Trucking," by Daniel MacFarland

1. Although it could be argued that the original version of the introduction is more dramatic, the revision is certainly clearer. MacFarland added a thesis statement to let readers know the point of his essay.

2. When the original first sentence of this paragraph is read as a topic sentence, the rest of the paragraph seems to be off the point. MacFarland's added topic sentence is broad enough to prepare readers for the whole paragraph.

3. MacFarland revised this sentence to keep the focus on the truckers. Without the revision, the paragraph seems to be straying from the point.

1

Hollywood Trucking

A beautiful new tractor and trailer rig comes barrel-
ing up the highway, heat waves shimmering on the road. A
small red convertible is in the way. The horn blares, the
girl smiles, and the movie begins. *We enter the* **1**
glamorous world of Hollywood trucking,
a world that is a far cry from
reality.

Perhaps Hollywood's greatest misconception surrounding the trucker concerns the CB radio, that magic box that
tells the drivers where the bears are hiding. Using the
CB, Burt Reynolds and Jerry Reed avoided Sheriff Jackie
Gleason throughout Smokey and the Bandit. The Rubber Duck
was able to hold together one thousand trucks which toured
the country in song and movie, recklessly breaking toll
gates and speed limits galore.

In reality the CB is used constructively **2**
more than it is used to evade the law.

(Real-life truckers use CB's to find parts, equipment, **3**
Truckers often tune in to
food, lodging, and whatever else they may need.∧ Channel
9, an emergency channel reserved for emergency transmis-

4. The added topic sentence acts as a transition between major chunks of text: the two paragraphs about the CB radio and the two paragraphs about the trucks. Notice that the new topic sentence contains the words "misconception" and "distortion," which remind readers of the main point of the essay.

5. The added topic sentence echoes the main point of the essay: that trucking movies do not depict reality.

2

sions only, is monitored by a national organization called
REACT. Many times a trucker has been the first to respond
to an emergency call. But is this service shown in the
movies?

The misconception about the use of the CB is not the only distortion of trucking in films.)

4

(Did you ever notice the type of tractor and trailer
rigs the stars drive? Their brand new trucks are equipped
with every chrome ornament available —— chrome gas tanks,
chrome exhaust stacks, even chrome wheel lugs. The paint
is clean, bright, and unscratched. As for the trailers,
there's not a hint of road dirt on the mudflaps. All in
all, the rigs are spotless, with no dust on the wind-
shield, no bugs on the grill, not even exhaust deposits on
the trailer. And who owns these rigs? Why, the driver,
of course.

The silver screen, however, is not life.)

5

(Most rigs, ~~however~~ are company owned or leased. The
few privately owned rigs actually belong to the banks.
The trucks are often dirty, with dull paint and bent bumpers, and little or no chrome. In the movies, if a tractor

6. Again, the new topic sentence acts as a transition between major chunks of text. We have read about two distortions and are about to learn of a third: the image of the driver.

7. The word "wrong" is not as accurate as "distorted." Also, by echoing one of the essay's key words, "distortion," MacFarland ends his essay right on focus.

Note: For more about focusing an essay, see Chapter 6, "Focusing on a Point." See also Chapters 8 and 9 on organization and paragraphing.

3

breaks down, a tow truck is called and a genuine mechanic works on it. In real life, nine times out of ten the driver is also the mechanic.

Perhaps the greatest distortion on the screen is the image of the driver.)

6

(Many people believe, thanks to Hollywood, that a truck driver is a young, free-wheeling, single guy who is good-looking enough to pick up a beauty queen within minutes of hitting the asphalt. But most drivers are actually middle-aged and attached to a family. If the driver is lucky enough to own a rig, he (or she) also owns a house, a station wagon, and a dog.

Trucking is a vital form of commercial transportation. But it's dull. To make it sell, producers had to create an appealing image, dispelling the loneliness of the long haul. So the screen trucker was born. Although the image may be attractive, it's ~~wrong~~. *distorted.*

7

Daniel MacFarland

Strengthening the Content

"Irish vs. American Education," by Margaret Stack

1. The original two-sentence paragraph only begins to describe the atmosphere of the convent. Before coming up with the details included in her revision, Stack spent five minutes brainstorming ideas on scratch paper. Her memory of the slippers led her to recall the other details.

1

Irish vs. American Education

During my junior year of high school, my family moved from a suburban American community to a small village in rural Ireland. The change was pleasant once we got over the initial cultural shock, and we learned a great deal from the visit. My biggest discoveries came from being enrolled in the local convent, a school that was very different from my old high school. The difference lay not in the subjects that were taught, but rather in the way they were taught and the surroundings and atmosphere they were taught in.

In contrast to my ordinary brick high school, the convent was a Gothic mansion with tall, narrow windows and doors, vaulted ceilings, and endless, winding corridors. To run or yell in a hallway was unthinkable. *Included in the school uniforms were soft slippers that wouldn't mar the marble floors or teak staircases. Not only were our steps hushed, but the gloomy, ancient decor intimidated us into speaking in whispers when walking along passageways.*

Unlike its American counterpart, the convent was

2. Instead of the generalizations and abstractions of the original, Stack's revision presents readers with specific details: one stove and seven sinks, one record player, and a tape recorder dating from World War II.

3. Although the contrast between *Love Story* and *War and Peace* is dramatic even by itself, Stack felt she should back it up with further details, to let readers know that this was not an isolated instance.

2

badly heated and had almost none of the educational facil-

ities or equipment believed necessary in America. There

was no cafeteria or food service. There were no science

labs (although one day my biology teacher did bring in a

dead frog and dissect it for us). The home economics de-

                    consisted of one stove and seven sinks.

partment ~~was equipped with only the bare necessities.~~
          ^

There was no library, really, just a box of paperback

                                              There

books that the English teacher let us borrow from. ~~In~~

was one record player for the entire school and a

~~contrast, just think of the many facilities in almost any~~

tape recorder that dated from World War II.

~~high school in America.~~

    Strangely enough, instead of being academically infe-

rior to my American high school, the Irish convent was

superior. In my class at home, <u>Love Story</u> was considered

pretty heavy reading, so imagine my surprise at finding

Irish students who could recite passages from <u>War and</u>

<u>Peace</u>. In high school, I didn't even begin algebra until

the ninth grade, while at the convent seventh graders (or

their Irish equivalent) were doing calculus and

trigonometry. *In high school we complained about*

having to study <u>*Romeo and Juliet*</u> *in one semester,*

whereas in Ireland we simultaneously studied

<u>*Macbeth*</u> *and Dicken's* <u>*Hard Times*</u>*, in addition*

to writing a composition a day in English class.

2

3

4. The original paragraph is too skimpy to suggest the truth of its topic sentence or its clincher sentence. The added sentence gives the paragraph more substance.

5. Stack felt that her rhetorical question and personal comment at the end of this paragraph were distracting, so she deleted these two sentences.

3

Not that the Irish were completely superior in educational standards. Many of the students at the convent had
never even heard of chemistry, much less sex education.

4

The average Irish student seemed to have a firm knowledge
of the classics but was out of touch with the world of
today. *They knew by heart the exploits of Cuchulain (a legendary Irish warrior) but knew nothing of Freud or Marx or any religion but their own.*

The main reason for this contrast may be the way the
classes were taught. In America the teacher is usually
approachable, and his or her teaching style is informal.
Disruption and disorder are normal. The students feel
relaxed, and very often daily life is discussed, ranging
anywhere from politics to personal problems, even at the
risk of wasting time. ~~Why are American teachers so willing to let students get them off the point? The nuns at
the convent would be shocked.~~

5

At the convent there was no disruption, no disorder,
no wasted time. Classes ran smoothly and on a tight
schedule. Unfortunately, this made for dull, regimented
We stood when asked questions and fired off the answer, never asking
classes where tension ran very high. ∧ ~~We never asked ques-~~

6. An additional detail makes Stack's description of the "dull, regimented classes" more vivid.

Note: For more about the content of an essay, see Chapter 7, "Supporting Your Point."

4

6

tions for fear of being singled out and drilled for lack
of knowledge.

After experiencing these two systems of teaching, I
am not sure which is better. Perhaps a combination of the
two would be ideal —— a system in which there is order and
discipline but without suppression and fear.

Margaret Stack

Clarifying the Organization

"Time Out," by Judith Burgin

1. Although Burgin's original introduction clearly states her point, it does not suggest the organization of the essay. The added sentence maps the essay for readers, telling them to expect a three-part organization.

2. Realizing that a sentence buried in the third paragraph worked well as a topic sentence for the second paragraph, Burgin moved it.

3. The added topic sentence helps readers see how the details in the third paragraph differ from those in the second. Notice that the topic sentence echoes the word "overstatements," one of the key words mentioned in the revised introduction.

1

Time Out

Howard Cosell is not the only offender. Most television sports announcers set my teeth on edge. I enjoy televised professional sports, especially football, but I
cannot understand the low quality of sports broadcasting
provided by the networks. I could forgive the numerous
technical errors and the consistently mispronounced names
if the persistent running commentary were tolerable. *Every*
Sunday during football season, overstatements
abound, clichés cascade, and maudlin anecdotes
turn this viewer's stomach.

1

(Insert from page 2)

↓ Each rookie who displays any talent is proclaimed a
future Hall of Fame nominee. Each participating team becomes the "toughest, meanest, and most fascinating to
watch." Any pass completion is "fantastic," and every
call by an official is "controversial." A second stringer
having a good day is said to be the "most undervalued
player in the league."
  Such overstatements are not limited to the players.
ʌ The local fans each week are dubbed "the most loyal"
in the world" and "the best to be found in any stadium."
The head coach always seems to be "the most respected man

2

3

4. Burgin added a clear topic sentence to help readers move from the first chunk of her essay to the second (as mapped in the introduction).

5. Burgin deleted this two-sentence paragraph because it interrupted the organization of her essay and because its informal, chatty tone seemed out of place.

6. The added topic sentence serves as a transition to the third section of the essay (as mapped in the introduction).

2

move to page 1

around" and has always "done a great job with the boys."

According to our announcers, there are no adequate athletes performing well, only superb superstars gaining
glory. During the pre-game chit-chat, the weather is described as "picture perfect" or "unbearably miserable."
Even the elements are not allowed to remain ho-hum in television land.

*Howard Cosell and friends are masters of the cliché.*Quarterbacks are "men of great courage" and specialty
teams are "suicide squads." Every person on the field is
"a real man" with "a lot of heart." If a team is losing
by twenty-eight points in the fourth quarter, we are instructed not to "count this team out" because those "tough
competitors" have been known to "turn it around."

~~What ever happened to originality in broadcasting?~~
~~These guys are earning hundreds of thousands of dollars a~~
~~year for sounding redundant.~~

*Even more offensive than the overstatements
and clichés are the maudlin personal stories
that sportscasters force upon us.*)

When they deplete their supply of handy statistics,
~~sportscasters~~ *they* turn to pathos. The viewer is informed that
a certain hulking linebacker was a sissy in second grade.
Another bought "dear old mom" her dream house with his

4

5

6

7. The original conclusion was not bad, but with the added sentences, which survey the essay, the conclusion rounds off the essay more completely.

Note: For more about organizing an essay, see Chapter 8, "Organizing."

3

first playoff bonus. We hear vivid descriptions of previous injuries and suffer through some poor guy's excruciatingly painful experience with a pulled groin muscle.
One player, who was not expected to walk after his car
accident, has a daughter with cerebral palsy for whom he
"plays his heart out" weekly. Another is enduring a
period of great stress. He wants to be near his family in
California, but is forced by his contract to earn millions
of Buffalo. If players are aware of these gushy interludes, they must find them embarrassing. "Dear old mom"
could be watching and might not want her neighbors to
realize that she doesn't make her own mortgage payments.

Why not allow the reality of a well-played game to
project its own excitement, and let the tension of the
competition provide the color? It doesn't seem like an
unreasonable request. I wonder if Howard and friends
could stop chattering long enough to consider it.

7

Judith Burgin

*I would prefer impersonal, objective announcing.
I'd like valid appraisals of athletic ability and
relevant statistics. Descriptions should contain
honest adjectives and fewer trite phrases.*

Reparagraphing

"Learning to Decide," by Ethel Ramsey

1. There is no need to put the thesis into a separate paragraph. Ordinarily, readers expect to see the thesis at the beginning or at the end of the first paragraph.

2. Certainly the original paragraph was too long for easy reading. Ramsey decided to break to a new paragraph at the point where her discussion shifts from her father's domination of her mother to his domination of his children.

1

Learning to Decide

To some extent, we are all affected by our environment. And among the most powerful influences upon us are
the personalities of the significant people in our lives.
These influential people can either nurture and promote
our growth and development as individuals, or they can
inhibit it.

1

Having been raised in the home of my father and
mother and now living in my own home with my husband, I am
acutely aware of the value of supportive personalities.

In our home, my father was the indisputable authority. Male supremacy was assumed by my father and accepted
by my mother. He considered it to be his prerogative to
govern every facet of life for anyone who resided in his
domain. My mother was not even permitted to select a new
piece of furniture or carpet. If he liked a particular
chair but she thought the fabric or color was inappropriate for our large family, he bought it and she tried to
keep it clean. With my mother having virtually no voice
in most subjects, it followed that we, as children, had
even less. This was inhibiting to all of us, but it was

2

3. Although Ramsey is still discussing the father's domination over his children, she decided to break to a new paragraph for two reasons. First, the paragraph would have been long without a break. Second, the dramatic short sentence "Dad insisted that we spend our leisure time together" receives greater emphasis when it appears at the beginning of a paragraph.

2

worse for my sister and me than for my brothers. Naturally my father did not share our interests, so he proclaimed them frivolous and unnecessary. On the other
hand, since my brothers shared many of his interests, they
had the opportunity to participate in activities they
enjoyed. ¶ Dad insisted that we spend our leisure time   3
together. He liked boating and fishing, so we all went
boating and fishing. And my being subject to motion sickness was completely irrelevant. Therefore I spent countless Saturdays and Sundays with clenched teeth and a
queasy stomach. Although there were four children in our
family, we never went to the zoo or to an amusement park.
Only once did we ever go to a movie. But we never missed
the annual boat and auto shows. We were expected to enjoy
Dad's interests and given little opportunity to enjoy normal childhood activities.

    What little individuality Dad did not crush, Mom dis-
couraged. An "A" in algebra—trig was trivial, because
she managed a house and family with a knowledge of only
basic mathematics. But a disinterest in home economics
was unforgivable. She totally rejected the idea that I
might be anything other than a wife and mother. Any mention of a career was met with murmurs concerning the

4. As a rule of thumb, one-sentence paragraphs should be avoided, since they seem choppy, but Ramsey decided to break this rule in order to highlight a sentence that sums up the first section of the essay.

5. Breaking to a new paragraph at this point adds emphasis to an especially vivid sentence: "After a week of stumbling around in our dark apartment, I selected some lamps." Also, the new short paragraph following this sentence serves well as a transition to the next full paragraph.

3

immoralities of unmarried women and her opinion that a
mother's place was with her children. ¶ Between the two of   **4**
them, my parents tried to mold us into duplicates of themselves, complete with their hobbies, professions, and
opinions.

After marrying, I found it confusing to be expected
to have my own point of view. My new husband insisted
upon knowing my preference before purchasing any household
items. At first, this was extremely difficult for me, because I discovered that I usually did not have a preference. Whenever that occurred, Bill would assume that I
needed more time to decide, so he would suggest that we
wait until I had made my decision. After a week of stumbling around in our dark apartment, I selected some lamps.
¶ Eventually, forming my own opinions and making decisions   **5**
became easier. Vacations, activities, and purchases were
mutually planned. I truly realized how much progress I
had made when we started to build our house.

We had decided, for economic reasons, to use a precut
or package-style house. After obtaining floor plans and
brochures from several companies, we found ourselves overwhelmed by the task of selecting the right house. Finally
I sorted through the plans and eliminated those that did

6. Because the original paragraph looked a bit long, Ramsey found a convenient point at which to break it.

7. Since all of these sentences function together, as a conclusion, they should be in the same paragraph.

Note: For more about paragraphing an essay, see Chapter 9, "Building Paragraphs."

4

not meet our minimum requirements or that were too large.
Next I considered which ones either included the extras we
wanted or could be altered to include them. I was left
with three plans, one of which I felt was the best house
for us. ¶When I showed Bill the plans and explained my   6
method of selection and ideas for alterations, he immediately agreed that my first choice was the best house for
us. It was built, complete with the alterations I had
suggested. Five years before I could barely choose a
lamp, but now I felt confident enough to select a house.

   As a child, I was expected to accept the opinions and
obey the decisions of others without questions. Now I am
encouraged to think, to reach, and to achieve whatever is
within my capabilities.   7

   For the first time in my life, I am expected to be
me, with my own interests, hobbies, opinions, and dreams.

                                          Ethel Ramsey

Improving Coherence

"Working the Water," by Kirk Brimmer

1. The phrase "Like most watermen" links the sentences about Robin to the opening sentence about watermen in general.

2. The original version, "Robin swore that there is no better way of life," is confusing because readers don't know when he swore this, or to whom. The revision clarifies this matter. Also, by mentioning his interview with Robin, Brimmer creates a context for the entire essay. Readers will not be surprised, later on, to hear Robin's words quoted directly.

3. By opening the revised sentence with an "Although" clause, Brimmer improves his sentence variety (see Chapter 11). Improvements in sentence variety, such as this one, often improve coherence as well. Sentences usually flow better when they are varied in structure.

4. In the original version, Brimmer simply drops the quotation into his text, without mentioning whose words are being quoted. The effect is jarring. In the revision, Brimmer integrates the quotation clearly into his own text by placing a signal phrase ("explained Robin") in the middle of the quotation.

5. The original draft moves from the crabbing season to the oyster season and then back to the crabbing season. By moving the paragraph about the oyster season, Brimmer keeps his discussion of the crabbing season all in one place.

1

Working the Water

Chesapeake Bay watermen have always been known as
hard-working individualists, and Robin Collier lives up to
this reputation. Robin has lived on Deale Island all his
Like most watermen, he
life. ∧ He learned his trade from his father, who learned

from his father. Working the water is hard and dangerous
when I interviewed Robin recently, he
work, but ∧ Robin swore that there is no better way of life.

At the age of eight Robin began working the water
although he
with his father. ∧ He began working as a carpenter when he

turned eighteen, but after two years he was back. "I
,, explained Robin. "When
didn't like having a boss ∧, When you work the water, you

are your own man."

~~Robin's main source of income comes from the summer~~
~~crab season, but he also works in the off season.~~ Occasionally he tongs for oysters (pronounced "arsters" on the
shore) at the mouth of the Moniac Bay and Menoken Creek,
but mainly he works as a custom cabinet maker. He also
carves decoys and has been known to act as a guide for a
hunting party every now and then.

Move to page 4

A typical day for Robin during the crabbing season
after
starts at 2:00 A.M. ~~He begins by~~ powering up the Chrysler

1

2

3

4

5

6. The revision corrects a confusing shift from the present tense, "pulls," to the past: "rebaited" and "sorted." Notice that Brimmer has also combined two sentences by using a colon, thereby avoiding a short, choppy sentence containing relatively unimportant information.

7. Clearly these are Robin's words, not Brimmer's, so they must be in quotation marks.

8. The revision adds a signal phrase ("he told me") to integrate the quotation smoothly into the text. Although signal phrases often precede the full quotation (see Chapter 20), Brimmer places his in the middle of the quotation for greater sentence variety.

2

engine of his twenty-seven-foot Baycraft, ~~and then~~ he

heads for Fox Island to buy ale-wives and menhaden, used

for bait. By 3:00 he is checking his six hundred crab

pots. He pulls up the pots, sunk in eight to twenty-five

feet of water, ~~rebaited~~ *rebaits* each of them and ~~sorted~~ *sorts* the crabs **6**

into three different groups~~.~~: ~~They are~~ males, females, and

crabs about to molt. Robin sells the crabs that are about

to molt for five dollars a bushel to a friend. Why does

he sell them so cheaply? "There's too much work involved

with soft-shelled crabs," said Robin. "You have to check **7**

the boxes every two hours, and I am out on the water up to

ten hours a day."

The crabbing season begins April 1st, on the last day

of the oyster season. Maryland watermen can't enter the

market until June because the crabs haven't yet moved into

their pots, but the Virginians on the other side of the

bay start dredging for crabs from the opening day on.

After saying ~~Robin said~~ a few choice words about the Virginia watermen,

Robin he explained that when you dredge for crabs you take all

the crabs off the bottom, large and small. "Some Virgini- **8**

ans keep 'em all, *" he told me, "even* ~~even~~ the ones under four inches." The

practice of dredging keeps many of the young crabs from

even reaching Maryland waters and is just one of many rea-

9. The signal phrase "He also said" is unnecessary because Brimmer has already introduced the quoted material with a clear signal phrase: "he replied."

10. The original transitional sentence, "And then there are the jellyfish," is too casual in tone. The revised transition is more formal, and because it mentions the people discussed earlier in the paragraph, it also works better as a transition.

11. The revision corrects a confusing shift from the present tense ("are" and "are covered") to the past: "got."

12. Here again, Brimmer integrates his quotations more smoothly into his text.

3

sons why there is so much hostility felt toward the Vir-

ginia watermen.

When I asked Robin what he disliked about working the

water besides the Virginians, ~~and~~ he replied, "These days

if people can't find jobs they work the water, and right

now the market is flooded. The price for bait is up, and

the price of a bushel is down. ~~He also said,~~ "With so   **9**

many people on the water you have some jokers fishing your

pots and sometimes stealing them." Even worse than the people, according to Robin, are the jellyfish. ~~And then there are the~~ **10**
~~jellyfish.~~ When the water warms up, the jellyfish move up

the bay, and they make crabbing miserable. When the

jellyfish are bad, Robin's arms are covered with red welts

up to his shoulders, and sometimes the poison gets ~~got~~ into his

eyes and he can ~~could~~ hardly see.   **11**

     It's hard to make a living from crabbing, says Robin, ~~In Robin's~~ **12**
because "anything ~~words, "Anything~~ can go wrong." Robin is kept from his

pots if his boat breaks down, and some storms can keep him

from going out. "You can crab in the rain but not in the

wind," explained Robin. "And ~~And~~ when the wind whips up the waves, I also lose

pots. The current will roll the pots and pull the floats

right down under."

     To supplement his income from crabbing, Robin must work in the off season.

13. The signal phrase "He ended with" is not very informative. The revision creates a clearer context for the final quotation.

Note: For more about the coherence of an essay, see Chapter 10, "Making Connections."

4

Occasionally he tongs for oysters (pronounced "arsters" on
the shore) at the mouth of the Moniac Bay and Menoken
Creek, but mainly he works as a custom cabinet maker. He
also carves decoys and has been known to act as a guide
for a hunting party every now and then.

Insert from page 1

Although working the water is a hard life, Robin
plans to stay with it. "I like being my own boss, ," he said. "I know

13

that if I don't work hard, I'm not hurting anyone but
myself." *And, he confessed, a life on the water does have its appeal:* ~~He ended with,~~ "You see things on the bay that
you can't see anywhere else. I probably see more sunrises
in a month than most people see in a lifetime."

Kirk Brimmer

Introducing Variety

"Who Goes to the Races?" by Tom Weitzel

1. By using a colon, Weitzel eliminated a boring repetition of "there are."

2. To vary his language, Weitzel replaced the word "group" in two places. Notice that Weitzel chose synonyms carefully in light of their connotations: the once-a-year "bunch" are undisciplined and only loosely connected; the clubhouse "set," like the "jet set," share a certain social status.

3. The original sentences are short and choppy. By deleting "They also use," Weitzel combined the second sentence with the first, making "intuition, lucky numbers, favorite colors, or appealing names" parallel items in a series.

4. Weitzel combined two needlessly short sentences by subordinating the second one to the first. As he revised the sentences, Weitzel also varied his language. Notice that in the original version the word "bet" appears four times — twice as a verb, once as a participle, and once as a noun. Weitzel's revision substitutes the synonym "gambling" for the participle "betting," and it eliminates the second use of the verb "bet."

5. Although there was nothing wrong with his original topic sentence, Weitzel decided to restructure it. The key word, "professionals," receives greater emphasis when it appears at the end of the sentence.

6. Weitzel combined two short sentences by presenting information as items in a series.

1

Who Goes to the Races?

A favorite pastime of mine is observing people, and
my favorite place to observe is at the horse races. After
about fifteen encounters with the racing crowd, I have
discovered that there are four distinct groups who appear
at the track: ~~There are~~ the once-a-year ~~group~~ lunch, the   **1**
professionals, the clubhouse ~~group~~ set, and the unemployed.   **2**

The most typical and largest group at the track are
those who show up once a year. They know little about
horses or betting. They rely strictly on racetrack gimmick sheets and newspaper predictions for selecting possible winners. If that doesn't work, they use intuition,   **3**
~~They also use~~ lucky numbers, favorite colors, or appealing
names. They bet larger amounts as the day goes along,   **4**
~~betting~~ gambling on every race, ~~They even bet~~ including long-shot bets on exactas and daily
doubles ~~(long shot bets)~~. The vast majority go home broke
and frustrated.

~~The professionals are a~~ A more subtle and quiet group are the professionals.   **5**
They follow the horses from track to track and live in
campers and motor homes. Many are married couples ~~and~~   **6**
some are retired, ~~All~~ and all are easily spotted with their lunch

7. By turning a compound sentence into a complex sentence, Weitzel varied his sentence structure. He put the subordinate "Since" clause first in order to vary his sentence openings.

8. The inverted sentence pattern, with the subject "they" appearing between parts of the verb "do bet," adds a touch of sentence variety.

9. Both in the original version and in the revision, the subject of the sentence, "clubhouse set," appears out of its normal order, at the end. The revision is more effective, however, because it replaces the weak "there exists" structure with a more descriptive sentence opening: "Isolated from the others are. . . ."

10. Here Weitzel has combined two related sentences by turning the first one into a participial phrase. The revision is more dramatic than the original because it withholds the subject "they" until the middle of the sentence. Notice too that "Found" is a more interesting sentence opening than "They can be found. . . ."

11. The added phrase, "members of the racetrack population," makes the topic sentence more complete. Without the phrase "and welfare group," the topic sentence more closely echoes the thesis statement, which refers to this group simply as "the unemployed."

12. This sentence is more emphatic with the list at the end. Also, the original version is in the passive voice, with the subject of the sentence receiving the action. By changing the sentence from passive to active, Weitzel made the sentence more straightforward.

13. By beginning this sentence with a subordinate "If" clause, Weitzel varied the sentence opening and the sentence structure.

2

sacks, thermos jugs, and binoculars. ~~Most~~ *Since most* are familiar

with one another, ~~so~~ they section themselves off in a par-

ticular area of the stadium. All rely on the racing form

and on personal knowledge of each horse, jockey, and track

in making the proper bet. They bet only on the smart

races, and rarely on the favorites. *Never do they bet on* ~~They always avoid~~

exactas and daily doubles. More often than not they

either break even or go home winners.

Isolated from the others are
~~In addition, there exists~~ the clubhouse ~~group~~ *set.* ~~They~~

~~can be~~ *F*ound either at the cocktail lounge in the restau-

rant, usually involved in business transactions*t*, ~~T~~hey

rarely see a race in person and do their betting via the

waiter. It's difficult to tell whether they go home sad,

happy, or in between. They keep their emotions to

themselves.

members of the race track population
The most interesting are the unemployed ~~and welfare~~

~~group~~. They won't be found in the clubhouse, but right

Here one can discover the
down at the rail next to the finish line. ~~The~~ real emo-

tion of the track -- the screaming, the cursing, and the

pushing ~~. is discovered here~~. The unemployed are not

Betting is
sportsmen. ~~It's~~ not a game for them, but a battle for

If they
survival. ~~They usually~~ lose, ~~and then~~ they must borrow

enough money to carry them until the next check comes in,

7

8

9

10

11

12

13

Note: For more about sentence variety, see Chapter 11, "Constructing Sentences." See also sections 20 and 21 of the handbook.

3

and then, of course, they head right back to the track.

This particular group arrives at the track beaten and

leaves beaten.

~~Financially speaking,~~ I have probably lost more money

than I have won at the track, but~~^~~ these *observing* four interesting

groups of people make^s^ it all worthwhile.

Tom Weitzel

Pruning Excess Words

"A Dangerous State of Mind," by H. C. McKenzie

1. McKenzie substituted "our" for "the United States's" partly to save words and partly to connect more directly with readers.

2. The fact that the senator held high rank in the military is interesting, but McKenzie deleted this sentence in order to get to his point faster.

3. The revisions in the first two sentences of this paragraph simplify the original sentences without loss of meaning.

4. McKenzie felt, on second thought, that the word "apprehension" carried his meaning very well without the modifier "extreme." He also realized that by splitting the sentence in two he could streamline his meaning.

5. Since the sentence says that the senator "sat quietly," the phrase "without speaking" is redundant.

1

A Dangerous State of Mind
~~Conflict, Black and White~~

our
I once served as an aide to one of ~~the United~~

~~States's~~ most powerful senators. ~~He was and still is not~~

~~only a powerful senator; he was also once a high-ranking~~

~~man in the military.~~ The senator made me more aware than

white
I had ever been before that some of our ~~caucasian~~ leaders

are still the victims of an early-nineteenth-century men-

tality; they're still stereotyping black people.

one time when the
I don't think I will ever forget ~~the time that I had~~

senator and I were alone.
~~the unhappy experience of being alone with the senator.~~ I

to drive him
had been assigned ~~the task of driving the senator~~ from his

senate office to Washington National Airport. As soon as

he got into the car, I could feel his ~~extreme~~ apprehension .

He couldn't decide what to
~~and total uncertainty as to what he should~~ say to me or

to
how ~~he should~~ say it. He shook my hand and said, "Good

afternoon, young man." Then he sat silently, ~~without~~

~~speaking.~~ for a few seconds. Finally, he began by asking

me my age, my educational background, and my place of

birth. I wondered if he was going to ask me if I liked

girls; he didn't, and I breathed a sigh of relief.

1

2

3

4

5

6. Here McKenzie has deleted needless repetitions and statements of the obvious.

7. McKenzie struggled with this sentence, since it was nearly impossible to explain what he felt. The revision at least suggests his numb feeling, while at the same time leaving room for the reader's imagination.

8. In addition to being less wordy, the revised sentence is more emphatic.

2

we drove in

For approximately two miles, ˄total silence. ~~filled the air. And~~ ᴛ˄hen the senator began telling me about a friendship he and his wife had with a "colored girl," *who had been his daughter's classmate at* ~~According to the senator, this young "colored girl" was a classmate of his daughter, and his daughter attended~~ a prestigious university. According to the senator, when-ever he and his wife visited their daughter, ~~at this pres-tigious university,~~˄ they would always request the presence of the "colored girl." She would play the piano and sing while he and his family had a merry time. I sat there behind the steering wheel, listening, but ˄ *not hearing.* ~~my mind was in a state of utter boredom.~~ When we finally reached our des-tination, I breathed another sigh of relief.

My drive back to my office was not ᴀ˄ pleasant. ~~one.~~ I wondered to myself: What is the senator telling me? Is he saying that all black people have musical talent? Is he saying that his only exposure to black people has been on a master-servant level? I finally concluded that the sen-ator is still living in the early nineteenth century when black slaves would sing and dance while their masters drank whiskey and clapped their hands. A dangerous state of mind for a modern-day senator, I thought to myself.

6

7

8

9. The original concluding paragraph takes readers beyond the narrative, allowing their emotions to simmer down. McKenzie felt, upon re-reading the essay, that this was not the effect he was after. Also, he noticed that the essay ended quite dramatically with the words "A dangerous state of mind for a modern-day senator, I thought to myself." As a matter of fact, these words suggested a more powerful title for his essay, "A Dangerous State of Mind," clearly an improvement over the original title, "Conflict, Black and White."

Note: For more about wordiness, see Chapter 12, "Choosing Words." See also section 17 of the handbook.

3

~~I wondered how the senator would react if the world~~
~~conflict between black and white came to a state of armed~~
~~warfare. Would he order total destruction of the enemy?~~
~~I shudder at the thought.~~

9

                                        H. C. McKenzie

Refining the Style

"Journey Under Water," by John Curley

1. Curley simplified his introduction by eliminating the parts that were overdone. There was no need, he decided, to mention "the rolling waves" of the sea, especially since his essay focuses on a world far beneath those waves. As for the line alluding to divers as "fools treading water where angels fear to go," Curley decided that this attempt at cleverness was more distracting than descriptive.

2. In the original draft, Curley waits until the third paragraph before asking readers to join him on a journey under water. In his revision, he puts this invitation at the beginning of the second paragraph. Notice that the revised invitation, "Had you traveled with me over the past ten years, you would have experienced . . . ," is much more natural sounding than the stilted sentence that originally opened paragraph three: "A description of the ultimate might be appropriate enticement to urge you to join me undersea."

3. "There is no McDonald's" is more emphatic as a separate sentence.

1

Journey Under Water

Each time I've tried to describe the beauty I have discovered under the ~~rolling waves of the~~ sea, my friends have countered with ~~their movie-going experience~~ *scenes* from Jaws **1** and its toothy sequel, Jaws 2, ~~which portray divers as fools treading water where angels fear to go.~~ In Jaws 2, you may recall, the bride of Jaws snacked on two scuba divers, a fast-moving water skier, a helicopter pilot, and the resident diving instructor before the local sailboat regatta became the main course.

Had you traveled with me
~~In my travels~~ over the past ten years, *you would* ~~I~~ have experi- **2** enced a far more peaceful world under water: from coral gardens along the Pacific shores of Thailand, to an under- water wedding in Australia, to oil tankers sunk by Nazis along the New Jersey coast, to the pastel hues of the Caribbean Sea.

~~A description of the ultimate might be appropriate enticement to urge you to join me undersea.~~ My favorite spot is Davis Beach, St. Croix, in the Virgin Islands. Picture, if you will, a deserted sandy beach graced with palm trees. ~~Of course, although~~ There is no McDonald's. **3**

4. Curley felt that the personification in the original version was a bit overdone, so he simplified the image.

5. The word "crevasse" is too elegant for the context, so Curley replaced it with the simpler word "cut." He also divided the original sentence into two, to create a more dramatic effect.

6. The image of the coral turning "blood red" where "nibbled by the parrot fish" is a vivid replacement for the cliché "red as rubies." Although coral does not literally bleed, the image "blood red" makes poetic sense, since one living thing is being nibbled by another.

7. The sentence "Enormous sponges ensconced at this depth become our royal thrones," struck Curley as far-fetched, upon a second reading, so he decided to cut it.

2

We
~~we~~ may come upon a little squirrel monkey or a strolling

peacock taking an interest in our visit. Usually the wel-

comed tradewinds sway the palms in the 80 degree tropic

heat. Here even the waves pause, *allowing sunlight* ~~taking an indolent~~   4

to dance through
~~pleasure in inviting the sunbeams to play upon~~ them as

they break over the reef.

Let's wade out through a century-old *cut* ~~crevasse~~ in the   5

This cut, I've been told,
reef ~~which it is believed~~ was made by early Danish

explorers.

After snorkeling around a few rocks, we begin the

dive. As we descend to the first level, about thirty feet

down, colorful parrot fish, butterfly fish, and damsels

greet us in a field of red and yellow coral. This coral

where nibbled
is yellow, courtesy of Mother Nature, but ~~the effect of~~   6

by the parrot fish, it has turned blood red.
~~the nibbling parrot fish is to turn it as red as rubies.~~

~~Enormous sponges ensconced at this depth become our royal~~   7

~~thrones.~~

Our descent
The coral reef guides our downward path, ~~which~~ is

carefully monitored with frequent and meticulous readings

on the depth gauge that I carry. The living reef of coral

drops to 1,800 feet. Our limit is 100 feet. Descending,

the effect of the warm
we see the clear water turning dark, ~~in color as it becomes~~

8. Curley felt that his simile comparing the layers of water to oil and vinegar was effective but that the direct reference to "salad dressing" should be cut because it called up inappropriate connotations. As he eliminated this reference, Curley also revised the stilted language of the original ("This appearance is analogous to . . ."), replacing it with a more straightforward description.

9. Here again Curley's revision corrects his tendency to indulge in clever remarks and complex sentence structures. The revision simplifies the original without loss of content.

10. The word "Thus" seems out of place in an essay taking readers on a journey under water.

water settling on the darker, colder water like that
~~colder. This appearance is analogous to oil floating on~~
of oil floating on vinegar.
~~vinegar in a salad dressing.~~ **8**

Now, down to sixty feet. We look about for Mo and

Maureen, a photogenic couple who have startled divers new

to the North Star Cliffs. These moray eels have never, as

far as anyone knows, behaved like the ~~famous -- or should~~

~~I say infamous --~~ man-eaters of movie notoriety. *They look forward* ~~but prefer~~ **9**

instead *to* the snacks the divers have saved from their lunch.

On our way back, we ascend slowly, relaxing and hov-

ering over purple fields of filigree coral fans reminis-

cent of old Spanish lace. *Apart from their beauty,* ~~Not only beautiful,~~ they are

functional navigational guides. The waves, rolling into

shore, create an underwater current which flutters the

fans in an off-shore and on-shore undulating motion. ~~Thus~~ **10**

*G*uided by the reef, we head for the land, loitering along

the way in crystalline waters warmed by the sun.

Perhaps on our next dive we will chance upon a sting-

ray, as I did recently off the coast of St. Thomas. With

a little encouragement, he spread out his magnificent

wings, and with more grace than a ballet dancer, lifted

himself to unfurl an eight-foot wing span. He then with-

drew, feeling perhaps his obligation to perform completed.

11. Curley deleted the last sentence because it seemed leaden. The sentence preceding it works better as a conclusion. It is more fluid and rhythmic, and it ends the essay with a lighter touch.

Note: For more about the style of a descriptive essay, see Chapter 13, "Describing."

4

Awed by his performance, I forgot to snap a picture. But

there will be other journeys under water for me, and, if

I've whetted your interest, I hope for you too. ~~It is all~~   **11**

~~there, just waiting for you, whenever you are ready.~~

John Curley

Quickening the Pace

"Fish Story," by Melvin White

1. By cutting unnecessary comparisons, White keeps readers focused on the action. Also, comparing Dirty Harry to a human being in the introduction ruins the surprise effect of the essay's conclusion.

2. Because these sentences do not move the action forward, White chose to eliminate them. The paragraph begins much more dramatically with the original second sentence.

1

Fish Story

Pipsqueak, a freshwater selvini, would eventually grow to be a terror in the tank, but only if he could manage to live long enough to become one. Pipsqueak's problems began when I placed Dirty Harry, a larger selvini, in the tank, to ease his loneliness. ~~~Though~~ I had hoped for peaceful coexistence, ~~but~~ Dirty Harry ~~proved to be like a contemporary human being.~~ He attacked Pipsqueak relentlessly, never allowing the child to rest. ~~Dirty Harry pursued his "companion" as if Pipsqueak were a punching bag.~~ This imbalance of power was so great and the ensuing battles were so alarming that something had to be done.

1

~~Since I had forced Pipsqueak to be subject to these inhuman acts of barbarism, I had to insure law and order, allowing this "little guy" the right to live peacefully until he was large and strong enough to defend himself and make it on his own.~~ To establish law and order, I had several alternatives: I could separate the villain from the victim, I could destroy the evil one, or I could hire a policeman. After considering the homeland, I had to eliminate the first alternative, *for there was no way to* ~~The homeland consists of~~

2

3. The original descriptive details add flair to the narrative, but because they take up several sentences, they bring the story to a halt. In his revision, White retains as many details as he can smoothly work into one sentence. The details no longer seem to interrupt the story.

4. White cut these sentences for two reasons. First, they were filled with clichés: "day of reckoning," "main attraction," "top dog," and "king of the castle." Second, they commented on the action without really moving it forward.

separate its eastern territory, consisting of colorful [2]
~~twenty gallons of clean fresh water, rising from a base of~~
grasslands, from its rocky, more desolate west end.
~~immaculate white pebbles. The eastern end of the homeland~~

~~consists of the grasslands, from which colorful elephant~~

~~grass rises and flows with the tide. The far west end is~~

~~rocky and desolate. Obviously, there was no way to sepa-~~

~~rate the eastern and the western territories.~~ The destruction of Dirty Harry would be nothing short of murder,

a punishment far greater than the crime. Alas, I had no

alternative but to seek the aid of a policeman.

After reviewing several potential employees, I found

my man. His name, Big John. His breed, Jack Dempsey.

His manner, tough. Big John wouldn't accept the job un-

less I allowed him to bring along his deputy, a mild-man-

nered Jack Dempsey who goes by the name of Murph. ~~The~~
~~stage was set; the day of reckoning had come. As the cur-~~

~~tain rose for the main attraction, Dirty Harry was busy~~

~~trying to mutilate poor Pipsqueak. At first Harry didn't~~

~~realize that he was no longer top dog. Harry didn't quite~~

~~understand that he was no longer king of the castle.~~

Big John made his rounds majestically, with Murph at

his side. Pipsqueak hovered in fear among the weeds,

hoping that the attacks upon his life would soon cease.

Suddenly an eerie silence fell over the homeland. Dirty

3

4

5. The original version chops up the action by presenting it all in verbs connected with "and": "moved" and "strolled," "examined" and "moved." The revision subordinates some of the action ("moving," "examining"), thereby focusing the reader's attention on Big John's overall movement from the eastern grasslands to the more dangerous west end.

6. White decided to delete the sentence describing Big John's careful approach of the dragon, since the dragon is only a minor player in his narrative. The real conflict is between Big John and Dirty Harry.

3

Harry stopped dead in his tracks. "Who the hell are you?"

he bellowed. Ignoring him, Big John continued his patrol.

He ~~moved from the eastern boundary and~~ strolled through   5

the high grasslands, *moving westward* toward a clump of orange vegetation

hiding the skeleton of an unfortunate seaman. *After examining* ~~He examined~~

the ~~seaman's~~ remains, *he* ~~and~~ moved into the west end,

patrolled by an air-blowing dragon. ~~Seeing the air~~   6

~~bubbles coming from the dragon, he carefully approached.~~

Realizing that the dragon was no threat, the peacekeeper,

~~Big John,~~ moved on, inserting his nose among the boulders

where Dirty Harry loved to bask.

Dirty Harry could hold back no longer. His back

arched and his fins stuck straight out. His whole body

began to shake in the ritual manner that precedes attack.

Big John did nothing. The shaking intensified. Fear and

hate were in the air.

When the shaking stopped, the attack began. First

Dirty Harry attacked face to face. The next attack came

toward Big John's midsection. The counterblow sent Dirty

Harry to a tunnel beneath the dragon to lick his wounds.

When Dirty Harry emerged, executing a sneak attack from

the rear, Big John whipped around and with a frontal as-

sault drove Dirty Harry back to the tunnel. ~~This time he~~

7. The editorial comment interrupts the story, so White cut it.

8. Big John is a more dramatic figure if his words are short and to the point.

Note: For more about the pacing of a narrative, see Chapter 14, "Narrating."

4

~~suffered defeat without dignity.~~ "They call me Big John

and I was hired to keep the peace. There's enough room

for everyone to live in harmony, Dirty Harry/. ~~so when you~~

~~come outside again you'd better act right."~~ Big John

didn't have to say more.

Peace and harmony have finally come to the homeland.

Pipsqueak has grown a little larger, and Dirty Harry has

learned to respect the rights of others. Big John and

Murph have adapted to their new positions well. Outside

the homeland, however, there is another territory, a land

filled with hatred, political unrest, and turmoil. I won-

der if Big John has any friends.

Melvin White

7

8

Changing the Format

" 'Popsicle,' " by Pat Napolitano

1

"Popsicle"

It makes me laugh when you say that we "spoil" Chris because she's handicapped — that we give her whatever she wants. Let me tell you what the procedure is in teaching a three-year-old deaf child one word.

One of the tools you'll need is a small table and chairs set so that the child can get up and down easily. Children generally are unable to sit still for long periods of time and get frustrated if they have difficulty climbing up and down when they need a break. Deaf children have a particular problem here since they do not expend the energy the rest of us do in talking.

Another necessary tool is a set of 3 X 5 cards containing pictures of the words that Chris has already mastered, such as pictures of her mom, dad, sister, a cat, and a dog. The other tools you will need are a lot of patience and a ready smile. Since deaf children cannot hear the tone of your voice, they "listen" to your expression and depend on your pleased response for reinforcement.

Okay, you're ready to start the warm-up exercises. Sit in one of the little chairs across from Chris. Show

1. Although there is nothing wrong with the original version, written completely in paragraphs, Napolitano decided to present this central section of her essay in list form. The purpose of her essay is to persuade readers that teaching a deaf child even one word is an amazingly complex task composed of many individual steps. The paragraph format does not highlight the separate steps because more than one step must appear in each paragraph (otherwise the paragraphs would seem very choppy).

2

her each picture whose word she has already mastered;
praise her when she says the word.

    Now you're ready for the new word -- "popsicle."
First, show her the picture of the popsicle and say "popsicle" slowly and distinctly. Next, hold the palm of her
hand in front of your mouth and say "pah, pah" (so she can
feel the puffs of air from the "p" sounds). Repeat this
until she's mastered "pop."

    Again hold her hand in front of your mouth while you
make an exaggerated "s" sound. She must see how your
teeth are positioned and feel that the "ssss" produces air
from your mouth. For the "c" sound, place one of her
hands in front of your mouth so she can feel the air.
Place her other hand on your throat so she can feel the
sound you make. Show her how to place her tongue on the
roof of her mouth to get the hard "c" effect. Repeat all
of this until she's mastered "kah."

    Now practice the "s-c" sounds together, "sica," using
the same methods as used for doing the sounds individually. Finally, show Chris how you roll your tongue to
get the "l" sound. Hold your hand against your throat so
that she feels the sound.

    Now you're ready to put it all together. Show her

1

2. The list format highlights the separate steps without creating a choppy effect. Listing, Napolitano decided, was an effective way to dramatize her main point: that teaching a deaf child one word is a complex, several-step process.

3

~~the picture of the~~ popsicle, place her hand ~~on your~~

~~throat, and say~~ "pop-si-cul," exaggerating every ~~syllable.~~

Now you're ready for the new word —— "popsicle."   2

(1)   Show her the picture of a popsicle.

(2)   Say "popsicle," slowly and distinctly.

(3)   Hold the palm of her hand in front of your mouth and
      say "pah, pah" (so she can feel the puffs of air
      from the "p" sounds).

(4)   Repeat step 3 until she's mastered "pop."

(5)   Again hold her hand in front of your mouth while you
      make an exaggerated "s" sound. She must see how
      your teeth are positioned and feel that the "ssss"
      produces air from your mouth.

(6)   For the "c" sound, place one of her hands in front
      of your mouth so she can feel the air. Place her
      other hand on your throat so she can feel the sound
      you make. Show her how to place her tongue on the
      roof of her mouth to get the hard "c" effect.

(7)   Repeat step 6 until she's mastered "kah."

(8)   Now practice the "s-c" sounds together, "sica,"
      using the same methods as in steps 5 and 6.

(9)   For the "l" sound, show Chris how you roll your

Note: For more about formatting, see Chapter 15, "Reporting."

4

> tongue to get the "la" sound. Hold her hand against
> your throat so that she feels the sound.
> (10) Now you're ready to put it all together. Show her
> the picture of the popsicle, place her hand on your
> throat and say "pop-si-cul," exaggerating every
> syllable.

You may not get through all ten steps in one day. If
she gets tired, push her further than she wants to go, but
not to the point where she's frustrated. Or to the point
where you're frustrated either. For if you aren't happy
and smiling, you'll lose her for sure.

When at last she mastered the word "popsicle," give
her a popsicle. After you've both gone through "popsicle"
every day for two or three weeks, every time Chris says
"popsicle" you will both want to celebrate the victory.
What better way to let her know she's got the idea than by
giving her a popsicle?

Imagine this process with every word Chris learns,
and maybe you'll understand why we tend to give her everything she asks for. Everything she asks for is to be
celebrated.

Pat Napolitano

18 A Collection of Student Essays

Like the twelve essays-in-progress in Chapter 17, the twenty essays in this chapter were written by our students at Prince George's Community College. Here we are printing only the final drafts.

We hope that you will browse through these essays the way you might browse through a favorite magazine — for your own pleasure and enrichment. Don't be surprised if you pick up some writing ideas along the way: You can learn much about writing by seeing what has worked for others.

Life as a Stewardess

Broadway Joe enters the cabin, smiles at the camera and says, "When you've got it, flaunt it." Such an inducement was hard for a nineteen-year-old to ignore, so I sent in my application for the position of airline stewardess.

All potential employees were flown to Dallas for their interviews. On the day of my appointment there were two of us in first class. We received a great deal of champagne and an equal amount of advice. It seemed to me that Riley's life was rough when compared to that of a stew.

During the testing and interview, I remained unusually calm and poised. Of course, I owed most of my relaxed demeanor to half a bottle of bubbly. When the acceptance letter arrived ten days later, I was thrilled and so was my family.

The schooling was a six-week course consisting of early curfews, room searches and weekly dismissals. In between these regimental restrictions, we attended classes on makeup, on nail and hair care, on walking, talking, and serving. The apex of the course was a week of training in first aid, federal safety standards, and evacuation procedures. During this week, we were brainwashed into thinking the main reason for being on the plane was to fill the role of safety expert. We were responsible for the lives of every passenger. In case of emergency, this knowledge would be vital. The spirits of all the students soared with the understanding of how important our jobs would be.

On my virgin trip, I soon learned that I functioned more as a coffee and soda dispenser than a safety expert. While we were refueling at the San Antonio airport, a woman in first class lighted a cigarette. I informed her that smoking was not allowed because of the fire hazard. "Go away, you silly girl," she replied. "I've been flying much longer than you. When you get a chance, bring me another martini." So much for safety expertise.

As for the excitement and glamour, I never saw it. When you first work in this job, you are on reserve. This means you fill in when a pattern-holder can't. By the time you have enough seniority to hold a monthly pattern, you've become so hardened that you either hide in the galley hoping no one will board or you quit. I chose the latter, but not before experiencing some very sad and lonely times.

The most lonely times were the "layovers," a normal part of the working trip. They involved spending the night in a motel room, eating cold sandwiches for dinner, and washing out a dirty uniform for the next day's flight. Sometimes I wasn't lucky enough to make it to a motel. I can remember spending my first Christmas eve away from my family sleeping on a bench in the Kansas City airport. Of course when I was really lonely, I could always refer to the stack of calling cards that were passed out by deplaning salesmen — "If you're ever in Chicago, give me a call and I'll show you around."

Flying did provide me the opportunity to visit places I might never have seen. I was also able to establish some close friendships and absorb some realities about people and life that have proved invaluable. But where was all the glamour behind those exotic places and beautiful faces? It existed in the Fifth Avenue ads and in the minds of those who had never been there. — Kathleen Lewis

So He's Driving You Crazy?

So he's driving you crazy? That soft, rosy bundle of joy you welcomed into your life just a short time ago has, seemingly overnight, become an iron-willed perpetual motion machine. He has the curiosity of a cat, the agility of a mountain goat, and more energy than most power plants are capable of producing. He's faster than a speeding bullet, more powerful than a locomotive, and today he learned to climb the shiny new fence that just set you back $800. Take heart, dear friend. Do not despair. Save your strength, because things are definitely going to get worse. The "terrible twos" can't hold a candle to the traumatic teens.

This is not to say that the care and feeding of young children is not a difficult, time-consuming task. Your aching back and weary step are living proof of that. But, after all, how much trouble can a three-year-old really get into? How far from home can he get? By the time he is fourteen, there will be hours on end when you really have no idea where he is. No matter how good your lines of communication may be, all you really know about a teenager's whereabouts is what he tells you when he leaves the house.

Of course your child would not lie to you. He really does plan to go to Tommy's house. Indeed, he does. But therein lies the rub! He and Tommy, finding things dull there, go on to Jim's, and then to the drugstore, the ballfield, Charlie's, the library, back to the drugstore and, finally, hours later, home — where you, his innocent parent, greet him by asking if he had a nice time at Tommy's.

All of this is, of course, compounded when, at the magic age of sixteen, the State decides he is mature and responsible enough to drive a car. The State, however, does not know him as well as you do. He is also not driving the State's car. He is driving yours. And who do you think will be up calling the hospitals when he is an hour late getting home? Not the good old Department of Motor Vehicles, that's for sure!

What all this really means is that now when he leaves home to go to Tommy's he will drive. And when he and Tommy get bored, they will seek adventure at (you hope) speeds up to 55 mph. The wonderful world of the Capital Beltway will open to your Precious Baby, and the wonderful world of Lady Clairol will open to you as you discover at least ten new gray hairs every morning.

One of the biggest traumas of the toddler years is toilet-training. I have seen strong women — and stronger men — reduced to quivering heaps while trying to coax their Little Darling into the bathroom. Years later, these same people will spend an equal number of hours pleading with him to come out.

While the rest of the family lines up in the hall with soap, towels, shampoo, etc., the Crown Prince is using the last drop of hot water for his shower and will be at least another twenty minutes blow-drying his hair. One parent I know read *War and Peace* waiting to take a shower while her offspring lounged in the tub shrinking his jeans; and while cold showers are certainly invigorating, too many too often are not conducive to pleasant intrafamily relations.

"But," you protest, "at least teenagers eat. My toddler will surely come down with malnutrition, beri-beri, or bubonic plague if I don't convince him to eat something!" Relax. By the time he is fifteen, he will be eating everything in sight that isn't either nailed down or still moving. In ten years your grocery bill is bound to make you see those times when you finally got him to eat two green beans and a bite of roast beef as the good old days they really were. I predict that at some time during your child's teen years you will seriously consider the purchase of (a) a cow; (b) a peanut farm; (c) stock in the McDonald Corporation; or (d) all of the above.

Of course, while he is doing all of this eating, he is growing at a fantastic rate. Right out of the clothes you paid $100 for last week. It is not enough that his clothes keep him warm and dry. They must be "in." Unfortunately, what is "in" is usually expensive. There is no point in buying what is "in" when it is on sale, because by that time it is most assuredly "out," and will remain unworn in the closet until you donate it to Goodwill.

I do hope that the foregoing has not been too discouraging for you. Do press on in the marvelous adventure of parenthood. You have not yet begun to fight. While coping with teenagers can be an exercise in frustration, the rewards are many and varied. A team of scientists at Harvard is working under a federal grant conducting research to determine just what those rewards are — and when they find out, they have promised I'll be the first to know. — MARY KENNY

Borrowings from Black Culture

Although the sixties saw blacks struggling to attain civil rights, blacks are still a long way from equality. However, for a group that has been oppressed in this country for two-hundred-odd years, the black population has been socially significant. In fact, blacks have influenced the white middle class by their modes of dress, language, music, and dance.

There was a time when the African look was threatening to whites. But times changed. In the sixties love beads became a unique means of expression for blacks and whites alike. Whether made of elephants' ivory tusks or plain old plastic, beads were commonplace. Dashikis also started a style of their own, along with bandeaux and shawls. And the Afro hairstyle became popular with Caucasian men as well as women.

The English language has picked up so many words from "Black English" — as it is sometimes referred to — that even Henry Higgins would find decoding difficult these days. How can anyone accurately explain the meaning of *soul food,* or *boogie,* or *funky,* yet these words are frequently heard. Nouns which originated in Black English and slipped into our everyday conversation include *dude* (male), *bama* (someone who doesn't dress well), *brother* (friend), *blood* (fellow back), and *honky* (white person). Some adjectives that many of us are familiar with are *solid* (good), *bad* (great), *phat* (well built), *cool* (no problems, all right), *hip* (up to date), and *uptight* (nervous). Verbs which have achieved considerable acceptability are *jam* (improvise), *rap* (converse), *jive* (exaggerate), and *hassle* (badger). Phrases also abound: *dig it, strung out, old lady,* and *out of sight* are all mainstays.

Black music has also been a trend setter. Starting with rhythm and blues, this music developed into a rage yet to die down — rock and roll. Black musicians who helped create rock include Muddy Waters, Chuck Berry, and Little Richard. Later came black vocal groups which helped develop the sound known as "soul music": the Temptations, the Supremes, the Miracles, and the Four Tops. Then we were introduced to disco, as interpreted by Van McCoy, Natalie Cole, and the Tramps. Other forms of music developed by black artists which have come to appeal to white ears include jazz, reggae, acid rock, and funk.

One of the stereotypes of blacks is that they all have rhythm and can dance. This, of course, is a fallacy. But blacks must be credited with introducing many new steps. The Twist, the Funky Chicken, and the Locomotion are black dances from years back. More recently have come the Robot, the Hustle, and many variations of disco. These steps have been adapted, improved, and literally sold to whites.

Clearly black culture has had much influence on the mainstream culture in our country. Blacks have given as well as received customs to help develop the style that is known as American. — CHARLES GANLEY

Coming Home

While my family and I were stationed in England for three and a half years, it took time getting used to having no ice in the drinks, calling french fries "chips," and remembering to drive on the wrong side of the road. But as we got to know the English people, with their colorful history and culture, and as we assimilated ourselves into their lifestyle, America grew farther and farther away.

In England, my wife made it a ritual to have tea at five. I became a regular at the local pub's dart tournaments, and we made our weekly trip to the village's market. Our daughter attended the local British school. Within a few weeks it was difficult to tell her from the other five-year-old lasses. Her cookies became "biscuits," warm became "warrrm," and my wife was "Mum."

When orders to Washington, D.C., came in, we had mixed feelings. We were excited about going home to family and friends and getting back into the mainstream of the American way of life. As much as we loved the Cotswold, it was isolated. Yet it would be painful to say goodbye to a country and its people, knowing that we might never see them again.

Although I had anticipated some cultural adjustment when we went overseas, I expected none on our return. After all, we were going home, right? But America hit me like a tidal wave. As soon as I got off the jetliner at John F. Kennedy International Airport, I felt as if I were seeing Technicolor for the first time. Someone had also turned up the volume and speeded up the film. America was in a very big hurry. Everybody talked and walked as if there were a prize for being the fastest. I was shocked when I went to the airport newsstand. I didn't recognize one face on the magazine covers.

Shopping malls overwhelmed me with their glitter, pizazz, and acres of parking lots. There were enough cars there to give every bicycle rider in Oxfordshire his own "motorcar." In Bicester (pronounced "Bister"), I had had two varieties of sunglasses to choose from. Here I had thousands. It took me two hours to select a pair.

America was a smorgasbord. But within two weeks, I had indigestion; there was simply too much of everything. I began to question our cultural values. Why did Americans have such big gas-guzzling cars? Why were all the commercials telling me that I had to buy their product in order to be liked? Material possessions and dressing for success were not top priorities in the Cotswold, and American TV was nothing like the excellent BBC "telly" that I missed so much.

I felt guilty for thinking this way. How could I possibly think that America was anything but the biggest and the best? I could not share my doubts with my neighbors; they'd think of me as a traitor and a snob. I was confused, and so was my daughter. She was used to a strict headmaster right out of Charles Dickens. Her Washington, D.C., principal strolled the corridors in a leisure suit and clogs. "You'll find American schools far superior to English schools," he assured us. Yet within two weeks my daughter had moved up one grade because she was bored in class and always seemed to know the answers.

Our family was suffering from re-entry shock. Reverse culture shock has been around ever since Uncle Sam began sending families overseas. When you come back from overseas, you see America as a foreigner does. You view America through a sharper lens that lets you pick up the strengths and weaknesses of your country much more clearly.

It's been seven years since our family left Oxfordshire. I haven't played darts since then, and although I was the most laid-back person when I returned, I now work at a feverish pace. Sometimes when I get into a traffic jam on the Beltway, I recall the lush green and quaint country side and the jovial British people. I'm glad for having lived there, and coming home to America was an experience I will never forget. — ALAIN GOLDSTICKER

A House of Cards

At first glance, I thought the room was unoccupied. It was dark, still, with none of the usual clutter that hospital patients tend to surround themselves with. Only the steady beeping of the heart monitor betrayed the presence of the fragile woman in the bed just a few feet away.

Lying there, unmoving, she looked like a picture that somebody forgot to paint. The soft lines around her eyes, the silvery gray hair that framed her face, were the rewards of a life well spent. She used to joke that people who didn't look their age had never learned to live, only to exist, because Time would never leave his signature on an incomplete work of art. Then she would laugh a laugh that would tickle the spirit of everyone around her. Her eyes would sparkle like a child's at Christmas, with a combination of vitality and mischievousness that was envied by women half her age.

Now her body was frozen, her face empty of expression, as it had been since the stroke a few days before. Looking at her, I felt as if an injustice had been committed, a mistake had been made. She had been a companion throughout my childhood, a confidante during my teenage years, and a treasured friend in adulthood. She was my grandmother, who always had the right words for me. My grandmother, who could do anything she set her mind to. So why was she just lying there?

I waited for her to get up and tell me it was only a joke, that she was rehearsing a part for the theater group she was so active in. I waited for her to get up, so we could both have a good laugh and stop for lunch on the way home and she could fill me in on everything she had been doing since I saw her the week before. I waited for her to get up. She didn't.

When I looked into her eyes, I could see that her mind was as alive as it had always been. The twinkle was still there, and slowly it diluted some of the bitterness I felt.

We shared many memories that day. We didn't talk; her condition wouldn't allow it, and neither would mine. But words had been nothing more than a formality with us, anyway, since we always seemed to know what was on the other's mind.

I recalled the story she told me after I had my first nightmare. She said that the angels would come and watch over me while I slept if I would build them a house of cards to keep them warm. So every night I built a house of cards, and felt quite safe from the monsters and goblins that haunted other children's bedrooms in the dark.

I could almost hear her laugh when we thought about the dozens of banana peels and orange seeds we planted in her garden. It was years before I realized that some people ate fruit because they actually liked the taste, and that planting the leftovers was not necessarily their main objective.

I thanked her for finding an excuse for me to spend the weekend with her when that Elvis Presley movie was playing around the corner from her house. And for sitting through it with me four times, because she used to feel the same way about Rudy Vallee.

I told her how hurt I had felt when she did nothing about the abuse she knew I had been growing up with, and she told me of the pain she had felt in not having the courage to do anything about it.

We had a long conversation that day; somehow we knew it would be our last. After the funeral, I went home and built her a house of cards. — LINDA WHITE

Goat Woman

Twenty-five years ago, at the age of thirteen, while hiking in the mountains near my hometown of Vancouver, Washington, I came face to face with the legendary Goat Woman of Livingston Mountain. When the Goat Woman invited me to her home for a bite to eat, I learned that her real name was Gladys Fulton and that she had been born in Switzerland. We hit it off and have been friends ever since. Gladys left a very deep impression on me; to this day I would have to say she is the most remarkable person I have ever met.

In 1936 a doctor advised Gladys that goat's milk would help alleviate or possibly cure an arthritic condition she had. One week later she bought 300 acres of mountain land (at $1 an acre) and 150 goats. She then built a barn, which she shared with the goats until she had completed her house. The original barn and house are still being used by Gladys today.

Gladys's house is small, consisting of two rooms. One room has a small table with one chair and a wood stove, which is used for both heating and cooking. The other room holds a bed and a piano. Both rooms contain stacks and stacks of newspapers, magazines, and books. A kerosene lamp hangs over the bed and on the bed lies a Bible. Oliver, the parrot, is housed on top of the piano. In the winter, baby chicks and geese sometimes share the house with Gladys. There are no toilet facilities, no running water, no electricity. Gladys does have two luxury items, though, a 1940 vacuum-tube radio and a recently acquired CB radio, both of which are powered by car batteries.

Gladys is seventy-six years old now and in addition to raising 150 goats, she has chickens, geese, a cow, a horse, five dogs, two cats, a pet raccoon, and a parrot. A typical day for Gladys starts at four in the morning. She walks to the barn to milk about 125 goats. After milking she releases the goats to the countryside, chasing them to a particular area that she wants them to feed on. She then cleans the barn, shovels manure, and spreads clean hay around the milking stalls. Afterward she feeds the remaining animals and retrieves eggs from the hens. In between all these chores, people are arriving to pick up their allotted share of goat's milk, with the local hospital receiving the biggest share. If time permits, Gladys slaughters a few male goats. Most of the dead goats are drenched in arsenic and left in the fields for the coyotes to feed on. The remainder of meat is consumed by Gladys and her dogs. Just before dark she rounds up the goats, locks them in the barn, and calls it a day.

Gladys has a simple meal of cheese, goat's milk, bread, and fresh vegetables. While eating she listens to classical music from the radio. She spends the remainder of the evening reading a newspaper or magazine and she finishes the day with the Bible. On weekends the local CB'ers are treated to conversing with Gladys, or should I say "Goat Lady One," which is her call sign. About once a month Gladys and her retired forest ranger friend get together and indulge in a bit of merriment — drinking blackberry wine, playing the piano, and singing.

This remarkable woman is going on seventy-seven now and her way of life hasn't changed a bit. She is healthy, hard-working, self-supporting, and completely independent. I don't believe there's anyone who leads a fuller, happier, or richer life than Gladys Fulton, the Goat Woman of Livingston Mountain. — TOM WEITZEL

Memories of Parochial School

How do I feel about parochial schools? Well, the feelings are flying all over the place and with the feelings come the memories.

I remember a bell clanging in the large schoolyard filled with squealing, laughing, busy children. With the ringing of the bell came instant silence. The children would stop in their tracks, as if playing Statues. Then *click-click,* a large wooden clicker sounded, and in unison the children moved in silent drill-like choreography. Bodies formed perfect rows, two by two. *Click-click,* every voice was heard saying the Apostles' Creed, then silence again. I always wondered how the wind could dare tickle and tease the huge friendly oak which stood in the cobblestoned yard. How could it shake and crackle its leaves, even after Mother Superior had rung the bell and sounded the clicker? *Click-click,* the columns of children marched slowly and silently into the red brick school building and down the gray halls. The discipline was absolute.

At St. Stephens School you learned and you followed rules — school rules and the Golden Rule. At St. Stephens I learned many things, so many things, too many things. I learned fear and guilt. Fear when I learned that the more I sinned, the more my soul became stained, and that those stains or scars from sin would remain on my soul until they were burned off in the fires of purgatory. I was taught that no one could escape these fires if they wanted to get to heaven. It was either purgatory fires or hell fires; the former if we were good, the latter if bad. Guilt came when I learned I was bad because I put Jesus on the cross, and that I came into the world with sin and would leave with sin. Each time I forgot and committed some terrible sin, like talking in line, the fear and guilt increased.

I also remember that I learned. I learned to read, write, add, subtract, and multiply in my first two years of school. I learned all the building blocks of a good education, even though I was absent for days, weeks, even months. In those first two years of school I had mumps, chicken pox, flu, colds, pneumonia, strep throat, scarlet fever, Russian measles resulting in undiagnosed total loss of hearing in one ear, mild polio resulting in the use of corrective walking shoes for ten years, and an undiagnosed vision problem. The doctor who finally discovered the vision problem thought it a small miracle that I had ever learned to read. I could have gotten lost and left behind in a world of undiagnosed minor handicaps. But I didn't, because of the superior teaching skills of a dedicated group of nuns.

I remember a large airy classroom with forty-five fellow students who also learned the basics and a little more. We learned how to behave like ladies and gentlemen. We were taught to be polite by always remembering our manners and being aware of other people's feelings.

I have such conflicting feelings about parochial school. I feel gratitude for being taught so well, yet I feel anger for being taught fear. I ask myself how I can question the method when the results were so good, but I do. I learned so many things so well; I had to — my everlasting soul was at stake. — MARTINA SOLLIDAY

The Bowhunt

November 1st, at last. I'm finally here. I finish that last sip of coffee and climb out of the truck. A crisp coldness envelops me as I pull on that last sweater and don my camouflage jacket. I pick up my bow from the back of the truck and bravely stalk into the darkness.

Cursing the lack of a moon, I stumble through the undergrowth, shattering the eerie quiet of the woods. I finally arrive at my preselected spot on the side of a ridge overlooking several almost invisible animal trails. I settle in and huddle up against the cold.

Slowly the light increases as the sun struggles towards the horizon. The quiet is broken by a brave little bird somewhere, stirring to life. As if waiting for that cue, several more begin to chirp their morning songs, and as the shadows begin to fade more join in. A squirrel barks angrily at the dawn, as if cursing the prospect of a hard day's work ahead. Several crows fly overhead and cry the warning to the forest of the strange creature concealed in the shadows below.

As the light filters through the morning mist, the shadows begin to take form. The formidable giants of the night become stately trees, and the forest floor becomes a carpet of leaves.

Suddenly, a new sound assails me, a quiet shuffle of leaves. I tense in anticipation as I spot a grayish-brown patch in the bushes that just doesn't seem to belong. The spot shifts and begins to grow, and suddenly that spot materializes into a deer. He moves forward a few timid steps and cautiously surveys the area, as if searching for that sinister creature the crows warned of. His eyes fall on me, but quietly pass. The deer steps forward a few more steps and discovers something more interesting on the ground. I take advantage of this lapse in security and cautiously raise my bow. The deadly missile is pulled back to its tautest and the razor-sharp warhead seems to settle on the deer's shoulder as if by its own will. He looks up, as if some sixth sense has warned him of danger. His eyes seek me out again, but there is still no recognition.

I slowly release the tension of the bow string and lower the bow. The deer zooms in on me again, and finally realizes his danger. He bounds off, fading swiftly into the forest.

It was enough. I'll be able to face the world a little longer, and tell tales of "the one that got away." — ROBERT JEANOTTE

Final Rite

My memories of myself before the birth of my first son, Alexander, are remote, as if seen through the cold eyes of a television camera. I was black and white then.

Before Alexander, I was responsible only to the Marine Corps. I had to appear for work five mornings a week in a neatly pressed uniform. That was it. Contrary to what most people believe, the Corps is very flexible. Any hastily contrived story can get you out of most trouble.

One of the weekend trips that I was fond of taking extended longer than it was supposed to, and I showed up at base a day late. I ended up standing at attention in front of the Major's desk, weaving many lies into an excuse involving engine trouble, a stolen wallet, and general bad luck. It worked! I strutted out of the office, not once pausing to think what a demotion would have meant.

Freedom was my constant companion. It was tangible, a fact of life. Except for working hours, my time was *mine*. My wife, Nickol, and I went dancing, dining, partying, all at a whim. One bright Friday afternoon, she blurted out that it would be nice to go to Florida. We did. In less than forty minutes we and two friends had squeezed into my purple Javelin and were cruising for Daytona beach, sand, and margaritas by the pitcher. We dragged back to the base in South Carolina twenty minutes before Monday morning muster.

I was as emotionally unattached as I was free. I never bothered to return the love that Nickol had for me. She was just another aspect of my environment. There were people whom I called friends, but I didn't care about them either. I thought only of myself, my needs, and those things which directly affected me. I didn't worry about hungry children, flooded homes, or bankrupt farmers. After all, how did their fate affect me?

Alexander was born in the middle of my year-long deployment to Japan. I flew home for the birth but left five days later. After arranging for money to be sent every month, I went back to life as a single marine in Japan. It wasn't until my return to my new family in the U.S. that the realities of fatherhood struck me.

Suddenly there was an infant who was totally dependent on his parents and a wife who craved emotional support. They needed me.

Loving Alexander has helped me to love Nickol. We rely on one another for support, and this has been a new experience for me. In my adult life, I've never before been dependent on anyone. I work during the day, go to school at night, and spend the rest of my time with Nickol and Alex. There is no time to think of myself.

I've begun to plan for our future. Currently I am a candidate for a highly competitive program in the Marine Corps which would allow me to go to college and be commissioned as an officer. The pressure is very disheartening, but I want for the sake of my family to succeed.

My love for my family has stirred the compassion inside me. I actually care about people now. I realized this recently when I wanted to buy a small parcel of land for us in western Maryland, a country retreat with a small stream on one side and apple trees galore. For $2,500 it seemed perfect. But on the day of the sale, I met a man whose family farm was being sold, acre by acre, to people who wanted a hideaway from urban life. I couldn't buy his child's fishing spot.

I also find myself identifying with people much older than me, my own father in particular. We are closer now than we ever were when together. We now share the "bond of fathers." Whenever Alexander does something particularly annoying, Dad laughs and calls it divine justice.

There are as many rites of passage into manhood as there are cultures in our world. But for me, fatherhood has been the final rite of manhood.
— TOM WHITE

Orphaned at Five

Celery sticks served as slugger bats; olives substituted for baseballs to be smashed across the kitchen. Cousins Sonny and Guido were pitcher and catcher, and my sister Dorrie was a combination of infield and outfield. I came up to bat for the first time just as Gramps called for us to come into the living room.

A policeman stood in the doorway. Nonnie and Aunt Sandy were crying. All morning we had been told to stop touching the Thanksgiving dinner or we would be punished. Who expected to go to jail because of olives!

Gramps pulled Dorrie and me onto his lap and hugged us close. "Your momma and daddy were going to get Uncle Vince and a truck hit their car. God took them to heaven." He started to cry. I wished he would let us down. His prickly sweater smelled of tobacco and his mouth was purple from wine.

Dorrie and I went home with Aunt Sandy. My stomach was hurting and making tiger noises, but everyone was crying so I was afraid to say I was hungry.

In the morning we went to a dark room where Mother and Daddy were lying in coffins. It smelled so sweet in that room, and the red-glassed candles burning everywhere made it sticky hot. Mother wore a lacy pink dress. A pink satin blanket covered her feet. Daddy looked so white, as if he wore makeup like Mother. Folded newspapers were hidden inside his trouser legs.

At night we all knelt down on the blue carpet and prayed a long, long time with Father Minnorra from Our Lady of the Angels Church. My knees were sore and I shifted my weight from one leg to the other. Aunt Sandy touched my shoulder and said, "Marie, stop that rocking. Kneel up."

The morning of the funeral was very bright. The curtains were opened in the coffin room. Aunt Sandy held my hand. She wore a black hat with a big black feather. Her eyes were red-circled from tears. With her bright red lipstick she reminded me of the clown in my circus coloring book.

Aunt Sandy kissed Daddy and lifted me to do the same. I touched his cheek. His skin was stiff. I kissed his forehead. We moved to Mother. Aunt Sandy lifted me again. I kissed Mother, then stood on the kneeler. I moved down and lifted the pink satin cover. Mother's shoes were pink. I moved back toward her head. Touching, touching as I went. Her hair was soft. Her lips were not soft. I pressed her mouth. It was tight. I pushed my fingers into her mouth. I saw and felt cotton. Aunt Sandy pulled me away.

A man in striped pants pulled down the backs of the coffins. Nonnie was crying. Gramps was blowing his nose. Someone took Dorrie and me to a big car. We sat on two little pull-down seats behind the driver.

At the cemetery everyone was crying and praying. Aunt Sandy fainted when the two men with ropes lowered the coffins into the graves. Father Minnorra gave Dorrie and me each a white flower. Mine was turning brown and its petals were falling. I gave the flower to Gramps so I could put my cold hands into my coat pockets. — MARIE VISOSKY

Behind the Eight Ball

"Breaker one nine . . . breaker one nine!" It's two o'clock in the morning on Route 50 and I am heading toward the beach.

"Go, breaker one nine," comes the welcome response, a female voice that is crisp and clear.

"You got the Wild Turkey here," I offer. "What's your 20?"

"Hey, Wild Turkey, I'm eastbound on 50 just past the bridge, come back," she replies.

"You must be on my back bumper. What are you driving?"

"I'm in a Ford van . . . blue and yellow. Is that you in the bronze Dodge just ahead?"

"That's me," I answer, "in the number two lane. What's your handle there?"

"You got the Eight Ball here. Where are you heading?"

"Ocean City, by the sea. And I got a problem. My speedometer isn't working and I'm worried about the smokies, come back."

"You say your speedometer went bad?" Eight Ball comes back. "Well, let me cruise past you and you can hitchhike on me all the way."

"That's a big 10-4," I reply as I sign off.

The handsome Ford van roars by me in a blink and I barely make out a quick wave from the woman behind the wheel. The next thing I know, I am staring at her rear bumper, and the fatigue I was starting to feel is gone. In the next twenty miles we change lanes three times to chatter about a variety of subjects. All I have to do is steer and throttle and talk. What I forget to do is think. When the flashing lights go on behind me, I suddenly realize that Eight Ball and I have forgotten about the "double nickels" speed limit.

"Hey, Eight Ball, there's a smokey on my butt," I let her know. "How fast were we going?"

"Sorry about that, Wild Turkey, for sure. Catch you on the flip-flop."

I pull the Dodge van over on the shoulder and play that old familiar scene again. I fumble for my license and registration. I smile weakly. My mind races for the right things to say.

"What's the trouble, officer?"

"I just clocked you at 68," replies the Maryland state patrolman, pleasantly but firmly.

While he writes the ticket, I decide to save the story about the broken speedometer and the woman in the Ford van I was trailing. It wouldn't matter anyway, I'm sure, I tell myself.

As I sign the ticket, I can't resist the pun. "I guess this is what it means to be behind the eight ball," I say, smiling.

"I guess," he answers. "Take it easy now."

I start my engine, turn off my CB, and head off — slowly — toward my destination once more. — HENRY BERTAGNOLLI

A Viennese Waltz It Was Not

The heavy bomber group of B-17s circled awhile, gaining altitude. It took time, since there were full loads of bombs, ammunition, and gas. It was November, 1943. We were flying out of central Italy, headed north for the railroad yards near Vienna.

As we passed over the Italian Alps, the air was clear, with white clouds drifting across the bright blue sky. Looking down, we could see neat little farms, looking like miniatures, on the mountains and in the valleys. The scene seemed so peaceful, but we knew that in a short time all hell could break loose.

We had started using our oxygen masks at 9,000 feet. When we reached 30,000 feet, we test-fired the twin caliber .50 machine guns and checked the intercom system. The unheated plane became cold, so we turned on the heated units under the heavy flying suits.

In the distance we saw a squadron of P-51s, the fighter planes that would escort us to the target area and then wait to bring us back. The markings on the planes were those of a squadron of black pilots. The planes seemed so graceful, compared with the lumbering bombers.

Standing at the waist windows, weighted down by heavy clothing, pistol and belt, and a parachute harness, we passed the time gossiping on the intercom system and telling obscene jokes that we had all heard many times before.

We passed Salzburg and Linz in Austria. Then, as we approached the target area, First John (the pilot) ordered radio silence. The bombing run began. We opened the door in the waist cabin floor and started throwing out the chaff, long strips of aluminum foil which would distort the radar used by the ground gunners to track the bombers. The railroad yards were heavily defended by ground guns, since the Germans had made them into a central transportation point for middle Europe. We had heard that the gunners were women and, from experience, knew that they were very good.

The bomb bay doors rumbled open, and freezing air whipped through the plane. Puffs of black smoke were layering upward from ground firing. The plane rattled and shook with flak hitting the metal. It reminded me of times when, as a small boy, I had thrown handfuls of gravel onto a tin roof.

Suddenly the plane shuddered and seemed to stop. Two engines had been hit. The pilots and flight engineer worked desperately to prevent an explosion or fires. We heard the First John tell the flight engineer to turn them off.

"We've had it — toggle the bombload and let's get out of here," First John yelled to the bombardier. The bombardier flipped the toggle switch and dumped the whole load of bombs at once, without regard for what they might hit.

First John banked sharply left to leave the group and return home alone. At first he did not see the other bomber. The next few seconds we watched helplessly as the two B-17s maneuvered desperately to avoid a mid-air collision. We rose and the other dropped, but it was a moment that caused nightmares for weeks to come.

We headed home, escorted by a couple of P-51s who broke off from their squadron to prevent German fighters from jumping a crippled American plane.

We made the return trip on two engines without further problems.

After we landed, we watched a B-17 land with its brakes shot out. The pilot zigzagged wildly on the dirt runway to slow the careening giant, with ground crews diving out of the way. He finally made it with clouds of dirt spewing into the air.

As we headed for the equipment room to store our gear, we passed the two pilots.

"Happy Thanksgiving, you sorry bastards," grinned First John.

— BILL ZACHEM

Escaped Prisoner

One busy Friday evening the police department had me assigned to the Bureau of Patrol at Woodland Grove. There weren't even enough seats to go around for all the prisoners. I was working the desk, and another shoplifter had just come in. With a recent directive requiring him to be handcuffed and with no space left on the bench, I was at a real loss. So I went into a nearby office and came out with a chair. Setting the chair next to the coatrack, I handcuffed the shoplifter to the rack until I could get to him. After all, I thought, he's only a shoplifter and the rack stands nearly six feet high. Where's he going to go?

It hadn't been ten minutes until someone went to get his coat. All the coats and jackets were on the floor and both rack and man were gone. The ultimate embarrassment had befallen me — an escaped prisoner. We searched the neighborhood for the rack-laden shoplifter, and after an hour I would have settled for almost anyone who happened to be handcuffed to any six-foot coatrack. Then the call came. A lady near Central Avenue had seen a man climbing backyard fences carrying what looked like a coatrack. A quick run to her house — but the man and the rack were gone. How could anyone move so fast with such a cross?

I rode around for about another hour or so and then pulled into an empty lot to sit a while. I looked down Central Avenue and suddenly there he was. Coatrack and all. The tired shoplifter was cautiously making his way up the street. I was in a dark spot so I decided to sit it out and watch him for a few minutes. I couldn't believe it. He stopped at the Metro bus stop, and with his own jacket covering the handcuffs, pretended to be leaning against the coatrack waiting for the bus.

Almost immediately a bus showed up, and there he was — a 160-pound, five-foot-four man trying to maneuver a six-foot coatrack onto the bus and trying to be cool about the whole thing. After he had made several unsuccessful attempts at boarding, one of which knocked the driver's hat off, I pulled up next to the bus. The exhausted shoplifter was almost relieved to see me. His burden had been too much, even for the search for freedom.

Once back at the station, the shoplifter found himself facing charges of escape, but even that didn't keep him from rolling with laughter as he recounted his trials at crossing all those backyard fences with his special companion. With my own embarrassment gone, I could laugh too. — Frank Cohee

A Close Call with Death

I'm twenty-seven years young and glad as hell to be here. My close call with death takes me back about four years ago. It was February. A week-old snow, or what was left of it, thawed and refrozen several times over, covered the ground.

There were four of us — Thomas, Derrick, Beavis, and me. We are all the same age, except for Derrick, who is two years younger. I would give you some background on these guys, but I don't feel it's necessary — except for Beavis.

Beavis was involved in a freak accident at the age of twenty-one. The rear door of a van flew open and he fell out, head first. He ended up with a cracked skull and hasn't been right since. End of background.

We didn't have anything better to do, so we pitched in and bought a fifth of Bacardi rum and a liter of coke. Afterwards we piled into Thomas's car, which we affectionately referred to as the Blue Goose, and went on a joy ride. Since we ran out of rum before we ran out of gas, we figured we'd stop at the nearest liquor store and buy another fifth. After all, the night was still relatively young. And that's when our trouble began.

The nearest liquor store turned out to be at 14th and something. It was decided that since Derrick and I were the more sober of the lot, we would go in and make the purchase. We went in, made our purchase, and turned to leave. Just then, Thomas and Beavis walked in to buy some chips, so Derrick and I decided to wait for them. Beavis paid for the chips but decided he wanted popcorn instead; on his way out, he switched. The owner wasn't too happy about this since the popcorn cost a nickle more than the chips.

The owner exchanged a few unkind words with Beavis, and the next thing I knew, he was yelling to his wife Buella to "lock the damn door." She did exactly what she was told. A big woman this Buella was, and I could see that there was no way I could wiggle around her and out that damned door.

Here we were, trapped in a liquor store, drunk, with Buella guarding the locked door. A quick look around confirmed my suspicion that the door was our only way out. The plate glass windows were covered with wrought iron.

In the meantime, the mad proprietor had ducked into the back to retrieve a bat that Hank Aaron would have been afraid to use. With mighty weapon in hand, he confronted the four of us, offering us a taste of the grain should we give him any more lip.

Actually, what he thought was lip was Derrick and me asking him to cool down and let us pay the difference, Thomas cursing at Beavis to shut up and stop giving lip, and of course, good ole unhinged Beavis giving lip.

For some reason the owner decided that the bat wasn't sufficient protection; he went into a back room grumbling, "I've got something for ya'lls asses." I could feel my bladder start to quiver, and a boulder grew inside my intestines. What could he have back there that was more intimidating than an outsized bat? Even as I asked myself this question, I knew the answer. I realized that I could be dead in less than two minutes if this guy decided to carry out his threat.

I was gripped by a fear I had never experienced before. I could feel my internal panic button begin to glow and flash ever so slowly, increasing with every breath I drew.

My mind began to race. Adrenaline had me going full tilt. I figured that by the time the police arrived on the scene, identified us, and located our next of kin, it would be about two o'clock in the morning. I toyed with a scene in which a policeman stood at our front door: "Mr. and Mrs. Hayden? Excuse me for disturbing you, but I thought you might like to know that early last evening a lunatic liquor store owner with a wife named Buella shot and killed your son. Please don't feel singled out. He also killed three of your son's buddies. Have a nice day."

All of a sudden I got mad as hell with myself for wasting time on such and for allowing a feeling of helplessness to crowd into my already overstuffed bank of emotions.

My mind began to race. I felt at that moment that my adrenaline could carry me not only through the glass unscathed but through the wrought iron mesh as well.

Suddenly Buella turned and unlocked that damned door, yelling something to the effect that we best get our "black asses" out of there quick. Which was a waste of air as far as I was concerned. When the tumblers clicked, we tried to climb over Buella to get to safety. The four of us took the door in two's and scattered.

I make light of this experience now, but for months afterwards I couldn't find anything humorous about our little encounter with the mad batter and Buella. And today, as a sober twenty-seven-year old, I still can't stop wondering whether the price of youthful indiscretion and a bag of popcorn might have been death. — CLARENCE HAYDEN

My First Quarter Mile

The lights changed: red, yellow, and then green. I watched with apprehension as the two cars went screaming down the track. I was next. I had finished my last water burn-out in the staging area and could tell my car was getting good traction. My palms were sweaty and my nerves were tight as I inched my way up to the starting line. I adjusted my helmet to fit more snugly on my head and glanced over at my opponent. Catching my eye, he gave me a sarcastic smile. I turned and looked down the track. It was a black streak stretching into the horizon.

I looked at all my instrument gauges and made sure everything was running normally. Oil pressure, check; gas pressure, check; engine temperature, check; transmission temperature, check. I was ready.

The staging lights began their descent. "Here it is, Lisa," I thought to myself. "All those hours in the garage turning wrenches and setting gauges have paid off." When it was twenty degrees outside and it hurt just to hold onto the ratchets and screwdrivers, I had known that the day would come when it would all be worth it. That day was now.

I could feel the tension mount, like a balloon stretched to its limit. One hand was on the steering wheel, the other on the gear shift lever. Then, GREEN! My foot slammed down the accelerator. I was pinned in the seat as the powerful engine hurled my car forward.

The needle on the tachometer climbed quickly to 8,000 revolutions per minute and I threw the shifter into second gear with practiced, timed precision. The stands flew by in a blur. I noticed my opponent gaining on me. With a silent prayer I clicked the shifter into third. "C'mon, C'mon" was all I said as my car picked up more speed and started to pull ahead. Then all else was forgotten. My eyes were glued to the finish line.

I slowed the car down and brought it to a screeching stop. I could see my pit crew jumping up and down in the back of the pickup truck as they rushed to haul my car back to the pit area. When they were within hearing distance, I could tell from their joyous yells that I had won the race. I felt like doing cartwheels all the way back down the track.

I had clocked in at 10.03 seconds, with a top speed of 134 miles per hour. My opponent's time was 10.98 seconds. As he got out of his car and came over to congratulate me, I could tell I had gained his respect. He extended his hand and said, "I never thought I would get beaten by a rookie driver in her first race. You definitely have what it takes."

I had raced my first quarter mile drag and won. I was on top of the world. — LISA FORTUNATO

The Phillips Collection

Washington is a unique city for art lovers. There is something for everyone, and it is all free. On the Mall, the Freer offers its Oriental treasures, the pristine marble of the National Gallery houses the old masters of the Kress and Mellon collections, and the dynamic new Hirshhorn contains the work of artists of this century. Not far away, one can browse in the National Portrait Gallery or experience the Corcoran, where something new is always happening. Georgetown and Capitol Hill boast clusters of small commercial galleries abounding with contemporary efforts for those of more adventurous tastes. My favorite Washington gallery, however, is located in the once elegant and still interesting neighborhood surrounding Dupont Circle. There, on 21st Street, just above Massachusetts Avenue, you will find the Phillips Collection.

Duncan Phillips was an art collector extraordinaire. He and his wife, Marjorie, loved the Impressionists, Post-impressionists, and modern masters. Fortunately for us, they acquired their works by the score and hung them with care and pride in their red brick townhouse on 21st Street. When in 1918 Duncan Phillips decided to turn his hobby into a public institution, the house was included. To me, this is the great charm of the Phillips Collection. Many of the paintings still hang in that original residence.

As you stroll up 21st Street, the townhouse facades conjure up a feeling of a bygone era — an era of teas and debutante parties and glittering balls. Enter the door at 1612, and you find yourself not in a museum but in a gracious home whose owners have been kind enough to ask you in to view their treasures.

Wander at will through the rooms. Bask in the beauty of the Van Goghs, the Degas, the Cézannes. On a quiet day — and it usually is quiet and uncrowded there — you will swear you can hear the tinkle of crystal and the music and laughter of an elegant, long-ago party.

Suddenly, in the midst of your musings, you find yourself in a room ablaze with light, color, and life. There on the wall is Renoir's "Luncheon of the Boating Party." Take a seat and treat yourself to a longer look. Settle back and feel the joy and warmth of the painting. Smell the early summer breeze off the Seine. Hear the rustle of the leaves and the hum of the conversation. Stay as long as you like, but remember, there is more.

As the collection grew, it became evident that the Georgian townhouse could not adequately display the new acquisitions. So in 1960 a new wing was opened adjoining the Phillips home. It too is beautiful in a different way, and houses the more nearly contemporary part of the collection.

As you enter the new wing, you will feel a quickening, a transition from yesterday to today. Gone are the lovely mantelpieces and views of the charming walled garden. Here all is clean and uncluttered to display to best advantage the blazing colors and stark lines of the modern masters. You will find Picasso and Pollock and Dali and Braque in profusion.

Don't miss the Rothko room. Here, against a black background, are hung Mark Rothko's huge color paintings. As you sit there, you will find yourself surrounded by pure, pulsating, sensuous color. Relax. Clear your thoughts and allow yourself to absorb the impact of the blazing reds and yellows, the soothing tranquility of the blues and greens. The results are unforgettable.

Assuming that you now can't wait to visit the Phillips Collection and claim it for your own, I must warn you that getting there is not half the fun. The neighborhood, while interesting and charming, is a maze of narrow one-way streets totally devoid of parking spaces. However, a Metro stop within two or three blocks, and I promise you the walk will be interesting.

In any event, go and see the Phillips Collection. On Sunday afternoons at five, there is the added bonus of a free concert by talented young musicians. If you are an art lover, you can't miss. If you are not an art lover, you just might become one. — Mary Kenny

Bathing: A Japanese Ritual

For centuries the ritual of bathing in Japan has been second to none in the world. The Japanese word for hotbath is "ofuro," and until you have sampled this aspect of Japanese life, you really don't know anything about good healthy bathing habits.

Normally before going to bed, the entire family take their baths one after the other — the father first, the mother last. In the "furoba," the bathroom, is a deep wooden bathtub made of cypress. It is usually built into the floor so that the bather's shoulders are even with the floor.

On the bottom or side of the bathtub, a gas burner is attached. Although Westerners like their bath temperatures about 90 degrees with bubbles and all, Japanese prefer their bath temperature between 104 and 120 degrees with the bathtub cleared of all soap. Once the water has reached the desired temperature, it it usually kept there by leaving the gas burner on low, as the water will not be changed even once until the last family member has bathed.

Regardless of what you may be thinking, this system of bathing is neither dirty nor unsanitary. As a matter of fact, Japanese bathing — whether done at home or in a public bath house — is a purification rite, a ritual deriving from the Shinto religion.

When you go to a Japanese bath house, it is best to bring along your own bar of soap, a wash cloth, and shaving utensils. This will save you from putting out more money than you have to. As you enter the "sento," or bath house, you will be provided with a wicker basket in which to deposit your clothes. They will be perfectly safe.

At the entrance of the sento there will be a man or woman collecting the entrance fee. He or she will give you a bath ticket. As you make your grand entrance, you may do as you like concerning your discreet Western habits. The Japanese couldn't care less whether you use your wash cloth as a fig leaf. It is said that the Japanese do not see bathtime nudity.

As you enter the sento, which is tiled from ceiling to floor, you will see two or three large pools (one with cold water only), either round or square, each containing a submerged bench. In any event, do not immediately jump into a pool to soak and wash at the same time. It just isn't done that way in Japan.

Instead, look along the walls for hot and cold water taps marked red and blue respectively. Then pick up a bath stool, a wash basin, and a dipper for rinsing (you'll find these close to the entrance), and head for the taps. You squat on the stool, mix your desired temperature of water from the taps, and pour it over yourself. After you have poured several buckets of water over yourself, you can soak in the pool. But only for a few minutes. Then you must get out and get to work. Thoroughly shampoo, soap, scrub, wash, and rinse away the suds with clean water from the tap. Then you may resoak indefinitely in one of the pools.

In Japan the tub is for relaxation, and soaking is a favorite pastime. You may rewash and resoak as long as you like, but never mix the two. Feel free to temper the heat with cold water when it becomes unbearable for you, even though others will change it back to its lobster-boiling temperature later on.

Once you've dipped into a steamy hot pool and gotten accustomed to its penetrating temperature, you will find that the Japanese way of bathing is more relaxing, soothing, and sanitary than the dull Western way, which you will learn to abhor. — ANDREW WOYCITZKY

Last Rites for Dolores Cockrell

Nelson and Chris, although I don't plan to die any time soon, I want to help you both in making the arrangements for my funeral and last rites.

Immediately upon my death, it is my intention to have my organs (eyes, heart, liver, and whatever else may be of use to the medical world) donated to help others live a more complete life. This is very important to me and must be done immediately. If this request is too difficult for either of you to handle, let someone outside the family make the arrangements.

After my organs have been removed, I would like my remains moved to Chambers Funeral Home in Riverdale, and I would especially like Kathy Chambers to handle the arrangements. Please make sure that Maria does my hair because I don't want to spend my time in eternity with a lousy hairdo. Don't laugh at this request; I have enjoyed having Maria do my hair for over fifteen years and certainly would not want anyone else to mess with it. Another request is to have beautiful red roses on my casket. Don't spend too much money for a casket because it will only be put in the ground in a cement vault. The roses, however, will be enjoyed by all, and they are my favorite flower.

Funeral services are to be held at St. Jerome's at 11:00 a.m. If Father Day is available, he is my choice to celebrate the Mass, and it should be a celebration, not a sorrowful time. Please try to keep this in mind. Contact my dear friend Alice Metrick to do the gospel readings. She has a vibrant voice and will read with heartfelt emotion. One of the readings should be the 23rd Psalm. You may select the others.

As you know, religious music is very special to me. The entrance hymn "Be Not Afraid" should be sung by the congregation. Later in the service I would like our friend Dorothy Behan, who has such a beautiful voice, to sing "Ave Maria" and "I Believe." Remember, Nelson? She sang at our 25th anniversary. For the concluding hymn, I would like the congregation to sing "Peace on Earth." These musical selections should be meaningful to our family because they were sung at Mark's funeral. I feel close to Mark whenever they are sung.

Pallbearers could be selected from our many nephews. Children mean a lot to me, so I want as many included in the service as possible. They can help the elderly family members and friends to their seats, and they can pass out prayer books. Remember to have envelopes with checks and cards of appreciation for Father Day, Dorothy, Alice, the organist, as well as the altar boys. St. Jerome's parish has played an important role in my life, so I want to make sure those close to me know I have appreciated all the contributions they've made to my life and now, my death.

Interment will, of course, be in Davidsonville. What a lovely place for a final rest. My funeral procession will take the old road down Central Avenue so I can have one last ride on my favorite lane. Be sure to go slowly. I want to enjoy all the memories. Recite a prayer at the graveside, say goodbye, and then take everyone home for a huge wake. There should be lots of good food. Carol Barrett can help you get the meal organized. Everyone is to come back to the house because I want you to have a good time, talking about the old days and how much we all meant to each other.

My final instructions to you both: Do not be sad. Remember that your wife and mother enjoyed her life on earth, and she intends to enjoy her life in eternity as well. I will miss you and know you'll miss me, but I wouldn't have traded lives with anyone else.

Love,
Dolores
— Dolores Cockrell

Children's Hospital

The little children in their gowns dart in and out of the playhouse. Laughing and shrieking, they scurry from one plaything to another, overwhelmed by the abundance of toys, books, and games. Except for the nervous parents sitting quietly among the toys, this room could be any well-stocked playroom. But it is a very special playroom. It is exceptional simply because it is here — in the operating suite of a large hospital. And it is only one of the ways in which Children's Hospital strives to alleviate the fears of its young patients.

I imagine that most parents dread taking their child to the hospital for surgery. Perhaps this dread is due to our own vague recollections of childhood surgery. Do you recall being confined to bed and rolling down the hall toward the operating room, as you looked back at concerned, nervous parents and wondered if Mom would be there when you got back? You may even have wondered if you would be coming back. The people who work at Children's Hospital endeavor to change this frightening experience.

To effect this change, they invite the future patients and their families to a guided tour of the hospital on the Sunday before the scheduled surgery. The first stop on the tour is a semiprivate room in a surgical unit. Here the guide demonstrates the use of the call button and the bed controls. She carefully points out the two extra beds that are provided for the mothers and assures the future patients that Mom will be allowed to remain with them. Next the guide shows the children the bathroom and warns them they may not feel capable of walking immediately after surgery. Then she shows the bedpans and kidney basins to the children, as she explains how they are used.

The guide then leads the group to an examining room. Here, with the assistance of some of the future patients, she demonstrates the use of the digital thermometer, blood pressure cuff, stethoscope, ophthalmoscope, and auriscope. The volunteers in these demonstrations assure the other children that these instruments are completely painless. All the children are then encouraged to try these items on each other. They peer into each other's ears and eyes, listen to their hearts beat, and wrap the blood pressure cuff around each other's arms. By the time the children leave the examining room, they are all certain that these instruments will not inflict any pain.

The next stop on the tour is the O.R. playroom. This is the playroom in the operating suite, where, on the morning of their surgery, the children will play until the anesthetist is ready for them. The guide explains that the anesthetist will help the children go to sleep and make sure they do not wake up until the surgery is completed. During the tour the children are not allowed to play in this enticing room, but they are promised that they will be permitted to play here on the day of their surgery.

Then the guide escorts the group next door to the parents' waiting room. She tells the children that Mom and Dad will be with them until they are asleep but will wait here while they are in surgery and recovery, which she calls the wake-up room. Next the guide helps the children dress in surgical gowns, hats, masks, and shoe covers, as she explains that the doctors and nurses will be wearing these strange garments in the operating and recovery rooms. The black mask, she informs the children, is to help them go to sleep. As the future patients try on the ether mask, she asks each child what he or she thinks the mask smells like.

The group is then escorted to the cafeteria and served cookies and punch. The guide circulates among the tables, answering questions and giving any further reassurance that may be needed. After the children have finished their cookies and punch, they are taken to see a puppet show about a little girl who has her tonsils removed.

When the day of surgery arrives, only Mom and Dad appear to be nervous. The patient — in this instance, our son Jon — seems perfectly at ease as he joins the other patients in the O.R. playroom. When the anesthetist comes for him, the patient is accompanied by his parents into the induction room, where he is gently anesthetized while holding hands with Mom and Dad. After the child is asleep, the anesthetist collects any pacifier, security blanket, or favorite stuffed cuddle-buddy that the patient has brought with him. These comforting objects are sent to the recovery room to help soothe the child as he wakes up.

Instead of being confined to bed following the surgery, the patient is encouraged to visit the unit's playroom. A child may be up and playing within two or three hours of his operation. If he feels like it, he is even allowed to accompany his parents to the cafeteria for meals.

From the pre-surgical tour to the postoperative care, the people who work at Children's Hospital strive to comfort, inform, and reassure their young patients. As a result of these innovative procedures, surgery is no longer a frightening and bewildering experience at Children's Hospital. — ETHEL RAMSEY

Dogs, Cats and Beethoven

Pets may not know much about music, but they know what they like. Just try turning up your favorite record of Stravinsky or Hindemith and watch how Fido or Felix reacts. Chances are good that they will tell you plainly you're insulting their eardrums; taste has nothing to do with it.

I happen to be fond of classical music and have a modest library of recordings from Elizabethan lute music to composers like Lukas Foss. Whenever I play anything dissonant or atonal, my dog J.J. disappears under the bed or runs out of the room. If our other dog, Ginger, is awake, her ears twitch as though she were suddenly afflicted with mites, but if she is upside down on the rug asleep, she doesn't move a muscle. She is blessed with that kind of imperturbability that allows her to go through life with her nerves virtually intact. On the other hand, she displays real pleasure if I put on Schubert's "Trout" Quintet or a Bach Brandenburg Concerto. She faces the record player and hunkers down as though to concentrate. Coloratura sopranos and solo violins drive both dogs into a frenzy. Mozart is received happily no matter what the selection; popular music is ignored.

Since the hearing range for both dogs and cats is much wider than for humans (my neighbor swears her cat comes running from half a block away whenever she slams the refrigerator door), it is not surprising that they are sensitive to music. Both dogs and cats can distinguish between two notes separated by as little as one-fourth the range between two notes on the piano. But though they may be able to distinguish quartertones and halftones, they seem to prefer harmony.

Moppet, a white Persian who lives in New York, has a passion for strings: chamber orchestras, quartets, trios, whatever. I have seen her stretched out on an ottoman in front of the record player, eyes shut, the expression on her face nothing short of ecstatic, listening to the famous "Canon in D Major" by Pachelbel. At Haydn's "Trumpet Concerto" she yawned and walked out.

A beagle I knew used to throw his head back and bay at the ceiling every time he heard a violin playing solo. The cello, however, didn't bother him at all. Something to do with pitch, no doubt. A miniature poodle of my acquaintance barks frantically at both violins and flutes but seems to enjoy, of all things, ragtime.

I have known pets who paid no attention whatever to music coming out of a box: radio, television, or tape recorder. Other animals, however, respond as well to canned music as to the real thing. Many years ago a friend told me her cat positioned itself in front of the radio every Sunday afternoon in time to hear the concert from the New York Philharmonic. The cat never missed a season. An owner of three collies told me that two of them sit up at attention whenever they hear band music on the radio or television, especially "Stars and Stripes Forever," while the third dog ignores it completely. "I think she's tone deaf," her owner says.

In the evening paper recently I read about Muff, a stray cat adopted by a Pasadena, California, gentleman who plays the organ. One evening the man said to his wife, "Here's a tune for Muff," and dashed off a song he remembered from his childhood: "Kitty, my pretty gray kitty, why do you scamper away? I've finished my work and my lessons, and now I am ready for play." Immediately Muff came over and jumped onto the bench beside him. From that day on, every time he plays that song Muff comes over to sit beside him. She knows her theme song.

— JOYCE SPRING

Part Six

Research Writing

19   *Researching*

What is research but a blind date with knowledge? — ANONYMOUS

Many composition courses devote a section to research writing, a section designed to teach you how to find information and how to document the sources of the information in your papers. Finding such information and documenting it may seem at first an awkward and bewildering process, but a sincere attempt at preparing the paper your instructor assigns should begin to convince you otherwise. You will learn that information on almost any subject is readily available, that within ten minutes you can find lists of articles on everything from the commercial use of musk-ox fur to 1950s rock music. You will also learn that incorporating information from sources in a paper does not need to be much more difficult than repeating a story your grandfather once told you. Basically, the statement, "When I was ten, my grandfather told me . . ." is replaced by something like "According to the *Statistical Abstract of the United States.* . . ." In formal research papers, you add a citation in parentheses to indicate exactly where in that volume you found the information. This citation is keyed to a list of works cited, which appears at the end of the paper.

Choosing a Topic

Many instructors provide students with a choice of specific topics or general subject areas, but others prefer for students to work with topics of their own choosing. The student who wrote the sample paper on the whooping crane, which appears at the end of Chapter 20, was asked to find a topic within one of the following general subject areas:

a significant breakthrough in medicine
the use of animals in medical research
the use of lie detectors by businesses
mandatory drug testing
state laws on drunk driving

nuclear waste disposal
an alternative source of energy such as solar or wind power
competency tests for teachers
a significant archaeological discovery
some aspect of the culture of an Indian tribe
a controversy surrounding the life of a famous historical figure
the fight to save an endangered species

The student, Nick Culver, chose to write about an endangered species, the whooping crane, because of a personal interest in the subject. Culver, a bird-watcher, had recently viewed along the Texas gulf coast the only surviving flock of whooping cranes in the wild.

If your instructor has given you free reign in choosing a topic, keep in mind that a topic should be narrow enough to allow in-depth investigation and significant enough to be worth exploring. To pick up topic ideas, you might browse through such library reference works as *Hot Topics*, which includes recent articles on controversial issues, or *Editorial Research Reports*, which contains digests of articles on both sides of an issue. Or you might take a look at current issues of magazines such as *Time, Newsweek, Scientific American,* or *Smithsonian.* Of course, your own interests — both scholarly and extracurricular — are an excellent source of ideas. You might consult with a professor in your major field to discover scholarly topics that are currently generating discussion.

Narrowing the Topic

Let's say that you are assigned a paper on some aspect of American history from 1776 to 1865. The professor obviously does not want a summary of George Washington's life or the sequence of events at Bull Run, but rather prefers a paper that develops a fairly precise thesis. You clearly do not want a subject like "The Causes of the Civil War," which would involve vast amounts of reading and to which you could contribute few insights of your own. What you should do is find a subject that has caught your interest — for instance, Thomas Jefferson — and then find of topic about Jefferson that is limited enough (his interest in music, his theories of architecture, his relationship with Lafayette) for you to emerge from the paper with a reasonable expertise.

Some background reading can help you narrow your topic. If you are interested in Jefferson but know little about him, you might first go to an article on him in either the *Encyclopaedia Britannica* or the *Dictionary of American Biography,* a standard reference work with articles on most notable Americans of the past. While reading one of these reference works, you might become interested in the fact that Jefferson frequently condemned slavery and yet owned slaves until the end of his life. (It is possible that he even had several children by one slave, Sally Hemmings.) At this point you might decide that your topic is "Thomas Jefferson and slavery."

Your finished paper would focus the topic more narrowly still — on a thesis making some assertion about Thomas Jefferson and slavery. But in order to formulate a thesis, you would first need to track down sources, read, and draw conclusions from what you had read.

Creating a Search Strategy

Librarians recommend that you spend a few minutes devising a search strategy appropriate for your particular topic. To create a search strategy, first consider what kinds of sources are most appropriate for your topic and then decide on the most efficient order in which to consult them.

For example, if you were writing about Thomas Jefferson and slavery, books would be a more likely source of information than magazines or newspapers. You would probably begin with articles in one or two general reference works, for background information, and then turn to books. Unless you had a great deal of time, you would focus on books (or chapters of books) dealing primarily with the paradoxes of Jefferson's attitudes toward slavery. Later, after acquiring some expertise, you might turn to scholarly articles in historical journals — perhaps articles frequently mentioned in the books you had consulted — and to some of Jefferson's own writings.

On the other hand, if you were writing about an endangered species such as the whooping crane, magazines and newspapers would be more appropriate than books, since they are more up-to-date. (By the time a book is published, its information is usually a year or so old.) You might first turn to a specialized reference work or to a book for an overview of the subject, but most of your investigation would focus on periodicals.

Finding Sources

As you begin researching in the library, it's a good idea to keep track of sources on 3″ × 5″ index cards. The information about sources that you put on these cards (known as "bibliography cards") has two purposes:

It will help you find the source in the library, and it will help you construct the list of works cited that will appear at the end of your research paper. For books, you should write down the following information:

> the call number (in the upper left-hand corner)
> the author or authors
> any editors or translators
> the title (underlined)
> the place of publication, the publisher, and the date of publication

For magazine or newspaper articles, write down this information:

> the author or authors
> the title of the article (in quotation marks)
> the name of the magazine or newspaper (underlined)
> the date of the issue
> the page numbers of the article

For scholarly journals, you will also need to note the volume number and perhaps the issue number.

Here are examples of bibliography cards, the first for a book, the second for a magazine article. If you are curious about the exact form required for the bibliographic entries in the list of works cited, consult pages 375–376.

Bibliography card for a book:

QL
696
S8
M23
1966A

Faith McNulty
The Whooping Crane
New York
E. P. Dutton + Co.
1966

Bibliography card for a magazine article:

Paul Johnsgard

"Whooper Recount"

Natural History

Feb. 1982
pp. 71-75

Reference Works

Many students make the mistake of reading highly specialized material before they have a clear overview of the subject itself. If you know very little about a subject or need to brush up on what you once knew, go first to an encyclopedia or other reference work. (These, which cannot be checked out, are usually kept in a separate section of the library.) With the background obtained from this general reading, you will better understand more specialized material you will read later, and you may find that other aspects of a subject interest you more than the one that attracted you initially. For instance, a student who was going to write a paper on the relationship between oil companies and the Ute Indians of Colorado and Utah decided after reading a general article that he preferred to write on the use of the drug peyote in Ute religious worship.

Encyclopedias most widely used by college students include *Academic American Encyclopedia, Collier's Encyclopedia, Encyclopedia Americana,* and the *Encyclopaedia Britannica.* The *Encyclopaedia Britannica* is divided into a ten-volume micropedia (with brief articles on tens of thousands of subjects) and a twenty-volume macropedia (with longer, more detailed articles on thousands of subjects). The micropedia will indicate where in the macropedia you will find more detailed discussions of your subject.

Almost all areas of study have specialized encyclopedias and reference works that go into more detail than even such a large reference as the *Encyclopaedia Britannica* can. There are hundreds of these, and while there is no reason for you to learn the names of all of them, you might want to become familiar with those in your major field. Here is a list covering a variety of disciplines and professions.

Encyclopedia of Anthropology
Encyclopedia of Banking and Finance
The Encyclopedia of Biological Sciences
Encyclopedia of Computers and Data Processing
Encyclopedia of Crime and Justice
The Encyclopedia of Management
The Encyclopedia of Philosophy
The Encyclopedia of Psychology
Encyclopedia of World Art
An Encyclopedia of World History
Harvard Guide to American History
McGraw-Hill Dictionary of Modern Economics
The McGraw-Hill Encyclopedia of Science and Technology
The New Grove Dictionary of Music and Musicians
The Oxford Companion to American Literature
The Oxford Companion to English Literature

If your subject is a person, consider turning to a biographical reference for background information. Here is a short list of such references:

Current Biography
Dictionary of American Biography
Dictionary of Literary Biography
McGraw-Hill Encyclopedia of World Biography
Notable American Women, 1607–1950
Notable American Women: The Modern Period
Who's Who in America

Of course there are many reference works not mentioned in this chapter. The student who wrote on the whooping crane consulted *The Audubon Society Encyclopedia of North American Birds*, a standard reference work found in most libraries. Such reference works can be located in one of three ways: (1) by consulting the library's catalog; (2) by consulting a reference work on reference works (there actually are such books); or (3) by consulting the reference librarian, whose job is to help you find source material.

Books

With almost any subject, you will want to check the library's catalog for its book holdings. Traditionally most libraries have used card catalogs: drawers of cards alphabetized by author, title, and subject. Today, however, some libraries have converted to microform catalogs, with the information formerly on cards appearing on microfiche or microfilm, or to computer catalogs, accessed through a keyboard.

The student writing on the whooping crane found one book entirely on the crane and one partly on it in the card catalog under the subject heading "Whooping Crane." If your subject is Thomas Jefferson, abortion, or Stoicism, you will find a great many more books than you would on the whooping crane and will be forced to select carefully those you are going to read in whole or in part. By surveying the table of contents you can usually tell whether a book is relevant to your narrowed topic, and by consulting the index you can often locate valuable information without reading the whole book.

Below is a sample of a card catalog entry under the subject "Whooping Crane." The letters and numbers in the upper left-hand corner are the "call number," the book's address on the library's shelves. The catalog card gives more information than you will need. If you think the book is worth consulting, copy down on a bibliography card only the call number, the author's name, the title of the book (underlined), the place of publication, the publisher, and the date of publication.

```
QL            WHOOPING CRANE
696.
G8     McNulty, Faith.
M23         The whooping crane; the bird that defies extinction. In-
1966a    trod. by Stewart L. Udall. [1st ed.,] New York, Dutton,
         1966.
            190 p.   illus.   25 cm.


            1. Whooping crane.
            QL696.G8M23   1966a        598.3          66–11544
                               O
            Library of Congress    [3]
```

If you fail to locate books under the first heading you try, consult *The Library of Congress Subject Headings (LCSH)*, two large volumes usually kept close to the card catalog. The student writing on the whooping crane first looked up "endangered species" but found no books listed under that heading. By consulting *LCSH*, he learned that the library files information about endangered species under the headings "rare animals" or "rare birds."

Magazine and Journal Articles

Many students choose topics of current interest when writing a research paper, and material on such subjects is most readily found in magazine articles.

If you want to find magazine articles written within the last five years, go to one of the microform indexes that most libraries now own. The best-known of these is *The Magazine Index*, an easy-to-use machine that lists by author and subject articles in hundreds of periodicals of general interest. The compilation covers the last five years and is frequently updated. Don't give up if you don't find what you are looking for under the first heading you try; you may need to try a more general heading.

Following is a sample of what will appear on the screen when you use *The Magazine Index*. The shorthand technique of *The Magazine Index* may appear puzzling at first, but it is easy to read once you get the hang of it. In each entry under the subject heading, the title comes first, followed perhaps by a brief description of the article in parentheses. Next you will find the name of the author (if the article has one), the name of the magazine, the date of the issue, and the page number on which the article begins. The number in parentheses at the end of the entry tells you how many pages long the article is.

```
        Whooping Crane
            The ambassador of cranes.  (Wisconsin's
                George Archibald & International Crane
                Foundation) by Patricia Daniels il
                National Wildlife v21-April-May '83-
                p33(5)

            This year's whooping crane countdown
                shows a probable gain of eleven birds.
                Audubon v82-Nov '80-p18(1)
```

If an article looks promising, check your library's list of periodicals, which is usually kept close to the magazine indexes, to see if the library owns the magazine. Then, if the library owns the magazine (or if you are willing to look for it in another library), write down the following information on your bibliography card: the author's name, the name of the article (in quotation marks), the name of the magazine (underlined), the date of the issue, and the page number on which the article begins. Once you find the actual article, put the inclusive page numbers on the bibliography card, since you may need them later.

If you are in search of articles written more than five years ago (or if you need current articles and the line at *The Magazine Index* is too long), turn to the indispensable *Reader's Guide to Periodical Literature,* an annual compilation by author and subject of articles in about 160 periodicals of general interest. Articles published in the current year may be found in paperback indexes that come out every month. When you are looking for current articles, however, you are better off using *The Magazine Index* because it covers five years in one shot and because — unlike the individual volumes of *Reader's Guide,* which often get scattered over the reference room — the machine stays in the same place and is lost only when its gears fail to function properly.

For most undergraduate papers, the *Reader's Guide* or a microfilm resource like *The Magazine Index* will provide sufficient material, but periodical indexes in specific fields cover the many scholarly and technical publications that the *Reader's Guide* and *The Magazine Index* do not. These specialized indexes are not always found in public libraries, but in most college libraries they will be on the shelves near the *Reader's Guide.* Here is a representative list:

Art Index
Biological Abstracts
Business Periodicals Index
Education Index
Engineering Index
General Science Index
Historical Abstracts
Humanities Index
MLA International Bibliography of Books and Articles in the Modern Languages and Literature
Music Index
Psychological Abstracts
Social Sciences Index

Indexing today is marvelously efficient, but there is still no easy way to find articles about an event that took place last month. In that case, go to the magazine section of the library and start thumbing; *Time* and *Newsweek* at least will have articles on any very recent event of importance.

Newspaper Articles

If you need up-to-date information or an account of a recent event of importance, the newspaper is probably your best bet. The most thorough newspaper index is that of the *New York Times*. (It is also the oldest, going back to 1851.) Like the *Reader's Guide*, the *New York Times Index* is an annual compilation with biweekly compilations for the current year. As can be seen in the sample below, the index also includes a handy one- or two-sentence summary of the story's content. Don't despair if there is nothing under the first subject heading you try; whooping cranes, for instance, are listed here under "Birds" and the subheading "Cranes."

Coots. See also Hunting, F 24
Cranes
Wildlife biologists reptdly are hopeful that 4 young whooping cranes that were born in Idaho during summer of '75 and recently migrated into wildlife refuge near Monte Vista (Colo), will form nucleus of new flock of endangered species (S), Mr 6,50:2; birdwatcher John Savage describes visit to Bosque del Apache Natl Wildlife Refuge (Sorocco, NM); notes 2 young whooping cranes raised by 'foster parent' sandhill cranes during '75 in Canada are wintering in area; says they are 1st whoopers to visit NM since 1850s; Tom Smylie notes there are only 48 wild whooping cranes in existence, excluding '75 hatch; illus (L), Mr 7,X, p9; Patuxent Wildlife Research Center head Dr Cameron Kepler says whooping crane chick was hatched May 5; birth expands whoopers' world population to 85; if chick survives, it will be 1st whooper successfully hatched and grown from parents raised in captivity (S), My 6,23:1
Fed Appeals Ct, New Orleans, refuses to consider decision

A shorthand entry like "Mr 6,50:2" gives first the date, then the page number, and then the column; this one would be translated as March 6, page 50, column 2. Note that titles and authors are not usually given, so you will need to take them down when you read the story.

In the past it was very difficult to find articles in newspapers other than the *New York Times*, but today several other handy indexes exist. For instance, there is the *National Newspaper Index*, a compilation of articles in five of the nation's leading newspapers: *Christian Science Monitor*,

New York Times, Los Angeles Times, Wall Street Journal, and *Washington Post.* Access to selected articles in over one hundred other American newspapers is provided by *Newsbank,* a continually updated collection of articles printed on microfiche.

Other Sources of Information

Most, if not all, of the source material you need may be found in the card catalog and in newspaper and periodical indexes, but if at some point you need further information, you almost certainly can find it in the library. There are, for instance, a number of sources for statistics. The United States Bureau of the Census each year publishes the *Statistical Abstract of the United States,* a compilation of the principal statistical information produced by the federal government. Statistics for the past may be found in *Historical Statistics of the United States, Colonial Times to 1957. Statistics Sources* will show you where to find data on industrial and business matters.

For some topics, information in pamphlets may be useful. These are usually stored in hanging files in a large file cabinet known as the "vertical file." Be aware, however, that not all pamphlets are equally reliable. If a pamphlet has been published by a group with a strong political interest in the subject, check the information carefully against other sources that are clearly unbiased.

Information relevant to many topics can be found outside the library. Depending on your topic, you might request information from a government agency, interview an expert, attend a political or a scholarly meeting, or conduct a survey or an original experiment. Information from such sources can provide a welcome touch of human interest in a paper that draws most of its facts and ideas from books and periodicals.

Taking Notes

You will not be far into your reading before your thesis will begin to take shape, however much it may later have to be modified. At this point you should begin taking notes. The best method of taking notes is to put each quotation, piece of information, or observation of your own on an individual note card, giving that card a label that will correspond to one of the sections of the paper.

The student writing on the whooping crane realized early in his reading, for example, that his thesis would be a generally optimistic statement about the crane's chances for survival. He also realized what the major sections of his paper would probably be about and labeled his cards accordingly. He soon could even see subheadings developing — for instance "Texas-Canada Flock — Hunting Dangers."

Although it is not necessary to take thorough notes on everything you read, the notes you do take must be accurate. Summaries should reflect what the text actually says, and quoted passages must be put down in quotation marks *exactly* as they appear in the source. Be sure to include the exact page numbers on which information appears. You will need these page numbers later if you decide to cite the source in your paper.

There are three general ways of noting a passage. The first is to summarize part of the article, as on the card below. Be certain that when you summarize, you do not "half-copy" — that is, rely too much on the wording of the text. Obviously you will be repeating some of the words in the text in your summary; but in general, when a series of words on your note card is exactly the same as a series of words in the text, you should put the words in quotation marks. To prevent half-copying, you may find it best to summarize without looking at the article and *then* check for accuracy. (See page 342 for an example of the form of plagiarism known as half-copying.)

> Texas – Canada flock – Hunting Dangers
> Pressure to open up more access to swan and sandhill crane hunting could endanger whooper because of its similarity to these birds.
> Author thinks, however, that fear of public wrath if a whooper shot will prevent this. North Dakota, e.g., will not allow sandhill crane hunting until certain all whoopers gone for year.
> — Sherwood, 84

The second method of noting is to quote directly. This method is most frequently used for statements of opinion or for particularly eloquent passages. Make sure to take down the quotation *exactly* as it appears in the original source, and place it in quotation marks.

> Human responsibility
> "Can society, whether through sheer
> wantonness or callous neglect, permit the
> extinction of something beautiful or grand in
> nature without risking extermination of
> something beautiful and grand in its
> own character?"
> —editorial in C. S. M.
> (quoted in Allen, 31)

The third method is to summarize, but to quote key words and phrases, especially those that are skillfully used.

> Life-Cycle — Mating Dances
>   Mating dances begin in late December —
> but only become intense 2-3 months later. In
> dances birds leap, bow, posture. Because of
> crane's "immense size," this is "one of the
> great dances of the bird world." By March
> dances are "an almost daily occurrence."
> Allen, pp. 68-70

Since the development of duplicating machines, students are more and more using other methods of note-taking. Particularly if you are working from magazine or newspaper articles, you can duplicate some or all of your source material inexpensively, which allows you to work from it at home rather than take notes in the library. One Soviet researcher now living in the United States calls our duplicating machines "the best thing about working in the United States." In the Soviet Union, he says, "I spent 50 percent of my time sitting in the library copying notes out of books." In recent years, some students have developed ingenious methods of avoiding the laborious task of note-taking. One student, writing on Stanley Kubrick's classic science fiction film *2001: A Space Odyssey*, decided what the divisions of her paper would be and bought five different colored pencils, with which she marked the duplicated articles as she read.

Most likely, however, even if you are going to duplicate articles, you are better off sticking to some variation of the traditional method of note-taking, as the student writing on the whooping crane did in the following note. He described part of an article briefly and indicated where the discussion could be found.

Life-Cycle — Summer
Describes in detail nesting, hatching, rearing process.

— Guthery, p. 19

Although duplication may enhance accuracy because the sources can be checked quickly, it may encourage the rushed student to rely too heavily on the wording of the source, sometimes unintentionally. *Don't* — both because this is plagiarism (copying someone else's work without giving proper credit to the source) and because such heavy reliance on someone else's wording will interrupt the smooth flow of your own style through the paper.

As you approach your final thesis, you may tend to note only those opinions or that information that will support it. But remember also to note information and opinions that may weaken or oppose your position, to be fair, and to make your argument most impressive by facing up to the strength of its opposition.

20 *Writing the Research Paper*

Scholarship is polite argument. — PHILIP RIEFF

Students who otherwise write clearly often lose their voices when they write research papers. They turn in papers that resemble patchwork quilts or scrapbooks, papers that are merely collections of other people's ideas. Don't let yourself be intimidated by your sources. Unless your paper is a simple factual report, it will, like all your other essays, revolve around an idea or opinion or conclusion that is your own. Your contribution may seem small and may consist primarily of a thesis statement and topic sentences, but the thesis statement and topic sentences are *your* conclusions, even if all your supporting evidence comes from sources.

For instance, three students in one class each decided to write a paper on Laetrile, a controversial cancer drug that is legal in Mexico but illegal in the United States. All three students read approximately the same articles, but came to somewhat different conclusions.

> Although individual cancer patients claim to have been helped by Laetrile, scientific study after scientific study has found no evidence that its use stops or slows down the spread of cancer.

> No scientific evidence exists that Laetrile retards the growth of cancer, and therefore the United States government should continue to ban its use. Its legalization would only encourage people with cancer to avoid legitimate treatment and to put money into the hands of unethical physicians.

> Although no scientific evidence exists that Laetrile stops or slows down the spread of cancer, neither does sure scientific evidence exist that its use is harmful. Until evidence that it is harmful does exist, the government should allow its use, for Laetrile at least provides victims of cancer a hope, a hope that could give them strength.

The three students seem to agree that there is no scientific evidence that Laetrile is effective in fighting cancer, and each goes on to establish that through reference to books and articles. The second student, however, has decided also to argue that the ban on its use in the United States should continue — a position he will probably bolster with the arguments of government officials and physicians and with his own observations about human nature. The third student apparently agrees with the other two about the scientific evidence, but has decided that legalizing the drug will do no harm and might even help patients psychologically. This student had an uncle who went to Mexico for cancer treatment in the last year of his life. What she knows about her uncle's treatment and death adds little to our scientific knowledge about Laetrile, but is very relevant to her decision as to whether Laetrile should be banned.

All three theses are legitimate, and they are the students' own. Each student decided after reading a number of sources what he or she wanted to say, and organized the thesis and paper accordingly. Each decided how seriously to take personal testimonials on the effectiveness of Laetrile and how conclusive the scientific research had been. And each grouped the various opinions in ways that fit into his or her paper.

Formulating a Thesis

For most of the papers you have been writing this semester, you probably began with a thesis and then found evidence (usually from personal experience) to prove it. For the research paper you will need to reverse the process: You'll look at the evidence first (primarily in books and magazines) and then come to a conclusion. That conclusion will be your thesis.

For instance, let's say that you have chosen to write your research paper on the controversy over grizzly bears in the national parks. You will find as you read that attacks on people by grizzly bears have increased dramatically in Yellowstone and Glacier National Parks in recent years, mostly because more people are in the parks and the bears are becoming aware that they can find food where humans camp. Some individuals have even advocated removing the bears from areas where they might come in contact with tourists or campers. Others argue that if the national parks are to preserve what is left of wild America, visitors to the parks must accept the possibility of danger — that to remove all dangers would turn Yellowstone and Glacier into Disneylands.

Unless you have encountered a grizzly bear yourself, you will probably take all your information on attacks from sources. You will read different opinions about what should be done. But in the end it is you who must formulate the thesis, which will depend on how you feel about dangerous wildlife. Don't make the mistake of accepting the first written opinion you find and trying to compose a paper to back up that writer's opinion; other writers may think differently, or you may change your mind. And accepting the first opinion you read violates a basic principle of research, that you choose from and use a number of sources.

When finally you arrive at a thesis, you will put it into an introductory paragraph in pretty much the way you have been doing for your other papers. The research-paper thesis may differ from the theses you have been writing in two ways, however: (1) Because the subject may be more complex, the thesis may be more than one sentence long; and (2) because the research paper may be longer than essays you have been writing, the thesis is more likely to set up the major divisions of the paper, as an aid to both you and the reader. (For an example of a research-paper thesis, turn to the sample paper following this chapter.)

Planning and Drafting the Paper

After you have finished taking notes and have some rough idea of your thesis, you will want to polish the thesis and sketch an outline before beginning your rough draft. By this time you will know a great deal about your subject, probably more than you realize. It is therefore best to set aside your notes and work on your thesis and rough outline without them. With so many facts, figures, and opinions in front of you, it is sometimes difficult to see the forest for the trees. A good way to start — and to prove to yourself how much you know — might be to take a friend aside and tell him or her what you plan to say about your subject in the paper. If you feel you have presented a reasonably well-organized argument in support of your thesis, that presentation can lead to a preliminary outline.

In your preliminary outline, try to block out the overall structure of the paper, limiting yourself to the thesis statement and two or more (but probably no more than five) major supports. Then, to get a rough idea of whether this initial plan will work, sort your note cards in stacks representing the major divisions of the outline. If at this point you're not happy with your preliminary plan, it will be a simple enough matter to adjust it and to rearrange your note cards accordingly. Once you have settled on an overall plan, you will be ready to fill in the details of the outline. By looking through the note cards in each stack, you should have little difficulty settling on a logical arrangement of ideas within each of the major sections of the paper. For an example of a research paper outline, see Nick Culver's outline for his paper on the whooping crane (pages 356–357).

After you have refined the outline and again referred to your notes, you should be ready to begin writing. As you write, you will for the most part simply back up the statements in your outline with your own observations and material from your notes. Whenever you quote a source or borrow ideas that are not common knowledge, you will cite the source. To do this, you will use a system of signal phrases and parenthetical citations, a system discussed in detail later in this chapter.

When quoting a source, you will need to look at your note card or at the source itself as you write, since quotations (which should appear in quotation marks) must be word-for-word accurate. When putting the ideas of a source in your own words, however, do *not* work closely with your sources. If the wording of a source is in front of you — as it might be if you are working from photocopied articles rather than summary-style note cards — it is practically impossible to avoid echoing the language of the source too closely as you attempt to put it in your own words. Simply by putting the source aside and working from memory, you can be certain that passages "in your own words" are in fact in your own words. You can always turn to the source later to check for accuracy.

Avoiding Plagiarism

Plagiarism — using the language or ideas of another writer as if they were one's own — is a serious form of academic dishonesty. Most students understand that they must give credit to an author for his or her ideas (at least those that cannot be considered common knowledge). What many students do *not* understand is that it is equally dishonest to borrow language from a source without putting such borrowings in quotation marks — even if the source is cited.

All too often students half-copy from a source, simply substituting synonyms here or there and modeling their own sentence structures on those in the original. Following are a passage from an article in *Smithsonian* magazine and a paragraph in which a student relied too heavily on the wording and organization of the *Smithsonian* original.

Original Source	Plagiarized Version
Allowing the entire wild population to remain concentrated at Aransas in winter, and Wood Buffalo in summer, also seemed imprudent. They were — and are — vulnerable to a wide variety of disasters. Epidemic illness is one. At Aransas, a late-season hurricane could decimate the band. So might an oil spill, or a toxic chemical that leaked from one of the many barges that pass through the refuge on the intracoastal waterway.	It seemed unwise to allow the entire wild population to remain concentrated in one place in winter and one place in summer. There are many disasters that could strike. Epidemic illness could eliminate the flock. A late-season hurricane could wipe out the band. An oil spill might occur, or chemicals could leak from one of the barges that pass through the refuge on the intracoastal waterway (Zimmerman 53).

Notice that the student has borrowed too many phrases from her source and that she has modeled the organization of her paragraph too closely on that of the original. Such borrowing, even though it ends with a source citation, is theft — perhaps unintentional, but theft nonetheless.

To protect yourself from the charge of academic dishonesty, you need to present your source material in one of two ways. Either quote the material word for word, put it in quotation marks, and end with a citation or present the material wholly in your own words and end with a citation, as this student has done:

Acceptable Use of the Source

When the entire wild population of whooping cranes is concentrated in one area, it is vulnerable to disasters that might wipe out the entire flock. *Smithsonian* cites the possibility of epidemic illness, hurricanes, oil spills, and chemical leaks from passing barges (Zimmerman 53).

Obviously some repetition of words and phrases from your sources will occur in your paper (there are only so many ways of saying, for instance, that Gray's Lake is in southeastern Idaho at an elevation of 6,400 feet), but if your sentences follow the sentence patterns in the original and repeat a large number of words and phrases, they need to be rewritten.

As mentioned earlier, the best way to avoid echoing too much language from a source is to set the original aside, write your paragraphs without reference to it, and consult the source later to check for accuracy.

When to Cite Sources

Except for common factual knowledge (of which there is a great deal), all information taken from a source, whether it is quoted directly or put in your own words, must be followed by a source citation — all quotations, all ideas and opinions, all precise factual information such as statistics.

Much that you have read, however, is common knowledge for which a source need not be cited (as long as you put this information into your own words), whether you knew the information before your reading or not. No absolute distinction exists between what is common knowledge and what is not (if you aren't sure, cite the source), but information can usually be called common knowledge if it passes two tests: (1) if such information (that whooping cranes mate for life, that William Faulkner won the Nobel Prize for literature) appears in general reference works and is mentioned without source citations in more than one article you have read; (2) if you can honestly say, "I know this."

Thus, what you tell your friends in the cafeteria about a subject (for instance, the grizzly bear) is in all likelihood common knowledge. But you wouldn't claim as common knowledge the thirty-some uses that the Plains Indians made of the buffalo.

At times you may wish to cite a source even for what is common knowledge. For instance, except for a few recent nips at biologists, no verifiable evidence exists that a wild wolf has ever attacked a human being on the North American continent; however, there are so many myths to the contrary that writers may wish to protect themselves by citing a source for this common knowledge.

How to Cite Sources:
In-text Citations

The form used in this chapter for source citations is that of the Modern Language Association (MLA) in the 1988 edition of its style manual. In place of the traditional footnotes or endnotes, MLA now recommends a combination of signal phrases and parenthetical citations appearing in the text of the paper itself. The following models illustrate the possible combinations of signal phrases and parenthetical citations.

Author in Signal Phrase, Page Number in Parentheses. Ordinarily, the signal phrase includes the author's name, and the parentheses include only a page number.

> As late as 1967, James C. Greenway said that the survival of the whooping crane "would be a miracle" (208).

The signal phrase "James Greenway said that" tells readers to expect information from a source, and the page number in parentheses tells them exactly where in the source the information can be found. To learn the title of the source, readers consult the list of works cited at the end of the paper, where works are listed alphabetically according to the last name of the author.

Author and Page Number in Parentheses. If the author's name is not mentioned in a signal phrase, it must be included in the parentheses. Use the author's last name only, and do not put any punctuation between it and the page number.

> As late as 1967, one scientist said that the survival of the whooping crane "would be a miracle" (Greenway 208).

Including a Title. Ordinarily a title need not be included either in the signal phrase or in the parentheses. There are two exceptions, however. A title must be included if a source has no author or if two or more works by the same author (or by authors with the same last name) appear in the list of works cited. In such instances, either include the title of the work in the signal phrase or put a short form of the title in the parentheses. Titles of books are underlined, to indicate italics; titles of magazine and newspaper articles are put in quotation marks. In the parentheses, no mark of punctuation separates the short title from the page number.

> As late at 1967, James C. Greenway said in <u>Extinct and</u> <u>Vanishing Birds of the World</u> that the survival of the whooping crane "would be a miracle" (208).

> As late as 1967, James C. Greenway said that the survival of the whooping crane "would be a miracle" (<u>Extinct</u> 208).

In the rare instance when it becomes necessary to put the author's name, a short title, and the page number in the parentheses, place a comma between the author's name and the short title.

> As late as 1976, one scientist said that the survival of the whooping crane "would be a miracle" (Greenway, <u>Extinct</u> 208).

Use some care in abbreviating titles. If you are abbreviating a work like the *Guiness Book of World Records*, which has no author, the work should be abbreviated *Guiness* rather than *World Records*, for the work will appear under *G* in the list of works cited. One-word abbreviations are usually acceptable, though at times they may seem silly. You would commit no crime in abbreviating Adrian Desmond's *The Ape's Reflexion* as *Ape's*, but it would be less awkward to write *Ape's Reflexion*.

A Work with Two or More Authors. When a source has two or three authors, name all authors either in the signal phrase or in the parentheses. Use only last names in the parentheses.

> According to <u>Wildlife in Danger</u>, the preservation of the whooping crane's nesting territories now seems "reasonably well-assured" (Fisher, Simon, and Vincent 244).

When a source has four or more authors, use only the name of the first author followed by "et al." (meaning "and others") either in the signal phrase or in the parentheses.

> Researchers at Patuxent argue that their captive breeding program was necessary in the early 1980s (Carpenter et al. 76).

An Unknown Author.   If the work (such as a magazine or newspaper article) has an unknown author, use a short form of the title of the work in the parentheses or mention the title in the signal phrase.

> One newspaper recently reported that the latest word on a
> healthy diet is coming "from an unlikely source -- our
> prehistoric ancestors" ("Nutrition" C1).

A Multivolume Work.   If you are citing a multivolume work, include the volume number before the page number and follow it by a colon.

> Page Smith points out that "it was to be more than a year
> before the French and Americans tried once more to combine
> forces in a military engagement against the British" (2:
> 1122).

An Indirect Source.   If you are citing a quotation found in an article or book written by someone else, begin the citation in parentheses with the abbreviation "qtd. in" (meaning "quoted in").

> Noam Chomsky once said, "Acquisition of even the barest
> rudiments of language is quite beyond the capacities of an
> otherwise intelligent ape" (qtd. in Crail 157-58).

Incorporating Source Material into Your Paper

When incorporating source material into your paper, be sure that you make clear to the reader what is from a source and what is not. As a general rule, quotations, opinions, and ideas that appear in your paper are preceded by a signal phrase, such as "According to Carl Jung" or "As Mario Pei has observed." The quotation, opinion, or idea is then followed by parentheses enclosing a source citation. Readers will know that everything between the signal phrase and the source citation is from the source, whether directly quoted or put into your own words.

Here are two examples of the proper form for introducing direct quotations.

> In June of 1977, Keith M. Schreiner, associate direc-
> tor of the Fish and Wildlife Service, said of the whooping
> crane's future, "The outlook has never been brighter"
> (14).

> So successful have hunting regulations and educa-
> tional campaigns been that Wildlife in Danger could say in
> 1969 that "the losses on migration by uncontrolled and

```
ignorant shooting have certainly become small" (Fisher,
Simon, and Vincent 225).
```

Notice that the writer of these sentences was careful to let readers know in the text itself the source of the quoted material. Readers understand immediately that the first quotation is from Schreiner, the second from *Wildlife in Danger*. In addition, readers learn who Schreiner is.

Factual material is also usually preceded by a signal phrase and followed by a citation in parentheses, but it is more often put in one's own words, as in the following example:

```
According to Faith McNulty, by 1938 there was only
one migratory flock of twenty-two birds left (15).
```

Except for numbers, the writer is not borrowing wording from his source and thus doesn't need to use quotation marks. The page number is cited to let the reader know exactly where the writer obtained the information.

To keep from sounding like a stuck record repeating over and over "Faith McNulty says," you will want to have at hand a variety of signal phrases and to learn to place them at various points in the sentence. In the following sentence, for instance, the student has cited the author in the middle of the quotation: "If chimpanzees have consciousness, if they are capable of abstractions," Carl Sagan asks, "do they not have what until now has been described as 'human rights'?"

Incorporating source material into your own writing may be a bit awkward at first, but you will quickly learn how to work such material into the texture of your paper. Following is a quotation about human hatred of wolves and three examples of ways you could incorporate this source material in a paper.

```
Wolf Hatred

     "How can one hate the wolf and love the dog as
his best friend at the same time? Without the
wolf on the evolutionary ladder, there would be
no dog. Yet there are people in Minnesota and
Alaska who would lay down their lives for their
huskies and German shepherds and forgetting the
origin of things, go gladly into the great void
still ungrateful to the wolf."

                    Mitchell, 20
```

Many people feel very differently about the wolf and
its descendant, the dog. John Mitchell points out that
"there are people in Minnesota and Alaska who would lay
down their lives for their huskies and German shepherds,"
yet die "still ungrateful to the wolf" (20).

A puzzled John Mitchell asks, "How can one hate the
wolf and love the dog as his best friend at the same
time?" As he observes, the dogs for which humans even
risk their lives are descended from wolves (20).

Since dogs are descended from wolves, this human
hatred of wolves seems inconsistent and irrational. John
Mitchell points out that the same Minnesotans and Alaskans
who hate wolves would risk death for their huskies and
German shepherds (20).

Once you have learned how to use signal phrases, you will find it
fairly simple to incorporate material from several sources into one paragraph and yet always make clear to the reader which information is
from what source, as in the following passage from the sample research
paper on the whooping crane. Any material between the signal phrase
and the parentheses, whether quoted directly or put in the student's
own words, is from the specific source indicated.

This bird [the whooping crane] of which so few remain
has a long history. James Fisher, Noel Simon, and Jack
Vincent describe it as a "Pleistocene relict": bones found
in Idaho are 3,500,000 years old by potassium—argon dating
and "are not distinguishable from modern bones of the species" (223). According to Fred Guthery, when glacial ice
was receding from North America 10,000 years ago, whooping
crane numbers were high, and the bird was distributed over
all of North America except eastern Canada and New England. The receding ice, however, meant the replacement of
marshes by forest and grasslands, so that the whooping
crane population had greatly declined even before humans
began further to diminish its numbers (18).

Information Notes

You may wish to include in your research essay one or more information
notes. These notes will be numbered at the end of your essay, and the
numbers will correspond to numbers in the text of the paper itself.
Although some instructors discourage this kind of note, an information
note is handy when you want to give the reader further information

about a subject, even repeat a delightful story you came across, but think that putting this more detailed information in the text of your essay would divert attention from the essay's main points or muddle your organization. The student writing on the whooping crane has used two such notes, one to give more detailed information about mating among whooping cranes, the other to tell the reader where to find more information about a subject.

When you wish to indicate to the reader that additional information about a subject will appear in note form at the end of your essay, insert a number in the text of your essay, usually at the end of a sentence. The number is raised half a space and corresponds to the number of the note.

For an illustration of how to insert information notes, see the text of the sample research paper and the page of notes that follows it.

Preparing a List of Works Cited

A list of works cited, which appears at the end of your paper, provides bibliographic information about each of the works that you have cited in the paper.

To prepare the list of works cited, first collect your bibliography cards for all of the sources actually cited in the paper. Unless your instructor requests otherwise, do not include bibliography cards for sources that you read but did not cite. Next arrange the bibliography cards in alphabetical order, according to the author's last name or, if there is no author, according to the first word of the title other than *a, an,* or *the.*

Now you are ready to construct the list. Begin it on a separate page and center the title "Works Cited" an inch from the top margin. Begin each bibliographic entry at the left margin, and indent any additional lines for that entry five spaces. (See pages 375–376 for an example.)

As you write each entry, consult the appropriate model below to see exactly how to order the bibliographic information. Be sure to observe all details of punctuation.

A Book with a Single Author. Begin with the author's name, last name first, followed by a period. Next write the title of the book, underlined to indicate italics, followed by a period. Finally, include the publishing information: the place of publication followed by a colon, the publisher's name followed by a comma, and the year of publication followed by a period.

```
Bettleheim, Bruno.  The Uses of Enchantment: The Meaning
     and Importance of Fairy Tales.  New York: Knopf,
     1977.
```

You can abbreviate the name of the publisher as long as your abbreviation is easily identifiable. In the entry just given, "Knopf" is an abbreviation for "Alfred A. Knopf, Inc."

A Work with Two or More Authors.   If a work has two or three authors, name all of the authors. Begin with the name of the first author, last name first, followed by a comma; then write the other authors' names in normal order.

```
Berrigan, Daniel, and Lee Lockwood.  Absurd Convictions,
     Modest Hopes.  New York: Random, 1973.
```

The names of three authors are separated by commas: Renshaw, Betty, Anne King, and Sandra Kurtinitis.

For four or more authors, use only the first author's name followed by a comma and "et al." (meaning "and others"): Smith, James J., et al.

An Unknown Author.   If the author of the work is unknown, begin the entry with the title of the work. Alphabetize the entry by the first word of the title other than *a, an,* or *the.*

```
Illustrated Atlas of the World.  Chicago: Rand, 1985.
```

A Book with an Editor.   If the book has an editor rather than an author, begin the entry with the name of the editor, last name first, and follow it with a comma and the abbreviation "ed." (for "editor").

```
Bell, Bernard W., ed.  Modern and Contemporary Afro-Ameri-
     can Poetry.  Boston: Allyn and Bacon, 1972.
```

If there is more than one editor, invert the name of the first editor only, and use the abbreviation "eds." (for "editors").

A Book with an Author and an Editor.   Begin with the author and title. Then write "Ed." (for "Edited by") followed by the name of the editor or editors.

```
Shakespeare, William.  Hamlet.  Ed. Louis B. Wright and
     Virginia A. Lamar.  New York: Washington Square,
     1959.
```

A Work with a Translator.   After the title of the work, write
"Trans." (for "Translated by") followed by the name of the translator
or translators.

> Leonov, Leonid. <u>The Thief</u>. Trans. Hubert Butler. New
> York: Vintage, 1960.

A Selection from an Anthology.   When citing a work (such as
an article, a poem, or a play) that appears in an anthology, begin with
the author of the work, not with the editor of the anthology. After the
author's name, put the title of the work in quotation marks (for articles,
poems, or short stories) or underlined (for plays and novels). After the
title of the work, give the title of the anthology, underlined, followed
by a period. Next write "Ed." (for "Edited by") followed by the name
of the editor and a period. Next present the publishing information
followed by a period. End with the page numbers of the work cited.

> Murray, Gilbert. "Beyond Good and Evil." <u>The Dimensions
> of Job: A Study and Selected Readings</u>. Ed. Nahum N.
> Glatzer. New York: Schocken, 1969. 194–97.

An Edition of a Book Other than the First.   When the book
you consulted is not the first edition, include the number of the edition
after the title of the book. Use the abbreviation "ed." (for "edition").

> Franklin, John Hope. <u>From Slavery to Freedom</u>. 3rd ed.
> New York: Knopf, 1967.

Multivolume Work.   If your paper cites only one volume of a
multivolume work, write the volume number after the title. At the end
of the entry, write the number of volumes in the work.

> Graves, Robert. <u>The Greek Myths</u>. Vol. 2. New York: Bra-
> ziller, 1967. 2 vols.

An Article in a Reference Work.   Rules for citing reference works
vary, for reference works vary. For a signed article, begin with the
author's name. For an unsigned article, begin with the title of the article.
When a reference work is arranged alphabetically, there is no need for
volume or page numbers.

> "Minerva." <u>The Oxford Classical Dictionary</u>. 1970 ed.

A Magazine Article.   Begin with the author's name, last name first, followed by a period. Then write the name of the article, followed by a period and placed in quotation marks. Finally, include the name of the magazine, underlined to indicate italics, followed by the date of the issue, a colon, and the page numbers on which the article appears.

> Carter, Snowden.   "All Along's International Victory Caps
> Win Streak."   <u>Maryland Horse</u> Dec. 1983: 24–28.

If the article's pagination is interrupted, appearing, for instance, on pages 24 to 28 and later on pages 40 to 41, put down the number of the article's first page followed by a plus sign: 24 + .

For weekly magazines, give the exact date of the issue, not just the month and year. Put the day of the month before the month, with no punctuation between the month and the year: 12 Dec. 1983.

A Journal Paginated by Volume.   Scholarly periodicals are called "journals," not "magazines." Many journals paginate from the beginning of the year to the end of the year continuously and then bind the issues together in yearly volumes. For such journals, put the volume number after the title of the journal and follow it with the year in parentheses. The other details of the entry are the same as for magazines.

> Tangley, Laura.   "Captive Propagation: Will It Succeed?"
> <u>Science News</u> 121 (1982): 266–68.

A Journal Paginated by Issue.   When each issue of a journal begins with page 1, put the number of the volume, a period, and the number of the issue before the year in parentheses.

> Gilbert, Janet R.   "Patterns and Possibilities for Basic
> Writers."   <u>Journal of Basic Writing</u> 6.2 (1987): 37–
> 52.

A Newspaper Article.   The author, the title of the article, and the name of the newspaper are handled as for magazines. After the name of the newspaper, put the date, with the day of the month appearing before the name of the month and the year. After the year, put a colon and follow it with the section letter and the page number.

> Kriegsman, Alan M.   "ABT Fires Two Stars."   <u>Washington
> Post</u> 10 Dec. 1980: D1.

If the section is numbered rather than lettered, handle the section and page number as follows: 10 Dec. 1980, sec. 4:1. If you have consulted a special edition of a newspaper, name the edition after the date and before the section and page reference: late ed., natl. ed., eastern ed., and so on. Handle multiple editors as you would multiple authors, and use the abbreviation "eds." (for "editors").

A Government Publication. Most government publications do not list an author. Begin with the name of the government followed by a period. Then give the name of the agency followed by a period. Conclude with the title and publishing information.

```
United States.  Internal Revenue Service.  Tax Guide for
     Small Business.  Publication 334.  Washington: GPO,
     1983.
```

Personal and Telephone Interviews. Begin with the name of the person interviewed, last name first, followed by a period. Next write "Personal interview" or "Telephone interview." Then give the date of the interview.

```
LaBruda, Steve.  Telephone interview.  17 Jan. 1988.
```

Two or More Works by the Same Author. If your paper cites two or more works by the same author, use the author's name only for the first entry. For subsequent entries, use three hyphens followed by a period in place of the name.

Sample Research Paper

On the following pages is a sample research paper, written for a class in which the students were asked to investigate the current status of an endangered North American animal species. This paper is approximately 3,000 words in length — not an unusual length for an undergraduate research paper, though good papers can be written with far fewer words. If you feel your paper is going to require more pages than you want to write, it is usually possible to narrow the topic further. This student, for instance, could have written his entire paper on the controversy over the captive breeding of whooping cranes.

In order to write this paper, the student read one entire book on the whooping crane and a section of one other book, two fairly short articles in reference works, four short news articles, and seven magazine articles. This is not an unreasonable amount of reading for a research paper. Your topic may demand more reading or less.

Unless your instructor specifies otherwise, submit the following material with the research paper:

1. *A title page.* The title should include the title of the paper, your name, the name of the course and the instructor, the name of the college, and the date of submission.

2. *An outline.* The thesis appears first in an outline. The major headings are logical divisions supporting the thesis.

3. *The text of the paper.* Most instructors require that the research paper be typed. It should be typed with inch-wide margins.

4. *A list of works cited,* arranged in alphabetical order.

A Miracle Almost Achieved:

The Status of the Whooping Crane in 1988

by

Nick Culver

English 101, Mr. Shaw

Prince George's Community College

February 28, 1988

A Miracle Almost Achieved:

The Status of the Whooping Crane in 1988

Thesis: Although the whooping crane's survival in the
            wild is far from absolutely assured, no one
            any longer sees extinction as inevitable, and
            many are optimistic about the crane's future.
            Developments in three locations provide the
            basis for this optimism.

Background: The background material briefly describes the
             whooping crane's life cycle and summarizes
             its history until its numerical low point in
             1938.

    I.   The Texas-Canada flock has grown, and its
         protection is relatively assured.
         A. The flock has steadily increased in
             number.
         B. The flock is better protected than in the
             past.
             1. The nesting and wintering territories
                 are now on government-protected land.
             2. Public protests would greet any
                 threat to the whooping crane.
             3. Hunting losses have become very
                 small.

II. Despite controversy, problems, and failure to meet proposed goals, the captive breeding program at Patuxent, Maryland, now appears to be a success.

    A. After long years of partial failure, the captive whooping cranes are now producing eggs.

    B. Some of the fears about the captive breeding program have been allayed.

III. Although the cranes have not yet successfully bred, a second migratory flock has been established in Idaho and New Mexico.

    A. Whooping cranes have been hatched by foster parents and have successfully participated in migration.

    B. Although there have been bad years, the number of cranes has steadily increased.

Conclusion: The conclusion briefly argues that humans should continue to protect the whooping crane.

Note: The numbers in the margins of the sample research paper correspond to the comments presented below.

1. In this first citation, the author was named in a signal phrase, so only the page number appears in parentheses. Note that the quoted material, which has been taken word-for-word from the source, appears in quotation marks. The closing quotation mark comes before the parentheses, the period after them.

2. The thesis of the paper usually appears in the first paragraph. Although the wording of the thesis in the text of the paper need not be exactly like the wording in the outline, it should closely parallel it. In this paper, the student has expanded the two-sentence statement in the outline to one paragraph, a paragraph which sets up the major divisions of his paper. The longer your paper is, the more important it is that you announce to the reader what the divisions of the paper will be.

3. Be sure to word your thesis carefully and don't hesitate to change the thesis if while writing the paper you decide that it is not quite what you want to say. In the process of his research, this student twice reworded his thesis. He reworded it first when he became more pessimistic about the whooping crane's survival than he had been after his initial reading. Later he returned to his original optimism when he read the most recent news reports on the successes of the breeding season in 1986 and 1987.

4. Because this is a fairly long paper, the student has decided to help the reader follow his organization by inserting a subtitle before each of the paper's main sections. He has done so here with the background section, which describes the whooping crane's life cycle and history.

5. Although personal experience and the *I* appear less frequently in papers making use of sources than in more subjective writing, there is no reason that they should not be used if relevant. Indeed, you will probably enjoy writing a paper more if you can make personal comments on the subject.

· 1

A Miracle Almost Achieved:
The Status of the Whooping Crane in 1988

In the 1930s the whooping crane seemed almost certainly doomed to extinction. As late as 1967, James C.
Greenway, Jr., in Extinct and Vanishing Birds of the
World, said that even with protection, "the survival of
the species would be a miracle" (208). Today, however,
though the bird's survival in the wild is far from absolutely assured, no one sees extinction as inevitable and
many are optimistic. Three developments have led to this
optimism: (1) the numerical increase and the more assured
protection of the wild whooping crane flock that nests and
winters in Texas; (2) the successes of the captive breeding program at Patuxent Wildlife Research Center in Maryland; and (3) the initial successes in establishing a second migratory flock in Idaho and New Mexico.

Background
On the Texas gulf coast in mid-February 1987, I
boarded a converted deep-sea fishing boat with two or
three hundred other tourists, most of them carrying binoculars and cameras. Our objective was to sight whooping
cranes from the last remaining established wild flock, a
flock the people on the boat far outnumbered. On that day
we saw 25 of the 110 whooping cranes that were wintering
at the Aransas National Wildlife Refuge.

1
2
3

4
5

6. The elevated number at the end of the fourth paragraph indicates that there is a note with additional information on this subject following the text of the paper.

7. The information on the whooping crane in this paragraph is common knowledge and thus does not have to be documented. The student has seen the information repeatedly during his reading and can honestly say that he knows it. If the student had presented a more detailed description of the incubation process, it might have become necessary to use a source citation.

8. Notice how the writer tells the reader through the use of signal phrases and parentheses where the use of material from a particular source begins and ends. The general rule is that the information between the signal phrase and the parentheses is from the source indicated. Therefore the reader can assume that all information from the phrase "According to Fred Guthery" to the parentheses is on page 18 of a work by Guthery. Since none of the material is in quotation marks, the reader should also be able to assume that the wording of the information from Guthery is put completely in Nick Culver's own words. None of it has been "half-copied" from the source.

2

We did not hear the distinctive call audible for miles that gave the bird its name (it was once called "bugle crane"), but we did see this tallest American bird in hunting stance and did see the size of its black-tipped snow-white wings as it glided over the Texas salt flats.

The whooping cranes arrive in Texas in late October, some singly, others in pairs, and others -- the most eagerly anticipated -- in pairs with a youngster. Each pair or group establishes a territory of around 400 acres, which it defends against intruders and rarely leaves.[1]

In April the whooping cranes migrate over 2,000 miles to Wood Buffalo Park in northern Canada. There the pairs, which mate for life, establish a nesting territory, usually the same one year after year. Two eggs are usually laid, and the parents alternate in incubating.

This bird of which so few remain has a long history. James Fisher, Noel Simon, and Jack Vincent describe it as a "Pleistocene relict": bones found in Idaho are 3,500,000 years old by potassium-argon dating and "are not distinguishable from modern bones of the species" (223). According to Fred Guthery, when glacial ice was receding from North America 10,000 years ago, whooping crane numbers were high, and the bird was distributed over all of North America except eastern Canada and New England. The receding ice, however, meant the replacement of marshes by forest and grasslands, so that the whooping crane population had greatly declined even before humans began to further diminish its numbers (18).

6

7

8

9. Because there is no signal phrase introducing this statistical information, the citation must include the last name of the author as well as the page number.

10. The section heading "The Texas–Canada Flock" tells readers that the background section is over and the main body of the paper is beginning. We are about to hear the first of the three reasons for optimism about the whooping crane's chances of survival. Section headings are usually unnecessary in short research papers, but Nick Culver decided to include them because his background section was rather long.

11. No page number is given in the parentheses because this citation is to a telephone interview.

3

In the nineteenth and twentieth centuries, destruction of habitat and hunting radically sped up the decline. By 1938 there was only one migrating flock of 22 birds left (McNulty 15). The only other flock, a nonmigratory group in Louisiana, had even fewer birds and would be almost entirely destroyed by storm in 1940, never to recover.

9

Today the whooping crane is well on its way to recovery. The total in the wild and in captivity is far greater than in 1938. Despite the persisting threats of oil spills, hurricanes, disease, and even the potential mistakes of well-intentioned biologists trying to replenish the whooping crane stock, the whooping crane is surviving.

The Texas-Canada Flock

10

The first reason for the new optimism about the whooping crane's future is the increase in the number of the Texas-Canada flock and the greater protection given it. Despite small declines in individual years, the Texas-Canada flock has steadily increased in number, especially in the last two decades. In the winter of 1988, according to the Assistant Refuge Manager at Aransas, 130 whooping cranes, including 25 young, were at Aransas, Texas. For the fourth consecutive year, both the total number of birds and the number of chicks brought from Canada had increased (Schwindt).

11

For several reasons this increasingly large flock will be much safer than its ancestors in the 1930s were.

12. When a work has two or three authors, all must be given credit in the citation, either in the signal phrase or in the parentheses. If there are four or more authors, give the first author's name, followed by "et al." Since the signal phrase in this instance names only the title of the work, which cannot be found listed alphabetically in the list of works cited, the parentheses must contain the names of the authors.

13. The newspaper article being cited has no author, so it will be found in the list of works cited alphabetized under the first important word of its title. A shortened version of the title must therefore appear in the parentheses along with the page number.

4

First, although much of the bird's former habitat can of
course never be recovered, the preservation of its wintering and nesting territories now seems "reasonably well-
assured," to use the words of <u>Wildlife in Danger</u>, a survey
of the world's endangered species (Fisher, Simon, and Vincent 244). In 1937 the United States government purchased
the approximately 50,000 acres on the Blackjack Peninsula
near Corpus Christi, Texas, where the bird wintered. When
the nesting grounds of the whooping crane were finally
found in 1954, they were in an established Canadian
national park, Wood Buffalo, on the Alberta-Mackenzie
border. So swampy and isolated is this area that danger
from human interference is minimal.

12

Not only are these areas government-protected, but
today any threat to the crane's territory would be greeted
by a public outcry, as it was, for instance, in 1981 when
Interior Secretary James G. Watt considered ceding 19,000
acres near Aransas to the state of Texas for recreational
use ("U.S. Considers" A10). More recently, conservationists have been opposing dam and water-diversion projects
on the Platte River in Nebraska, which they feel would
endanger feeding grounds where the whooping cranes stop on
migration (Gilliland 12-19).

13

Hunting was of course a major cause of the whooping
crane's decline in the last century.[2] However, severe
penalties now exist for shooting whooping cranes, and public and private groups conduct intensive campaigns to edu-
cate hunters along the migration route in bird identifica-

14. When you use quotations of more than four lines, set them apart from the text of the paper. Introduce the quotation with a full signal phrase followed by a colon, then double-space, then indent ten spaces from the left side and double-space the quotation. The indentation replaces the quotation marks as a signal that this is quoted material.

15. The words in brackets are Nick Culver's own. The sentence in the original source began with the pronoun "he," which would not have been clear to readers in this context. The brackets are a convention allowing readers to know exactly what is from the original source and what is not. If your typewriter has no brackets on its keyboard, you can put them in with ink.

16. Frequently, especially in long quotations, you will want to omit something that appears in the middle of a quotation you are using. If the omission is a group of words, it is marked by an ellipsis (. . .). If the omission occurs at the end of a sentence or consists of an entire sentence, add an extra dot for the period. In the quotation from Allen, the student omitted an entire sentence.

5

tion. <u>Wildlife in Danger</u> could say in 1969 that "the losses on migration by uncontrolled and ignorant shooting have certainly become small" (Fisher, Simon, and Vincent 225).

Strange as it may seem in the conservation—conscious 1980s, the attempts to protect the whooping crane did not always go unopposed. Robert Porter Allen describes a time of despair in 1949:

> [A farmer in Saskatchewan] told of certain of
> his neighbors who were outspoken in their opin—
> ion that all this fuss about the whooping crane
> was a lot of nonsense. They proposed that the
> best way to put a stop to it would be to kill
> the few birds that remain and then forget the
> whole thing, thus saving the taxpayers a lot of
> money. . . . They likewise announced their
> intention of using their guns at every opportu—
> nity to promote such results. (74–75)

One writer to a leading newspaper, unsympathetic to the whooping crane, called it "a dim—witted gawk of a bird . . . not quite sharp enough mentally to be up to the fundamentals of procreation" (qtd. in Allen 75).

I hope to give my children a view of an even stronger flock than my parents showed me, and therefore do not begrudge the relatively small amount of tax money spent on protecting the Texas—Canada flock.

14

15

16

6

Captive Breeding at Patuxent

Despite controversy, problems, and failures to meet proposed goals, the second reason for the growing optimism about the whooping crane has been the captive breeding program at Patuxent Wildlife Research Center in Maryland. By the 1980s the Patuxent flock, which was inaugurated in the 1960s, numbered between thirty and forty birds, and a number of eggs produced through artificial insemination of captive females had been transferred to Grays Lake National Wildlife Refuge in Idaho to be hatched by sand- hill cranes as part of a project to establish a second mi- gratory flock.

The captive flock at Patuxent was established because biologists and conservationists were aware of the Texas- Canada flock's fragility even with maximum government pro- tection. For example, Science News reported that in the spring of 1975, just before the whooping cranes flew north from Aransas, a severe epidemic of avian cholera broke out among waterfowl at Nebraska refuges where the whoopers customarily stop to feed and rest. The disease had already killed 15,000 of the 140,000 waterfowl at Sacra- mento Game Refuge. Only by scaring the whooping cranes away with airplanes was contact with the contaminated birds in Nebraska avoided ("Whooping" 271).

Because of such threats of disaster, proposals were made to maintain in captivity a reserve flock whose young or eggs might replenish the wild stock. The plan, which began in 1966, was to retrieve one of the two eggs usually

7

laid by whooping cranes at Wood Buffalo and to transport them with great care to Patuxent for hatching. Dr. Ray Erickson, who headed the Patuxent program, anticipated that the taking of eggs would not diminish the number of wild birds. He maintained that only one chick usually survives anyway because "newborn whooping cranes are so hostile and aggressive toward each other that when there are two, one often kills the other" (qtd. in Zimmerman 8).

These proposals were further supported by research that seemed to show that if the eggs of captive birds were removed soon after they were laid, the birds could be stimulated to produce more eggs. This has proved to be the case. James Carpenter, head of the propagation section, pointed out in 1982 that Patuxent females were laying "as many as 11 eggs per season" (qtd. in Tangley 266).

The successes at Patuxent have allayed some, though not all, of the fears about captive breeding, a very controversial subject. The fears were raised again recently when in 1987 a mysterious disease struck the Patuxent flock, killing 14 birds, although scores of other infected whooping cranes just as mysteriously recovered ("Ailing" D11).

In an article in Natural History, D. R. Zimmerman (a writer who has misgivings about captive breeding) describes the bitter debate that ensued when the Patuxent program was proposed, a debate between the "protectionists" and the "propagationists." "Protectionists," according to Zimmerman, felt there was too little proof of suc-

8

cess in captive breeding to warrant removing eggs from the
wild. They saw risks in releasing captive-bred birds or
their eggs into the wild flocks, for these birds might be
unable to adjust to the wild and might carry disease.
"Propagationists," on the other hand, argued that the
cranes were "too close to extinction not to try captive
breeding to increase their numbers" (7-8).

Initial Successes in Idaho and New Mexico

The third reason for the new optimism about the
whooping crane is the initial success of biologists in
establishing a second migratory flock. These birds, which
summer in Grays Lake Wildlife Refuge in Idaho and winter
at Bosque del Apache National Wildlife Refuge in New Mexico, have not yet mated, but by February of 1988 they numbered around 40 (Schwindt).

The development of this second wild flock began in
1974, when Canada and the United States approved what has
been called "the biggest gamble ever in the . . . 40-year
effort to save the whooping crane from extinction" (Scarbrough 88). The plan was to move eggs from Wood Buffalo
and Patuxent to Grays Lake, where the eggs would be
hatched by sandhill cranes acting as foster parents. It
was hoped that the flock would follow the sandhill cranes
to wintering grounds in New Mexico, and in later years fly
the route independently.

In a 1977 Natural History article, Rodney Barker
cites four major reasons for the gamble. First, in 1974
Patuxent did not seem to be meeting its goals. Second,

many subadult whoopers were disappearing in the Canadian wilderness for unexplained reasons. Third, cranes summering in Idaho and surrounding areas would have a much shorter -- and thus less dangerous -- migration route to wintering grounds. Fourth, and perhaps most important, new developments in biology suggested that such a plan might succeed (24–26). After a long study of sandhill cranes, the nearest American relative of the whooping crane, biologists had come to the conclusion that crane behavior was primarily learned through early experience rather than being innate and that therefore young whooping cranes could learn to survive and to migrate from sandhill crane foster parents (24).

Thus, in May, 1975, fourteen eggs were taken from Canadian nests and flown to Idaho -- flown with many questions. Would the whooping cranes, if they hatched, survive in a new environment? Would the chicks be rejected by their foster parents? Would the whooping cranes take on the traits of sandhill cranes to such a degree that they might even interbreed, producing sterile hybrids? Would the whooping cranes learn and adopt on their own the sandhill crane migration route?

In 1988 it is clear that the chicks will not be rejected by their foster parents and that they can learn the migration route from their parents, but, as Shannon Brownlee points out, "Unless sandhill-reared whoopers mate, the costly attempt to reestablish them in the Rockies will have been a bust" (4). And according to Jim

10

Lewis, coordinator for whooping crane conservation efforts
in the United States, unless the Grays Lake whoopers soon
mate, plans to establish another flock in northern Michigan or southern Ontario "will probably be dropped" (qtd.
in Brownlee 43).

As Brownlee observes, a number of reasons have been
proposed as to why the cranes have not yet mated. First,
"With whooping cranes picky about their mates even when
plenty of prospects are nearby," the summer range of over
37,000 square miles may be "too large for Grays Lake-
reared whoopers to find one another." Second, for unknown
reasons, "more males have hatched and survived than
females," and the females frequently summer in Wyoming,
apart from the males, who summer at Grays Lake. Third,
and most troubling, "the whoopers may have become
imprinted on their sandhill foster parents, and thus they
might not fancy members of the opposite sex of their own
species" (43).

Conclusion

Because whooping crane numbers were low before human
interference, there may be some question as to whether the
decline of the whooping crane, unlike that of the bald
eagle, stems more from humans or from natural selection.
However, humans have certainly sped up the decline and
should be humane enough to try to abate it. As an editorial in the Christian Science Monitor once asked, "Can
society, whether through sheer wantonness or callous
neglect, permit the extinction of something beautiful or

grand in nature without risking extermination of something beautiful and grand in its own character?" (qtd. in Allen 31). The contributions of Americans and Canadians to whooping crane survival indicate that society is not risking such extermination.

Notes

[1]According to Faith McNulty, whooping cranes are among the few birds in which the family does not fully break up at the end of the breeding season. If a pair returns to Aransas with a youngster, they will "defend their territory with greater determination than a childless couple." A mated pair, through childless, will in turn defend their territory more fiercely than single birds (69–70).

[2]For an account of the losses from hunting, see Allen.

13

Works Cited

"Ailing Cranes Rally from Mystery Illness." New York
    Times 12 Oct. 1987: D11.

Allen, Robert Porter. On the Trail of Vanishing Birds.
    New York: McGraw-Hill, 1957.

Barker, Rodney. "A Whooper Rally." Natural History Mar.
    1977: 22-30.

Brownlee, Shannon. "Fostering Hope for the Whooper."
    National Wildlife June-July 1987: 38-43.

Fisher, James, Noel Simon, and Jack Vincent. Wildlife in
    Danger. New York: Viking, 1969.

Gilliland, Martha W. "Trouble Downstream: Migrating
    Cranes Force a Showdown on Platte River Water Proj-
    ects." Sierra Club Bulletin Mar.-Apr. 1984: 12-19.

Greenway, James C., Jr. Extinct and Vanishing Birds of
    the World. 2nd ed. New York: Dover, 1967.

Guthery, Fred S. "Whoopers in Idaho." National Parks and
    Conservation Magazine Oct. 1976: 18-21.

McNulty, Faith. The Whooping Crane: The Bird that Defies
    Extinction. New York: Dutton, 1966.

Scarbrough, Linda. "The Ugly Duckling Updated." New York
    Times Magazine 30 Nov. 1975: 88-93.

Schwindt, Kenneth. Assistant Refuge Manager, Aransas
    National Wildlife Refuge. Telephone interview. 24
    Feb. 1988.

Tangley, Laura. "Captive Propagation: Will It Succeed?"
    Science News 121 (1982): 266-68.

Terres, John K. The Audubon Encyclopedia of North Ameri-
    can Birds. New York: Knopf, 1980.

14

"U.S. Considers Ceding Control of Crane Refuge." New York
      Times 8 July 1981: A10.

"Whooping Cranes Survive Disease Threat." Science News
      107 (1975): 271.

Zimmerman, D. R. "Captive Breeding: Boon or Boondoggle."
      Natural History Dec. 1976: 6+.

Some Endangered Species Topics

If the sample paper has whetted your interest, perhaps you too would like to research an endangered species. Here is a list of possible topics.

1. *Grizzly bear.* Because the grizzly is one of the most dangerous of American animals, it has more and more been driven into a few national parks such as Yellowstone, where its presence, coupled with the greater and greater influx of visitors, causes problems. (There is a good book on this subject by the Craighead brothers, two men who have strong opinions about what should and should not be done with the bears.)

2. *Timber wolf* (also called grey wolf). Today the wolf is pretty much confined to the states of Minnesota and Michigan in the "lower 48." You might want to write on the conflict between wolves and Minnesota hunters and farmers. Or you could write about the wolves that live on an island in the Great Lakes.

3. *Red wolf.* Less material will be available on this wolf than on the timber wolf, but it too is endangered. Recently this wolf has been reintroduced into areas of North Carolina.

4. *Blue whale.* The largest animal that has ever lived, the blue whale has been overhunted; only a few thousand still survive in the North Atlantic and North Pacific.

5. *Bowhead whale.* Both Canada and the United States still allow Eskimos to hunt the bowhead, but otherwise this greatly endangered species is protected.

6. *Polar bear.* The polar bear is only moderately endangered, but oil and gas interests do encroach on its territory.

7. *Black-footed ferret.* This animal, which was not discovered until 1851, is the rarest mammal on the North American continent.

8. *Mountain lion* (also called puma, panther, and catamount). The mountain lion is an endangered species in the American West, although a small population still exists in Florida, and there are more and more reports of its return to the mountains of the eastern United States.

9. *Harp seal.* Although the harp seal is not seriously endangered, there is much material on it because of the practice of killing pup seals for their white pelts.

10. *Manatee* (generally called Florida manatee). A large percentage of Florida manatees bear scars from motorboat propellers passing over them.

11. *Caribou.* You will find much material on the effect of oil drilling and pipelines on caribou migrations in Alaska.

12. *Bison* (popularly known as the buffalo). This animal, millions of which once roamed America, now exists only in maintained herds.

13. *Bald eagle.* Although plentiful in Alaska, this national symbol has had a rough twenty years in the eastern United States primarily because of poisoning from the now-outlawed DDT. Today, the bald eagle seems to be recovering.

14. *Peregrine falcon.* Like the bald eagle, the peregrine falcon was hurt by DDT, but it is now recovering because of extensive efforts in captive breeding. After captive breeding, the birds are released into American cities, where they nest in tall buildings and feed on pigeons.

15. *California condor.* This seemingly doomed bird has caused much controversy among naturalists, who cannot seem to agree on a program to arrest its decline.

16. *Giant panda.* You will find much material on the panda's problems in China and on attempts to breed the panda in captivity.

17. *Gorilla.* The loss of any species is a sad thing, but because the gorilla is such a close relative of humans, its probable loss is especially sad. The gorilla is very much endangered.

Part Seven

A Writer's Handbook

Punctuation and Mechanics

1. The period

The period, the most common mark of *terminal* punctuation, is used to end sentences that make a statement or convey a request.

- Jeannie was lonely at first, but she soon came to like having the house to herself.
- Please arrive fifteen minutes before curtain time.

2. The question mark

The question mark is used as terminal punctuation for direct questions.

- Did you know that yogurt originated in Turkey?

Use a period, not a question mark, for indirect questions. An indirect question is reported rather than asked directly.

- Jane asked if she was eligible for the scholarship.

3. The exclamation point

The exclamation point follows expressions of exclamation.

- Leave that poor terrapin alone!
- We watched the sun set over the Grand Canyon — an awesome spectacle!

Caution: Do not overuse the exclamation point. It is intended to make a statement emphatic; if you use it too freely, the emphasis is lost. Deleting the first and third exclamation points in the following passage will increase the effect of the second one.

INEFFECTIVE   We went to the swamp early to observe the alligators before they awoke. As we stood on the bank, they began to move slowly — exactly at the moment the sun came up! What strange creatures they are! We felt as if we had stumbled into a prehistoric era!

381

IMPROVED   We went to the swamp early to observe the alli-
            gators before they awoke. As we stood on the
            bank, they began to move slowly — exactly at
            the moment the sun came up. What strange
            creatures they are! We felt as if we had stumbled
            into a prehistoric era.

4. The semicolon

The semicolon is used to join elements of equal rank.

4a. Use the semicolon between two closely related independent clauses not joined by a coordinating conjunction.

An independent clause is a word group that can stand alone as a sentence. When two independent clauses appearing in the same sentence have not been joined with a coordinating conjunction (*and, but, or, nor, for, so, yet*), the clauses must be separated with a semicolon.

- My old country school is no longer standing; it has been replaced by a ten-room elementary school and a modern regional high school.

The semicolon should be reserved for closely related independent clauses. If the relationship between two independent clauses is not clear with a semicolon alone, use a comma and a coordinating conjunction (see #5a) or use the semicolon with a conjunctive adverb or transitional expression (see #4b).

4b. Use the semicolon between independent clauses joined by a conjunctive adverb or transitional expression.

When a conjunctive adverb such as *however, furthermore, nevertheless,* or *moreover* or a transitional expression such as *in fact* or *for example* is used to join two independent clauses, the clauses must be separated by a semicolon.

- Joseph wants a job like the one in India; however, he does not want to leave this country.

Caution: Be sure to use a semicolon, not a comma, to separate independent clauses that have not been joined with a coordinating conjunction (*and, but, or, nor, for, so, yet*). To use a comma alone creates a serious error known as a *comma splice*. See #23.

4c. Use the semicolon to separate items in a series when the items themselves are punctuated by commas.

- There are three major divisions in the new college: humanities, which includes English, art, speech, philosophy, and drama; social sciences, which includes history, psychology, sociology, and political science; and science, which includes biology, chemistry, geology, physics, and astronomy.

You will find an exercise on semicolons and commas following Section 5.

5. The comma

The comma, which provides most of the punctuation *inside* sentences, has many uses. A relatively weak mark, it indicates a brief pause to readers.

5a. Use a comma before a coordinating conjunction that joins two independent clauses.

A coordinating conjunction is a word on this list: *and, but, or, nor, for, so, yet.* An independent clause is a word group that can stand alone as a sentence.

- We were tired and hungry after hiking, *but* we stopped to pick wildflowers before we returned to our car.
- The tall man in the shiny red top hat and the rainbow-striped boots led the parade, *and* all of us cheered as he marched by.

Note: You may omit the comma before the coordinating conjunction if the two independent clauses are short and misreading cannot occur.

- Charles left early *but* Mary stayed till midnight.

Caution: Do not put a comma before the coordinating conjunction unless there is an independent clause on either side of it:

FAULTY   Joel tried to call the police, but accidentally dialed his mother.

REVISED   Joel tried to call the police but accidentally dialed his mother.

5b. Use a comma between all items in a series.

- We made a fruit salad of oranges, apples, raisins, bananas, and figs. Then we ate, sang, danced, and talked.

- Gen teaches dancing in a private school in the city daily, at a dance club in the suburbs weekly, and out on Long Island during the summer.

- Jennifer played the flute, William picked his guitar, and the rest of us tried to sing along.

5c. Use a comma between coordinate adjectives.

Coordinate adjectives are those that might have been connected with the word *and* or that might have been scrambled.

- The awkward, velvety-eyed, shy giraffe entertained us for a long time.

  The awkward and velvety-eyed and shy giraffe . . .

  The shy, awkward, velvety-eyed giraffe . . .

But: Do not use a comma between cumulative adjectives. Cumulative adjectives, which often designate number, size, age, color, material, or substance, cannot be connected with *and;* nor can they be scrambled.

- Polly's mother made six large new green canvas tote bags for the fair.
  NOT: Six and large and new and green and canvas tote bags
  NOT: Canvas green new large six tote bags

Caution: Do not put a comma between a final adjective and the noun:

FAULTY	In the Rothko room of the art gallery, you find yourself surrounded by pure, pulsating, sensuous, color.
REVISED	In the Rothko room of the art gallery, you find yourself surrounded by pure, pulsating, sensuous color.

5d. Use a comma after an introductory word group.

- *Although most mice are not very strong,* we found our refrigerator had been moved three feet from the wall during the night.
- *To get to know more people,* you need to become involved in more activities.
- *After drinking the vanilla by mistake,* I had a peculiar hangover.
- *Fighting for her dignity,* she refused to open her mouth.

Note: Short introductory constructions do not have to be set off by a comma.

- After lunch we lay in the sun and talked quietly.

But: Be alert to possible misreading. The following short introductory constructions need commas to prevent misreading.

CONFUSING	Soon after Nicole was well and happy again.
CLEAR	Soon after, Nicole was well and happy again.
CONFUSING	When the helicopter hit the gas tank broke loose and exploded.
CLEAR	When the helicopter hit, the gas tank broke loose and exploded.

5e. Use commas to set off modifiers and appositives that are not essential to the basic meaning of the sentence.

Modifiers describe, and appositives rename. If removing a modifier or appositive does not change the meaning of a sentence dramatically, commas are necessary — to signal that the information is nonessential.

- Jack Lucas, *who made those brownies,* lives over by the river. (modifier)
- The vinegar, *which has begun to cloud,* is still usable. (modifier)
- One of Adrienne Rich's poems, "Orion," has a special appeal for me. (appositive)

But: Do not use commas if the modifier or appositive is essential to the basic meaning of the sentence.

If the meaning of a sentence changes dramatically or becomes nonsense when a modifier or appositive is removed, omit the commas — to signal that the information is essential.

- The man *who made those brownies* lives over by the river. (modifier)
- Vinegar *that has begun to cloud* is still usable. (modifier)
- Adrienne Rich's poem "Song" appeals to readers of many ages. (appositive)

5f. Use a comma before a concluding construction when the added material is not essential to the basic meaning of the sentence.

- Three of the dancers decided to skip the afternoon rehearsal, although they knew they might lose their positions in the new production.
- Your letter arrived late on Friday, after the office had closed for the weekend.

But: Do not use a comma if the added material is essential to the basic meaning of the sentence.

- Don't visit Paris at the height of the tourist season unless you have made hotel reservations in advance.
- We have not seen our pet pigeon since she escaped a week ago.

5g. Use a comma to set off parenthetical insertions: transitional words and phrases, opinion indicators, and other miscellaneous inserted material.

- Maple syrup, *I believe,* is a major native product of Vermont.
- Eating raw limpets, *I found out,* is like trying to eat art gum erasers.
- Many minority groups, *especially blacks and Hispanics,* encounter racial prejudice and language barriers when they try to obtain health-care services.
- The elephants, *according to their trainer,* look forward to their bath in the big pool in their enclosure.

5h. Use commas with expressions such as *he said* to set off direct quotations.

- In *Working It Out,* Alice Walker comments, "What . . . are we to make of Phillis Wheatley, a slave (and a poet), who owned not even herself?"
- "That tree looks like a good hiding place for the treasure," Terry said to himself.
- "When Tom's train arrives," said Ruth, "let's greet him with balloons and streamers."

5i. Use commas to set off nouns of direct address.

- *Jim,* come here.
- You, *sir,* will have to come in later.
- Hurry up, *Mary.*

5j. Use commas to set off mild exclamations and the words *yes* or *no.*

- *Oh, yes,* I will join you for dinner.

5k. Use commas between elements of dates and addresses (except for zip codes).

- My mother left for Russia on October 13, 1988.
- June 19, 1991, is the last date you may apply for that grant.
- My best friend lives in Silver Spring, Maryland.
- Send the letter to Redding Thompson, 93 N. Prospect Street, Burlington, Vermont 05401.

5l. Use commas between contrasted elements in a sentence.

- She found on the shore only colored pebbles, not the exotic shells she was looking for.
- As a stranger in the African desert, I felt not only deaf, but also blind whenever I encountered a native tribe.

5m. Do not use the comma in the following places:

Between a subject and its verb:

FAULTY	Eating pizza and drinking beer, are her favorite pastimes.
REVISED	Eating pizza and drinking beer are her favorite pastimes.

Between a verb and its object:

FAULTY	After months away from the farm, Michael found, digging potatoes hard on his back.
REVISED	After months away from the farm, Michael found digging potatoes hard on his back.

Between a final adjective and the noun it modifies:

FAULTY	The soft, silky, cape flowed gracefully.
REVISED	The soft, silky cape flowed gracefully.

After a coordinating conjunction:

FAULTY	Yet, he cares enough for me to pick me up when I'm financially down and out.

|REVISED|Yet he cares enough for me to pick me up when I'm financially down and out.|

After *such as,* *like,* and similar terms:

|FAULTY|Some countries, such as, Brazil, Mexico, and Chile, schedule their school years quite differently from ours.|
|REVISED|Some countries, such as Brazil, Mexico, and Chile, schedule their school years quite differently from ours.|

Before *than:*

|FAULTY|She is both more talented and more disciplined, than most of the other ballerinas in the company.|
|REVISED|She is both more talented and more disciplined than most of the other ballerinas in the company.|

Before a parenthesis:

|FAULTY|In *Kind and Unusual Punishment,* (an exposé of the American penal system), Jessica Mitford describes a disturbing night she spent in the District of Columbia's Detention Center for Women.|
|REVISED|In *Kind and Unusual Punishment* (an exposé of the American penal system), Jessica Mitford describes a disturbing night she spent in the District of Columbia's Detention Center for Women.|

Exercise   The Comma

For practice in using commas, try these sentences.

1. Scott and Helen Nearing lived off the land for many years.

2. I first read about the Nearings in the book *Ways Americans Live* a collection of essays on life-styles by Andrew Greene.

3. The Nearings the pioneers of the back-to-the-land movement left city life long before the return to rural life became fashionable.

4. They developed their plot of land into a reasonably comfortable pleasant attractive place to live; however there was always work to be done.

5. When people interested in their way of life came to visit the Nearings they were put to work building planting harvesting or otherwise using whatever skills they brought with them.

6. The Nearings built their house using stones that were too heavy for persons their age.

7. Therefore one of the jobs that visitors were sometimes assigned was hauling stones for the Nearings continued to add buildings to their property.

8. According to visitors both the Nearings although they were aging still fiercely supported their choice to live as they chose.

9. A friend of mine who visited the Nearings some years ago commented to me on her return "It made me wish I had the courage or whatever it takes to live that way."

10. "Not me" I replied "no indeed; I'm a person who likes comfort too much!"

Exercise   Semicolons and Commas

Here are some practice sentences to test your use of semicolons and commas. Some of the sentences are punctuated correctly; others need to be corrected. Sometimes you may prefer to use a period rather than a semicolon.

1. Last summer I participated in our college's New England Literary Tour; which was sponsored by Dr. Fry of the English Division.

2. Dr. Fry reserved two large buses for the tour, later he had to locate a third bus to accommodate additional travelers.

3. The tour included visiting Emily Dickinson's home in Amherst, Massachusetts, the House of Seven Gables, featured in Hawthorne's novel, Walden Pond, made famous by Thoreau, and many other sites, such as famous churches, a one-room schoolhouse, and a silversmith shop like Paul Revere's.

4. Most of our sleeping accommodations during the tour were very comfortable, however one night I rolled off a hard bed while having a nightmare about Washington Irving's headless horseman.

5. One night we stayed at an old-fashioned country inn built in the mid-1800s, where I was tempted to leave a sign saying "G.K. slept here."

6. The food on the trip was so plentiful that I could never finish a meal although some people asked for seconds on desserts almost every night.

7. A pleasant feature of the trip was the long afternoon rides through a rolling New England countryside; during which some passengers napped, some read, and the rest of us laughed joked and exclaimed over the scenery.

8. We reached one church just in time for a candlelight service it was a peaceful way to end a long day.

9. We were on the tour for college credit and therefore we had to spend some of our evening hours writing in our travel journals.

10. I recommend Dr. Fry's Literary Tour of New England to you; but only if you have stamina and a sense of humor, you'll need both if you go!

6. The colon

The colon, a rather formal punctuation mark, is used after an independent clause to direct attention to a list, a clarification, or a quotation.

- The reasons for a low energy level include the following: poor diet, heavy smoking, inadequate rest, metabolic difficulties, and blood deficiencies.

- There are only two places in the world where time takes precedence over the job to be done: school and prison.

- In an article in *New Times*, Karla Brown describes her enthusiasm for Manhattan: "Living in New York is still like living at the hub of the wheel of the world."

7. The dash

The dash, a rather informal mark of punctuation, is used to set off material that deserves emphasis. Use a single dash to emphasize what follows it. Use a pair of dashes to set off material appearing in the middle of a sentence.

- I have but one goal on this trip to Ireland — to kiss the Blarney Stone.

- In the 1920s, liberals argued that the opposite of repression — sex education, freedom of talking, feeling, and expressing — would have healthy effects.

Caution: Do not overuse dashes. Doing so suggests that you have not constructed sentences very carefully.

Note: In typing, use two hyphens to form a dash.

8. Parentheses

Parentheses are sometimes used around explanatory or other added material.

- The two leading female gymnasts of the world (one Russian, the other German) moved with flawless timing on the double bars.
- The hypothalamus (our bodily temperature regulator) sometimes functions less adequately with aging.
- May Sarton (1912–   ), author of *The House by the Sea*, lives on the Maine seacoast.

Caution: Don't overuse parentheses. If you tend to put much sentence content inside parentheses, restructure your sentences. When you do so, you may find your parenthetical details are not important enough to include.

Note: Generally, surrounding inserted material with dashes will make it stand out more; with parentheses, it stands out less.

9. The apostrophe

The apostrophe is used to form the possessive of nouns and of some pronouns; to indicate contraction of words and omission of letters; and to make plurals of numbers, letters, and words used as themselves.

9a. Use the apostrophe to form the possessive.

1. Add the apostrophe plus "s" to singular nouns.

- That cat's game with the barn mice is hilarious.
- Smokers should respect the nonsmoker's right to a smoke-free environment.

2. Add only the apostrophe to plural nouns ending in "s."

- Those cats' games with the barn mice are hilarious.
- Have you seen the Schultzes' new speedboat?

But: Add the apostrophe plus "s" to plural nouns not ending in "s": women's, children's.

3. Add the apostrophe plus "s" to *indefinite* pronouns: everybody's, other's, someone else's, no one's, and so on.

But: Omit the apostrophe with the possessive of *personal* pronouns: ours, yours, his, hers, its (*it's* means "it is"), theirs.

Note: You hear a few common expressions so often that you may forget that they require an apostrophe. Be alert to them: "a day's work," "your money's worth," "a week's rest" are some examples.

9b. Use the apostrophe to substitute for deleted letters or words in contractions and omissions.

1. Contractions: it's (it is); don't (do not); you've (you have); that's (that is); we'll (we will); can't (cannot); let's (let us); and so on.

2. Omissions: seven o'clock (seven of the clock); the radical '60s (1960s).

9c. Add the apostrophe plus "s" to make the plurals of numbers, letters, and words used as themselves.

• The two *A*'s, five 9's, and three *of*'s on the poster are all printed in ink that glows under black light.

Caution: Sometimes the apostrophe plus "s" will create a sentence that is hard to read. Watch out for such awkward constructions and recast sentences in which they occur.

AWKWARD	Our local newspaper's editorial page's make-up is confusing.
IMPROVED	The make-up of the editorial page of our local newspaper is confusing.
AWKWARD	Our barn mice's favorite game is hide and seek with the cat.
IMPROVED	The favorite game of our barn mice is hide and seek with the cat.
AWKWARD	I borrowed my father's sister's friend's suitcase.
IMPROVED	I borrowed a suitcase that belongs to my aunt's friend.

Caution: Do not drop in apostrophes where they don't belong. Apostrophes do not belong in simple (nonpossessive) plurals of nouns.

FAULTY   Soap opera's are absurd.

REVISED   Soap operas are absurd.

Nor do they belong in verbs.

FAULTY   Janet want's to ride the carousel.

REVISED   Janet wants to ride the carousel.

Exercise   *The Apostrophe*

Add or delete apostrophes as needed.

1. Our countys fair is a highlight of every autumn for me and my three brothers, Terry, David, and Michael.

2. We dont ever go to the fair on weekends because its too crowded then; we've found that the best time to go is about two oclock on a weekday.

3. The fair is better these days than it was in the 70s because more handicraft's are shown.

4. One of the most beautiful items I've ever seen was the Blue Ridge Mountain quilt exhibited last year by our preacher's wife's best friend.

5. Another feature of the fair my brothers and I especially like is the livestock area. One year we saw some oxen's yoke's get entangled, and those oxen nearly went crazy.

6. Another time there was a great rattling over at the monkey's cages, where one monkey had wrapped it's tail around a long stick somebody had poked into the cage and wouldnt let go.

7. Anyone who enjoy's watching roosters strut and pigeon's pout surely wouldnt want to miss the area of the fair marked "Fowl's and Poultry."

8. One of the best parts of any fair is the food, and our's is no exception.

9. Our fair feature's Tonys pizza, Christopher the Greeks baklava, Macks Scottish barley soup, and Johnnys American subs, among other mouth-watering culinary attractions.

10. After a visit to the fair, my brother's and I definitely need a days rest to recuperate, because weve walked and gawked and stuffed ourselve's nearly out of existence by the end of the day.

10. The hyphen

10a. Use the hyphen to divide a word at the end of a line.

- Scarves can be used to achieve many different fashionable effects.

10b. Use the hyphen to connect the parts of compound
words.

- double-header, self-reliance, half-moon

10c. Use the hyphen to connect two or more words
forming a single adjective before a noun.

- the long-awaited costume ball, the Nielsen-rated program, the
two-year-old child, the well-known acrobat

But: When a compound adjective completes a sentence instead of
coming before its noun, no hyphen is used: That acrobat is well
known in gymnastic circles.

Note: For more about how to handle compound words, see #16,
"Spelling."

11. Underlining (italics)

Underlining in either handwriting or typing equals italics (slanted
type) in print.

11a. Underline titles of major publications and of long
literary and musical works.

- books: Poetic Celebrations, The Web and the Rock, Exploring
Canada
- magazines: Psychology Today, Rolling Stone
- newspapers: Washington Post, Christian Science Monitor
- plays and musicals: Hedda Gabler, The Sound of Music
- full-length films: Kramer vs. Kramer, The Black Stallion
- long poems: The Love Song of J. Alfred Prufrock
- long musical compositions: Mozart's Little Night Music,
Schubert's Trout Quintet

11b. Underline terms used as themselves inside a sentence.

- The word <u>pajama</u> originated in the Hindi language.
- It is easy to confuse the letter <u>s</u> and the number <u>5</u> if they are not formed carefully.

Note: Quotation marks may be used instead of underlining to set off terms used as themselves.

11c. Underline names of ships, trains, and aircraft.

- My grandparents crossed Europe on the <u>Orient Express</u>.
- <u>The Spirit of St. Louis</u> hangs in the Air and Space Museum.

11d. Underline foreign words used in an English sentence.

- Martha, the first in her family to attend college, graduated <u>magna cum laude</u>.

11e. Occasionally, underline to give added emphasis to a word or words in a sentence.

- While they were hiking, she said to him, "Don't you <u>dare</u> drop that rock on my lunch!"

Caution: You should not often need to use underlining for emphasis. Strong sentences can stand on their own. Excessive underlining suggests hasty, lazy writing; avoid it.

12. Quotation marks

Quotation marks are used to punctuate minor titles, to set off direct quotations, and to set off dialogue, either spoken or internal.

12a. Use quotation marks around minor titles.

- essays, articles, chapter or section headings: Thoreau's "Civil Disobedience"; Beth Thompson's column "Getting There"; "People and Places" in *Holiday* magazine; "Five Ways to Stop Smoking" in Dr. Jennie Albertson's book *Improving Your Health*
- short stories: "A Worn Path"
- short poems: "Whose Lips I've Kissed"

- short musical compositions: Neil Diamond's "Stargazer"
- paintings: Helen Frankenthaler's "Red Slash"

12b. Use quotation marks to set off direct quotations.

- Janet told Theodore, "My introductory physics class is full of practical information about everyday life."
- In *A Room of One's Own*, Virginia Woolf says that "a woman must have money and a room of her own if she is to write fiction."
- "I swing out over the earth over and over again," from Audre Lorde's "Love Poem," is one of my favorite lines of poetry.
- When we talk about meeting child-care needs in the United States, our first question is too often "How much is it going to cost?"
- In her fantasy stories about the future in *The Wanderground*, Sally Gearhart defines what she calls "grace-making" as "the creation of extra attention and love" toward one or more persons who may be suffering.

12c. Use quotation marks to set off dialogue.

- "Do you like the Alvin Ailey dancers?" John asked Sam.
- "I don't know. I've never seen them perform," replied Sam.
- "Then, let's go! You'll like their exciting choreography, I know," John urged.

12d. Use single quotation marks when a title or quoted material appears inside a quotation.

- Laurie asked her father, "Can you recite 'Macavity: The Mystery Cat,' the poem by T. S. Eliot?"

12e. Use quotation marks with other punctuation marks according to convention.

Periods and commas go inside quotation marks.

- One of my favorite folksingers is Joni Mitchell; I especially like her "Both Sides Now."
- I also like Olivia Newton-John's "Country Girl," Jim Croce's "Time in a Bottle," and John Denver's "Country Roads."

Semicolons and colons are placed outside quotation marks.

- One of Emily Dickinson's riddle poems is "A Narrow Fellow in the Grass"; by the time you finish reading the poem, you can see the snake that is the answer to the riddle.
- Ernest Hemingway achieves highly dramatic conflict among the characters in his short story "The Short Happy Life of Francis Macomber": Francis, the weak male; Margot, the strong female; and Robert, the strong male.

Question marks and exclamation points go outside quotation marks, unless the question or the exclamation itself is being quoted, in which case they go inside.

- Did you hear her say, "All aboard"?
- Stop smiling and saying, "Yes, yes"!
- I wondered aloud, "What shall I do next?"
- Thomas kept saying to the hungry bear, "No, stop that!"

Caution: Do not use quotation marks around questionable words in a sentence, or to try to achieve a humorous effect. Using quotation marks in this way has the unfortunate effect of calling attention to what they surround. If you are tempted to write this kind of sentence, you probably need to look for more precise language.

INEFFECTIVE	Nancy suggested to her parents that smoking marijuana was no more harmful than getting "bombed" on alcohol.
IMPROVED	Nancy suggested to her parents that smoking marijuana was no more harmful than getting drunk on alcohol.

Exercise   *Quotation Marks*

Add, remove, or move quotation marks as needed. Note: Words used as words may be put in quotation marks or they may be underlined (to indicate italics). For the purpose of this exercise, put them in quotation marks.

1. My son asked me, "Why is it so important to write "he and she" instead of just "he"?

2. He was irritated by sentences like, Every student should bring his or her textbook to class.

3. His English teacher told him that many women are offended by the use of just "he" to refer to men and women and consider it "sexist language."

4. "I agree with your English teacher, I said."

5. "Remember how angry I was, I went on, about my not getting the promotion at work? When women are discriminated against, as I was, they lose their sense of humor about "sexism"."

6. My son's English textbook, *Writing with a Voice,* shows how to avoid sexist English without using the wordy "he or she" construction.

7. Since 1980 we have been using in the office a book by Casey Miller and Kate Swift titled *The Handbook of Nonsexist Writing.*

8. My grandfather's 1895 "Webster's Dictionary" has a silly definition of "breast" that uses "man" to refer to the human race.

9. According to the 1895 dictionary, a breast is "a soft protuberance on the anterior part of the thorax, in man and some other mammals . . . for the secretion of milk."

10. Included in its definition of sex is the information that "the female sex is characterized by softness, sensibility, and modesty.

---

13. Brackets and the ellipsis mark

13a. Brackets are used when you need to insert a word or words into a quotation.

• In a book about Dr. Mary Walker, I was amazed to read the following statement: "The medal awarded her for service in the [Civil] War was taken back by the United States government."

13b. Ellipsis dots (three spaced periods) are substituted for deletions from quoted material.

Original:

"When my sons grow up, then, Gentlemen, I ask you to punish them, you hurting them the same as I hurt you, if they seem to you to care for money, or aught else, more than they care for virtue." (Plato, *The Apology of Socrates*)

With ellipsis:

- Near the end of *The Apology*, Socrates asks the court: "When my sons grow up . . . I ask you to punish them . . . if they seem to care for money, or aught else more than they care for virtue."

If deleted material is at the end of a sentence, then add one more dot to the three, to indicate a period.

Exercise 1 Punctuation

To discover how well you understand punctuation after studying this section, punctuate the following sentences.

1. Harry please bring pecans walnuts and chestnuts when you come for the weekend we need those I think for between meal snacks

2. One of my favorite short stories is Shirley Jacksons The Lottery which has been filmed for classroom use

3. Its too early to take a taxi to the theater but lets think about going by Johns fathers horsedrawn carriage

4. Have you seen Natalie Smorgavich in Shaws play Major Barbara

5. My youngest aunt Katharine Jones is in line for a diplomatic appointment but she is reluctant to leave Washington

6. Look at that dancer leap

7. Any person who wishes to apply for work at that record store must take a lie detector test

8. My neighbors cat will climb any tree in sight however that habit creates a problem when she cant get back down without a firefighters assistance

9. Whether you like it or not Im going to include the quotation To thine own self be true from Shakespeare in my psychology paper asserted Tom

10. Ruth asked the little girl How old are you

Exercise 2 Punctuation

Now punctuate the student paper below, dividing it into paragraphs as you work. Be sure to capitalize letters that begin new sentences.

i was suddenly awakened at four o'clock one morning by my wife its time to go she exclaimed gazing across the room and seeing her standing with suitcase in hand i realized that this was the moment for which we had been waiting nine months i sprang out of bed grabbed whatever clothes were available and started dressing while simultaneously calling the doctor ill meet you at the hospital in forty-five minutes was the doctors reply to a very nervous father-to-be on the way to the hospital i tried to remain calm as i tried to remember the training we had received in prepared childbirth classes and the reading we had done in having your baby naturally inhale exhale breathe deeply and slowly i repeated to my wife over and over again as we drove into the city arriving at the hospital i drove right up to the front door and carefully ushered my wife to the admitting office after rushing through much paperwork not really knowing what we were signing we finally made it to the labor room then it began the timing of contractions the breathing in unison and the waiting three long hours later when my wife was fully dilated the doctor sent me out to dress in the delivery room garb a green cap mask gown and shoes once in the delivery room i held my wifes hand and assisted whenever possible twenty short minutes later a beautiful six-pound twelve-ounce girl was born one does not realize how much pain a woman can tolerate or the strength she possesses until he can witness a childbirth i shall always treasure having shared my daughters birth with my wife it was an event i shall not forget

14. Numbers and abbreviations

14a. Numbers

Spell out one- and two-word numbers or numbers that begin a sentence.

- Please send *twenty-four* daffodil bulbs of the King Alfred variety.
- *Two hundred fifty* employees have been moved to the Rockville plant.

Use figures for numbers that cannot be spelled in one or two words and for dates, times, addresses, temperatures, amounts of money, decimals and fractions, page references, scores, results of surveys, and the like.

Please send 125 daffodil bulbs of the King Alfred variety.

May 18, 1984	4.66
3:30 P.M.	5½
608 Porter Street	page 16
85	a score of 95
$6.82	6 in favor, 6 against

14b. Abbreviations

Use only generally accepted and widely understood abbreviations in most writing. Titles are abbreviated when they precede or immediately follow a name, and names of corporations or government agencies are abbreviated when their initials are commonly known.

Mr. Thomas Webner	AFL-CIO
Ms. Kate Lidfors	CIA
Mrs. Darelene Smith	IBM
Prof. William Mullinix	ABC
Dr. Robert Barshay	NASA
Patricia Tatspaugh, Ph.D.	NAACP

Do not abbreviate personal names, names of courses, units of measurement, divisions of written works, days of the week, months, or holidays.

Robert (not Robt.)	Tuesday (not Tues.)
economics (not econ.)	February (not Feb.)
pounds (not lbs.)	Christmas (not Xmas)
chapter 6 (not chapt. 6)	

15. Capitalization

Usually you know what to capitalize without thinking much about it. But when you're not quite sure, these rules will help.

15a. In general, capitalize the names or titles of *specific* places, persons, organizations, historical events, or educational courses.

Capitalize the complete names of specific geographic places.

Spring Street   t**ḥ**e *Illinois River*
Grand Island, Nebraska   the *West*
Lake Superior

Also capitalize words that derive from names of specific geographic places.

a *New Yorker*   *Indian* food
French blue jeans   the *English* language

But: Do not capitalize the points of the compass or geographic terms that do not name a specific region.

drive *west*   *a* beautiful *river*
the *plains*   the *suburbs*
downtown

Capitalize titles of persons if they are used with the person's name or as the person's name.

Although she had been poor all her life, *Mother* always kept her dignity.

Professor Stevens   *Uncle* Jake   *Mayor* Baldwin

But: Do not capitalize titles of persons when the title is not used as a name or part of a name.

Jim's *uncle*   Stevens is a *professor.*
my mother   Joe Baldwin, the *mayor*

Capitalize all significant words in the names of specific organizations and institutions.

Girl Scouts of America   *Department of Commerce*
American Cancer Society   *Largo High School*

But: Do not capitalize words that refer generally to groups or institutions.

steelworkers   the *unemployed*
pacifists   *high school*

Capitalize names of specific historical events and names of historical eras.

the *Civil War*   the *Middle Ages*

the *Age of Reason*   the *Nuremberg Trials*

But: Do not capitalize words that refer generally to historical happenings or developments.

war crimes   *industrialism*

ancient *democracy*   the rise of *capitalism*

Capitalize the names of specific educational courses.

Math 285   *English* 102   *Philosophy* 101

But: Do not capitalize names of subjects in general, except languages.

Have you thought of taking *philosophy* this semester?

Have you completed your *math* requirement?

Will you take *French* along with *English* next semester?

15b. Capitalize the days of the week, months of the year, and holidays.

Friday   *Thanksgiving*   *September*

15c. Capitalize all the words in titles except for articles, prepositions, and conjunctions. Capitalize even these if they are the first words of a title.

The House of the Dead   "The Lottery"

The World of Zen   "All Things Considered"

Sex and Power in History   *A Time to Remember*

15d. Capitalize religious names and terms of especially sacred significance.

God   the *Annunciation*

Buddha   the *Koran*

Mosaic law   the *Bible*

But: Do not capitalize the word *god* when you use it generally.

the Greek *gods*

belief in a *god*

15e. Capitalize the first word of a full sentence quoted inside another sentence.

Corrine said to Marie, "*That* shrub beside your pond is very rare."

Don't forget to make the following announcement before the tour of historical sites: "*No* smoking is allowed in the restored homes."

Caution: Do not use a capital letter after a semicolon.

All the audience left the play early; *they* had seen enough of poor acting.

Exercise   Capitalization

Correct the following paragraph for capitalization.

I think everyone these days should take a course in Economics. People often think that the Law of Supply and Demand is about all that is taught in economics. But I can assure you that you will learn far more if you enroll in Professor Susan Brown's course entitled the American economy. There you will learn about the Rise and Fall of Revolutions — such as the agricultural revolution and the industrial revolution — as well as how the Technological/Electronic Revolution has influenced Economic Development in America. You will also learn why the Columbia River is so important to the economy of the Pacific northwest and how economic vibrations have moved from there eastward. You will even study how the german economy has affected the economy of the World in the Twentieth Century. Furthermore, you will come to realize that charitable and social service groups like the united way and Big Brothers have more of an effect on our National economy than might be expected. You may be wondering how a single Professor could pack so much material into one Economics course. Why not take The American Economy with Professor Brown and find out?

---

16. Spelling

"Anybody who can think of only one way to spell a word is a damn fool." We have heard that remark credited to at least three persons: Mark Twain, Will Rogers, and Andrew Jackson. We would not be surprised to hear it from anyone who has ever tried to write in the English language. Because the spelling of our language is so unpredictable, you should not allow yourself to feel like a blockhead if you can't spell. Spelling ability is not an index to intelligence; some of the smartest people we know can't spell. However, it is true that spelling errors distract readers. So you will want to look carefully for misspellings as you proofread.

Read the following paragraph.

> Most of us know at least one women who is begining colledge in her fourties. Her family may find this new arangement dificult to acommodate to. However, once they become acustomed to it, they frequently speak proudly of her. She, on the other hand, may have to struggle to overcome certian guilt feelings; somehow, the principal of self-development for her own being is hard for her to except, despite the advise of her freinds who have allready traveled the same path. Gradualy, though, she realizes that she truely is a whole person, seperate from her husband and her childern, and she learns to function outside the wife-mother role. Then she can relax, let down her gaurd some, and finaly begin to recomend "comming back to school" to her neighbors. The growth observeable in such women is exciteing to watch; its one of the real pleasures of being in the collage enviroment today.

How many misspelled words did you spot? There are twenty-seven. If you as a reader found the misspellings in this paragraph distracting, you'll appreciate the importance of proofreading for spelling.

As we pointed out in the chapter on writing and rewriting, stopping to worry about spelling while you are writing can do more harm than good, because it can hinder the flow of your writing. Ignore spelling as you write; attend to it later.

If you often misspell you may want to do a separate proofreading just for spelling. To do so, read your writing aloud, making yourself say *exactly* what you wrote down, not merely what you *intended* to write, which no doubt will still be lingering in your head. In proof-reading for spelling you must train your eye to pay equal attention to each individual letter of a word, rather than reading groups of words in the usual way.

One way in which to make yourself concentrate on single words as you proofread for spelling is to read your paper backwards. Start at the bottom righthand corner and read each line from left to right. If you meant to write "preserve" but you wrote "perserve," this method should force you to see "*per*serve." And you will realize that *unusal* cannot spell *unusual,* that *quite* cannot be *quiet,* that *conscience* cannot mean *conscious.*

If you handwrite your papers, be sure every letter of a word looks like what you meant it to be; otherwise, illegibility can be taken for misspelling. If you type your work, be especially alert to typographical errors, which can be read as spelling errors.

16a.   Improving your spelling

Once you learn to spot your errors, you will begin to recognize your "spelling demons" — words that consistently trip you up. Make a list of these on a 3 × 5 card — or a 5 × 6 or a 6 × 8, if you are tormented by a horde of demons — and keep it handy when you write. In this way you will save yourself the time and trouble of looking up these words. Almost everybody has some spelling demons. One of us, for example, never can remember how to spell *guarantee, obsession,* and *license.*

If you misspell many words in addition to your demons, we urge you to buy a spelling dictionary. Spelling dictionaries give just the spelling and the division of words, without any definitions, so that it is easy to locate words in them. Most spelling dictionaries will also distinguish between sound-alike words such as *affect/effect* and *advise/advice.*

Your regular dictionary can help you with spelling in a way you may not be aware of. Most hardbound dictionaries and some paperback ones feature a section on spelling rules. Look there if you need help with such spelling dilemmas as how to form irregular plurals (*children, mice*), how to form the plurals of words ending in -*y* and -*ey* (*ferry, ferries; donkey, donkeys*), how to add prefixes and suffixes (*renegotiate, finally*), and so on.

How to handle compound words (new words composed of two or more old words) is also clarified in your regular dictionary. If a compound word should be written as a single unbroken word, it will be divided by only the syllable-division marker, a dot in the middle of the line: *fel·low·ship.* If the word is hyphenated, a tiny hyphen will appear between the two older words: *self-con·fi·dence.* If the compound word remains two separate words, an empty space appears between the original words: *cross section.*

Because our language changes, you may find compound words treated differently in different dictionaries. Don't fret about that. We do suggest, though, that you should avoid spelling a compound word in such a way that deciphering it creates a problem for your reader. *Cross section* may be *cross-section* in some dictionaries. Just don't write it *crosssection;* all those *s*'s in a row are hard to read!

Over the years people with spelling problems have devised various mnemonics (pronounced *knee-mahn'-icks*) to help them remember how to spell certain confusing words. *Mnemonic,* from Greek, means "a memory aid." Probably the most common of these is the one that goes "*i* befoe *e,* except after *c*" — to help us remember how to spell *believe, sieve, receive,* and so on. Perhaps you know of some others you could share with the class.

You can make up mnemonics to help you remember how to spell your demon words, as we have done for one of ours:

> *obsession:* Oscar banned Sally's elephants seven Saturdays in Owen's neighborhood.

Mnemonics are often easier to remember if they are funny, so play around as you devise yours.

Some words in our language are demons for so many people that over the years, lists of frequently misspelled words have been compiled. Here is such a list to help you. You will not find sound-alike words here; those are handled separately in the section that follows.

List of Frequently Misspelled Words

absence	analyze	beautiful	characteristic
abundance	anticipate	becoming	chief
accessible	anxiety	before	column
accidentally	apology	beginning	comfortable
accommodate	apparatus	belief	comfortably
accomplish	apparent	believe	coming
accumulate	appearance	beneficial	commission
accurately	appreciate	benefited	committed
accustomed	appropriate	boundaries	committee
achievement	approximately	breath	companies
acknowledgment	area	brilliant	competition
acquaintance	arguing	Britain	competitive
acquire	argument	business	completely
adequate	arising	calendar	comprehension
adolescence	arrangement	candidate	conceivable
advantageous	article	career	conceive
advertisement	athlete	careless	concentrate
aggravate	athletic	carrying	condemn
aggressive	attendance	category	confident
allotted	audience	ceiling	confidential
amateur	authority	cemetery	conscientious
among	balance	challenge	considerably
analysis	basically	character	consistent

continually
continuous
convenience
convenient
coolly
courageous
courteous
criticism
criticize
cruelty
curiosity
curriculum
dealt
deceit
deceive
decision
definite
definitely
definition
dependent
description
despair
desperate
devastate
development
difference
different
difficult
dilemma
dining
disappear
disappoint
disastrous
discipline
disease
dissatisfied
doesn't
dominant
during
ecstasy
efficiency
efficient
eighth
eliminate
embarrass
embarrassment

emphasize
endeavor
enough
entertain
environment
equipped
erroneous
especially
exaggerate
excellent
exceptionally
exercise
exhilarate
existence
experience
explanation
extraordinary
extremely
familiar
fascinate
finally
financial
foreign
friend
fulfill
fundamentally
generally
genius
government
grammar
guaranteed
guidance
happily
height
heroes
hindrance
humorous
hundred
hypocrisy
hypocrite
ignorant
imaginary
imagination
immediately
immensely
incidentally

indefinite
independent
indispensable
influence
ingenious
intellectual
intelligence
interest
interpret
interrupt
irrelevant
knowledge
laboratory
leisure
likelihood
literature
loneliness
losing
magnificence
maintenance
manageable
manufacturer
marriage
mathematics
meant
medieval
merely
mileage
miniature
mischievous
muscle
mysterious
naive
necessarily
necessary
ninety
noticeable
obstacle
occasion
occasionally
occurred
occurrence
opinion
opponent
opportunity
optimism

original
parallel
paralysis
paralyze
particularly
peculiar
perceive
perform
performance
permanent
persistent
persuade
pertain
phenomenon
philosophy
physical
possess
possession
practical
prejudice
prevalent
privilege
probably
procedure
professor
prominent
propaganda
psychology
pursue
quantity
recommend
relief
relieve
religion
repetition
representative
resource
rhythm
ridiculous
roommate
safety
satisfactorily
schedule
seize
separate
sergeant

shining	strictly	tendency	useful
significance	studying	therefore	using
similar	subtle	thorough	various
sincerely	succeed	tragedy	vengeance
sophomore	successful	transferred	villain
sponsor	surprise	undoubtedly	weird
strength	temperament	unnecessary	writing
stretch			

16b. Sound-alike words

Words that sound either exactly or approximately alike but that have different meanings can be troublesome. Here is a list of some of these troublemakers, with sample sentences.

1. accept (verb) — Will you *accept* the offer?

except (preposition) — Put all *except* the spoiled ones into the basket.

2. advice (noun) — Give me some *advice.*

advise (verb) — I'll be glad to *advise* you.

3. affect (verb) — Will it *affect* my promotion possibilities?

effect (noun) — The *effect* of the collision was slight.

4. already (adverb) — They have *already* come.

all ready — I am *all ready* to go. (means "completely ready")

5. altogether (adverb) — Carolyn was *altogether* wrong.

all together — They are *all together* at the station already. (means "everyone gathered")

6. capital — What is the *capital* of Brazil? (place)

capital — Marie has a large amount of *capital* invested in that office building. (money)

capitol — Maryland's State House, in Annapolis, is the oldest *capitol* in the United States. (building)

7. choose (present tense)

Be sure to *choose* the best.

   chose (past tense)

Yesterday she *chose* a desk for her study.

8. cloths

Those silk *cloths* come from Taiwan.

   clothes

Put the *clothes* in the dryer.

9. coarse (adjective)

The texture of those rugs is too *coarse*.

   course (noun)

Is that *course* required for your degree?

10. conscience (noun)

His *conscience* troubled him because he had lied.

   conscious (adjective)

I was still *conscious* when the dentist began to drill.

11. desert (noun)

The sands of the *desert* sparkled in the sun.

   desert (verb)

Did you *desert* your friends at the party?

   dessert (noun)

We had grasshopper pie for *dessert*.

12. effect

See *affect*.

13. except

See *accept*.

14. fair (noun)

Let's go to the county *fair* this fall.

   fair (adjective)

She is a very *fair* executive.

   fare (noun)

The bus *fare* has gone up.

15. formally

We dressed *formally* for the costume ball.

   formerly

Formerly he worked as a firefighter.

16. forth (adverb)

Step *forth* and assert yourself.

   fourth (adjective)

Beth sat in the *fourth* row. (from *four*)

17. hear (verb)

Did you *hear* Frank play "Tally Ho" on his horn?

here (adverb)

The parade should begin *here*.

18. its (possessive pronoun)

Its head is small for its body.

it's (it is)

It's perfect weather for skiing.

19. know (verb)

I *know* everybody in the class.

no

His answer was *"no"* — in *no* uncertain terms.

20. later (adverb)

We will follow you *later*.

latter (adjective)

The *latter* third of the concert was too modern for my taste.

21. lead (noun)

That basket is as heavy as *lead*.

lead (verb, present tense)

Thomas will *lead* the way.

led (verb, past tense)

It's Thomas' turn, because Kate *led* yesterday.

22. lose (verb)

"Did you *lose* my turtle?" asked Jimmy.

loose (adjective)

The name of the bar is *The Loose Goose*.

23. no

See *know*.

24. passed (verb)

James *passed* the long, difficult test.

past (noun)

That happened so far in the *past* I wish we could forget it.

past (adjective)

The *past* few days have been hectic.

25. peace

That group works hard for world *peace*.

piece

Give me a *piece* of cheesecake.

26. personal (adjective)

Linda considers that her *personal* business.

personnel (noun)	Isn't it strange that all the *personnel* in that company have red hair?
27. precede	Let Richard *precede* you in the line. (go before)
proceed	Please *proceed* to the end of the block. (go forward)
28. principal (noun)	The *principal* was in his office. (person)
principal (noun)	The *principal* was $12,000. (money)
principal (adjective)	Their *principal* food was rice. (meaning "major")
principle (noun)	The *principles* Esther lives by are honesty and dependability. (rule, code of behavior)
29. quiet (adjective)	It was *quiet* in the house.
quite (adverb)	It was *quite* dark outside.
30. right (adjective)	You were quite *right* to tell John the truth.
right (noun)	All members have a *right* to their own opinions.
write (verb)	Louie is going to *write* his paper on computers in the home.
31. role	Sam will play the *role* of Helmer in "A Doll's House."
roll	He called the *roll* quickly.
32. sense (noun)	Most dogs have a *sense* of smell.
sense (verb)	Did you *sense* some hostility on Jenny's part?
since (conjunction)	*Since* your pet iguana will be on the train, Jake won't go.
since (preposition)	I have not talked with Betsy *since* yesterday.
33. stationery (noun)	Eleanor wrote on lavender *stationery*.

stationary (adjective) — Her desk is *stationary* in that corner.

34. than (used to compare) — Charlotte is more reflective *than* I.

then (adverb of time) — Jasper turned red and *then* left the room.

35. there (introductory word and adverb of place)
their (possessive)
they're (they are) — *There* are young people who, as soon as *they're* old enough to drive, think they should have a car of *their* own. Many want to keep *their* cars on the school grounds, over *there* near the playing field.

36. through (preposition)
threw (verb) — Timing her jump precisely, Sandy *threw* the ball *through* the hoop.

37. to (preposition and part of verb) — Is Ellen planning *to* go *to* the ballet?

too (adverb) — I want some frozen raspberry yogurt *too*. (means also)
It is *too* late to worry about whether your costume is *too* loose.

two (number) — Ed has *two* valuable comic books I want.

38. weather (noun) — The clear *weather* makes today just right for exploring the valley.

whether (conjunction) — David didn't know *whether* to laugh or cry.

39. where (adverb of place)
were (verb) — *Where were* you when the rest of us left for the art gallery?

40. whose — *Whose* pocket is housing a croaking frog?

who's (who is, who has) — *Who's* coming scuba-diving with us?

41. woman (singular)

Harriet Tubman, a somewhat fragile *woman,* was nevertheless a major figure in the Underground Railway during the Civil War.

women (plural)

Are you taking the course *Women in Art?*

42. your (possessive pronoun)
you're (you are)

You're likely to lose *your* coat if you take it off in this trolley car.

Polishing Sentences: Style

wordy

17. Tighten wordy sentences.

A wordy sentence is one that can be trimmed *without losing any meaning*. Sometimes you can tighten wordy sentences simply by deleting words; other times you'll need to restructure the sentence.

WORDY	Some of the mentally retarded can be taught to lead productive lives through training.
REVISED	Some of the mentally retarded can be trained to lead productive lives.
WORDY	The basic principle of a parochial school mainly involves receiving a good education along with discipline.
REVISED	Parochial schools provide a good education and a healthy dose of discipline.
WORDY	The males are classically known as being dumb jocks.
REVISED	The males are stereotyped as dumb jocks.

Note: For more about wordiness, see Chapter 13.

Exercise **Wordiness**

The following sentences are so wordy that they require major surgery. Revise them by deleting excess words and, where necessary, restructuring. Each sentence may be improved in a variety of ways.

1. In the modern world of today, one reason why people write wordy sentences is because they're not sure about what they want to say when they start to write their rough drafts, so they kind of ramble on in the expectation that what they really mean will eventually come out on the page.

2. Despite the fact that such a method usually produces wordy first-draft sentences, I would say that it is a method preferable to attempting to form perfect sentences and then writing them down perfectly.

415

3. Well, it seems to me that trying to write a perfect sentence will probably cause writer's block because that goal is very difficult to achieve, and it is also frustrating because it takes too long.

4. A second reason why people write wordy sentences is that they read them all the time at work, where windy, inflated, pretentious, verbose, jargon-filled, tedious sentences are written by bureaucrats who think people will take them more seriously if they write the pretentious "in the event that" instead of the simple "if."

5. The appearance of this kind of motivation to impress people is usually seen in the use of long phrases like "with respect to" and "in regard to" instead of "about," as illustrated by the following example I received at work from my boss:

6. "With respect to your recent traveling expenses and in light of the company policy in regard to reducing traveling expenses by minimizing unnecessary trips to customers in lieu of placing telephone calls, please make an appointment with my secretary to discuss this matter as soon as possible."

7. As far as precise wording is concerned, it is my purpose to illustrate that sometimes a cause for wordiness is the overuse of phrases that state the obvious, phrases such as "what I am trying to say here is that" and "my chief purpose is to."

8. It is generally accepted that another cause of wordiness is the use of too many phrases to gain emphasis, such as "it is fundamental that" and "a key principle is that."

9. On the other hand, if a writer follows the advice about concise sentences too closely, ignoring advice about transitions and sentence variety, the wish to produce concise, emphatic sentences might produce a series of bold, aggressive sentences that pound on the reader's ears.

10. Last but not least, inflate the following concise sentence into the kind of wordy sentences in this exercise: Avoid excess words.

---

p-a 18. **Write in the active voice.**

In the active voice, the subject of the sentence performs the action: "Carlos called the police." In passive-voice sentences, the subject receives the action: "The police were called by Carlos." In the passive voice, the real actor — in this case Carlos — can disappear from the sentence altogether: "The police were called."

In general, prefer the active voice to the passive; it is more direct and forceful.

PASSIVE   The skills I need to master will be worked on.

ACTIVE	I will work on the skills I need to master.
PASSIVE	Finally, after two hours of bumbling, the pie was completed by Harriet.
ACTIVE	Finally, after two hours of bumbling, Harriet completed the pie.

Exceptions: Though you should usually write in the active voice, you might sensibly choose to write in the passive voice when:

1. You do not know the actor of the sentence.

   • It was determined that her brain cells were slowly being destroyed.

2. You wish to focus on the action, not the actor.

   • You are shown how to pace through a book at a rate two or more times your normal reading speed.

3. The receiver of the action is more important than the actor.

   • *Weeds*, according to the paper, has been seen by approximately ten million people.

19. Put parallel content in parallel form.

When you put parallel ideas in unparallel form, the form fights the meaning. Readers will be grateful when the form of your sentences supports their meaning.

FAULTY	I have been accused of being rough, hardheaded, and a thoughtless individual.
REVISED	I have been accused of being rough, hardheaded, and thoughtless.
FAULTY	A person may pursue a goal at college, at a trade school, a military career, or in industry.
REVISED	A person may pursue a goal at college, at a trade school, in the military, or in industry.
FAULTY	The examiners observed us to see if we could stomach the grotesque accidents and how to cope with them.
REVISED	The examiners observed us to see if we could stomach the grotesque accidents and knew how to cope with them.

Note: For more about parallel sentence structure, see Chapter 12. Parallelism is also discussed in Chapters 11 and 15.

Exercise **Parallelism**

Revise these sentences so that parallel ideas are expressed in parallel structure. Some sentences do not need revision.

1. Most colleges usually require a speech course to give students some knowledge of communication theory, how to work in groups, and to practice public speaking.

2. In speech class we learned to write and deliver speeches.

3. Our speech instructor would not let us read our previously written speeches to the class because audiences usually prefer to be talked to rather than your reading to them.

4. According to a survey, speaking in public is feared more than any other common fear — more than people are afraid of heights, or water or the dark, or more than they fear even death.

5. Nearly 100 percent of us experience communication apprehension in certain situations or with certain people.

6. Communication apprehension is the fear of conversing with another person or persons or before large groups.

7. The causes of this fear may be in our own personality or be due to something about the type of communication or the people involved.

8. Unless they say something "wrong," the more people talk, the more highly other people will value their intelligence.

9. People who don't talk much have a problem making a good impression; the less they talk, the less smart they seem.

10. The most useful things I learned in speech class were to accept and understand my own communication apprehension, how I could cope with it, and speaking before a group.

---

ch

20. Combine choppy sentences.

In a rough draft, you may tend to overuse short, simple sentences, as this writer has done:

CHOPPY   *On Death and Dying* was written by Dr. Elisabeth Kübler-Ross. It describes the author's experiences with terminally ill patients.

Because short sentences demand attention from readers, they should be reserved for ideas that are truly important. The sample sentences above might be combined in a variety of ways:

> REVISED   *On Death and Dying*, by Dr. Elisabeth Kübler-Ross, describes the author's experiences with terminally ill patients.
>
> REVISED   Dr. Elisabeth Kübler-Ross's *On Death and Dying* describes the author's experiences with terminally ill patients.
>
> REVISED   Dr. Elisabeth Kübler-Ross's experiences with terminally ill patients are described in her book *On Death and Dying*.

In each revision the minor idea — the fact that Dr. Kübler-Ross wrote the book — has been subordinated. The important content of the sentence is carried in the subject and verb of the main clause, the words that receive most attention from readers.

For more about short, choppy sentences, see Chapter 12. An exercise on combining choppy sentences appears following Section 21.

wc

21. Restructure weak compounds.

In a rough draft, you may tend to string too many ideas loosely together with *and*'s. When this happens, at least some of those ideas — the ones that are less important — should be subordinated.

> WEAK   Linda was thrilled to be living in San Vito, Italy, and she stood at her window watching the rain falling gently on the red tile rooftops.
>
> IMPROVED   Thrilled to be living in San Vito, Italy, Linda stood at her window watching the rain falling gently on the red tile rooftops.
>
> WEAK   One day I checked the bulletin board, and I discovered that a position was open in the Customer Service Department.
>
> IMPROVED   One day, when I checked the bulletin board, I discovered that a position was open in the Customer Service Department.
>
> WEAK   I saw Aunt Nora taking her "leg" off, and I could see the raw, sore stump, and I knew that it must be causing her terrible pain.

IMPROVED   When Aunt Nora removed her "leg," revealing
the raw, sore stump, I realized that it must be
causing her terrible pain.

For more about weak compounds, see Chapter 12.

Exercise   ***Choppy Sentences and Weak Compounds***

Combine any short, choppy sentences and restructure any weak
compounds in the following groups of sentences.

1. Discrimination cases are numerous in our agency, and because
   there are so many cases, a challenge can take as long as five years
   to be brought to a decision.

2. My friend Marie was discriminated against. Marie is a college
   graduate and a certified paralegal.

3. Marie worked for three months in the legal department. Her
   performance exceeded all expectations.

4. Then one secretary decided not to cooperate with Marie. This
   secretary was known to be prejudiced against blacks.

5. Eventually Marie decided to take the problem to her supervisors,
   and a meeting was arranged to try to resolve the problem.

6. The secretary was surprisingly open about her feelings. She said
   in the presence of her supervisors that she would not take orders
   from blacks.

7. Two weeks later Marie was called back to the office of her two
   supervisors, and they suggested that it would be best if she would
   resign.

8. Marie didn't know what else to do, so she signed her release
   papers the next day.

9. She thought better of her decision the next day. She began the
   lengthy process of filing a complaint with the Office of Equal
   Opportunity.

10. Marie hired an attorney. She met with her Congressperson. The
    supervisors then changed their minds, and they rehired her and
    moved the secretary to another branch of the agency.

Editing Sentences: Grammar

frag

22. Revise sentence fragments.

Don't treat fragments (pieces) of sentences as if they were complete sentences. That is, don't begin a series of words that is not a sentence with a capital letter and end it with a period.

Sentence fragments are usually phrases or subordinate clauses that have been detached from the sentences in which they belong. To correct a fragment, you can often simply attach it to a nearby sentence, usually with a comma.

FRAGMENT	There is a great need for female doctors. Especially in obstetrics and gynecology.
REVISED	There is a great need for female doctors, especially in obstetrics and gynecology.
FRAGMENT	Jim's gaily wrapped package sat waiting in the closet. Safely hidden from inquisitive little fingers.
REVISED	Jim's gaily wrapped package sat waiting in the closet, safely hidden from inquisitive little fingers.
FRAGMENT	The school has been dubbed SERE. An acronym for survival, evasion, resistance, and escape.
REVISED	The school has been dubbed SERE, an acronym for survival, evasion, resistance, and escape.

You can also correct a fragment by turning it into a sentence.

FRAGMENT	Europe's rail system is quick, cheap, and efficient. While European roads are primitive.
REVISED	Europe's rail system is quick, cheap, and efficient. In contrast, European roads are primitive.

Exception: Sentence fragments are permissible when you use them deliberately, for emphasis.

- The plane took off with a mighty roar. Off toward the unknown.

421

- I sometimes think as I look at my child: "I love you, but you remind me of my mistakes and I can't bear to look at you. Or talk to you. Or think about you."

You will find an exercise on fragments following Section 23.

cs/fused

23. Revise comma splices and fused sentences.

Independent clauses, word groups that could stand alone as sentences, may be joined together in one sentence in *only* two ways.

1. With a comma and a coordinating conjunction:

, and   , for
, but   , so
, or   , yet
, nor

2. With a semicolon:

;

When a writer uses a comma alone between independent clauses, the error is known as a *comma splice*. When a writer uses no punctuation between the clauses, the error is known as a *fused sentence*.

There are four possible ways to correct a comma splice or a fused sentence.

1. Split the two independent clauses into two separate sentences.

FAULTY   The worst thing about hell is that there will be no one to turn to you will be all alone.

REVISED   The worst thing about hell is that there will be no one to turn to. You will be all alone.

FAULTY   I don't mind cooking, in fact I enjoy it.

REVISED   I don't mind cooking. In fact, I enjoy it.

2. Put a coordinating conjunction (*and, but, or, nor, for, so, yet*) between the two independent clauses, and place a comma before the coordinating conjunction.

FAULTY   I have thirty more years before retirement by then I should have reached my goal.

REVISED   I have thirty more years before retirement, and by then I should have reached my goal.

FAULTY   Jim said it looked snug around the waist, I thought it looked perfect.

REVISED   Jim said it looked snug around the waist, but I thought it looked perfect.

3. Insert a semicolon between the two independent clauses.

FAULTY   He could not respond it seemed hopeless.

REVISED   He could not respond; it seemed hopeless.

FAULTY   Water conditions of the soil can be a real source of trouble when camping, however, your camp should be located close to a spring of running water.

REVISED   Water conditions of the soil can be a real source of trouble when camping; however, your camp should be located close to a spring of running water.

4. Restructure the sentence.

FAULTY   This is why there are so many robberies, murders, and rapes people are just bored.

REVISED   Many robberies, murders, and rapes are committed out of boredom.

FAULTY   The plains Indians were a trusting people, many of the tribes didn't even have a word for *lie.*

REVISED   The plains Indians were so trusting that many of the tribes didn't even have a word for *lie.*

Note: Whenever a conjunctive adverb such as *however, therefore, furthermore,* or *nevertheless* is used to join two independent clauses, the clauses must be separated by a semicolon.

- Society often forgives the criminal; however, it rarely forgives the dreamer.

Exercise   *Fragments, Fused Sentences, and Comma Splices*

Each of the following items contains one of the errors mentioned above.

    1. Before the snows come, I would like to go to the Appalachian Mountains. Where I hear you can still find some authentic banjo-picking.

2. I think I'll ask some friends, like Chip, Joan, and Martha, to go along, we could take turns driving those mountain roads.

3. Charlotte Blackman, who's in my art class, grew up in those hills, let's ask her to come.

4. Keep in mind that we need to find people who really want to listen to bluegrass it will be an unhappy outing if we ask the wrong folks.

5. Tom O'Hare says that comparing the bluegrass of different regions is one of his hobbies. Although I've never seen him at a local festival.

6. I'd vote for taking a chance on Tom, he's good company no matter where he is.

7. Let's leave early on a Saturday morning everybody should be free then, and we can stop for brunch instead of eating breakfast before we leave.

8. The trip should take about three hours if we don't run into problems driving in the mountains. Which could surely happen.

9. We should take some cheese and bread and wine for lunch you tell Charlotte to bring a treat the mountain people would appreciate.

10. Maybe we could take our own instruments and play some with the mountain people, that could be the best part of our trip.

---

mix

24. Revise mixed constructions.

A mixed construction is a sentence that got out of control as you were writing it. It begins with one grammatical plan and then shifts confusingly to another. You can think of a mixed construction as having the head of one sentence and the tail of another. Here is an example:

MIXED   If I can help out just by listening to a child's small but pressing problems gives me satisfaction.

The "head" of this sentence is "If I can help out just by listening to a child's small but pressing problems." The "tail" is "gives me satisfaction." The problem is that the head and tail don't go together.

To revise this sentence we can change the tail to fit the head:

REVISED   If I can help out just by listening to a child's small but pressing problems, I am satisfied.

Or we can change the head to fit the tail:

REVISED   Just listening to a child's small but pressing prob-
           lems gives me satisfaction.

Sometimes, though, a construction will be so badly mixed that you
can't even find its head and its tail. What should you do then? Just
throw it out, then try again to express your idea — this time in a
clear, straightforward sentence.

MIXED   I found that getting involved in working with stu-
           dents on their reading problems a new and enlight-
           ening experience.

REVISED   Helping students with their reading problems was a
           new and enlightening experience for me.

MIXED   I think that would be the most important thing
           about a job is satisfaction.

REVISED   The most important thing about a job, for me, is
           the satisfaction I receive from it.

MIXED   Not being able to go to her mother and talk to her
           the way she once did and the love for her husband
           not being returned, made her feel very depressed.

REVISED   Her husband no longer loved her, and she could no
           longer talk over personal problems with her
           mother. Her isolation made her feel very depressed.

An occasional mixed construction is nothing to worry about. Just
revise it when you discover it. But if many of your sentences are
spinning out of control, try to discover why. Here is a list of common
causes of the problem, each of which suggests its own cure.

Cause: You're trying to write in a style that is more formal and
        complex than you can handle.
Cure: Write in a simpler, more direct style.
Cause: Your only purpose for writing is that you have to complete
        an assignment. Attempting to spin something out of
        nothing, you wind up in a tangle of words and phrases.
Cure: Choose writing topics that are more "real" for you —
        on subjects you know something about. And as you write,
        focus on writing for readers who want to hear what you
        have to say.

Cause: You treat writing as a one-step process. Once you start writing, you just plunge forward, even when you can feel sentences escaping from your control.

Cure: Change your writing habits. Practice writing the way professionals do — use a several-step process involving false starts and lots of crossing-out and rephrasing. Control your sentences instead of letting them control you.

Cause: You're not sure which sentence structures are acceptable in written English. You know that certain "loose" sentence structures are all right in spoken English, but you're not sure which ones will work in written English.

Cure: This cure will take time — a whole semester at least. Purchase a workbook or work through programmed materials on the basic sentence patterns of written English. Your instructor can advise you on books and materials available at your school.

You will find an exercise on mixed constructions following Section 26.

shift

25. Avoid confusing shifts.

If you begin writing in one tense, such as the past, don't make a confusing shift to another, such as the present.

SHIFT We left early to go to the circus. Once there, we wander around, eat popcorn, and some of us get lost.

REVISED We left early to go to the circus. Once there, we wandered around, ate popcorn, and some of us got lost.

If you are using one pronoun, such as *they,* don't shift without warning to another, such as *you.*

SHIFT The other members of the team must accept all decisions made by the leader, even if that means they won't make it to the top. You must be willing to trust the leader without question.

REVISED The other members of the team must accept all decisions made by the leader, even if that means they won't make it to the top. They must be willing to trust the leader without question.

If you have been writing in the active voice, with the subject doing the action, don't shift suddenly to the passive voice, with the subject receiving the action.

SHIFT   The teacher focuses on main events. Trivia is included only when it helps the student understand the material.

REVISED   The teacher focuses on main events. She includes trivia only when it helps the student understand the material.

Note: For more about confusing shifts, see Chapters 4 and 11. You will find an exercise on confusing shifts following Section 26.

om   26. Do not omit necessary words.

Though the word *that* may often be dropped in the interest of economy, include it whenever it helps readers understand how the parts of a sentence fit together.

CONFUSING   Dave saw his four-year-old brother was moving too close to the cliff.

CLEAR   Dave saw that his four-year-old brother was moving too close to the cliff.

CONFUSING   I knew then that everything would be all right but there would be other patients just like her.

CLEAR   I knew then that everything would be all right but that there would be other patients just like her.

In compound structures, be sure to include any words necessary for grammatical completeness.

INCOMPLETE   Having grown up in the ghetto, Teresa was both gratified and apprehensive about her scholarship to Harvard.

REVISED   Having grown up in the ghetto, Teresa was both gratified by and apprehensive about her scholarship to Harvard.

INCOMPLETE   Though he runs for mayor every four years, Stevens never has and never will be elected.

REVISED   Though he runs for mayor every four years, Stevens never has been and never will be elected.

In comparisons, be sure to include any words necessary for logical completeness.

ILLOGICAL
In my opinion her dependence on tranquilizers is no healthier than the alcoholic or the addict.

REVISED
In my opinion her dependence on tranquilizers is no healthier than the alcoholic's dependence on alcohol or the addict's need for a fix.

ILLOGICAL
The children's shoes here are much higher than those in Winston-Salem.

REVISED
The children's shoes here are much higher priced than those in Winston-Salem.

Exercise   Mixed Constructions, Confusing Shifts, and Omitted Words

Edit these sentences for the errors mentioned above.

1. An experience that happened to my sister was arrested by mistake for shoplifting.

2. It's embarrassing when that happens to you, but it was as embarrassing to the store guard who arrested her.

3. The guard said that she was seen to put the store's gloves into her purse without paying for them.

4. The guard asks her did she know she put the gloves in her purse and failed to pay for them?

5. My sister said she had tried the gloves on and they were put back on the counter.

6. A customer who saw the whole thing and the guard trusted said my sister was wearing a similar pair when she entered the store.

7. Though my sister had never before been arrested by the guard remembered seeing her somewhere.

8. Suddenly the guard recalls where he's seen her before.

9. She sings in the choir in which he had just joined.

10. The guard looks embarrassed, and since then he has not, and will not be able, to look her in the eye at choir practice.

`mod`

27. Position modifiers clearly.

A modifier is a word or group of words that gives readers additional information about some other word in the sentence. Position modifiers so that readers will understand at once what they modify.

CONFUSING	Our dog Gregory nipped the blind man on the leg who was delivering light bulbs.
CLEAR	Our dog Gregory nipped the leg of the blind man who was delivering light bulbs.
CONFUSING	Marlboro ads often depict a man on a horse smoking a cigarette.
CLEAR	Marlboro ads often depict a man on horseback smoking a cigarette.
CONFUSING	Our next-door neighbor has a black Corvette whose reputation for driving wildly down the block is notorious.
CLEAR	Our next-door neighbor has a notorious reputation for driving wildly down the block in his black Corvette.
CONFUSING	Lloyd decided on his way to the office to buy flowers.
CLEAR	On his way to the office, Lloyd decided to buy flowers.

Be particularly careful in the placement of the words *not* and *only*.

FAULTY	All Air Force members are not aviation experts.
REVISED	Not all Air Force members are aviation experts.
FAULTY	To complete the transaction, only push the button once. If you push it twice, you'll have to begin again.
REVISED	To complete the transaction, push the button only once. If you push it twice, you'll have to begin again.

You will find an exercise on misplaced modifiers following Section 28.

dng

28. Repair dangling modifiers.

A modifier is a word or group of words that gives readers additional information about some other word in the sentence. Only certain kinds of modifiers, those that suggest an action but fail to name an actor, can be said to dangle. When a sentence opens with such a modifier, the modifier will dangle unless it is followed by the name of the actor.

One way to repair a dangling modifier is to insert the name of the actor after the modifier.

Dangling	Gazing from the hillside, the early morning fog blanketed the slough like a damp overcoat.
Revised	Gazing from the hillside, I watched as the early morning fog blanketed the slough like a damp overcoat.
Dangling	Seeing her standing with suitcase in hand, it dawned on me that this was the moment for which we had been waiting.
Revised	Seeing her standing with suitcase in hand, I realized that this was the moment for which we had been waiting.

Another way to fix a dangling modifier is to add a logical actor to the modifier itself.

Dangling	Already failing one test, my spirits were low.
Revised	Since I had already failed one test, my spirits were low.
Dangling	While running an EEG one day, the pens started clacking and throwing ink about the room.
Revised	While I was running an EEG one day, the pens started clacking and throwing ink about the room.

Exercise   Misplaced Modifiers and Dangling Modifiers

Revise sentences containing misplaced and/or dangling modifiers.

1. Balcony gardening is becoming more and more popular to grow both flowers and vegetables.

2. Gardening in pots of several sizes, plants grow especially well for the couple living just opposite me.

3. This year they have tomatoes, roses, and geraniums, as well as old-fashioned blue morning glories, which add a pleasing touch of red to their balcony.

4. Watching my neighbors enjoy their balcony garden, it occurred to me that I should try my hand at planting something.

5. Having planted petunias without much success last summer, this year's garden on my balcony will be all vegetables.

6. To pot-garden successfully, the pots must not be crowded with plants, which should be of clay or wood.

7. The orange tree is an attractive small tree for balcony gardens that bears both fragrant blossoms and colorful miniature fruit.

8. To outdo their neighbors, small rock gardens are set up by some people on their balconies.

9. Insects are beginning to invade some of our balcony gardens, which could get to be a real nuisance if they find our houseplants.

10. Maybe I'll just give up on pot-gardening and make a terrarium (a small indoor garden under glass), which is beginning to take up too much of my time.

S-V

29. Match your subjects and verbs.

Verbs in the present tense must be selected to match or "agree with" their subjects. If the subject is third-person singular, the verb takes an -*s* ending; otherwise it does not. Here, for example, are the present-tense forms of the verb *to dance:*

	Singular	*Plural*
first person	I dance	we dance
second person	you dance	you dance
third person	he/she/it dances	they dance

All present-tense verbs in English follow this model except for the highly irregular verb *to be:*

	Singular	*Plural*
first person	I am	we are
second person	you are	you are
third person	he/she/it is	they are

Though most past-tense verbs do not need to be matched with their subjects, the verb *to be* is an exception. Here are its past-tense forms:

	Singular	*Plural*
first person	I was	we were
second person	you were	you were
third person	he/she/it was	they were

If you speak standard English, your ear will match subjects and verbs almost automatically; it will tell you to write "he dances" (not "he dance") or "they were" (not "they was"). There are certain troublesome situations, however, in which your ear may mislead you, and those situations are discussed in this section.

If you speak a dialect of English, such as Appalachian English or Black English, your ear may not match subjects and verbs according to the rules of standard English. For advice on this matter, turn to Section 37.

29a. If several words come between the subject and the verb, do not mistake a noun close to the verb for the subject.

FAULTY   The large boxes of mixed candy was on sale.

REVISED   The large *boxes* of mixed candy *were* on sale.

FAULTY   The role of the police officer in these shows seem stereotyped.

REVISED   The *role* of the police officer in these shows *seems* stereotyped.

29b. If the subject follows the verb (reversing the usual order), do not mistake a noun that comes before the verb for the subject of the sentence.

FAULTY   Behind the defensive line is several young linebackers.

REVISED   Behind the defensive line *are* several young *linebackers*.

FAULTY   Hiding in the corner behind the plants are the long-sought-after runaway child.

REVISED   Hiding in the corner behind the plants *is* the long-sought-after runaway *child*.

Note: Sentences beginning with "There is" or "There are" present a special problem because they seem to have no subject. Actually the subject follows the "There is" or "There are" construction.

FAULTY   There is not many people on Assateague Island.

REVISED   There *are* not many *people* on Assateague Island.

FAULTY   There wasn't even enough chairs to go around.

REVISED   There *weren't* even enough *chairs* to go around.

29c. Treat indefinite pronouns such as *each, one, none, either, neither, any, everyone,* and *somebody* as singular.

In casual speech many people treat indefinite pronouns as plural, but in writing, especially in formal writing, they have traditionally been treated as singular.

FAULTY   Each of the twelve stamps are worth fifty dollars.

REVISED   *Each* of the twelve stamps *is* worth fifty dollars.

FAULTY   Everybody in the local jail have been released.

REVISED   *Everybody* in the local jail *has* been released.

29d. When the two parts of a compound subject are connected with *and,* treat the subject as plural.

FAULTY   My mother's natural *ability and* her *desire* to help others has led to a career as a psychic medium.

REVISED   My mother's natural ability and her desire to help others *have* led to a career as a psychic medium.

29e. When the two parts of a compound subject are connected with *or* or *nor,* match the verb with the part of the subject that's closer to it.

• Neither the *students nor* their *instructor was* able to find the classroom.

• Neither the *instructor nor* her *students were* able to find the classroom.

29f. When the subject is a collective noun like *committee* or *team* or *jury,* treat the noun as singular if you want readers to view the group as a unit.

- The *committee was* more successful than we had hoped.

- Our *team is* expected to win.

If you want readers to view the group as a number of individuals, treat the noun as plural.

- Unable so far to agree on a verdict, the *jury continue* to debate the case.

Exercise   Subject-Verb Agreement

Correct any sentences containing errors in subject-verb agreement.

1. Import stores, where you can find a jeweled bracelet or an inlaid card-holder or pieces of Asian pottery, all reasonably priced, is a good place to shop for presents.

2. My sister, who can afford to buy very expensive gifts, shops at such stores every Christmas.

3. A group of women I know go to the import store in a nearby town every fall; once there the group break up so that everybody is on her own to circulate and look for treasures.

4. Everyone who rummages around import stores are almost sure to come up with unexpected treasures.

5. Last year, tucked away in a poorly lighted far corner, was some beautiful bookcovers of Moroccan leather, which Jane Tucker unearthed.

6. Unfortunately, neither Jane nor her friends were interested in Moroccan leather bookcovers.

7. Also in that corner were a collection of hand-painted wooden canes from Switzerland.

8. One of my best import store finds were a large, heavy, ornate marble-topped washstand from England — which I would have bought if I had been driving a truck!

9. Once when I was at an import store, there was some excellent buys still crated in their shipping boxes.

10. Long lines of adults, and now and then a restless child, stands in line waiting for import stores to open each Saturday.

n-p ## 30. Match your nouns and pronouns.

Pronouns are words that substitute for nouns. Each pronoun should agree in number with its antecedent (the noun it refers to). Use singular pronouns to refer to singular nouns, plural pronouns to refer to plural nouns.

FAULTY   The sermon reminded us that even though temptations to be unkind are great, we must learn to resist it.

REVISED   The sermon reminded us that even though temptations to be unkind are great, we must learn to resist them.

For the most part you probably follow this rule quite easily, without even thinking about it. But in certain situations you may run into problems.

30a. Do not use plural pronouns to refer to singular antecedents.

Writers are often tempted to use plural pronouns even though the antecedents are singular, as in this sentence: "The average student is worried about *their* grades." Traditionally this sentence would have been corrected to "The average student is worried about *his* grades"; but this sort of sentence, which ignores half the human race, is becoming less and less acceptable.

A more acceptable form is "The average student is concerned about *his* or *her* grades." This sentence is socially sensitive, because it includes both men and women, and it is grammatically correct, because the singular *his* or *her* agrees with the singular *student.*

However, too many repetitions of *his or her* can begin to sound awkward. To avoid such awkwardness, you can recast your sentences. You can write "The average student is worried about grades" or "Students are usually worried about grades."

Problem sentences	*Acceptable revised versions*
If an individual on approved leave wishes to continue hospitalization coverage, they must pay the full premium.	If an individual on approved leave wishes to continue hospitalization coverage, he or she must pay the full premium.

	Persons on approved leave who wish to continue hospitalization coverage must pay the full premium.
When a person goes to the hospital, they are put on a schedule that is convenient for the hospital staff.	When a person goes to the hospital, he or she is put on a schedule that is convenient for the hosptial staff.
	Patients are put on schedules that are convenient for the hospital staff.

30b. In formal English, treat indefinite pronouns such as *anyone, somebody, each, either,* and *everybody* as singular.

Many people treat indefinite pronouns as plural, especially in informal speech and writing. In formal writing, however, these words have been traditionally viewed as singular. Although informal practice seems to be changing the formal rule, you'll find it safer to follow the formal rule for now.

If "his or her" begins to sound awkward to you, you might write "Voters must cast their votes in person" or "You must vote in person" or "All votes must be cast in person."

Problem sentences	*Acceptable revised versions*
Everyone was told to make sure they attended class on Friday.	Everyone was told to make sure he or she attended class on Friday.
	All the students were told to make sure they attended class on Friday.
Has anyone lost their glove?	Has anyone lost his or her glove?
	Has anyone lost a glove?
Each of us wanted their fair share.	Each of us wanted his or her fair share.
	All of us wanted our fair share.

30c. Treat collective nouns such as *committee, jury,* or *audience* as singular or plural, depending on your meaning.

If you are speaking of the group as a single unit, write "The committee regrets its decision." But if you want to focus on the group as a collection of individuals, write "Unable to agree among themselves, the committee decided to delay their announcement."

You will find an exercise on noun-pronoun agreement following
Section 31.

31. Make pronoun references clear.

Pronouns are words that substitute for nouns. They are a kind of
shorthand. In a sentence like "When the queen issued the order, she
assumed everyone would obey it," the pronouns *she* and *it* are simply
shorthand for the nouns *queen* and *order*. The word a pronoun refers
to is known as its antecedent.

Make sure that readers will understand the antecedent of a pronoun.
Most of the time your pronoun references will be clear, but occasionally
they may be vague or ambiguous or too remote.

31a. Avoid vague pronoun reference.

Pronoun reference is vague when the pronoun's antecedent is only
loosely implied, not actually present. Usually the solution is to put
the actual word into the sentence.

VAGUE	The course consists of seven weekly sessions, each two hours long. *They* guarantee that you will increase your reading speed and comprehension.
IMPROVED	The course consists of seven weekly sessions, each two hours long. The instructors guarantee that you will increase your reading speed and comprehension.
VAGUE	Many people watch soap operas as a form of relaxation. Like watching Monday night football games, *this* provides viewers with a relaxing escape from everyday problems.
IMPROVED	Many people watch soap operas as a form of relaxation. Like watching Monday night football games, watching soap operas provides viewers with a relaxing escape from everyday concerns.
VAGUE	In the encyclopedia *it* states that only eight out of one hundred snakes are poisonous.
IMPROVED	The encyclopedia states that only eight out of one hundred snakes are poisonous.
VAGUE	"Like a Winding Sheet" is about a black man who feels victimized by white people; the story shows

how much friction *it* causes between him and his wife.

IMPROVED   "Like a Winding Sheet" is about a black man who feels victimized by white people; the story shows how much friction these feelings cause between him and his wife.

31b. Avoid ambiguous pronoun reference.

Ambiguous pronoun reference occurs when a pronoun could conceivably refer to two different antecedents. To correct the problem, you must usually restructure the sentence.

AMBIGUOUS   When Jack put the sculpture on the table, *it* broke.

CLEAR   The table broke when Jack put the sculpture on it.

Or

CLEAR   The sculpture broke when Jack put it on the table.

AMBIGUOUS   Mary Ellen said to Pamela that *she* was wrong to have repeated the rumor.

CLEAR   Mary Ellen apologized to Pamela for having repeated the rumor.

Or

CLEAR   Mary Ellen reprimanded Pamela for having repeated the rumor.

31c. Avoid remote pronoun reference.

The reference of a pronoun is remote when the pronoun is simply too far away from its antecedent. The usual cure for the problem is to repeat the antecedent.

REMOTE   Though they are presented as keepers of justice, the police on many television programs are cold-hearted killers. In one episode last week I saw a person choked, another run down by a squad car, and four people shot to death. Instead of trying to solve a situation, *they* seem to shoot first and ask questions later.

IMPROVED   Though they are presented as keepers of justice, the police on many television programs are cold-hearted killers. In one episode last week I saw a person choked, another run down by a squad car, and four people shot to death. Instead of trying to solve a situation, the police on these programs seem to shoot first and ask questions later.

Exercise   **Noun-Pronoun Agreement and Pronoun Reference**

Correct the following sentences for errors in noun-pronoun agreement and in pronoun reference.

1. According to some instructors, anybody can learn to swim if they try hard enough.

2. Learning to swim is one of the best ways to make sure all the body gets enough exercise; this is easy to do at the health clubs found in many towns.

3. A person just beginning to swim regularly should not push themselves beyond a comfortable endurance point; otherwise, it might discourage continuing this beneficial exercise.

4. A comfortable suit is a must for swimming, and a cap is required at some clubs; it must not restrict the swimmer's breathing.

5. Those who swim regularly often join a health club team. My team won their most satisfying trophy when we all swim in unison during a meet that excluded individual competition. In this, each of the swimmers have to coordinate their movements precisely in order not to interfere with each other's strokes.

---

case

32. Choose personal pronouns with care.

Often you will need to choose between the personal pronouns in the lists below, and usually your ear will lead you to the correct choice. When in doubt, however, you must turn to grammar. If the word in question functions as a subject or subject complement, choose one of the pronouns belonging to the "subjective case." If the word functions as an object — whether a direct object, an indirect object, or the object of a preposition — choose an "objective case" pronoun.

Subjective Case	*Objective Case*
I	me
he/she	him/her
we	us
they	them

32a.   Use subjective case pronouns for subjects or subject complements.

FAULTY   My brother's friend, my oldest sister, and me will prepare Thanksgiving dinner.

REVISED   My brother's friend, my oldest sister, and I will prepare Thanksgiving dinner. (subject)

FAULTY   Geoffrey is now taller than me.

REVISED   Geoffrey is now taller than I. (subject of an understood verb, "am")

FAULTY   Where is Marsha? That attractive woman talking to Laurel is her.

REVISED   Where is Marsha? That attractive woman talking to Laurel is she. (subject complement)

32b.   Use objective case pronouns for all objects.

The writers of the following sentences chose subjective-case pronouns in contexts demanding the objective case. Probably they were "hypercorrecting" their English, trying to choose what seemed to them the more educated version.

FAULTY   Management is short-changing we, the tenants.

REVISED   Management is short-changing us, the tenants. (direct object)

FAULTY   For Christmas we gave Karen and she each a music box.

REVISED   For Christmas we gave Karen and her each a music box. (indirect object)

FAULTY   I had to work two jobs to make ends meet, and for Chrissy and I, that was a disaster.

REVISED   I had to work two jobs to make ends meet, and for Chrissy and me, that was a disaster. (object of the preposition)

You will find an exercise on case following Section 34.

`case`

33. Choose *who* or *whom* with care.

The words *who* and *whom* ordinarily function within subordinate clauses, with *who* reserved for subjects and subject complements, *whom* for all objects. In making your choice, you must first isolate the subordinate clause:

> We visited friends in Denver who/whom live in a geodesic dome.

> We visited friends in Denver, who/whom we had not seen for years.

Focusing on the subordinate clause, your next step is to read off its subject, verb, and any objects, restructuring the clause if necessary:

> who/whom live

> we had not seen who/whom

At this point your ear should tell you to choose *who* in the first sentence, *whom* in the second:

> who live (*who* is the subject of the verb *live*)

> we had not seen whom (*whom* is the direct object of the verb *had seen*)

If the pronouns *who* or *whom* function within a question rather than a subordinate clause, again read off the subject, verb, and any objects, rearranging the structure, if necessary, to hear the correct choice:

> Who/Whom received first place in the literary contest?

> Who received first place . . . ? (*Who* is the subject of *received*)

> Who/Whom did the committee support?

> The committee did support whom? (*Whom* is the direct object of *did support*)

You will find an exercise on *who/whom* following Section 34.

`aj/av`

34. Choose adjectives and adverbs with care.

In the following pairs, the first word is an adjective, the second an adverb: good/well, happy/happily, strong/strongly, real/really. Notice that adverbs are often formed by adding an *-ly* ending to the adjective. Not all words ending in *-ly,* however, are adverbs, nor do all adverbs end in *-ly.* So when in doubt, you must check the dictionary. There you will find, for example, that *friendly* is an adjective, and that *fast* can function as an adjective or as an adverb.

Adjectives usually modify nouns or pronouns (a *plump* turkey), though they sometimes function as subject complements following linking verbs (The turkey is *plump*). Adverbs ordinarily modify verbs (She walked *slowly*), but some adverbs modify adjectives or other adverbs (*really* clean, *very* quickly).

Writers sometimes use adjectives when they should use adverbs, as in these sentences:

FAULTY　　　When your players perform especially good, let them know that you noticed.

REVISED　　When your players perform especially well, let them know that you noticed. (*well* modifies the verb *do*)

FAULTY　　　John had never before treated Alice so polite.

REVISED　　John had never before treated Alice so politely. (*politely* modifies the verb *treated*)

FAULTY　　　The bike path had become real bumpy.

REVISED　　The bike path had become really bumpy. (*really* modifies the adjective *bumpy*)

Only rarely do writers choose adverbs mistakenly. The error can occur, however, when a linking verb is followed by a subject complement. Subject complements can be adjectives, but never adverbs, because they describe or point back to the subject of the sentence, always a noun or pronoun.

Jennifer looks especially *pretty* in blue.

No one would write that Jennifer looks *prettily,* but some writers, perhaps trying too hard to be "correct," would claim that Jennifer looks *well* in blue. The correct form here is *good,* the adjective.

The verb that causes the most problems is *feel,* when it suggests a state of being rather than an action. Many educated speakers insist on saying that they feel "badly" about such and such a turn of events, but they are hypercorrecting their English. Because the verb *feel* is linking in this sense, the correct form is the adjective *bad.*

Exercise   Use of Personal Pronouns, Who *and* Whom, *and Adjectives and Adverbs*

Edit the following sentences for errors in the use of personal pronouns, the pronouns *who* and *whom,* and adjectives and adverbs. Some sentences are correct.

1. Me and my friends Rudy and Dan are going to give a real exciting party next weekend.
2. Now that Rudy has broken up with Irene, who will he ask?
3. Aren't Dan and he both planning to ask Nancy?
4. Nancy will have to choose quick who to go to the party with.
5. Surprisingly, Nancy chose two dates — Dan and me — for the party.
6. Dan can dance better than me, but I can tell jokes better than he.
7. Nancy felt badly about Rudy's hurt feelings, but she said she'd go to the party with whomever volunteered to clean up afterward.
8. Rudy didn't handle his disappointment too good.
9. No one at the party drank as much as he.
10. Playing music too loud caused complaints by whoever lives upstairs, and the party broke up as soon as we heard the police car's siren.

Exercise   *For Proofreading*

Proofread the following draft for punctuation, capitalization, spelling, and sentence problems.

1 Shortly after leaving High School I enlisted in the Navy
2 during the Korean War. Even if I didn't want to die on a
3 battlefield, I felt enough patriotism to want to serve my country.
4 By this I entered on the first of many paths that have shaped
5 my career and my life.
6   My choice of fire control school after basic training, was
7 not a carefully considered decision. Fire control simply sounded
8 like an intresting school and besides it was the longest in the
9 enlisted man's Navy, it would last for fifty-two weeks of my
10 four year enlistment. Learning fire control did not mean putting
11 out fires abroad ship. Instead it meant to know and control
12 the radar system by which the guns aboard the ships were
13 being fired.

14   During this long period of learning, I fell in love with and
15 married a local high school girl. We settled down in her Home-
16 town. After my enlistment was over, I enrolled in college,
17 feeling that would be a good way for you to get ahead. I had
18 the G.I. bill to help me through college and I knew I would
19 be expected to be the breadwinner in family in the future.
20 Meanwhile, my wife worked — for a small salery.
21   I was lead onto a path filled with Mathematics and weapons,
22 by the courses I selected in college; as well as by my background.
23 However, going to college on the money from the G.I. bill,
24 and liveing on my wife's small income, ment we had to live
25 frugally. As we set up housekeeping on our meager means.
26 A previously hidden talent in me for building began to emerge.
27   This discovery sparked an interest totally diffrent from the
28 one I was pursuing in my education. So I left the path of
29 mathematics and weapons, young and full of dreams, for a
30 new path to construction and being independent. Unfortunatly,
31 at the same time I started down this path the country went
32 into a deep recesion, putting many young hopefuls like out
33 of business and into debt.
34   By now my wife had stopped working to have a family,
35 and I became our familys sole support. Fortunately my back-
36 ground was good; and I had a freind who helped me get a
37 job in the Defense business. My college degree had to be
38 postponed, although I never stopped working toward it.
39   I never forgot the time spent in the building industry. Even
40 though my natural abilities training and later my college degree
41 helped me advance in my new career. For me hammering,
42 sawing, nailing and sweating during the creation of a building
43 held much satisfaction then solving the critcal problems related
44 to my job in defense.
45   A chance to go back to construction never came along, so
46 I put my energy into my career as a Math Analyst. A career
47 filled with details responsibilities and at times a great deal of
48 mental stress. Having time to think on the job, the times when
49 I could be building constantly occupied my mind. Building
50 was a rest, an escape and a pleasure. Although I felt I could
51 know longer begin a new career in construction; I became
52 dissatisfied even with my acheivements in my prospering career.
53   Always thinking of the future and at the same time recalling
54 the passed insecurity of my parents, I maintained my position
55 for it's retirement benefits as a math analyst, instead of venturing
56 out once more into construction. But like a sailor who counts
57 the days till his enlistment ends I count the time until I can
58 gain enough independence to try to re-enter my dream oc-

59 cupation. On that final path I expect to be a contented person
60 — but not until I am on that path once again.

Note: If you need practice beyond these exercises in any area
covered in the handbook, consult your instructor. Several kinds of
resources, including workbooks, a learning lab, and writing tutors,
may be available at your school.

Dialect Interference

This chapter is intended to help writers whose spoken dialect is interfering with their written English. A dialect, as you may already know, is a variety of spoken language typical of a regional or social group. For example, if you are from Appalachia, you may speak Appalachian English, or if you're black, you may speak a dialect known as Black English.

Writing is nearly always done in standard English, a language accessible to almost all English-speaking people. Dialects differ from standard English in two important ways, both of which can cause interference when a dialect speaker writes. First, a dialect has a system of pronunciation slightly different from that of standard English. Second, a dialect also has its own system of grammar that differs in small but noticeable ways from the grammar of standard English.

This chapter details common differences between some spoken dialects and standard written English. If you speak a dialect, you're probably already aware of some of these differences. Most dialect speakers are able to shift back and forth, depending on the situation, between dialect speech and standard speech. In very formal situations, or when speaking to people who don't speak the dialect, they have a tendency to shift to a more standard English.

As you read you will notice that we assume that dialect English is "different from," not "inferior to," standard English. Years ago many people thought that dialect speech was just sloppy — that it differed from spoken standard English in totally unpredictable ways. But more recently, linguists (scientists who study the ways people actually speak) have been steadily proving that the language of dialect speakers has a high degree of regularity. One linguist, William Labov, sums up these discoveries in a thought-provoking essay, "The Logic of Nonstandard English." * There he argues that nonstandard English is not illogical; it is just different from standard English. Nearly all linguists and a growing number of English professors agree with Labov.

* William Labov, "The Logic of Nonstandard English," *Georgetown Monographs on Language and Linguistics*, vol. 22, 1969, pp. 1–22, 26–31.

ir ## 35. Irregular verbs

When a verb is regular, its past tense and past participle forms both end in *-ed*. The past participle is the form of the verb that may be used following *have*.

PAST TENSE   Yesterday I *bicycled* to school.

PAST PARTICIPLE   I *have bicycled* to school many times before.

Irregular verbs vary from this pattern in a variety of ways. Consider the verbs *choose, build,* and *ring,* for example:

PAST TENSE   Yesterday I *chose/built/rang.* . . .

PAST PARTICIPLE   I *have chosen/built/rung* . . . many times before.

Native speakers of English usually choose the standard English forms of irregular verbs without thinking about it. In some parts of the country, however, it is common to say "he *seen*" instead of "he saw," or "they *brung*" instead of "they *brought*." To see whether you have been influenced by such variations from the standard, take a look at the list of commonly used irregular verbs listed below. Put your hand over the two right-hand columns, and test your ability to produce the standard English forms.

Whenever you're in doubt as to the standard English form, you can consult our list, or you can look up the verb in the dictionary, which lists past tense and past participle forms for all irregular verbs.

Commonly Used Irregular Verbs

Base Form	Past Tense Form	Past Participle Form
arise	arose	arisen
awake	awoke	awaked
bear	bore	born, borne
beat	beat	beaten
become	became	become
begin	began	begun
bleed	bled	bled
blow	blew	blown
break	broke	broken
bring	brought	brought
build	built	built
buy	bought	bought
catch	caught	caught
choose	chose	chosen

Base Form	*Past Tense Form*	*Past Participle Form*
come	came	come
cost	cost	cost
deal	dealt	dealt
dig	dug	dug
dive	dived, dove	dived
do	did	done
draw	drew	drawn
dream	dreamed, dreamt	dreamed, dreamt
drink	drank	drunk
drive	drove	driven
eat	ate	eaten
fall	fell	fallen
feel	felt	felt
fight	fought	fought
find	found	found
fly	flew	flown
forget	forgot	forgotten, forgot
forgive	forgave	forgiven
freeze	froze	frozen
get	got	got, gotten
give	gave	given
go	went	gone
grow	grew	grown
hang (suspend)	hung	hung
hang (execute)	hanged	hanged
have	had	had
hear	heard	heard
hide	hid	hidden
hit	hit	hit
hold	held	held
hurt	hurt	hurt
keep	kept	kept
know	knew	known
lay (put)	laid	laid
lead	led	led
leave	left	left
lend	lent	lent
let (allow)	let	let
lie (recline)	lay	lain
lose	lost	lost
make	made	made
meet	met	met
pay	paid	paid
prove	proved	proved, proven

Base Form	*Past Tense Form*	*Past Participle Form*
put	put	put
read	read	read
ride	rode	ridden
ring	rang	rung
rise	rose	risen
run	ran	run
say	said	said
see	saw	seen
sell	sold	sold
send	sent	sent
set	set	set
shoot	shot	shot
shrink	shrank	shrunk
sing	sang	sung
sink	sank	sunk
sit	sat	sat
sleep	slept	slept
speak	spoke	spoken
spend	spent	spent
spread	spread	spread
spring	sprang	sprung
stand	stood	stood
steal	stole	stolen
sting	stung	stung
stink	stank	stunk
swear	swore	sworn
swim	swam	swum
take	took	taken
teach	taught	taught
tear	torn	torn
tell	told	told
think	thought	thought
throw	threw	thrown
wear	wore	worn
weep	wept	wept
win	won	won
write	wrote	written

Exercise   *Irregular Verbs*

The verbs in parentheses are "base" forms, the ones you'll find listed in the dictionary. For each verb, choose either the past-tense form or the past-participle form.

1. The cold wind (blow) the chilling sound of a howling owl who (know) that six bodies (lie) beneath the murky, gassy swamp.

2. Thirteen years ago a (drink) cheerleader had (drive) a 1954 Pontiac into the swamp, and a group of teenagers who had (drink) too much had all (drown).

3. If only they had (know) what (lie) ahead, they would not have (ride) in that doomed car or (steal) that fatal case of beer.

4. Slowly a dark, hunched shadow (come) from behind a rooted, gray tree.

5. He carried a shovel on which he had (write) the single word *Rosebud*.

6. He (bend) his back over a small mud puddle and (sing) a loony tune.

7. The muddy water had (freeze), but ridges of dirt (prove) that he had (dig) at the spot before.

8. The old man (take) off his coat and (lay) it on the ground.

9. He (wear) only an old tee shirt which had (tear) years ago.

10. On it was (write): "Drinking and driving don't mix."

-ed 36. Omitted -*ed* endings

Some writers tend to drop -*ed* endings from verbs. They write "Lurleen *walk* home from school yesterday" instead of "Lurleen *walked* home." Or they write "As a supervisor, I am *charge* with the responsibility of evaluating my subordinates" or "After school the children were *suppose* to go straight home," when they should have written "*charged with*" and "*were supposed.*" Occasionally a writer with this problem will add an -*ed* ending when it's not needed. One student, for example, wrote "A traffic violator was *founded* dead in his cell." The word is *found,* not *founded,* but this student was so used to being corrected for leaving off -*ed*'s that he threw in an extra one just to be safe.

The -*ed* problem is caused by an important difference between speaking and writing. Linguists have discovered that nearly all speakers of English fail to pronounce their -*ed* endings at least some of the time and that some speakers drop their -*ed*'s more often than others. Most speakers don't even notice that they have done this. The context of their sentences usually makes the tense clear, so dropping -*ed*'s in speech really doesn't matter much. But in written English those

-ed's become conspicuous by their absence; a reader, unlike a listener, consciously misses them. If you tend to omit *-ed* endings in your writing, you need to become more aware of this difference between spoken and written English.

Just being aware of the difference will help you some, and more experience in both reading and writing will reinforce your awareness. But luckily there is a faster way to attack the problem. The same linguists who discovered that everyone drops at least some *-ed* endings in speech also discovered that people tend to drop these endings less frequently when they are speaking in formal situations.* The most formal situation of all, they discovered, was reading out loud. Even if you drop many *-ed* endings in casual speech, you will tend to pronounce them when you read aloud. A possible solution to your problem, then, is to read your rough draft *out loud,* using a formal reading voice.

For practice, try reading these sentences out loud in a formal-sounding voice. *Don't* be careful to read exactly what's on the page, as you ordinarily would when proofreading. Read the sentences the way you would say them in a very formal voice.

> The agency assists the batter wife or husband with temporary housing and counseling.

> She was scare out of her wits.

> My grandmother use to run a hotel in Denver.

> Last week I ask if he could get tickets for the Super Bowl.

Did you catch one *-ed* problem in each sentence: *battered wife* instead of *batter wife; scared* instead of *scare; used* instead of *use;* and *asked* instead of *ask?*

It's possible that you found some of the missing *-ed*'s but overlooked others. Linguists tell us that we're more likely to pronounce these word endings in some situations than in others. If the word following the *-ed* begins with a vowel (*a, e, i, o, u*), for example, we are more likely to pronounce the *-ed* than if the following word begins with a consonant. This matter is too technical for us to go into, but we mention it so you will understand why it is possible to catch some *-ed* problems and yet miss others.

---

* W. Labov, *The Social Stratification of English in New York City* (Washington, D.C.: Center for Applied Linguistics, 1966); Walt Wolfram and Ralph Fasold, *The Study of Social Dialects in American English* (Englewood Cliffs, N.J.: Prentice-Hall, 1974).

Exercise   *-ed* **Endings**

Proofread the following sentences for any *-ed* problems. Remember to use a formal, out-loud reading voice as you proofread.

1. Some of the children could be consider undernourished.
2. It was mention to me during the intermission.
3. Most of the characters have die by the end of the play.
4. I was surprise at the way he responded.
5. He beated her up so badly that he was thrown in jail.
6. Everything about the place has change since last year.
7. I already explain it.
8. The cost of bread has increase because of the increase cost of flour.
9. Though it was below freezing, I walk three miles to the hospital.
10. It's suppose to last for a lifetime, but it broke after a week.
11. He looked like a scare rabbit.
12. It happen to her when she was only eight years old.
13. Jack talk about the situation and then try to clear up the problem.
14. The story capture my imagination.
15. The police follow him until he stop and pull over to the side of the road.

-s

37. Omitted *-s* endings

If you have a problem with *s-* endings, it may be caused by dialect interference. Actually there are three distinct ways in which a spoken dialect can lead to *-s* problems in written English. Let's treat them one at a time.

37a. Use *-s* endings on present-tense verbs used with third-person singular subjects.

In standard English an *-s* ending is added to a present-tense verb when the verb is used with a third-person singular subject.

	Singular	*Plural*
first person	I work	we work
second person	you work	you work
third person	he/she/it works	they work

In at least one dialect, the -*s* ending does not appear: The verb is *work* no matter what the subject is. When a dialect speaker says "He *talk* too much for his own good" instead of "He *talks* too much for his own good," the -*s* has been omitted because the grammar of the dialect doesn't require it. It's not that the speaker fails to pronounce the -*s*. The -*s* is not there to be pronounced. Careful pronunciation, therefore, will not help the writer who tends to drop -*s* endings from verbs; the only cure is learning the present-tense verb system of standard English.

The present-tense conjugation of the verb *to work,* given above, will serve as a model for nearly all verbs. We would also like to give you the present-tense conjugations of two frequently used verbs, *to have* and *to do,* for easy reference.

to have		*to do*	
I have	we have	I do (don't)	we do (don't)
you have	you have	you do (don't)	you do (don't)
he/she/it *has*	they have	he/she/it *does*	they do (don't)
		(*doesn't*)	

Another frequently used verb is highly irregular, both in the present and the past tenses: the verb *to be.*

Present Tense		*Past Tense*	
I *am*	we are	I *was*	we were
you are	you are	you were	you were
he/she/it *is*	they are	he/she/it *was*	they were

Occasionally a writer who is conscious of leaving -*s* endings off verbs may supply them where they don't belong, as in "I goes to the movies at least once a week." This may be "hypercorrection" — overcorrecting the dialect in an effort to be safe. Standard English requires the -*s* ending for present-tense verbs in the third person singular *only.*

37b. Use -*s* endings on most plural nouns.

Some dialect speakers occasionally omit the -*s* ending from plural nouns, as in "He bought six book" or "They were my friend" or "I had to work two job to support my family." Standard English requires an -*s* to mark most plural nouns: "six books," "my friends," "two jobs." Certain exceptions, however, can cause problems for dialect speakers, since the exceptions may lead to hypercorrection.

454 A Writer's Handbook

Speakers who are conscious of leaving the -*s* endings off nouns some-times add them unnecessarily, as in *childrens, womens, feets.* The standard English plurals of these irregular nouns are not marked with -*s: children, women, feet.*

When in doubt, check a dictionary.

37c. Use -'*s* endings on nouns to indicate possession.

In at least one dialect, possession is not shown by *s* plus an apostrophe: "She welcomed her husband death." Standard written English requires both the apostrophe and the *s* to indicate possession: "She welcomed her husband's death." If you find yourself omitting the apostrophe and the *s,* as in "Harry car" or "Richard Wright story" or "Alice friend," make the corrections as you proofread: "Harry's car," "Richard Wright's story," "Alice's friend."

Exercise –s Endings

Proofread the following sentences for problems with -*s* endings.

1. The girl father was a doctor.
2. He seem to be doing well.
3. The story illustrate how one man, Howard, overcame his physical handicap.
4. In most instance the people do not pay attention to his sermons.
5. Poe stories can be read in one sitting.
6. Al travel to South Carolina once every two weeks.
7. Whenever he get a chance, he like to try to speak French.
8. Though I am forty years old, many time I am called a "girl."
9. The average farmer expenses have doubled in the past ten years.
10. The movie last only twenty minutes.
11. The film give the viewer a new way of looking at the Civil War.
12. Old people are not respected in today world.
13. Steve main problem is that he can't spell.
14. Many new career have opened up in the medical field.
15. He believe in justice for all peoples.

---

om ## 38. Omitted verbs

Most writers carelessly omit a word every once in a while, like this:

> It would be far more pleasant for if I could be accepted on the same basis as Charlie.

The writer meant to write "pleasant for *me*" but forgot to write the *me*. Perhaps this was just a slip of the pen, or maybe the writer's thoughts were racing ahead of his pen. But whatever the cause, careless omissions like these are easy enough to catch with careful proofreading.

Omissions of verbs, however, are not always so easy to catch. In some dialects certain helping verbs required by standard English may be omitted. For example, standard English requires "I have gone there" or "I've gone there," but some dialects allow the *have* or the *'ve* to be omitted: "I gone there." Below are three sentences with omissions that resulted from dialect interference. For each sentence, we have listed two versions that are acceptable in standard written English.

Dialect	*Standard English*
I gone there lots of times.	I've gone there lots of times.
	I have gone there lots of times.
He go there tomorrow.	He'll go there tomorrow.
	He will go there tomorrow.
They over there all the time.	They're over there all the time.
	They are over there all the time.

Exercise   *Omitted Verbs*

Proofread the following sentences for omissions.

1. It a subject most people don't want to talk about.
2. You're nervous because you been in school only a short time.
3. I don't think it fair.
4. Do you know someone who be good for the job?
5. They can't read as well as they supposed to.
6. In the opening lines, he saying that he afraid of death.

7. He be here in a few minutes.

8. In the movie she displaying all her talents.

9. Before you know it, it full of fish.

10. She mainly a career woman.

---

dd

39. Miscellaneous dialect differences

39a.   Standard English requires the use of the word *an* before nouns that begin with vowel sounds (*a, e, i, o, u*). Some spoken dialects do not.

Dialect	*Standard English*
a orange, *a* apple	*an* orange, *an* apple

39b.   Standard English does not allow the repetition of the subject of the sentence, as some dialects do.

Dialect	*Standard English*
That teacher, she likes me.	*That teacher* likes me.
My father, he works in Detroit.	*My father* works in Detroit.

39c.   Standard English requires the word *there* instead of *it* in sentences like this one, which are acceptable in some dialects: "It's a man in my class that I like very much."

Dialect	*Standard English*
It's a supermarket at the end of the street.	*There's* a supermarket at the end of the street.
Is it a Methodist church in this town?	*Is there* a Methodist church in this town?

39d.   Standard English does not allow the use of *they* to indicate possession, as do some dialects. Standard English uses *their*.

Dialect	*Standard English*
Mary and Mike brought *they* stereo to our house.	Mary and Mike brought *their* stereo to our house.
The three little kittens lost *they* mittens.	The three little kittens lost *their* mittens.

39e. Standard English requires the words *whether* or *if* in sentences like the following.

Dialect	*Standard English*
I wonder is he going.	I wonder *if* he is going.
Ask him can you do it.	Ask him *whether* you can do it.

39f. Standard English does not permit the double negatives that are allowed in some dialects.

Note: In standard English the word *hardly* counts as a negative.

Dialect	*Standard English*
They *don't* know *nothing* about it.	They *don't* know *anything* about it.
I *can't hardly* believe it.	I *can hardly* believe it.

39g. Standard English does not recognize a use of the verb *be* that occurs in at least one dialect.

In this dialect *be* can be used to refer to an action stretched out in time. A simple translation into standard English is not possible, as can be seen from the following examples.

Dialect	*Standard English*
He be working hard.	Does *not* mean "He is working hard." Means "He works hard habitually."
She be sick.	Does *not* mean "She is sick." Means "She has been sick for some time and continues to be sick."
They be waiting for me to make a mistake.	Does *not* mean "They are waiting for me to make a mistake." Means "Habitually, they have been waiting and continue to wait for me to make a mistake."

Note: This use of the verb *be* should not be confused with the dialect rule that allows dropped contractions in a sentence such as "They be here soon," which means "They'll be here soon." See Section 38.

Exercise 1   Dialect Interference

Proofread the following sentences for problems caused by dialect interference.

1. Some of the student work full time.
2. Jill was dress up for the party.
3. Where you been lately?
4. As far as I'm concern, he's innocent.
5. I'd like to know who stole they car.
6. Her childrens were born two year apart.
7. My job keep me very busy.
8. Did you see a ostrich at the zoo?
9. They be ready in a few minutes.
10. I worried unnecessarily because my answer prove to be correct.
11. Jack been living there since 1975.
12. Student with good grades can get tutoring jobs.
13. The carp is place on a board and cook in the oven for an hour.
14. Your sister, did she win the tennis match?
15. I feel faint. Is it a place where I can sit down?
16. There are two basic method of preparing hard-shell crabs.
17. Larry founded out too late.
18. If you give him a raise, he be happy.
19. It doesn't seem like the kind of story that Flannery O'Connor usually write.
20. Ask him is it suppose to rain tomorrow.
21. Suzanne be sick.
22. When she was young my daughter ask me all kinds of strange questions.
23. Their argument don't amount to nothing.
24. Last week she fix up my brother room for my grandmother.
25. This story tell about a young man who destroys a house.

Exercise 2   Dialect Interference

Edit the following paragraphs, taken from student papers, for problems caused by dialect interference.

1. Tami McAllister was born in Atlantic City, N.J., but she was raise in Washington, D.C. She attend Coolidge Tech, where she took art classes until she graduate in 1979. She especially enjoy her drawing class. Two years later she got married and had two children, a boy and a girl. The boy is four year old and the girl two. She met her husband at Metro in Washington, where they both use to work. He is now a police officer, and she work for Woodies. Although she say Woodies be OK for her, she'd rather paint than be a salesperson. She has enroll in college to major in commercial art. After earning a associate degree, she hope to transfer to the University of Maryland.

2. My mother position as a housewife and mother of eight get rough at times, but she wouldn't give it up for the world. She does not mind getting up at 6:00 to cook breakfast and fix lunch for my father. My father have told her many times that she don't have to get up so early, but she enjoy spending this time with us.

   My mother only have time for two hobbies, gardening and the CB radio. In the winter she collect all types of house plants, which she hangs in the living room, the den, the kitchen, and even the bathrooms. In the summer she usually work in the vegetable garden in the mornings; in the evenings she water and prune the bushes and flowers. Her favorite and main hobby is the CB radio. She have a base station in the den, which stays on nearly 24 hours, and she also have one in her car. She is one of the most active member of our local CB radio club. Her CB handle is "Foxy."

Appendix

A List of Writing Topics

A List of Writing Topics

A. The World of Work

1. Write about the way in which a particular job has been glamorized. Contrast the job's image with reality.

2. Describe your job to someone who is considering applying for a similar position.

3. Describe your job to a new coworker who needs to be broken in.

4. Explain what a person must do to get into the profession or vocation you've chosen. Aim the essay at readers who are considering the profession.

5. Interview someone who does work that is interesting. Describe the job to readers who are considering that line of work.

6. Sketch a popular stereotype of persons in your chosen profession. Then contrast the stereotype with the reality.

7. Have you rejected a career because pursuing it seemed too demanding, with too many barriers to overcome? Write an essay warning others about the difficulties.

8. Warn readers about a job or position that is not all it is advertised to be.

9. Are there features of your job that encourage you to treat customers or clients as though they were not really people? (For example, a doctor or nurse might be tempted to look at a person as a disease or a collection of symptoms.) Make readers see why it is so easy in your job or profession to forget that clients are people.

10. Describe to a new coworker the possibilities for advancement in his or her position.

11. What effect does prolonged joblessness have on a person? Make this topic come alive by talking with someone who has been out of work for a long time.

12. If your job tends to dehumanize you, convince your employer that this is so. Include specific suggestions for improvement.

13. Show interested readers that a college education is not necessary for a person to get a job that pays well.

14. Argue that a college-educated person is much better off in the world of work than a person with only a high-school degree.

15. Describe some of the difficulties involved when a person of the other sex enters a line of work previously considered all-male or all-female. You might want to give newcomers of your sex some hints on how to avoid difficulties that are likely to arise.

16. Do you feel that you have been discriminated against — in hiring, in assignments, in promotion, in firing, and so forth? If so, write a letter of protest to an appropriate audience.

17. If you are a supervisor, discuss one or more of the difficulties of overseeing other workers. Your audience is people who plan to become supervisors.

18. If you work for an agency that can help people in some way, write a newspaper article explaining how clients can obtain aid.

19. Some work places are experimenting with flexitime and/or job sharing to fit the scheduling needs of a variety of persons better. If you know of such a system, describe it to interested readers. Or write a letter in which you persuade an employer to try such a plan.

B. Education

1. Robert Frost said, "We come to college to get over our little-mindedness." Cite specific examples of ways in which college has "expanded" you. Your audience is someone who is thinking about going to college.

2. Describe something specific about your child's schooling of which you either approve or disapprove. Aim your essay at an appropriate audience, perhaps other parents in your community.

3. Choose an instructor from whom you are taking a course this semester. Describe in detail one actual class period in such a way as to communicate either your admiration of or your distaste for his or her teaching style. *No real names,* please.

4. If you have attended both parochial and public schools, contrast the two schools you attended. Your audience might be parents trying to decide where to send their children, or it might be young people whose parents have given them a choice.

5. Write a letter to one of your instructors suggesting changes he or she might make in his or her teaching. Assume that the instructor is interested in improving. *No real names,* please.

6. Choose a course that you're enjoying (other than college English!). Convince a friend to sign up for it next semester.

7. If you feel that one of your instructors is incompetent and if talking to him or her has not led to improvements, write a letter to the head of the department explaining the situation. *No real names,* please.

8. If one of your instructors gave a lecture this week, summarize it for a friend who missed class. Caution: Choose a good lecture.

9. If you have attended school in another country, contrast some aspect of that country's educational system with an aspect of ours.

10. Have you ever taken a course taught primarily with programmed (self-teaching) materials, through either machines or books? If so, how effective was the method? Your audience is people thinking of taking a similar course.

11. An ancient Greek scholar defined students as "lamps to be lighted, rather than vessels to be filled." Show readers that you agree or disagree — perhaps by contrasting two teachers with opposing philosophies.

12. Visit your child's school for at least half a day. Report on what you observe to interested parents in your community.

13. If you have attended high school recently, write a report to your county's board of education about how your high school could be improved.

14. Attempt to convince a classmate of the importance of taking some courses other than those directly related to his or her chosen career.

C. Religion

1. Retell last week's sermon for a member of your church who was away for the weekend. Comment on the sermon if you wish.

2. If you are a Jew or a Christian, describe your concept of God to someone unfamiliar with the Judeo-Christian tradition.

3. Encourage parents in your church to send their children to Sunday school.

4. What is the value of prayer, as you see it?

5. Do you disagree with your church's position on any important issue? Defend your own position. Your audience includes church members who disagree with you and those who have not yet made up their minds.

6. Should prayer be allowed in public schools?

7. Should women be ordained?

8. If you have recently converted to a religion (or to atheism), explain what led you to convert.

9. If your religious beliefs differ from those of your parents, contrast the two sets of beliefs.

10. Are the women and men in your church expected to serve it in different ways, or are all areas of participation equalized? Argue for or against the policies that presently exist.

11. If you have firsthand experience of some non-Protestant or non-Catholic religion in America (for example, Quaker, American Indian, Black Muslim, Jewish), explain some of the basic tenets of your religion to someone who knows little about it.

12. Read Hermann Hesse's *Siddhartha*, a short novel about a young Indian searching for spiritual understanding. Write a character study of Siddhartha.

13. Write an essay in which you compare the Judeo-Christian account of Creation in Genesis with that of some other religion — perhaps Hindu or American Indian. Ask a librarian to help you locate other accounts.

14. Contrast the religious beliefs of your childhood with those you hold presently.

D. Violence

1. Write about the way in which violence is glamorized in the media. Use specific television programs, films, newspaper stories, or comic strips to illustrate your insights. You will need to limit this topic.

2. If you have served in a war, write about a personal experience with violence.

3. How might a family provide harmless outlets for the aggressive impulses of children?

4. If you have seen a violent movie recently, describe it in a way that emphasizes the violence and shows how ridiculous, sordid, or painful it was.

5. There have been many complaints about violence in the news media. In your opinion, should unpleasant, disgusting, or painful pictures appear in newspapers or on television? Try to convince readers who disagree with you.

6. Write a humorous essay in which you show that certain fairy tales, or some other stories intended for children, are perversely violent.

7. Movies in which women are abused in some way have increased in recent years. Although such films are often advertised as "sexy," they may in fact have more to do with violence than with sex (or love). If you have seen any movies that might be analyzed in this way, write about one of them as an expression of violence.

8. If you have ever been the victim of police brutality, describe the incident. Your audience is a citizens' review board.

9. Write about an experience with guns, either a positive or a negative one. Make sure your paper has a purpose.

10. A number of modern phenomena are cited as possible causes of the high level of violence in contemporary society — among them noise pollution, urban density, lack of recreation facilities. Select one such possible contributing factor (preferably one you yourself have had to deal with) and show readers why violence results. Or if you know of a program that successfully counteracts one of these causes of violence, describe the program to interested readers.

11. If you are in a position to witness violence or the results of violence in your community, perhaps because you work in a hospital emergency room or for a community hotline, inform readers about what you have seen.

12. Violence between parents and children or between husband and wife has received much attention in the media. Write about a particular incidence of such violence, making sure you are telling your account for some purpose.

13. Write about the nonviolent philosophy behind the art of karate.

14. If you are a pacifist, explain your philosophy to readers who are skeptical of pacifists.

15. If you are concerned about unnecessary violence to animals, write about your concern.

16. Show readers how easy it is to become hardened to violence from continued exposure to it. If possible, write from personal experience.

E. The Arts and Creativity

1. Take your reader on a tour of an art museum you have visited. Write the essay to encourage a visit by your reader.

2. If you are in a position to encourage creativity in other persons in any way, how do you go about doing so? Share your insights with someone else who can provide this kind of support.

3. Write about the achievements of a favorite artist, musician, or writer. Explain why the work of this particular person is especially significant.

4. Argue that your city or county should establish a special high school for the arts.

5. Some people do not acknowledge that photography is an art form. If you are especially interested in photography, defend it as an art.

6. Review a play (or a film, an opera, a ballet, or a concert) that you have attended recently. Either encourage readers to attend the performance or discourage them from attending. Take notes during the performance or just after it.

7. If you belong to a working musical group that has survived for at least a year, explain your formula for success in this competitive business. Your audience is a newly formed group.

8. If you plan to enter the world of art — for example, as a painter, sculptor, musician, dancer, actor, or writer — explain the discipline required for success.

9. When schools trim their budgets during periods of recession, activities related to the arts are often among the first to be eliminated. Either support or argue against such priorities in education.

10. Contrast your expectations of a concert with the reality of it.

11. Explain to someone who is skeptical of avant-garde art, literature, or music why you feel certain works have merit.

12. If you have studied an art under a particularly effective teacher, describe the teaching techniques that helped you grow as an artist. Your audience might be either students or teachers of that particular art.

13. If you have recently worked behind the scenes during a performance, as a makeup artist, a lighting technician, or a set-builder, inform readers about your work.

14. If you have ever directed a group of performers (for a church choir, a school play, a fashion show), describe how you managed to lead your group from amateurism to professionalism.

F. Food

1. Write an article advertising a natural food store in your community.

2. Criticize from a nutritional standpoint the food served by a particular school, hospital, or other institution.

3. Give your neighbor advice on vegetable gardening. Your neighbor has a small plot, so limit your advice to how to grow three to five vegetables.

4. Write a review of a cafeteria, a fast-food chain, or a local restaurant.

5. Show readers that they can save money, be better off nutritionally, or both by substituting fresh foods for canned, frozen, or ready-mix ones.

6. Describe soul food (or some other specialized kind of food) to someone completely unfamiliar with it. Don't let your paper become a list of recipes.

7. Write a critique of your local supermarket.

8. Excess weight is a problem for many Americans. If you have found a diet that works for you, share your discovery. If there are any medical precautions about the diet, be sure to note them.

9. Certain conditions (such as hypertension and hypoglycemia) can be treated with special diets. If you know of such a diet, describe it to someone who has just learned that he or she has the problem.

10. Inform your reader about some particular nutritional issue he or she is unlikely to know about, such as the dangers of nitrites or the need for fiber in the diet.

11. Suggest low-cost, nutritious menus to a family on a tight budget.

G. Death and Dying

1. Write out instructions for how your body is to be handled after your death — with a traditional funeral, a memorial service, cremation, a donation to medical research, or whatever. Your

audience is your parents, spouse, or a close friend whom you trust to carry out your wishes.

2. If you have known someone who knew that he or she was dying, describe that person's resistance to and/or acceptance of the fact of death.

✓ 3. Describe a funeral you attended recently so that your readers will understand how you felt about the ceremony.

4. If you have ever had a close call with death, describe the experience. Make sure your paper has a purpose.

5. Write about the death of someone you loved, if you can do so without being sentimental. Remember that most of your readers will not have known the person.

6. Choose a religion (Judaism, Hinduism, Buddhism, Unitarianism) and explain how that religion deals with the fact of death.

7. How would you inform a child of the death of someone he or she loves? Write from personal experience if possible, and include the age of the child you're writing about.

8. Write about the suicide of someone you knew. Focus your paper as you see fit.

9. Read the first seven chapters of Elisabeth Kübler-Ross's well-known book *On Death and Dying*. Summarize what she says for someone who has not read the book.

10. Have you ever known someone who was dying? Describe your own reaction to his or her impending death. What did you do and say?

11. If you have worked with terminally ill patients (as a nurse, hospital technician, or volunteer), what have you been able to do to ease their suffering? Share your insights with others who work with such patients.

12. Write your own obituary. Or write the obituary of a family member who is (or was) important to you.

13. Should parents have the right to decide whether their deformed or mentally defective child should be allowed to live?

14. Should either passive or active euthanasia be legalized? Passive euthanasia involves *allowing* someone to die by withholding certain medication or by not utilizing life-sustaining machines; active euthanasia involves *helping* someone to die by administering drugs or by "pulling the tubes."

H. Justice

1. Write about some inequity in our judicial system. Use at least one true anecdote to illustrate the inequity.

2. Have you ever been in jail? If so, write about the experience, focusing your essay as you see fit.

3. Write about a time when you were the victim of a crime. Make sure your paper has a purpose.

4. Interview a police officer — or better yet, accompany the officer on his or her beat (many communities have ride-along programs). What did you learn about the officer, the job, or both? Give the essay a focus.

5. Why are our prisons filled with a disproportionate number of black people?

6. If you know of a police officer who deserves special praise, write a letter of commendation to his or her supervisor. Or write a letter to the editor of a local newspaper, expressing your admiration for the officer.

7. In what areas of your life are you called upon to act as judge (for example, as a parent or as a supervisor)? Share your experiences as a judge, focusing your paper as you wish.

8. Find out what kind of vocational rehabilitation is offered to prisoners in a jail near you. Is the program realistic, in view of the employment likely to be available to such a person once he or she has been released?

9. Show that comparable behavior is unjustly labeled as "lawful" or "criminal" depending on a person's status (age, social position, sex, color, religion, professional position, and so on). Be sure to narrow this topic.

10. Write about the experience of visiting someone in jail or prison, focusing your paper as you wish.

11. Some communities have alternatives to the punishment system of committing lawbreakers to traditional "holding facilities" — local jails, state and federal prisons, and so on. Find out about one of these alternatives in your community, such as a halfway house, and report on your findings.

12. If you have a supervisor who is prejudiced against a particular group or who shows favoritism to certain persons, write a letter to an appropriate audence protesting that injustice.

I. Sports/Exercise

1. If you are very good at a team sport, summarize your qualifications to impress a coach or a scholarship committee.

2. If you've coached a team, give advice to a new coach.

3. Argue against football, ice hockey, or some other team sport for its physical danger or violence. Or argue in favor of such a sport as an important training in teamwork, cooperation, how to deal with winning and losing in life, and so on.

4. Write a paper about the exaggerated language of sportscasters and sports reporters.

5. Argue that schools should emphasize sports that any individual can participate in and benefit from throughout life (for example, swimming, bowling, tennis) instead of such sports as football and basketball.

6. Title IX states that schools receiving any federal funds must provide equal sports programs for male and female students. Investigate whether your college complies with Title IX; if not, write a letter pointing out the inadequacies and submit it to your college newspaper.

7. Write about the high cost of some sport such as skiing. Or advise readers on how to cut the costs of an expensive sport.

8. Write a letter to your local TV news program suggesting any improvements you would like to see in their sports coverage. Or write a letter praising their sports coverage. Before writing the paper, watch the program several times and take notes.

9. Explain why you admire a favorite sports figure.

10. Write about the extreme discipline required for ballet or for a sport such as gymnastics.

11. Write about some program that uses sports or physical activity as therapy for persons with physical, mental, or social handicaps.

12. If you're familiar with a sport popular in another culture, such as cricket, describe it to American readers.

13. Encourage a friend to take up a particular sport such as jogging, tennis, golf, bicycling, or swimming.

J. Growing Old

1. Write a paper about someone you know who has aged in a way that you admire and respect.

2. *The Coming of Age*, a book by Simone de Beauvoir, contains an interesting chapter on old age in historical societies. Read this chapter and summarize it for someone who doesn't have the time to read it.

3. We hear a great deal about the disadvantages of growing old. Talk to some older people (sixty-five or over) about some possible advantages of age, and then write a paper about these advantages.

4. Be alert to how people about sixty or older are portrayed on television. Does stereotyping occur? Watch enough situation comedies and similar programs to be able to describe two or three stereotypes.

5. Find out whether your college has a continuing education program for senior citizens. If it does, try to get some retired person who seems to need new interests involved in the program.

6. If you know of some especially good community program for senior citizens, describe it to readers who might be interested in taking advantage of it.

7. Write about a close friendship you have with someone who is much older (or younger) than you are. What have you gained from this friendship that you could not have received from someone your own age?

8. Describe someone you know who is over sixty-five and who defies the commonly accepted assumption that old age is horrible.

9. If you are fairly familiar with either a retirement home or a nursing home, write a letter suggesting some changes that might make living there more pleasant. Try to make realistic suggestions. Or write a letter commending some feature or features of the home.

K. Race and Ethnic Identity

1. Describe someone you know who has lost his or her ethnic character in the attempt to become assimilated into the mainstream of American culture.

2. Write a jazzy description of "soul."

3. Write a positive description of your ethnic background — Italian, Polish, Irish, Afro-American, Jewish, or whatever.

4. If you have experienced interracial or intercultural dating, write about that experience, focusing your paper as you wish.

5. If you experience a cultural conflict between your world of work or school and the world of your friends, describe it.

6. What picture of American Indians, black Americans, Italian-Americans, southern whites, Chinese, or other minority group is presented in movies or television dramas? Limit this topic radically, perhaps by discussing the image of one of these groups as presented in one film or TV series.

7. It is often said that the liberation struggle of the black woman and the white woman differ. If you are a woman, talk about this question with a woman of the other race and report your findings in a paper.

8. Describe a stereotype of any ethnic group and then write a character sketch of someone you know who disproves that stereotype.

9. Have you ever been stereotyped? Contrast the stereotype with the real you.

L. Men and Women

1. Write about the way a television series depicts male-female relationships.

2. If you have lived in another culture, describe the position of women in that culture.

3. Should prostitution be legalized?

4. Write about the extremes to which some women will go to look beautiful.

5. Argue that men will benefit as much as women from women's liberation.

6. Are you acquainted with any couples in which the woman has a career and the man maintains the home and looks after any children they have? Interview such a couple and shape your paper around your interview, using whatever focus most interests you.

7. If you are a woman who combines motherhood with a job, tell readers how you manage to cope. If you've decided that such a lifestyle is more than you can manage, explain why you came to such a conclusion.

8. Compare and contrast your expectations of marriage with the reality.

9. Write about the problems of being married to a person of another faith, culture, or race. Or write about how you have overcome such problems.

10. What effect does divorce have on a woman who has not worked outside the home and who has no marketable skills?

11. If you know any divorced parents who have split custody of the children, describe how well the arrangement works.

12. Under what conditions, if any, should alimony be awarded to either spouse?

13. If you know a gay person who will talk freely with you, interview him or her concerning his or her life-style. Write an article based on the interview, focusing it as you see fit.

14. If you have been married more or less "happily" for a long time, share any seasoned insights with a young couple about to marry.

M. Parents and Children

1. Describe someone you know who is, in your opinion, a bad parent. Or describe someone who is an ideal (or nearly ideal) parent.

2. Write a character sketch of one of your children.

3. Contrast your expectations of motherhood or fatherhood with the reality as you have experienced it.

4. Find out about family life in another culture, preferably by talking to someone who has experienced it firsthand. Report on your findings in an interesting, readable style.

5. Write about the difficulties or satisfactions (or both) of being a single parent. Your audience includes people who have recently become single parents.

6. Write a paper based on the following statement: "If you think raising a toddler is hard, wait until your child is a teenager."

7. Write a review of a favorite children's book. Your purpose is to steer parents toward the book.

8. A problem for working parents is adequate child care. If you have discovered a good solution to this problem, such as an excellent day-care center, share your discovery with other parents in your community.

9. Warn parents about a poor child-care center.

10. Write a love letter to one of your children, showing why you are glad you had him or her. Try not to be too sentimental.

11. Describe some older person in your family whom you would you like to emulate as you grow older. Or describe someone after whom you would not like to pattern yourself.

12. Explain your philosophy of discipline for a particular age group, giving real examples of the kinds of rewards and punishments you find workable.

13. Show readers that a parent can often steer a child in the right direction without resorting to rewards and punishments.

14. Write about an interracial or intercultural adoption with which you are familiar. Shape this topic as you see fit.

N. Ecology and Nature

1. Describe your neighborhood as it is. Then describe how you would improve it if you had the power to make it more beautiful and more livable. Use enough details so that your reader can visualize the changes you suggest.

2. If you are happy in your neighborhood, describe its virtues to readers looking for a place to live.

3. Select some area other than your own neighborhood and describe how you would redesign it to make it more pleasant and functional. You might work with one block, part of one street, a shopping center, or an entire residential area.

4. If you or someone you know is using solar energy in any way, describe the system to readers interested in trying it.

5. How would ordinary Americans need to change their living habits if the government were to decide seriously to combat pollution and environmental decay?

6. If you enjoy country living, try to explain its appeal to persons who prefer city living.

7. If you or anyone you know has been involved in a wilderness survival program such as Outward Bound, describe the program.

8. If you know of unusual ways to conserve energy, persuade readers to adopt them.

9. Write a letter to the editor in which you warn against the dangers of noise pollution. Or compile a set of suggestions to your city council for decreasing noise pollution.

10. Assume that the federal budget for the upkeep of national parklands is in jeopardy. Grass-roots views are being collected, and you

plan to testify at a local citizens' hearing. Write up your testimony for or against budget-trimming in this area.

11. If "getting close to nature" is therapeutic for you, encourage a reader to try your method by describing how the experience helps you.

12. If you have been involved in a successful community effort to save a historic building or to preserve parkland, describe the methods that led to your group's success. Your readers are people interested in organizing a similar effort in their own community.

Sources of Quoted Material

Page

3   Toni Morrison, quoted by Mel Watkins, "Talk with Toni Morrison," *New York Times Book Review* (September 11, 1977).

3   Anne Tyler, "Because I Want More Than One Life," *Washington Post* (August 15, 1976), p. G-7.

11 Toni Morrison, interviewed by Karen De Witt, *Washington Post* (September 30, 1977), p. C-1.

11 Jacques Barzun, *On Writing, Editing, and Publishing* (Chicago: University of Chicago Press, 1971), p. 12.

11 Barzun, p. 5.

11 Flannery O'Connor, source unknown.

12 Carson McCullers, *Playbill* (October 28, 1957).

12 Van Wyck Brooks, source unknown.

12 Gene Olson, *Sweet Agony* (Grants Pass, Oreg.: Windyridge Press, 1972), p. 35.

20 Ezra Pound, *ABC of Reading* (New York: New Directions, 1960), p. 62.

23 Samuel Johnson, quoted in *Bartlett's Unfamiliar Quotations,* edited by Leonard Louis Levinson (Chicago: Cowles Book Co., 1971), p. 334.

23 Bernard de Voto, source unknown.

23 Louis Brandeis, source unknown.

23 James Michener, source unknown.

23 Ernest Hemingway, quoted in Samuel Putnam, *Paris Was Our Mistress: Memoirs of a Lost and Found Generation* (Carbondale, Ill.: Southern Illinois University Press, 1970).

23 Ben Lucien Berman, quoted in Donald M. Murray, *A Writer Teaches Writing* (Boston: Houghton Mifflin, 1968), p. 232.

23 Dorothy Parker, *Writers at Work: The Paris Review Interviews (First Series),* edited by George Plimpton (New York: Viking Press, 1959), p. 79.

24 John Updike, quoted in Donald M. Murray, *A Writer Teaches Writing* (Boston: Houghton Mifflin, 1968), p. 244.

24 Raphael Hamilton, quoted in an interview by Michael V. Uschan, *Washington Post* (September 4, 1977).

Page

25 John Steinbeck, *John Steinbeck: A Life in Letters,* edited by Elaine Steinbeck and Robert Wallsten (New York: Viking Press, 1975).

26 Jonathan Swift, *On Poetry* (1712).

39 Walker Gibson, *The Limits of Language* (New York: Hill and Wang, 1962), p. 104.

39 Gerald Levin, *Prose Models,* 3rd ed. (New York: Harcourt Brace Jovanovich, 1975), p. 161.

46 Walker Gibson, *Persona,* p. 5.

47 Mary McCarthy, *Writers at Work: The Paris Review Interviews* (*Second Series*), edited by George Plimpton (New York: Viking Press, 1963), p. 302.

47 Anthony Burgess, *Writers at Work: The Paris Review Interviews* (*Fourth Series*), edited by George Plimpton (New York: Viking Press, 1976), p. 326.

47 Laurence Sterne, *Tristram Shandy,* II, 1760.

48 Wayne C. Booth, "The Rhetorical Stance," *College Composition and Communication* 14 (1963), p. 139.

51 Elizabeth Bowen, quoted in Donald M. Murray, *A Writer Teaches Writing* (Boston: Houghton Mifflin, 1968), p. 232.

54 Sojourner Truth, "Ain't I a Woman?" in Jacqueline Bernard, *Journey Toward Freedom: The Story of Sojourner Truth* (New York: Grosset & Dunlap, 1967).

54 José Ángel Gutiérrez, "Mexicanos Need to Control Their Own Destinies," *Pain and Promise: The Chicano Today,* edited by Edward Simmen (New York: New American Library, 1972), pp. 252–53.

67 Matthew Arnold, quoted in Donald M. Murray, *A Writer Teaches Writing* (Boston: Houghton Mifflin, 1968), p. 231.

69 *H.E.W. Training Manual #7:* "Getting Your Ideas Across Through Writing," p. 42.

80 Sholem Asch, *New York Herald Tribune* (November 6, 1955).

83 Stuart Chase, "Writing Nonfiction," *On Writing, by Writers,* edited by William W. West (Boston: Ginn, 1966).

87 W. Somerset Maugham, quoted in *A Treasury of Humorous Quotations,* edited by Herbert V. Prochnow and Herbert V. Prochnow, Jr. (New York: Harper and Row, 1969), p. 367.

87 E. B. White, source unknown.

87 Darcy O'Brien, source unknown.

88 Ivan Turgenev, quoted in *The Viking Book of Aphorisms,* edited by W. H. Auden and Louis Kronenberger (New York: Viking Press, 1962), p. 277.

Page

88   Emile Chartier Alain, source unknown.

88   Georges Simenon, source unknown.

88   Henry David Thoreau, *Journals*, July 14, 1852.

88   Patrick Dennis (Edward Everett Tanner), *Vogue* (February 15, 1956).

91   Donald M. Murray, *A Writer Teaches Writing* (Boston: Houghton Mifflin, 1968), p. 51.

95   Mortimer J. Adler and Charles Van Doren, *How to Read a Book* (New York: Simon and Schuster, 1972), p. 90.

96   Cyril H. Knoblauch, quoted in Edward B. Fiske, " 'Functional Writing' Course Catching On at College Level," *New York Times* (November 24, 1976), p. 59M.

97   Rudolf Flesch, *The Art of Readable Writing* (New York: Collier MacMillan Publishers, 1949), pp. 58–59.

97   Donald M. Murray, *A Writer Teaches Writing* (Boston: Houghton Mifflin, 1968), p. 7.

97   Rudolf Flesch, *The Art of Readable Writing* (New York: Collier MacMillan Publishers, 1949), pp. 58–59.

100   Donald Hall, *Writing Well* (Boston: Little, Brown, 1973), p. 143.

100   Hall, *Writing Well,* p. 144.

117   Anatole France, source unknown.

121   Jo Goodwin Parker, "What Is Poverty?" in *America's Other Children: Public Schools Outside Suburbia* (Norman, Okla.: University of Oklahoma Press, 1971).

131   Henry David Thoreau, "Sunday," *A Week on the Concord and Merrimac Rivers* (1849).

143   Eldridge Cleaver, *Soul on Ice* (New York: Dell, 1968), pp. 6, 18, 38.

145   Joan Didion, "Why I Write," *New York Times Book Review* (December 5, 1976), pp. 2, 98.

147   Mark Twain, source unknown.

148   George Orwell, "Politics and the English Language," *Shooting an Elephant and Other Essays* (New York: Harcourt Brace Jovanovich, 1974).

149   Wallace Stevens, "Adagia," *Opus Posthumous* (New York: Alfred A. Knopf, 1957), p. 169.

151   John O'Hayre, *Gobbledygook Has Gotta Go* (Washington, D.C.: Department of the Interior, 1966).

155   Sidney Smith, quoted in *Peter's Quotations,* edited by Laurence J. Peter (New York: William Morrow and Co., Inc., 1977), p. 545.

Page

155   Pliny the Younger, source unknown.
155   William Zinsser, *On Writing Well* (New York: Harper & Row, 1976), p. 6.
155   Oscar Levant, source unknown.
155   Somerset Maugham, quoted in Donald M. Murray, *A Writer Teaches Writing* (Boston: Houghton Mifflin, 1968), p. 240.
156   Abraham Lincoln, source unknown.
156   William Zinsser, *On Writing Well* (New York: Harper & Row, 1976), p. 18.
163   Flannery O'Connor, *Mystery and Manners: Occasional Prose*, edited by Robert and Sally Fitzgerald (New York: Farrar, Straus, and Giroux, 1969), p. 67.
167   Raymond Barrio, *The Plum Plum Pickers* (New York: Harper & Row, 1971).
167   Annie Dillard, *Pilgrim at Tinker Creek* (New York: Bantam Books, 1974).
167   Frank Walters, *The Man Who Killed the Deer* (Chicago: Swallow Press, 1970).
167   *Sappho: A New Translation,* translated by Mary Barnard (Berkeley and Los Angeles: University of California Press, 1966), fragment 3.
175   Ernest Hemingway, *Death in the Afternoon* (New York: Charles Scribner's Sons, 1932), p. 2.
179   Edgar Allan Poe, "The Fall of the House of Usher," *The Rinehart Book of Short Stories,* edited by C. L. Cline (New York: Rinehart and Company, 1952), p. 1.
179   Albert Camus, *The Stranger,* translated by Stuart Gilbert (New York: Alfred A. Knopf, 1946), p. 1.
196   William James, quoted in *The Viking Book of Aphorisms,* edited by W. H. Auden and Louis Kronenberger (New York: Viking Press, 1962), p. 277.
198   George Santayana, quoted in *The Viking Book of Aphorisms,* edited by W. H. Auden and Louis Kronenberger (New York: Viking Press, 1962), p. 332.

Index

Abbreviations and Symbols
for Marking Student Papers

abbr	faulty abbreviation (HB 14)
adj/adv	misuse of adjective or adverb (HB 34)
cap	capitalize (HB 15)
case	pronoun case (HB 32–33)
coh	improve coherence (Ch. 11)
cs	comma splice (HB 23)
dm	dangling modifier (HB 28)
-ed	error in *-ed* ending (HB 36)
frag	sentence fragment (HB 22)
fs	fused sentence (HB 23)
irreg	error in irregular verb (HB 35)
ital	italics by underlining (HB 11)
lc	lower case letter (HB 15)
mix	mixed construction (HB 24)
mm	misplaced modifier (HB 27)
nonst	nonstandard usage (HB 35–39)
num	error in use of numbers (HB 14)
om	omission (HB 26, 38)
P	punctuation (HB 1–13)
p-a	passive/active voice (HB 18)
pro-ante	pronoun-antecedent agreement (HB 30)
ref	faulty pronoun reference (HB 31)
-s	problem with *-s* ending (HB 37)
shift	confusing shift (HB 25)
sp	spelling (HB 16)
s-v	subject-verb agreement (HB 29)
trans	transition needed (Ch. 11)
var	sentence variety needed (Ch. 12, HB 20–21)
W	wordiness (Ch. 13, HB 17)
wc	word choice (Ch. 13)
X	obvious error
//	parallel structure (Ch. 12, HB 19)
¶	paragraph break (Ch. 10)
⌒	fasten together
∧	something omitted
∼	transpose

Note: HB means Handbook